THE FOOD OF
SOUTHERN ITALY

THE FOOD OF

Southern Italy

Carlo Middione

Edited by Maria Guarnaschelli
Color photography by Chris Shorten
Food styling by Sandra Learned
Line drawings by Dolores R. Santoliguido

WILLIAM MORROW AND COMPANY, INC.
NEW YORK

FOR THE PEOPLE
OF SOUTHERN ITALY,
PAST AND PRESENT, WHO HAVE
ALWAY HAD A PLACE IN THE SUN.
MAY THIS BOOK MAKE IT
SHINE BRIGHTER,
AND FOREVER.

Library of Congress Cataloging-in-Publication Data

Middione, Carlo.
The food of southern italy.

Includes index.
1. Cookery, Italian—Southern style.   I. Title.
TX723.M4874   1987   641.5945'7   87-15406
ISBN 0-688-05042-5

Printed in the United States of America

Book-of-the-Month Records® offers recordings on
compact discs, cassettes and records. For information and
catalog write to BOMR, Department 901, Camp Hill, PA 17012.

BOOK DESIGN BY RICHARD ORIOLO

Foreword

IT IS WITH CONSIDERABLE ENTHUSIASM and an appropriate sense of the importance of what I shall have to say that I write a foreword to this book on the bread and wine of Southern Italy. Its basic virtue, historical and perhaps unintended by the author, is redemptive. How so? Its very conception, and the fact that it will be published and distributed nationally, will contribute something toward the righting of wrong inflicted on the people of Southern Italy and endured by them with patience for centuries.

Carlo Levi, in exile from fascism, lived for a time in Lucania, one of the southern provinces. The natives there told him that when Christ came down the Italian peninsula, he stopped at Eboli, a town on the northern frontier of the province. The consequence of that historic stop, they said, was that they were not Christians, not members of the human family; they were more akin to beasts of burden. Their self-appraisal, as Levi discovered later, was entirely correct. They were passed by not only by Christ but by time, what we call history.

There is no need to elaborate on what Levi, a professional man from the North, has written with such compassion about Lucania and its peasants; for it is descriptive of all the southern provinces whose cuisine is recorded in Carlo Middione's book. They have been neglected by the Italian government and rarely visited by tourists. Whom do you know who has gone to Taranto, Brindisi, Reggio Calabria, Messina? Poor in natural but rich in human resources, Southern Italy deserves better than what it has been given. It has contributed to the Western world Caruso and some of the greatest scientists and philosophers: Campanella, Telesio, Vico, Giordano Bruno, sixteenth-century precursors of Sir Isaac Newton, and Benedetto Croce. The novelists D'Annunzio, Verga, Nobel Laureate Grazia Deledda, Ignazio Silone are Southerners.

Its men and women of labor, the peasants, called *contadini* in Italy, have generated their own civilization, recorded by Silone in *Fontamara* and in *Bread and Wine*. The cardinal principle of their way of life is hospitality, the most ancient and inviolable of virtues, for it requires one to open the door to a stranger without asking his name, and to share with him the bread no matter how scarce. They may not know that the words *company* and *companion* derive from the Latin *cum panis*, "with bread"; but they live by their ancient meaning: sharing, breaking bread together. Hence the symbolic title given above of Silone's novel.

There is an art in Italy known as *l'arte di arrangiarsi*. Translated literally, as "the art of arranging oneself," yields only an abstraction; for what it means is something quite concrete: having the ingenuity to come by one's daily bread; the art of making ends meet, of extracting something from little or nothing, of living by one's wits. The Neapolitans are the most ingenious practitioners of the art. When one was asked what he did for a living, he said that he was a painter. Did he paint pictures or houses? "Neither," he said. "I paint eyes on stale fish to make them look fresh." Thus the fish makes out, the fishmonger makes out, and the painter earns his bread.

From various other ways of making ends meet, one that relates immediately to cookery, note this: a poor shepherd in need of cash slaughters a very young lamb for sale. His wife, using the head, all the interior organs, including the intestine, and ingenuity born of necessity, prepares two dinners for the family. The cooking will be done over burning wood on the hearth; and since all fuel is scarece, the wood, mostly the larger prunings from trees and vines, must be used ingeniously. Instead of laying them horizontally as one does in the fireplace, she will lay them so that their ends meet in the center. As the burning proceeds, she will keep the flame at its maximum intensity by keeping the ends of the wood pieces burning together under the skillet. This concentrates the heat where it is needed, and no wood is wasted. What wisdom! What ethical propriety! If we in the land of plenty had thus conserved our natural resources, scarcity would not be the shape of the future.

Such are Italy's neglected southern provinces and their inhabitants; and what I have called the redemptive virtue of this book is that it tends to right that wrong by *celebrating* what has been for so long neglected. Unlike Christ, the government of Italy, and tourists, Carlo Middione does not stop at Eboli. Himself of Sicilian ancestry, following his nose and what is registered in his olfactory memory, he visits every province in order to record with accuracy the cuisine of those resourceful Southerners. In reading what he has written and testing the recipes in our kitchen, we learn by eating, so to speak.

He is, of course, an infallible culinary guide. An accomplished chef and purveyor of quality food, his guiding principle in preparing a dinner is an Italian proverbial edict: *Dai due regni di natura, piglia il cibo con misura.* "From the two kingdoms of nature, animal and vegetable, take your edibles in measured portions." Fresh and of prime quality. Add to this the indispensable potables: well-made wines of the region.

Another virtue of the book that will be much appreciated by the amateur in the kitchen is that each recipe is written clearly, with precision, and in a way that inspires confidence in the amateur by encouraging whatever variation one may think will improve the result. More butter? Less oil? Less tomato in the sauce? Furthermore, the cuisine as a whole, the soul of which is the use of culinary herbs, is simple rather than complex, lean rather than fat. Note, for example, Macaroni with Arugula and Fresh Tomatoes. And it is never more complex than the recipe for Rabbit, Sardinian Style, the distinct flavor of which derives from the amalgamation of oil, garlic, onion, parsley, wine vinegar, and capers. I can smell that amalgamation!

One final note, an inquiry regarding the author of this unique and eminently useful book. As the son of a Sicilian immigrant, was it written in his genetic code that he must honor the land of his father and more remote ancestry by writing some such book as *The Food of Southern Italy*? In any case: three edible and potable cheers for Carlo Middione.

—ANGELO PELLEGRINI

Ringraziamenti

Acknowledgments

NO MAJOR WORK IS UNDERTAKEN without the help of others. No major work means so much as when one can thank those who made it happen, the people who were so supportive, eager to help, and understanding while this book was gestating. I wish I could mention all of them but that seems impossible. The major champions in my life and of this work are, first of all, my wife, Lisa, who has the fortitude of a titan—and needs it to be with me; my mother and father, whose guidance still comes from above and who really should have been the ones to write this book; Maria Guarnaschelli, my editor, whose faith in this book has been immense and endless, and whose confidence in me was shaken many times but never abandoned; Ruth Fremes, for her support, generosity, friendship, and for trumpeting whatever virtues I have, resulting in my being asked to do this book; Julie Sahni, the maharanee of Indian cooking, for carrying my flag all the way to William Morrow; Ann Draper of Trilobyte Micro Resource, the newly canonized Saint Ann of the Computer, who has read this book many times; my cousins Roberto and Mary Middione, for their love and devotion and Mary's brilliance as a scientist and an artist; Chris Shorten, whose artistic and photographic skills have made my food into art; Sandra Learned, whose love for my food is obvious, her skill as the food stylist made it not only look fresh and edible—it was!; Molly Finn, who tested and corrected my recipes with an eagle eye; Giuseppe Bagnatori, who sent me on a Southern Italian odyssey that will never leave my mind, while his wife, Paola, advised and encouraged; Avv. Berardo Lazzaro, for immeasurable hospitality and for making me a Socio Onorario dell'Accademia Italiana della Cucina, Delegazione de L'Aquila; Dott. Roberto Simari, who, as a total stranger, did for me what only lifelong friends usually do; Dott. Luigi Marra, a fine journalist in L'Aquila who shared food ideas with me; Avv. Luigi Russo, for his historical recipe archives and his charming nephew Domenico, my sunny chauffeur, guide, and breakfast friend; Avv. Augusto Chiavara, a gastronome in every sense of the word; Dott. Medoro De Domenicis, a scholarly gastronome; Pino Pomo and his mother and father, whose information and generosity were boundless, and Julie Raymond, for introducing me to them; Gerald Asher, for his warmth and encouragement; Germano and Mirella (my food consultant) Nasi, for endless friendship, sharing, and eating; Contessa Giovanna Calini, for being graceful and generous and a fantastic cook; Gerald and Anna Adams, who were my tour guides to Italy in the early days and who have become family; Dale Harris for his inexhaustible library of

Southern Italian books and his friendship and interest; Dott. Gianfranco Savio, owner of Biordi Italian Imports, ever a gentleman, merchant prince, and friend; Romano Chietti, whose hospitality reaches across the sea; Andrea Bartolozzi, who is a talented cook and a generous host; Sue Fisher King, for her generosity; Anna Pisciotta, *Maestra della Raviolatrice* and a good friend; Rosario and Damilia Bonanno, two very special people who bless Sicily's soil; Mr. and Mrs. Pietro Bonanno, his father and mother, and his Aunt Benigna, whose combined formidable cooking skills are exceeded only by their generosity; Barone Diego Planeta, for his kindness and interest; Joel Butler, for his knowledge and help with Southern Italian wines; Manuela "Tena" Catena, who introduced me to her cousin Franco Borgia, thereby giving me a loving and special glimpse of Basilicata; Dott. Nicola Pisani, for his translation skills and friendship; Thomas "Tif" Birmingham, Vivande's loyal Chef de Cuisine, whose angelic face belies his strengths in cooking, administrating, and making my work life tolerable; my staff and clientele at Vivande, who are delighted that I have finally finished this book.

Introduction

MOST AMERICANS BELIEVE Italian food originates from a single national style of cooking. In fact, the opposite is true. Campania is the most heavily populated part of Italy. Naples is situated in its poorest region. Since the turn of the century, these two areas have given rise to the greatest numbers of immigrants. And, of course, for these people cooking skill frequently provided the most immediately accessible route to survival in an alien society.

Consequently, it is not surprising the food traditionally served in Italian-American restaurants is largely of Neapolitan origin, particularly in the eastern United States. The ubiquitous spaghetti and meatballs, lasagna, and pizzas have inevitably monopolized the image of Italian food in this country. In reality, these dishes represent only a fraction of the indigenous fare of even that cuisine.

Recently tourism expanded our exposure to Italian foods and wines. It also stimulated a steadily growing import market for these products. Most of this travel, however, is to Northern Italy—the country's wealthiest area. So, yet another stereotype has been produced: Northern Italian is the *best* Italian or the *national* Italian or the *only* Italian cooking.

To be sure, the cooking of Northern Italy deserves every attention that has been bestowed upon it. However, touting it as the *best* or *only* version of true Italian culinary art seriously distorts the picture. To put the foods of Italy into better perspective for Americans, it is obviously necessary to move beyond both the exported Neapolitan restaurant image, and the supposed monopoly of Northern Italian food. Rather surprisingly, very little has been written about the full range of Southern Italian cooking. A great deal remains to be done—and therefore this book. The delightful fact is your palate will be richly rewarded by an exploration of the vast variety of Italian culinary treasures waiting to be found in Southern Italy.

Background of Italian Food

The remotest routes of Italian cooking derive distantly from traditions inherited from classical times. Thereafter cooking in Italy was probably the first artfully cultivated cuisine in Europe. The great emphasis on refining the arts of life which flowered in Italy in the Renaissance of the fourteenth and fifteenth centuries included a renewal of creativity in preparing food. Italian cooking thereby became the cuisine from which the art of cooking elsewhere in Europe took its cue.

As the new queen of France, Catherine de' Medici brought her Italian cooks from Florence—rumored by some to have been Neapolitans. Soon thereafter, the sixteenth-century Venetian Gerolamo Zanetti wrote of the French—who had promptly claimed Italian cooking as their own—that they "ruined Venetian stomachs with meat and fish transformed to such a point that they were scarcely recognizable by the time they reached the table . . . everything masked and mixed with a hundred herbs, spices, sauces."

Back home in Italy, cooking styles continued in the course of their own development, producing soundly simple foods, which, without flamboyance, satisfied the tastes of the *grandi*, the movers and shakers of Italian Renaissance society.

The Italian peninsula remained divided into many small territories ruled by such princes or dukes until 1861. These principalities were often enough at war with one another. And there was little trade or even communication across the difficult mountainous terrain that separated them. As a consequence, these regions developed fiercely individual cultures and cooking styles so diversified that one area was practically foreign to another.

In 1861, Italy was finally unified as a monarchy under the House of Savoy. In 1946 Italy abandoned its monarchy to become a democratic republic of twenty regions and ninety-three provinces. There is now, obviously, more travel, interchange, and standardization of certain cultural styles throughout the Peninsula, which is nationalized at least to the extent of one language and one prevailing religion. But at bottom the Italian people remain diversified in outlook. And while such diversity might obstruct national political unity, it wonderfully enriches human development, creativity in music, art, cooking, and other imaginative endeavors.

The renowned food writer Waverly Root believes, "A great cuisine cannot develop within narrow limits, but needs to draw inspiration from a variety of sources." Although Root also feels that regional cuisines are more alike within Italy compared to foreign cuisines, to project a single national cooking style upon all Italy from sampling just a few of these regional foods is a profound mistake. It is truly impossible to cast all of Italy in a single mold. The Italian peninsula is seven hundred miles long, less than the state of California. It borders France, Switzerland, Austria, and Yugoslavia in the North. Yet the island of Sicily is only ninety miles from Africa. No point in Italy is more than 150 miles from the sea. Small wonder that fish is used plentifully in the Italian diet. Yet, the entire peninsula is also rugged and mountainous except for the Po River Valley in the north, the heel of the "boot" in the south, and a few coastal areas. Italy's climate is generally mild and Mediterranean, though, again, there are wide variations. Sicily and southern Italy compare to southern California, while the climate of the North is similar to that of the U.S. mountain states.

In Italy as a whole, the difficult terrain hinders both industrial and agricultural development, and, as nonagricultural industries are developed, agriculture suffers. Today, Italy imports more food than it exports, and that trend is increasing.

In sum, modern Italy is a relatively poor country, and Southern Italy is especially so. Perhaps for these reasons the Italians have been forced to make the best use of what they do have. In some areas crops have been adapted so that two can grow in the same soil for a greater return. Olive trees grow in the vineyards and row crops in the orchards. The general lack of arable land has imposed the most economic and ingenious uses of the available farming spaces. Small farmers and small-town residents grow their produce wherever they can eke out a few feet of garden space. Above all, the lack of land has fostered a keen respect for scarce food ingredients. It has also stimulated the Italians to use what they can find on the land, such as chestnuts, pine nuts, white truffles, wild *porcini* mushrooms, wild mustard greens, wild chicory, dandelions, and wild oregano, all of which are considered delicacies in other parts of the world.

This brings us to the one dimension of Italian cooking where generalizations about a single national Italian attitude and approach to food can, indeed, be safely and soundly made: Italians cherish their raw food materials. When preparing them for the table, they prefer to leave them in as natural a state as possible, with everything eaten fresh and in its proper season. Virtually no fruits or vegetables are grown in the hothouse or are picked green and allowed to ripen in storage; few are frozen; and very few are chemically preserved. According to a recent survey, only 13 percent of Italians use packaged foods. Only 2.3 percent currently eat processed foods. Nearly all Italian cooking methods are simple, yet they produce sophisticated and often elegant dishes. Italians insist on preserving the identity and integrity of each individual ingredient in preparation, exposing them freshly, separately, and purely, without complex saucing. The key to Italian cooking is thus to bring out the essence of each ingredient's natural taste. And it depends heavily upon ingredients of the best possible quality to ensure the success of the finished dish. Such standards require full sugar development in produce through sun ripening, and leaping freshness in fish and fowl.

Sauces per se do not constitute a major aspect of Italian cooking. Most sauces are produced simply by reducing natural juices and occasionally by adding a bit of wine. There are, of course, a few basic sauces, such as *besciamella* and marinara, that could be considered "mother" sauces, which are varied by adding additional ingredients. Most other saucing is done with light oil dressings flavored with fresh herbs, spices, and sometimes lemon, anchovy, or garlic.

Generally speaking, Italian meals begin in the marketplace. But there the generalities end. The term *Italian*, used in relation to cooking, would, in fact, mean very little to most Italians. To them there is Florentine, Venetian, Genovese, Piedmontese, Roman, Palermitan, and Neapolitan food, etc. Even the names of the same foods vary from region to region, especially when it comes to shapes of pasta and the names of fish. A given dish may differ from town to town and even from house to house. Much of Italian cooking is peasant cooking in the best sense of the word. It has not been greatly influenced by foreign sources. It is ingredient cooking, and it is mainly home cooking, prepared *con amore*, or "with love."

The regions of Italy can be broadly divided between those of the North and those of the South.* The dividing line is somewhere around Rome in Lazio. And the

*NOTE: The regions of Abruzzo and parts of Lazio are included in this book not only because they are part of the Mezzogiorno (as defined by the Italian government), or Southern Italy, but because they are kindred souls by temperament and food.

southern regions include Abruzzi, Molise, Calabria, Campania, Lucania (Basilicata), Puglia (Apulia), the major islands of Sicily and Sardinia, and, of course, the little islands scattered around the Tyrrhenian and Mediterranean seas, such as the Eolie and Lipari, Egadi and Pelagie. Once again, among these areas a few common traits can be discerned: In northern Italy and Sardinia butter and flat pastas are mainly used; in southern Italy and Sicily oil or salt pork and tube pastas are used; Northerners use more rice and polenta dishes as staples; Southerners use more pastas. The South grows an abundance of vegetables, olives, nuts, and fruits; the North has the only flat lands where beef can be effectively raised. The South has fresh cheese such as Ricotta, Provolone, and Mozzarella; the North makes more of the hard aged cheeses for grating, including the world-famous Parmigiano-Reggiano or Parmesan. The South serves pasta *al dente*, considered the classic way; the North tends to cook pastas slightly softer; sausages are more highly spiced in the South, blander in the North (both are marvelous!). Northern fare includes more butter, rice, truffles, seafood, and soups; the South, it is true, uses more olive oil, tomatoes, garlic, and pasta, but it uses a surprising array of less well-known and more-delicate local specialities as well.

While Italy produces and exports a relatively huge amount of wine, many delicious smaller vintages are known only locally, especially in the South. Wine is used affirmatively as food and as part of the meal. Little hard liquor is drunk. Italy is one of the more temperate countries in the world, and its social customs frown on drunkenness or even overindulgence.

The average per capita consumption of bread in Italy is at least double that in America. Tasty and expensive foods can often be used economically because they are even more delicious served in smaller quantities with bread. If pasta, as a form of bread or starch, is included in the bread category, Italians are possibly the greatest breadeaters in the Western world; but Italians do not like to double up on wheat products at the same meal. Breakfast throughout Italy is halfhearted, usually consisting of coffee with milk and a crust of good bread, although sometimes sweet rolls are eaten. When I was a kid in school in Buffalo, New York, the teacher asked the class what we'd had for breakfast. When my turn came, she was shocked when I said, "Coffee with a piece of bread dipped in it and some homemade peach brandy." The teacher embarrassed me in front of the class by making me very aware that I was so different. The next day she once again asked me what I had had for breakfast. I made up a fictitious meal of orange juice, cereal, eggs, bacon, pancakes, milk, and everything else I could remember that the other kids had mentioned the day before. Years later when I traveled to Italy, I noticed that the kids there were being raised on the same breakfast I had had. Although the American kids I grew up with thought our family "ate funny," my mother's kitchen was always crowded after school. My friends loved pizza and *pasta al forno* and rice balls, to say nothing of the wine and beer my mother offered them when they were as young as eleven or twelve years old.

The cappuccino, espresso, *caffe latte*, and other coffees served in Italy are superb, as are the ice creams and ices, confections, and pastries, with major contributions in the latter categories being made by Southern Italy. These are more often eaten between meals than as part of a menu.

The Western world's two great cuisines, Italian and French, won their respective places for simplicity on the one hand and complexity on the other. In the Italian school of basically peasant cooking, it is hard to turn out inedible food as long as one firmly commits to the principle of using the best-quality fresh ingredients. Many today believe that Italian cooking is best in tune with the requirements of a changing, modern world. It is undemanding, adaptable, and relatively inexpensive—characteristics that help it resist the pressures of rising costs. With the exception of a few dishes, most Italian foods are cooked quickly, suited to shortened kitchen schedules and the generally faster pace of today's life-style.

Bologna, situated in an area of abundance and wealth, is known as the food capital of Northern Italy; Naples, situated in an area of scarcity and poverty, is known as the food capital of Southern Italy. Increasingly, people are also discovering the delightful foods of Sicily and declaring them to be more delicate than they had imagined. Some are even proclaiming them their favorite foods in all of Italy! While Southern Italians may have less money in their pockets than Northerners, they nonetheless have a beautifully realized and delicious culinary tradition that has been handed down through the centuries. It is as simple, as elegant, as anyone could want. In this volume we will explore the foods and specialities of the regions of Meridionale, or southern, Italy; the *porcini* and *abbacchio* of Latium ("wild mushrooms" and "baby lamb"); the fish and *ragù* of Puglia; the saffron of Abruzzo; the cheeses, sausages, and chestnuts of Calabria; the clams, pastas, and pizzas of Naples; the sardines, zucchini, and sweets of Sicily; the *pecorino* cheeses, the fresh trout of Sardinia. In each case I have selected dishes you can prepare in America using fresh local ingredients with some imported food specialities.

Above all, I will try to supply sufficient knowledge of these southern regional Italian dishes to help you decide what is or is not an acceptable substitute or alternative recipe, if you need to find one, and thus avoid "manipulation of the recipes" beyond recognition of the original indigenous Italian foods. Only in this way can we take full advantage of what Italian cooking, in its full diversity and breadth, has to teach us about enjoyable and healthy cooking and eating to survive in the modern world. And only then will we be able to say with true authority, "That's Italian!"

The Italian Way of Eating

In restaurants in Italy the waiter brings courses out as you want them. Almost without exception he asks what more you want to eat after you have finished the previous course. Imagine being able to continue or terminate or adjust your meal as you are eating it. This also allows time between courses so that there is no assault on your alimentary system, only a gently progressive satisfaction of stomach and soul. With the possible exception of the antipasto or a "composed" dish, such as a casserole of pasta like *lasagne,* each item of food is presented unadorned on its own plate and as its own course in the Italian meal. When you are presented with your dish of pasta, it is complete and stands alone as a very important item of food. If it is followed by meat, fish, or fowl, these are served alone on a plate and undecorated. You will enjoy the solitary offering and begin to appreciate its taste, texture, color, and aroma without the distraction of three or four other foods heaped on your plate. This is the Italian way. If, perchance, you have a "contour" (usually a suitable vegetable) with your dish, it is served at the same time but in its own plate and off to the side so that you have to make a conscious decision as to when and how you are going to enjoy it. A single main course as such does not exist. And the whole meal is constructed according to its own theory. (But keep in mind that this is a framework and not a scientific formula and there are as many variations of it as people who use it.)

The most important meal of the day is eaten at midday, roughly equivalent to our lunch. However, much more time is devoted to eating than is common in America, and it is a highly social time. Meals have different names and can be called *cena* ("meal" or "supper") or *pranzo* (implying a more important meal, perhaps with more complicated dishes as well). A *pranzo* ("dinner party") might well begin with antipasto (which means, literally, "before the meal": *pasto* meaning "meal" and distinct from *pasta,* a dough).

Antipasti (*Before the Meal*)

Antipasto is usually eaten on festive occasions such as weddings, birthdays, or religious holidays, or as part of a restaurant meal, though it is usually omitted in the normal home routine.

Antipasto is less frequent in the South of Italy. The vast majority of old and new cookbooks on southern cooking don't even list it as a category. Southerners begin instead with *minestre*, which is almost incomprehensible to all but Italians. As confusing as it seems, *minestre* take the place of *antipasti* (plural) and can easily be what are *primi piatti* ("first dishes") on other menus! Don't despair, eventually you will understand. In restaurants, though, you almost always find a very nice array of *antipasti*. Antipasto can include diverse assortments and amounts of cured meats like *mortadella* and various salami, raw crunchy vegetables like celery and radishes, cured olives and perhaps freshly marinated fish or anchovies drizzled with extra virgin olive oil. The number of foods from which you can choose is endless. Use your own judgment. If a big meal follows, be judicious in the amount of and the type of *antipasti* you serve. You could have *bruschetta*—toasted bread prepared Roman style with fresh chopped tomatoes, garlic, fresh basil, and the best olive oil. You could have roasted peppers annointed with the best olive oil, cracked pepper, and perhaps a touch of garlic. In Sicily they say these *antipasti* are something to *grappi 'pittitu*, or "open up the appetite."

Minestre (*Soups*)

Although I have translated the word as soups, in Southern Italian terms *minestre* are often interchangeable with *antipasti. Minestre*, not meaning just "soups," but including pasta dishes and rice dishes, are used to open the meal. In Italian terms anything remotely considered a bit "soupy" and eaten at the beginning of a meal is a *minestra*. Strangely enough, you will not encounter *minestra di pesce* ("fish"). Depending on which region you are in or even what city or province, this dish is called various other things, the most popular being *brodetto* and *caciucco* in the North and *zuppa di pesce* in the South. *Minestra* per se, though, can be quite confusing because of the inclusion of some wonderful pasta and rice dishes that really should be called *primi piatti*. Even more confusing, you will see *pasta asciutta*, the generic name for pasta served on a dish with some sauce on it, listed under *minestre*.

When encountering that wonderful word *minestrone*, you get the satisfaction of knowing that here is a word that can be easily translated into a rather precise *idea* of what a soup can be. The endings *-one* or *-ona* in Italian imply that whatever something is, it is bigger than what would end in *-ino* or *-ina*, meaning "small"; hence, minestrone is a "big soup," which can be made with either stock as the base or, as is often done, with water as the base. Mountains of vegetables are put into the "big soup," your favorite herbs and other flavorings, and then it really must have some rice or pasta, potato or legumes such as beans or lentils in it to really make it a minestrone. You can also have combinations of the aforementioned ingredients. Very often this dish and a nice big piece of crusty bread constitute a meal. In smaller portions it starts a meal.

Primi Piatti (*First Courses*)

To confound you even more we have *i primi piatti*, the first courses, which are but one of many courses in the meal. The first dishes are often pasta or rice, but they can also be a *minestra* or *zuppa* or *brodo* of some type. One can safely say, though, that *primi piatti* are practically synonymous with pasta or rice. These first dishes or courses are so numerous that you would need something as big as a Webster's dictionary just to name them, let alone describe them.

For a Southern Italian, pasta is as necessary as water and air for survival. Since rich and poor alike have the same passion for it, I once claimed that pasta was the most democratic food on earth because it did the most good for the most people. On the more poetic side, pasta is like an artist's canvas. You can do virtually anything with it simply by imagining what would be good and then combining it with pasta. Pasta portions in Italy are fairly large, even when served as a first dish in a big meal. The usual standard is *un etto per una persona*. One *etto* is roughly four ounces. This is a dry measurement, which, when cooked, will at least double in weight. Add some condiments and you can see that this is a mighty portion. It is surprising to see how many people in Italy, men and women alike, easily consume this amount of pasta and then go on to other courses.

The typical style of preparation for rice is risotto, which is a very moist and wonderfully succulent dish. It becomes that way by cooking it in rich broths for the most part, but wine can be used as well.

The most essential characteristics of perfect risotto—after, of course, using the best rice you can—are its moisture and texture. The rice must be *al dente*, chewy yet tender, and its moisture should be as only the Italians can put it: *al onda*, like the waves. Actually, its texture should resemble a loose mud slide but not so wet as to be a soup, although it is eaten with a spoon and a fork.

Secondi Piatti (*Second or Main Courses*)

I secondi piatti, the second or main dishes or courses, are as varied and interesting as are the first courses. We begin to see in this course just a bit more substance, such as roasted wild game, roasted lamb or veal, or perhaps chicken, either simply grilled or in a stew. This course might include beautifully grilled fish. No doubt a fish stew could be in here, too, although it probably would not be preceded by a very wetly sauced pasta or a risotto. But remember that so far every course has been equal but different. It is a maddeningly complicated menu if you make it so. The Italians deal with it so swiftly, efficiently, and with such nonchalance that only when you partake of the meal do you see how perfect and enjoyable it all is.

Along with the *secondo*, sometimes just before or just after it, but never on the same plate, is the *contorno*, meaning literally the "contour." It actually rounds out or complements the second dish. With roast lamb you might well have artichoke as contour, which is so good with it and seems like the logical choice. Meat and vegetables and potatoes together on one plate is unheard of at the Italian table. Salads can be *contorni* (plural) and they can also be *antipasti*. This is another example of the marvelously perverse logic of the Italians.

Intermezzi (*Between Courses*)

Between any of these courses you might encounter (but only at the most important meals) an *intermezzo*, some small, either very delicate or rather potent, respite for your mouth. This could be a little dish of deep-fried vegetables or perhaps some tuna with olive oil and lemon or a little individual *frittata*. Nowadays, tart sherbet or *granita*-type ices are sometimes served, but this is mostly in very sophisticated homes or in very chic restaurants with an international influence and clientele. (Oddly enough, sometimes Italian restaurateurs speak of their "foreign" visitors and their strange ways, and the whole time they are really talking about Italians from other regions!)

Frutte, formaggi, dolci (*Fruit, cheeses, sweets*)

After the *secondo* and *contorni* comes *frutta di stagione* ("fruit in season"), *formaggio* ("cheese"), or *dolci* ("sweets or desserts"). A very important dinner might include cheese and then proceed to sweets. I can say categorically that in the Italian home the dessert is fruit. Cheese is common enough, but you don't encounter both of them as we so often find in America. Both have their own characteristics and merits. Sometimes it is a mistake to try to mix them, although that is not an immutable rule. Sweet desserts are usually saved for really festive occasions or taken at restaurant meals, although no self-respecting house would find itself without a nice big batch of hard cookies to munch on. Midmorning or midafternoon is when Italians really want sweets. Espresso and a sweet is a nice way to break up your mornings and afternoons. Italian sweets have their own character, but when you compare them to international desserts, you see that they are not as refined. Even those you find in a pastry shop have a homemade look.

Vino (*Wine*)

No Italian meal could approach completion without wine. Italians view wine as food and take it into account in menu planning just as they do pasta or chicken or bread. Italian wines are readily available and cost so little that every Italian not only has the chance to but expects to have a healthy daily ration of wine. There is little mystique about wines in Italy, and that is as it should be. Do you think there is any mystique, or should there be any, about a chicken? Wine in Italy is almost invariably drunk with food, whether at a large meal or with some cookies dunked in it. The wines so casually mentioned here are quite good by any world standard.

Red wine is by far the most available and the most popular in Italy. It is amazingly good with many kinds of delicately grilled fish and is especially good with grilled chicken with herbs. In fact, it is the preferred wine with just about every dish. With a *zuppa di pesce* made with a bit of tomato you would surely have red wine. Whites are appreciated and drunk often, but no hard and fast rule exists that white wine must be drunk with white meat, etc.

Italians manage to produce a great deal of excellent food and still have it look home-cooked. Keep in mind that in spite of the number of restaurants in Italy, the home is still the place where the majority of cooking as well as eating take place. Everyone compares the fare presented at shops and restaurants to what Aunt Benigna or Mama can cook. These are hard acts to follow! For that reason alone Italian restaurant cooking has remained essentially a *casalinga* ("home-style") cuisine, and also for that reason Italian cooking has remained a truly fine national art.

The
Italian Pantry

A FEW BASIC INGREDIENTS ARE essential for cooking Southern Italian food. Fortunately, most of them are readily available. In this section I provide advice on how to obtain those not as easy to find and on what to do with them after you've bought them. Substitutions are indicated wherever possible.

Almonds (*Mandorle*)

Whole, peeled, and unpeeled almonds are useful because you can knife-chop or, with a machine, grind or pulverize them to the degree you want. If you use lots of almonds buy large quantities and save time and labor later. For certain desserts you will need bitter almonds or, if these are not available, substitute apricot kernels usually found at ethnic food stores or at health food stores. (Sometimes these are difficult to buy because they contain prussic acid, a key element in cyanide and also the source of laetrile.) The flavor is wonderful and unique. If you have ever eaten the kernel out of a perfectly ripe peach pit that has split open, you know the taste. It is slightly bitter, hence *amaretto* (slightly bitter), the name for the famous cookies. You can use plum or peach kernels as well if you care to crack your own pits.

Almonds of any types are best used very fresh. Ideally they should be stored in a tightly sealed glass jar in the refrigerator as they become rancid quickly. If you are forced to buy large quantities, freezing them maintains their freshness almost perfectly. A tightly sealed glass jar is the most effective way to store them because it controls the moisture and it also eliminates the chance of their picking up any "freezer smell."

Anchovies (*Acciughe*)

These are essential to Italian cooking and are usually quite delicious by themselves. They are underrated as an antipasto ingredient or just as a snack. The best are large, whole ones with their silver skin and skeletons intact (save for their heads, which have been pulled off), beautifully crisscrossed and packed in salt. After they are opened you can leave them in the can in the salt, covered with plastic or foil and kept cool (wine cellar temperature is perfect, or keep them in your refrigerator). They last indefinitely. Simply take out the quantity you want, wash them in cold water, and then, using your thumbnails, separate the flesh and expose the skeleton. Grasp the skeleton with your finger and gently pull it out. The anchovies are then ready to be eaten or used however you like. The preferred kind, Margiotta-Recca, come from the seacoast town of Sciacca on the southwest Mediterranean coast of Sicily. The skinned and boned anchovies that are packed in olive oil and come mostly from Portugal are excellent. Angelo Parodi is the brand most commonly found and is consistently reliable.

Basil (*Basilico*)

Basil is pungent and powerful and is vaguely part of the mint family. It can be purple or small-leaved as is found in Liguria, where the famous *pesto* sauce originated, but mostly it is large-leaved. The variety found in America is the same as is commonly used throughout Italy. It is an easy and rewarding herb to grow. Use only the leaves for cooking because the stems tend to be bitter. However, if the basil is young with very fine stems, I am not compulsive about removing all of them. Dried basil is a waste of money. It actually becomes something else that is not good-tasting. If you are desperate, combine a tiny bit of fresh mint and bay leaf to impart the idea of basil in your dish.

Bay Leaf (*Alloro* or *Lauro*)

Californians are fortunate because the state is riddled with bay laurel trees. The leaves can be stored indefinitely in a sealed bottle. Bay leaf is critical to stews, marinades, and some soups. It imparts a wonderful depth of flavor when added to the scalded milk needed for *besciamella* (*Béchamel* Sauce, page 73).

Beans (*Fagioli*)

Stock several types because they have a long shelf life and are marvelous for impromptu meals. Red kidney beans are delicious cooked with rice or just on their own; they are great cold in a salad. Imported *cannellini* beans are perfect for soups and casseroles and are interchangeable for the most part with Great Northern white beans. Navy beans are as handsome-looking as they are tasty.

Fava beans are very good eating. They last forever dried, and if you can find them fresh and young in the market, they are a special treat just eaten peeled and out of hand. Fava beans are also called broad beans or Windsor beans. This is the original bean of Europe while the Great Northern white beans are from the American continent and did not show up in Europe until the sixteenth century.

Caciocavallo (*Caciocavallo*)

This is a very compact cow cheese with a consistency much like Gouda. It is wonderfully tasty and a very popular eating cheese in Southern Italy. It has the traditional shape of two gourds tied together with a piece of raffia (*palm*). The cheese gets its name (*cacio* = cheese, *cavallo* = horse) because when it is hung to cure with the raffia, it resembles saddlebags draped over the haunches of a horse. It comes in different shapes, perhaps some of them with large bottoms and little knoblike heads. It also comes in very charming shapes like little pigs, cows, elephants, or octopus and squid. There is a minimum of forty major types of Caciocavallo. The sub-types must be many times that number. The nice thing about this cheese is that you can eat it in chunks with bread or, if you purchase one that has been aged, you can grate it on pasta.

Capers (*Capperi*)

Capers are very pungent little buds that grow on a shrub that loves intense heat and is said to be native to Asia Minor and Southern Italy. The Arabs, Greeks, and Romans ate and liked them, and they are widely used in Southern dishes. Driving about the southern countryside on a hot day, you can see the plant growing in its favorite location: out of a rock's crevice or, even more typically, on the ancient stone walls of a city or castle. Being a desert plant, it needs virtually no water or other nutrients.

Generally, you should pick the buds while they are tiny. Young buds are known as *nonpareil* and are expensive. The biggest crops are grown in France. The Italians like them just a bit bigger, and these are either local or imported from Spain. The buds packed dry in salt are getting harder to find, but they also come in jars of salt water, which are the most common.

Capers are indispensable to several southern specialities, among them *capunatina*, Sicilian eggplant relish, and *baccalà al pomodoro*, a dish of fish, tomatoes, onions, capers, and wine all baked in the oven.

Chestnuts (*Castagne*)

After Japan, Italy is the largest consumer of chestnuts. The best chestnuts are reputedly from Calabria, but in fact they grow easily and well in most of Italy, with especially good ones from the hills around Euganea in the Veneto. However, in the mountains of Basilicata there are so many chestnut trees that a genus of flora there is called *Castanetum* (derived from chestnut). Sardinia produces nuts in abundance, not the least of which are chestnuts. Sicily, another great producer of chestnuts, was reputed to have the largest and oldest chestnut tree known to man. (Like olive trees, chestnut trees live hundreds of years. The best chestnuts are not yielded until the trees are about sixty years old.) It is reported that there existed in the foothills of Etna a chestnut tree that was planted by the Romans and had grown to a circumference of 205 feet! A wash of lava took it down in 1850.

Dry chestnuts from Italy are available most of the time in spring. Italian delicatessens in major cities should have them. They can be shipped easily and last at least a year kept in a sealed jar in a cool dry place. They can be soaked overnight in cold water and then used because they become soft and tender. These make wonderful additions to stuffings, or you could even make flamed chestnuts with sugar and rum in July!

Chick-peas (*Ceci* or, in Sicilian, *Cicciri*)

Garbanzo is another word for these tasty and pretty little round faun-colored peas. If you buy them dried, you can keep them indefinitely. Most supermarkets carry them, but try to buy them in Italian, Middle Eastern, and Indian specialty shops. Simply soak the dried peas in cold water overnight. They are utterly delicious simmered, the next day, in the least amount of water possible to make them soft and delicious. Meanwhile sauté plenty of diced onions until they are just tender and slightly gilded, then add some chopped garlic and cook until it, too, is gilded. Combine the *ceci* with the onion and garlic, cook them together for about 10 minutes, and then correct for salt. Serve the *ceci* piping hot in a rimmed soup dish, and at the table grind on plenty of fresh black pepper and drizzle on the best virgin olive oil. This makes a super first course in a meal followed by broiled fish. These peas, after simmering, are good pureed as a vegetable or added, when cooled, to salads. Garlic is perfect with them.

Some delicatessens in New York and New Jersey carry *ceci* that have been roasted and salted. These are more irresistible than peanuts. We used to make them by simmering the *ceci* until they were tender and then putting them into a pot of hot gravel over a fire, stirring constantly so that the heat of the gravel would toast the *ceci*. When they were cooked and still hot, we salted them. Eaten hot or cold, they are delicious.

This pea is not only nutritious and delicious, it is also historically very important because it released the Sicilians from the stranglehold of the French in the thirteenth century. The now famous Sicilian Vespers took place on Easter Monday in 1282, when a French soldier molested a young Sicilian girl who was suspected of concealing arms. The Sicilians were not happy with their occupiers anyway, and it was quite possible the girl was guilty. Whether by spontaneous reaction or by some design, the soldier was killed on the spot, setting off one of the bloodiest massacres in history. All who did not have a Sicilian accent were suspected of being French, French sympathizers, or French agents and were dispatched in a trice. The test word, apparently, was *cicciri*. Only a Sicilian knows how to say it right even to this day.

Fennel Seeds (*Semi di Finocchio*)

Indispensable for making sausage as they do in Agrigento, Sicily, these seeds are also wonderful on fresh slices of swordfish or tuna, panfried in olive oil. They are especially good on sautéed shrimp with a splash of white wine. And in the Italian style: Please do not strain out the seeds, they are meant to be eaten. They are also used in Calabrian *taralli*, a hard doughnut-shaped biscuit made a little like a bagel but very small.

You can buy fennel seeds most everywhere nowadays, and they keep very well for long periods in a glass jar.

Garlic (*Aglio*)

Garlic is not only abundantly available but abundantly necessary to Italian cooking. Raw garlic is used in a dish like *pasta Ericina*, which is a cold sauce of raw chopped tomatoes, plenty of chopped basil, olive oil, and salt and pepper, served over hot pasta. Chopped raw garlic is sprinkled all over. The taste of the garlic here is sharp and very pronounced. When garlic is cooked, however, it becomes sweet and very even and not so pervasive in flavor.

Garlic is best stored out of the refrigerator, uncovered, in a basket or bowl. Fresh garlic should be very firm and have a tightly closed head. The skin can be pure white or feature purple-colored tinges. It will keep fresh for at least a month or six weeks.

Glacé Fruit and Peel
(*Buccia di Frutta Candita*)

Most people do not like candied fruit peel, and I don't blame them, when one sees what is being sold in the supermarkets. Go to an Italian or Mexican store, a good health food store, or a nut and fruit shop to purchase really fine candied fruit. When you have eaten orange or lemon peel properly glacéed, you will experience a world of difference. It is easy to store, lasts a long time, and is a good buy, even the best quality. Just put it into a sealed glass jar and keep in a cool place.

Lard (*Strutto*)

Many doughs in Southern Italian cooking call for lard, whether they are for savory breads or for pastries. The best way to make it is to buy a nice piece of pork fat and cut it into small dice. Put the diced fat in a heavy pan on low heat, let the cubes render the fat slowly, and watch that you don't burn it. Adding water at the beginning ensures you won't burn the fat. Eventually the water evaporates and only the rendered fat remains. While it is very hot, carefully strain the liquid fat through a very fine sieve or cheesecloth (you will notice that it strains out crystal clear), put it into a glass jar, and let it cool. Store, covered, in the refrigerator until you use it. You can easily freeze it for long-term storage. I would divide it into smaller amounts before freezing for the convenience of easy thawing. Many foods are fried in *strutto*, and it is a perfect fat for browning meats for stew and roasts. It has a good, pure flavor and is of very high quality in that it takes high heat without readily smoking.

Buy lard that does not have any additives, but it will be hard to find. Even good commercial lards contain citric acid and BHT added for shelf life and appearance. Rendering lard is so easy that I think most people will want to do it. In my early life, even though we had a rudimentary icebox, we did not use it for things that were possible to conserve other ways. When we made large amounts of sausage, which was often, we conserved them by roasting, then layering them in a large five-gallon ceramic crock and pouring very hot liquid lard over the whole thing. Then during the season when we wanted sausage, we would scrape through the lard and dig out whatever amount we wanted. Crock and all had to be kept cool, so it was always stored in our cellar.

Lentils (*Lenticchie*)

Records show that it is probable that lentils were grown at least in 3000 B.C. They have never been very highly thought of, which is a pity because they are one of the most delicious legumes. These little charmers are perfect for using up pieces of *prosciutto* good enough only for soup. They are equally delicious stewed and served on a large dish with thick slices of boiled *coteghino* sausage or *zampone*. Boiled beef, short ribs, pieces of roast duck, goose, and pork roast all benefit in the company of lentils. Southern Italians in seacoasts and mountains alike have subsisted for centuries on dishes like lentils and pasta mixed together with some onion and garlic.

Marjoram (*Maggiorana*)

This herb (*Majorana hortensis*) is not oregano nor is it a substitution for it, as is commonly thought. It belongs to a different family and is much milder, softer in flavor, less intense, and very good in meat stuffings and minestrone-type soups. I am not saying that if you do not have any oregano you should not use marjoram, but I am saying that you should not assume the two are equal.

Mint
(*Menta, Mentuccia, Nepitella*)

What you know as mint is *Menta spicata*, the oldest known species of mint. While it is fresh and flavorful and loaded with that special tangy aroma, it does not have the subtlety of wild mint. To my knowledge, there is no wild mint to speak of in America. The Italians use *M. spicata*, which they find in the markets, but on their country outings (for many Italians that means walking out the door and turning either right or left) they find a wild plant called *nepitella*, sometimes called *mentuccia*. Once you have eaten this, you know how wonderful it is with lamb, or chopped and added to braised artichokes with garlic and bread crumbs. Recently a friend gave me cuttings for *nepitella*, but I cannot find anyplace to buy seeds.

To approximate the taste of *mentuccia*, put together two thirds basil and one third regular mint. You can also get lemon verbena at your local health food store or you can mail order it from an herb company. This mixed half and half with regular mint will also approximate *mentuccia*. You get a suggestion of flavor rather than an exact substitution with these mixtures, and I urge you to try them on lamb, chicken, or in stuffed artichokes, where they are particularly good.

Mortadella
(*Mortadella*)

Commonly known as baloney on these shores, *mortadella* is, in fact, a large pink sausage from Bologna, Italy, distinguished by chunks of fat and whole peppercorns mixed throughout finely ground pork and veal flavored with nutmeg. In Bologna I saw a whole *mortadella* bigger than a football player lying on three large sawhorses in that wonderful *salumeria* Tamburini. The best comes from Bologna, but you can get some mighty fine versions in other provinces in Italy. In America you can get a fairly respectable *mortadella* on both coasts and in the Chicago area. In San Francisco the best is made by Molinari, and nationally you can get Citterio.

The story goes—and it makes sense—that the name derives from the fact that the first sausage meat was ground up in a mortar with a pestle; hence, the root word *mortaio*, which means "mortar." To go one step further, you could say *mortaio della carne*, roughly, the "mortar used for the meat," and if you contract the two first words, you have *mortadella*. This sausage is very pungent, and a little goes a long way. In dishes like Eggplant "Sandwiches" (page 98), use just a little. A small amount, chopped fine, is delicious in lentil soup.

Mozzarella
(*Mozzarella*)

Mozzarella is buffalo or cow cheese made in Campania and now and then in other places. It is getting rare, indeed, to find real buffalo's milk Mozzarella. It is made by washing the curd (*casein*) in hot water and kneading by hand as you would bread, stretching it, and kneading some more. It is left to rest in warm whey, which eventually cools off. The cheese stays in that water until sold, usually that same day. There is also a version of Mozzarella called *affumicato*, which is smoked over damp straw that produces a white smoke. This imbues the Mozzarella with a beautiful deep chestnut color and the subtle flavor of smoke from burning straw. This is a very special cheese generally available at stores that carry a large assortment of fresh Italian goods.

The American version of Mozzarella is a world apart from the real stuff. As long as you don't compare the two, you can prepare some nice dishes with the domestic kind. It is not particularly good to eat as a table cheese, as is the case with the Italian version. In some restaurants you can start a meal with Mozzarella *bocconcini* ("little mouthfuls"). Also called *bocconcini di Cardinale* or *ovolini* (a speciality of Campania) or *fior di latte* or sometimes Mozzarella. This cheese is made into small oval shapes like eggs and, as distinct from Mozzarella, is packed in small crocks swimming with fresh cream.

Mushrooms
(*Funghi*)

To find good-tasting mushrooms, you will have to be resourceful in looking for local kinds. *Boletus edulis* (*porcini* or cepes) is the same species as is found in Europe. *Cantherellus cybarius*, otherwise known as chanterelles (which somehow do not work well in Italian dishes) is also available. You might find good cultivated mushrooms like *shiitake*, which are very meaty and quite delicious, although their stems are woody and generally not easily edible, so the yield is not as good as it should be. The most wonderful eating mushroom is the cepe (*Boletus edulis*), found mostly in the northern parts of Italy and shipped everywhere. Generally, they are gathered from the end of September through the first part of the year. They are shipped dried to the United States and are exceptionally good. They appear to be expensive, but are really not because you use so few of them. Beware of those that come from South America. They are tough and woody and the flavor is not nearly as good as the Italian mushrooms, although these are getting to be in short supply, despite their being harvested in Yugoslavia and shipped here via Italy. Also, fresh Italian *porcini* ("little pig") mushrooms are flown in while the season is on. I have seen them costing around fifteen to twenty dollars a pound. Frozen ones are also available, although their texture is not as firm as the fresh kind.

The nice part about dried mushrooms is that they keep for months in perfect condition in a closed glass jar. When you need them, simply take a small handful (I find that one ounce of dried *porcini*, which costs about three dollars, will easily flavor about six quarts of tomato sauce), place them in about one and a half cups of warm water, and let them stand for about half an hour. Gently scoop the mushrooms off the surface of the water and squeeze them dry, reserving the soaking water. Strain the water through a cheesecloth to hold back any sand or dirt that might have escaped. Add the water to the sauce or freeze it and add it to soups or sauces later. It is very flavorful, and to waste it would be a pity. If you get nice plump pieces of dried *porcini*, soak them as described and finish cooking by frying them quickly in a sauté pan with a little olive oil, some rosemary, and a hint of garlic. Eat them with bread and red wine.

Nutmeg
(*Noce Moscata*)

Unless you are using very large quantities of nutmeg, there is no reason not to use a fresh nut that you grate with a little metal scraper. The perfume is actually seductive. People who hate nutmeg probably have never had it fresh scraped. This is an invaluable ingredient for cookies and some sauces and even seems to spark up that famous dish *fettuccine all' Alfredo* known to Romans as *fettuccine doppio burro* ("fettuccine with double amounts of butter," see Fettuccine, Roman Style, page 132).

Olives (*Olive*)

All of Italy grows olives. Some trees are hundreds of years old, the average age is between three hundred and six hundred years old, although there are older ones about. They do not begin to give up good fruit until they are about twenty-five years old. They do not need a lot of water, and they can go for several months without a drop ever touching them. Too much water or even a humid climate prohibits the formation of fruit. Green olives are underripe, which accounts for their color, and black ones have been left on the tree to finish maturing; hence, their black color. Among the most famous olives are those of Gaeta, a coastal town above Naples, one third of the way to Rome, on the Tyrrhenian Sea.

The Italian way of treating olives, green or black, is to either leave them whole or slightly crush them open. First, though, they are soaked in water that is changed daily for eight days, and then they are left to soak in salted water for about one month, after which they are ready to be put up in crocks, bottles, barrels, etc. There is a salt-cured olive that calls for mixing rock salt and olives together and leaving them in the very hot sun for several days or weeks, stirring all the while. When they are shriveled, the salt is brushed off and they are stored in crocks or in wood barrels.

The characteristic flavor in these and all Italian cured olives is their bitter undertaste, without which they are worthless. The typical canned supermarket olives are cured with lye, which takes everything of value out of them.

Olive Oil, Virgin (*Olio d'Oliva Vergine*)

With so many virgin olive oils available at so many diverse prices, there is no reason not to use it as much as you want. Some Italians, and some makers and distributors of virgin olive oils claim that the best oils come from Lucca. I agree that these oils are excellent, but tell this to a southern Italian and you will get an endless speech about the virtues of southern olive oil. He may well be right, as the oils of the South are superb and have enormous character. In fact, I think they define virgin olive oil. The biggest producer of oil is Puglia, with 32 percent, followed at some distance by Reggio-Calabria, Sicily, and Tuscany. In my commercial kitchen I use nothing but extra virgin olive oil. It makes the difference.

The best olive oil comes from ripe olives that are loaded with their own natural juices and oil. The olives should not fall to the ground but be picked by people who really know what they are doing. The oil must be cold-pressed, which means that the olives and their pits are crushed under a giant stone wheel in a trough. The resulting juices are collected in a large vat, pressed to get the most oil out of the pulp, and then filtered through large woven discs of natural fibers. My father, who made his own olive oil for years, used an old but sturdy wine press for the pulp and newly washed burlap as a filter, and these worked quite well. He left the oil to float to the top of the juices, and very carefully ladled it off and put it into bottles or ceramic jugs. The oil on the very top was obviously the lightest and contained the least acid. This natural filtering was not as refined as modern methods so the resulting oils were a little cloudy. In Italy this cloudiness is regarded as a sign of quality. In America, if things look cloudy you might not be able to sell them. As a result, some of the Italian oils sold here are filtered to make them very clear and sparkly. They are excellent but not as fruity and full-bodied as the kind with some sediment. Commercial olive oil in Italy is made just as I have described except that the juices and the oil are put into a large centrifuge to separate them.

Virgin or extra virgin; that is an oily question. The degree of acidity determines what is extra virgin and what is not. If the acidity is 1 percent or under, then it is extra virgin; if it is over that amount and not more than 1.5 percent, then it is superfine virgin olive oil. If the oil is 1.51 to 3 percent acid, it is fine virgin olive oil. If it is 3.01 to 4 percent acid, it is pure virgin olive oil. Anything over that is just the dregs of the juice and oils from the processing and is sold to commercial manufacturers who extrude, under gentle heat, any remaining oil and then separate it from the juices, which are discarded. This is pure olive oil, and it can be very good. It certainly is reasonable in price, but since the product has had heat put on it and the acidity is high, it is not choice. For large volume cooking you might consider using this kind of oil.

Oregano (*Origano*)

Probably the most identifiably southern Italian herb is oregano (followed by basil). Oregano is one of those herbs that is wonderful dried. Some Italians even prefer it. It is handy to gather, or buy large bunches of it and save it to use whenever you need it. It is certainly recognized in Greece, for they produce mountains of excellent quality *Origanum* for export. The Italians import this or they use locally grown oregano. One handy characteristic of oregano is that it grows in arid soil that would not support much other growth. Plenty of it also grows wild. My friends in Sicily gather it every season and put some away for drying. I have tasted none better. The Neapolitans maintain that oregano is a must for flavoring their pizza.

Pancetta (*Pancetta*)

"Little belly" is how this name translates from the word *pancia*. In America we know a similar cut as bacon, but the traditional bacon is salt-cured, usually with plenty of preservatives, and then smoked. The Italians eat few smoked meats, although they eat lots of salt and air-cured meats like *salame* and *prosciutto*. *Pancetta* is made just like *prosciutto* and is, therefore, edible in its cured state (see *Prosciutto*, page 30). It should be sliced paper thin, laid out on crusty homemade bread, and then topped with equally thin-sliced red onion on which you grind fresh black pepper (a drop of virgin olive oil doesn't hurt); you eat this *crostino* with some sliced tomatoes and a glass of good red wine. If you ever try it cooked like bacon, you will love it.

Pancetta is very important in dishes like *spaghetti alla Carbonara* and in sauces and stuffings. The flavor is so different from bacon that I really get upset when I see bacon interchanged with *pancetta*.

Parmesan
(*Parmigiano-Reggiano*)

Parmesan is made from the best-quality cow's milk and is one of Italy's finest cheeses. It is produced in Reggio nel'Emilia and Parma, located in the Emilia-Romagna region, from which it gets its name. The best *Reggiano*, as it is commonly called, is aged at least two years. Three- or four-year-old Parmesans are exceptionally good but rarely found. *Reggiano* is included in this section because it is indispensable in all Italian cooking and is found everywhere in Italy.

Similar cheeses not from this area are called *grana* ("grainy"), which describes a characteristic of all Parmesan cheese. *Grana* is very good, but it is not as strictly controlled as *Reggiano*, nor does it tend to be aged as long.

Parsley (*Prezzemolo*)

Curly parsley, the most commonly available type, is actually not all that exciting to eat, which, perhaps, explains why so many people don't bother to do so. When you eat plain-leaved parsley, sometimes called Italian parsley, however, you can see how easy it is to enjoy it by the handful in a salad, on baked fish, or in a soup. It has a depth of flavor that is sweet, a strong and appetizing aroma, and sometimes just a hint of peppery taste. It is very special and delicious.

Pasta (*Pasta, Pasta Asciutta*)

See Pasta, page 123.

Keep a large supply of commercial pasta in your pantry. It has a very long shelf life and is very healthy indeed. Commercial pasta, whether made in Italy or in the United States, should be made solely with fancy durum semolina (hard wheat) and water. It may have some vitamins and minerals added for supplementary nutritional value. By all means eat lots of pasta because it is without question the original convenience food. With just a little or even no oil or butter and the addition of some vegetables or herbs you have a very low-calorie, high complex-carbohydrate dish. In my opinion Italian pasta products are better than their American counterparts. They taste better and they are better made, although the ingredients are the same.

Pecorino (*Pecorino*)

The most notable *pecorino* is from Lazio and is called *pecorino Romano*. There must be twenty-five major kinds of *pecorino*, but what they all have in common is that they are of sheep's milk, salty, aged, hard enough to grate, and just soft enough to eat as a table cheese. They travel well and keep a long time in perfect condition. Once you get used to the flavor of *pecorino* you will depend on it in your cooking. There is no question that *pecorino Romano* is considered to be the best or at least is the best known. They all have their virtues, and I use as many as I can find, but the Romano certainly is good.

Pepper, Black (*Pepe Nero*)

There is no reason not to have fresh ground black pepper at all times. When you smell the fresh earthiness and pungency of fresh ground pepper you begin to appreciate its value. Most Italians in the South do not use white pepper. It is the same pepper, but the black covering of the ripe peppercorn, which is allowed to mature a little longer than usual on the bush, is washed off. Therefore, you don't get little black specks in light-colored sauces. Actually white pepper is hotter without being as perfumed or as tasty as the pepper from black corns.

For an example of how zesty and balanced pepper can be and what it can bring to a dish, try the Orange and Lemon Salad (page 242).

For grinding large quantities of black pepper, I use a small hand coffee grinder, which I use exclusively for this purpose. Three or four turns of the crank provide a tablespoonful or more of fresh pepper. It descends into the little drawer provided, which I can take out and carry to the stove. If I have company and want to make life easier for my guests, I grind the pepper in my mill at the table and pass the little drawer around.

Polenta (*Polenta*)

Polenta is semi-coarse ground corn. The name derives from the Roman (Latin) word *pulmentum*, originally used to describe a gruel of wheat popular in ancient times. While corn is ground primarily in the North, polenta is seen regularly as far south as the Abruzzo and appreciated everywhere in Italy. Polenta should be bright yellow and ground to resemble heavy semolina, which is wheat. Semolina (wheat) and polenta are not interchangeable.

Prosciutto (*Prosciutto*)

Undoubtedly the best *prosciutti* are made in the North of Italy. The Langhirano hams from around Parma and the San Daniele hams from the Friuli region are legendary. All over Italy *prosciutto* is made essentially the same way: Pigs are slaughtered in early winter, when they have had their last season of fall food, sometimes comprised solely of corn or chestnuts or combinations of both, and their fat is thick, white, and firm. The ham (or in the case of *pancetta*, the belly) is put under salt in a cool place, usually in a stone barn or similar building. After forty days it is taken out of the salt and put into a cold-water bath for three days, preferably with the cold water running the whole time or else the water is changed about every six hours. Then comes the pressing down of the hams under a clean pine board with up to two hundred pounds of weight. This squeezes out any excess liquid and gives the ham its characteristic flat shape. After flavors are rubbed into the ham, it is hung and left to air-cure about nine months. A stone tower on a hill is ideal, as is an abandoned *campanile* ("bell tower") in a similar location. Then it is ready for eating.

This delicious and popular ham is eaten thinly sliced with fruit, such as melon or fresh figs, and it is also a valuable cooking ingredient. While not absolutely ideal, you can freeze *prosciutto* and slice off pieces as needed for eating or cooking. It should be bought in large pieces for best storage and can be mailed to any part of the country. Why not share some with friends if you can't use a whole one?

Provolone (*Provolone*)

Here is another example of confusion utterly understandable to an Italian but to no one else. This cow (or rarely, buffalo) cheese probably qualifies as a Caciocavallo but it is handled in different ways and at different temperatures, etc. The result is a cheese of several faces. When it is young it is slightly rubbery but quite good. In middle age it is more crumbly but still holds together and is much more flavorful.

Finally, it can be quite a dense hard cheese that can be grated although this is not considered a normal use for it. It is an excellent cheese to cook with: it loves the company of artichokes, tomato sauces, and meat and vegetable stuffings.

Red Pepper Flakes (*Peperoncino apena macinato*)

Red pepper (*Capsicum frutescans*) shows up in many guises, but this is one of my favorites. With flakes you get little jolts of hotness for just a few seconds and then in the next bite you may not get any at all. You can actually taste the food better because of all the little, but regular, "awakenings" that occur while you are chewing.

Rice (*Riso*)

Rice is considered a northern staple. And while it is true that the North is now the primary producer of arborio-type rice (short, fat, round, and very farinaceous), Southerners do their share of preparing some outstanding *risotti* such as *risotto di mare* with its dazzling array of fish and shellfish. And the charmingly named oval rice croquettes from Rome called *supplì al telefono* that are filled with soft Mozzarella cheese and when pulled apart resemble telephone wires strung out; or the famous and delicious Sicilian *arancine* ("little oranges"), a whimsical name for round rice croquettes, with tomato sauce and saffron in the rice, stuffed with chopped pork or chicken and peas. There is also the Neapolitan *sartù*, a large rice timbal filled with small meatballs and sausage.

Arborio is the standard Italian rice and is quite expensive. You can have it shipped to you if you can't find it locally. It travels well. Long-grain rice can be used, but the result won't be the same. Do not use processed rice; be sure it is simply polished and let that be enough.

Ricotta (*Ricotta*)

This delicious cheese comes from many parts of Italy, but the very best is from Rome, followed closely by that from Sicily and Calabria. A cow cheese that is essential to Italian cooking, from being mixed with garlic and spinach to being mixed with nuts and rum for desserts, Ricotta is not made as well in this country. Some producers on the East Coast make a very good product, though. *Ricotta* means literally "recooked." It is made with the leftover whey from cheesemaking. When the curds are skimmed off the top of the whey to make various other cheeses, the hot whey that remains has in it particles of residual milk solids. Some of the milk fats are left along with the protein, which is called albumen. Albumen becomes solidified when subjected to high heat, thus when you recook the whey (Ricotta) you get lovely little pillows of solidified albumen that are then skimmed off the top and put into a basket to drain. Eventually you get a whole basketful. You can eat or cook with the results and scarcely believe anything could be so good.

Ricotta is incredibly versatile. In Calabria they sometimes add red pepper flakes and then put the Ricotta in a warm oven to dry out. When it is semihard it is eaten with bread and it is divine. As you know, the world-famous Sicilian cannoli are stuffed with a sweetened Ricotta mixture.

Rosemary
(*Rosmarino, Ramerino*)

This herb is much misunderstood. It is native to the Mediterranean and grows best on parched land near the seacoast. Its name, according to the dictionary, comes from *ros* ("dew") and *marinus* ("ocean") thus, ocean dew or *rosmarino*. Many people find rosemary too strong for their tastes, and I think this complaint is legitimate. Put rosemary into a liquid such as soup or in a braised dish, and the taste will be overpowering if you were not stingy in the amount used. On roasts or for making a rosemary "brush" for spreading oil on grilled fish or chicken, you can use quite a bit. The Romans use a good deal of rosemary in cooking lamb, and the Sicilians use a fair amount on roast rabbit, but in the southern regions the use of oregano and basil probably outweighs the use of rosemary. I find rosemary indispensable with garlic in dishes like grilled or roasted pork, turkey, chicken, veal, lamb, or kid.

Fortunately, rosemary grows extremely well in most gardens. It is a perennial, as good in the winter as it is in the summer, and one medium-sized bush will take care of all of your needs plus those of one or two of your neighbors. It is also a very beautiful shrub. It is dark blue-green, and when it blooms, its tiny blue trumpet-shaped flowers are enchanting. Sometimes I break off small sprigs with the flowers and put one at each guest's dinner place.

Sage (*Salvia*)

This herb, while native to the Mediterranean, is not used in abundance in Southern Italy, but it does show up in some game and fish dishes. It is another you can easily grow. Be very careful in using dried sage: The powdered kind is unacceptable. It is better to buy dried whole-leaf sage.

Salami
(*Salami* or *Salame*)

Everyone knows this stick of ground meat that has been flavored, salted, and cured in a casing. It may be as American as it is Italian. The name is generic and means that salami can be made of most anything. The most popular and traditional are those made of pork, but there are some made with beef and pork and some made with veal and pork; the list is endless.

Salami is enjoyed as an antipasto ingredient or just eaten with a piece of bread as a snack, but Southerners also cook with it. My mother used to stuff bell peppers with little chunks of Caciocavallo cheese and thinly sliced and julienned salami. She drizzled on some olive oil, some cracked pepper, and a bit of oregano, and she baked the peppers until they were done. With bread and wine this was a special treat.

In Apulia and Basilicata they make a wonderful stuffed sausage called *soppressata*. The meat is cut, rather than ground, into medium-sized pieces, and then under great pressure (in the old days it took at least two people—one to hold the casing and the other to push the meat with all his might), the stuffing is completed. You have to press hard, as the name states, because if you don't, there will be air spaces among the chunks of meat that allow the growth of bacteria.

Salt (*Sale*)

In Italy the common salt is sea salt, and it is used extensively not only in cooking but in preserving. Suffice it to say that salt is a taste enhancer and only enough should be used to elicit flavors and not give you a taste of the salt itself. This is an indispensable ingredient for preparing pasta water.

Semolina (*Semolino*)

Winter wheat, red winter wheat, hard wheat all describe durum wheat. This is the wheat berry that becomes semolina, which in turn is used to make all commercial pasta. It is finely ground but granular and is a little bigger than grains of sugar. Semolina and water are the only ingredients used to make pasta in the extrusion method—that is, pushed through die plates under enormous pressure to produce hundreds of different shapes of pasta. The names are usually descriptive of the shapes, and some even have whimsical names. A large book would be needed to enumerate them all. Semolina is also used to make sweet or savory puddings and to make the mouthwatering *gnocchi alla Romana*, little dumplings that are bathed in butter and grated Parmesan, and then baked in the oven (see *Baked Semolina Gnocchi*, page 133).

Fancy durum flour is semolina except that it is ground finer, as fine as face powder. It can be used not only to make pasta commercially and at home, but also to make wonderful bread. It is essential for making *strascinati* or *orecchiette*, in the Pugliese specialty (see *Pasta Cushions with Meat Rolls*, page 140).

Sesame Seeds (*Sesamo* or, in Sicilian, *Giugiolena*)

These delicious little seeds, especially when put on bread and cookies, are loved by southern Italians. They are so nutty and flavorful it is hard to believe that only a few provide as much flavor as some larger nuts. There are two kinds of sesame seeds: One has a covering, like bran on wheat, and the other is polished and without a covering. I prefer those with a covering because they are a little crunchier and, I believe, a little tastier, especially when lightly toasted. These seeds are quite oily and should be stored in a jar and kept, covered, in a cool place lest they become rancid. The refrigerator or a wine cellar are the best places.

Tomatoes (*Pomodori*)

Ideally you should grow your own tomatoes or have someone who is a good gardener do it for you. Failing this, a good farmer's market might be a source. In most cases you are better off, if a recipe calls for tomatoes, using canned tomatoes. The reason is simple: Tomatoes for canning are generally picked ripe and processed at or near the field where they are grown, and there is much more control in how and when they are picked. I prefer the pear-shaped, so-called Roma tomatoes. The imported Italian ones are called San Marzano, and you can buy them for a very reasonable price.

Tomatoes should be firm but succulent, vine-ripened, smell delicious, and have a good plump appearance. Don't worry if vine-ripened tomatoes are not completely red; some green is all right and will not in any way detract from their goodness. In Italy many tomatoes to be eaten sliced or in a salad have a tinge of green. Those used for sauces, however, should be soft and red all over.

Tomato paste is still used a great deal in Italy, but Italians tend to make their own. I find the commercial paste available here good, but you cannot use too much of it because it has no real life to it. I prefer to cook down (reduce) fresh tomatoes if I can. Paste is handy if you need just a little for color or a hint of tomato flavor.

Vinegar (*Aceto*)

For salads and for some game dishes and liver, vinegar is critical. It should be made from wine. Distilled vinegar has no place in Italian cooking. The normal color for vinegar is red, but white is used now and then. This product should be easy to find, but if it isn't, you can buy some from a mail order source. It lasts, in good condition, a very long time.

Water (*Acqua*)

It seems silly to mention water—without which none of us could survive—but when it is used in cooking, it becomes another matter. If you have good local water you are fortunate. Some local water has a chemical taste. If the condition is very bad, I would recommend buying a reliable brand of bottled water for cooking and drinking. You could buy imported Italian mineral water for drinking and local bottled water for cooking. Or add a large filtering canister that has charcoal in it to your water supply; it softens and sweetens the water. Sometimes just putting water into a glass or enamel container and leaving it uncovered overnight will remove some of its chemical taste. To make it tastier before you use it, shake it thoroughly in a covered jar to put oxygen back in, or, if it is a large amount, use a big whisk and slosh the water all around.

If you think water is not very important consider this: Alfredo alla Scrofa, a restaurateur from Rome, introduced at the 1939 World's Fair his now famous *fettuccine all'Alfredo* made with lots of butter, cream, and cheese. He brought all his ingredients with him from Rome. When the pasta resulted in worldwide acclaim, was Alfredo happy? Well, sort of, but he said, "If only I had thought to bring Roman water with me to cook the pasta, then the dish would have been perfect." Roman water was thought, until very recently, to be the best on earth.

My mother used to make a fish stew with freshly gathered rainwater. Granted this was many years ago when we did not have acid rain to consider. Good-tasting water really does make a difference. You can gather rainwater and freeze it for a short period, but be sure to put it into a glass jar with a tight lid and fill it only about 80 percent full to allow for expansion when it freezes. A tight lid keeps other food flavors and odors out of the water. Consult your local Environmental Protection Agency to see whether the rainwater you might gather is safe to use.

Wine (*Vino*)

Wine is a requirement in the Italian diet and in Italian cooking. A glossary of Southern Italian wines available in this country is found at the back of the book. Menu suggestions and wine selections that follow the recipes provide specific recommendations.

Kitchen Equipment

YOU PROBABLY ALREADY HAVE ALL you need to cook from this book and it would be redundant to give a listing of every tool you should have in your kitchen. This section, therefore, is to give you a sense of what particular, or say, peculiar things you might need. In some cases you will be able to use tools you already have, but maybe not the way in which they were originally intended to be used.

Baking Sheets or Cookie Sheets

Baking sheets should be of sturdy design and fairly heavy weight or they will warp easily. You should have some that have no edges, which are good for sliding cookies off onto a cooling rack or onto a dish. You should also have some with edges so that you can make long, flat cakes to use in making a Sicilian Cassata, for example. These are often called jelly-roll pans. Buy heavy ones if you can. Bright shiny pans will give you tender, moist crust that is golden in color. Dark pans will give you darker, heavier, drier crusts, which is desirable if you are making tarts, pies, and yeast breads. There is a very heavy gunmetal blue steel pan that has very gently sloped edges and is called in baking catalogs and in most big baking supply houses a *plaque au four* (French for "baking sheet"). You can purchase one at any good kitchen store that carries a wide selection of equipment. It is perfect if you are using a flan ring for making tarts. This pan is preferred by many professional bakers, and I highly recommend it.

One of the best uses a *plaque au four* has is novel but works wonders: I cook pizza on it. I turn it upside down and place it on the bottom of the oven, if possible. Otherwise place a rack as close to the bottom as you can and set the plaque on that. Heat the oven to 500°F, or as hot as you can get it, 30 minutes before baking the pizza. Slide the pizza onto the plaque. This method works best for me, even better than the so-called pizza stones. The nice part about this is that you have a perfectly usable baking sheet as well.

Cookie Cutters

Cookie cutters are inexpensive and last a long time. Purchase several shapes, but be sure to select some rounds and squares of different sizes.

| Electric Mixer | This is handy indeed, and given the choice of having a mixer or a food processor, I would opt for the mixer in a minute. A good sturdy mixer can make a difficult job far less tedious. When I was a boy in my father's kitchen I used to knead, by hand, enough bread dough to make fifty loaves at a time. Until three years ago, I used to make my *genoise* cakes by beating eggs and sugar to the ribbon by hand. Then one day a student watching me asked why I didn't use a mixer. The truth is I never really thought about it, but since then I have enjoyed the convenience of a good strong mixer. I feel it is well worth the price, because it is a lifetime investment. It offers good results in making bread doughs, creaming butter, and whipping eggs to the ribbon and making mayonnaise. |

| Food Processor | The help of such new machines as food processors is marvelous but always be careful to judge the results of the machine's effect on the food. Onions tend to exude water when chopped *en masse* in a machine. If parsley is fresh, crisp, and very tender, and the blade of the processor is sharp enough to shave with, you can get good results, but don't rely on it. A food processor, however, can be an invaluable tool and I provide advice on when and how to use it in the recipes. |

| Grills | There is some confusion about the term *grill*. According to the dictionary, a grill is a grated utensil used to broil meat over a flame. Sometimes in restaurants you will hear the waiter say that the pancakes are "on the grill" or you can have "grilled" hamburgers. The big flat piece of iron or steel they are talking about is a griddle, on which you do make pancakes and can indeed make hamburgers.

You should get a grill, even if you live in an apartment; you need only a little outdoor space to set one up. The very popular hibachi is ideal for cooking small amounts of food. Larger, more complicated grills are nice, but unless you do massive amounts of grilling they can be messy and expensive. A grill permits you to make fish and mushrooms and meat dishes simply and deliciously, once you learn to control the heat and judge the timing. And you will find yourself grilling food you ordinarily wouldn't have thought to do that way. It is the original implement used for making *bruschetta* (Garlic Bread, page 91). That alone would make me rush out and buy one. |

| Matterello | This rolling pin is necessary if you are going to make handmade pasta. It is about thirty inches long and about two inches across. Without such a long stick you would be unable to make much pasta and the effort wouldn't be worth it. It is also handy for making large pieces of pastry dough for lining a cookie sheet or a large round tart. These are found at good kitchen-supply stores. |

| Mortar and Pestle | The Italians generally have excellent marble or wood mortars and pestles. Wood often harbors odors and flavors, but I have not found that to be true with the wooden mortar and pestle. The really heavy marble Italian mortars weigh about ten or twelve |

pounds, a heft needed for the workout they get. You can buy such a mortar at Biordi Italian Imports in San Francisco for about sixty-five dollars, and it is worth all of that and more. A very good English one made of unglazed bisque is called a chemist's mortar and pestle, and it is spotproof and odor- and tasteproof. It, too, is quite beautiful. It costs about the same as the marble one.

These implements are excellent for pounding and grinding. They are essential for making certain mashed combinations such as bay leaves, mint, black peppercorns, and garlic, the flavor base for putting into artichokes or sprinkling on rabbit. A blender or food processor is useless for these jobs.

Pasta Machine

A hand-cranked pasta machine with rollers six or seven inches wide is all you need. If the roller opening settings are infinite instead of being preset by notches, so much the better. This type of machine is rare and more expensive because it has to be more sturdily built and more precisely calibrated. I have found the most useful, average-priced machine to be the Excelsa. Purchase the kind with seven-inch rollers. It has preset notches for pasta thickness, but I find it no trouble, really, to use. Such a machine enables you to use stronger flour because it does so much of the work for you, and your pasta is superior. You can also use the pasta machine to make cannoli, which by hand are far more difficult to produce. In this case a machine is worthwhile because it does the job more easily, faster, and more accurately than by hand. This is not necessarily true of all machines. Electric pasta machines (roller type) and home extruder types are, in my opinion, not worth the money.

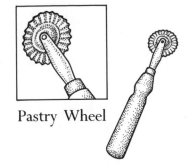

Pastry Wheel

This is a little wheel that has a wavy edge and is good for making fancy borders on dough, and when used on double sheets of dough, it makes a secure bond between them.

Potato Ricer

This handy little gadget enables you to make such things as potato croquettes with the right consistency and wonderful desserts such as Monte Bianco, which needs those little oblong shapes for the chestnuts. It is perfect for making my Cousin Mary's Potato Pudding (page 165).

Pots and Pans

You need frying pans of several sizes. Many good ones are available, but my favorites for most frying jobs are the black cast-iron pans. I know they supposedly have "hot spots" here and there. But, when you learn to use them properly, "hot spots" become a challenge; sort of like running seven miles to work or skiing downhill without bumping into trees along the way. (Among those I use are the two my mother gave me about thirty years ago. They were then already thirty years old. They work perfectly and are as pretty as any I have seen. They are pure black and glisten as though they had been dipped in enamel.)

Another good frying pan is the kind used in restaurants made of spun steel, but you can burn oil and food in seconds if you are not careful. Some of my best dishes are made in seconds or minutes with those inexpensive but indispensable pans. They are easy to season, just like the big black ones: Coat the bottoms and sides well with vegetable oil and then place the pans in a hot oven for about two hours. Carefully remove them and let them cool slowly on a rack, or just turn off the oven and wait until they are cool. From then on you should have a fairly nonstick surface unless you scrub them to death. After each use you should be able to build up and maintain that wonderful fireglaze, the shine that comes with use. If you are not satisfied, repeat the procedure one or two times more.

Other good frying pans are those of steel with a core of aluminum or copper sandwiched in between for heat dispersion. They are costly but good. Unless you are a restaurant cook, frying pans should take care of every frying and sautéing need you have.

Fragile as they are, one of my all-time favorites is the terra-cotta pan, a beautiful pan that serves as frying pan, sauté pan, and casserole dish. It can always be brought to the table after having been on an open flame or in the oven. Vesuvio makes an excellent one and if you want to spend a bit more, you can get them hand-painted from Brolli at most fine china stores that specialize in Italian products. These are generally made in Faenza, a name now generic for this kind of ware the world over that we know as faïence. They are available in New York and Chicago, and in San Francisco the best place to buy them is Biordi Italian Imports.

You will need an oblong lasagna pan, which can be metal (but preferably not aluminum), glass, or terra-cotta.

You will also need a large pot for cooking pasta. It should hold at least eight quarts, and it can be made of almost anything. Very good ones are available in either steel or aluminum, which is quite versatile. It has an insert about the same size as the pot itself, but it is a colander so that you can lift out the pasta and leave the water behind. This is handy if you are cooking more than one batch of pasta. Additionally, it generally has a smaller, shallow basket and sits above the water, making it an effective steamer for vegetables, fish, or chicken. It can be a marvelous little device for making *couscous*. Now there's a versatile pot. You can even use it for making soups and stocks.

You should have a heavier-weight stock pot or large sauce pan for making some of the longer cooking sauces. This helps to prevent scorching on the bottom.

Roasting pans are a must. You should have one small, one medium, and one large so that you will never be at a loss to roast various-sized pieces of meat or fowl, or just to brown bones for making a dark stock. They should be of the heaviest metal you can find. This makes for more even heating, thus better cooking results. It also prevents the heat from warping the pan. Roasting pans, even those with reinforcement straps, warp easily.

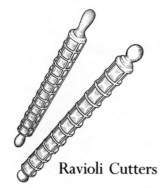

Ravioli Cutters

The crimp cutter previously described is good. You can also get ravioli forms made of metal or plastic, but my favorite and the one that provides the best yield is the fat rolling pin with small square holes. Its Italian name is wonderfully musical: *raviolatrice di legno* ("raviolimaker made out of wood"). This tool is designed specifically for making ravioli and it comes in two or three sizes. After laying out one sheet of pasta dough, cover about half of it with filling to about a half inch from the edge of the dough. Fold over the other half of the dough to cover. Then gently, but firmly and slowly, roll the pin with the little cut outs over the covered filling. You get little pillows, which you cut apart with the crimp cutter and line up, ready for cooking.

With a batch of pasta dough made with one pound of flour and rolled into a long sheet, and about one and a half pounds of Ricotta (obviously plus other ingredients), you can make, by this method, about one hundred ravioli in about five minutes.

Scales

Every kitchen should have the best quality scales built right in so that they would become "part of the woodwork," so to speak. Nothing is as bothersome, inaccurate, messy, and confusing as to have to measure things. It is better to weigh them. Try measuring and weighing one pound of flour and see what happens. The cup measure is constantly changing according to everything from the humidity in the air to who milled the flour.

Serving Dishes (Heatproof)

So many wonderful dishes made in casseroles or baking pans should be left undisturbed in their beauty and naturalness. They bring to the table a warmth not only from the fire but from the heart, and it is one of the most obvious signs of sharing. By having stove-to-table dishes you also save time and work. And somehow these dishes taste better when left in the pan they were cooked in.

Stoves

If you have a choice, buy a stove with gas burners. The flame will contour itself to the pan placed on it. Some of my trusty old pans don't have absolutely flat and perfect bottoms, and when you put these on an electric element, you get very uneven heat. If you have a good, really heavy quality pan like copper, you may be able to get away with it because copper, without a doubt, is the best heat distributor, and terra-cotta is a good runner-up. It is acceptable to have electric ovens. Many people have stoves with gas burners and an electric oven to very good effect. Electric ovens and gas ovens are like people; no two are alike. But even as good as some electric ovens are, I would still prefer a gas that has pilot lights because I can get a wonderful proofing box for bread with no extra room or cost.

If you have room for a small restaurant-quality range, you should purchase one. It is a sturdy workhorse that needs virtually no repairs. You will have to time the cooking of foods in the oven by experience and by thinking and observing.

Don't worry if you can't buy a restaurant range with a broiler. Most broilers are inadequate. They do not become hot enough, and you can't get the food close enough to it to do a satisfactory job of cooking and browning. A salamander in a commercial kitchen is the only thing that really does an effective broiling job, and this piece of equipment is not practical for even the most ambitious home cooks. Buy a small one that will hold a moderate-sized fireproof dish and let it go at that.

Wooden Kneading Board

When kneading any doughs by hand, wood is by far the best choice. You simply do not get the same grip on the dough on other surfaces. Formica, steel, and plastic are futile for this use. Purchase a piece of clear, well-sanded pine and cut it to fit your work space. That is all you need to do. To maintain it, dust it off with a clean, dry cloth. If any bits of dry dough stick to it, scrape them off. Keep it from getting wet and away from intense heat, and it will not warp and will last almost forever. If you have the kind of table on which you cannot leave the board permanently, or if you have severe sliding problems, you can do one of two things. One is to place a damp cloth under the board to create traction, but be aware that the moisture will cause warping after time. The other idea takes a little bit of carpentry, but it is worth the time and effort.

Buy a piece of half-inch- or three-quarter-inch-thick pine or birch plywood that is about four inches longer, in any direction, than you need for a kneading board. Cut off the four-inch length. Nail it onto the cut edge of the large piece of board, creating a 90-degree angle, using headless steel nails and a bit of glue, if you wish. (Looking at the board from the side you will have a long piece of wood with the short piece of wood forming an L shape.) When you put the board on the table, the little apron of wood will keep it from pushing away from you, and on return strokes, should it slide, your belly will anchor the four-inch strip of wood against the table edge.

Recipes are different things to different people. The ones that follow are guidelines, not scientific formulas. The vast majority of recipes have been handed down from one generation to another and, for the most part, not recorded in a book. Writing them down is a very recent phenomenon. In some professional cooking schools in Europe, recipes are still passed on from teacher to student, and that is how I was trained in my father's kitchen.

Think how this was done—the teacher (chef, parent, or grandparent) demonstrated with the student executing steps of a job before being able to (or given permission to) make the dish from start to finish. This is why so many recipes have been transcribed to tell you to add "just a pinch" of that and a "handful" of this. Subconsciously you can see the amount in your grandmother's hand and, in turn, imagine how it relates to your own hand. Real cooks learn this and never forget it. Writing down formulas for cooking dishes is not exactly futile, it is merely frustrating.

In my recipes it is best if you are a bit of an adventurer. I hope you will find them clearly written, which is not as much a problem as successfully conveying the meaning of what a teacher wants his students to know. In a cooking class a teacher has all kinds of guidance: he or she can look at and feel the ingredients, and step in, if necessary, to demonstrate a technique.

When you are alone with a book in your own kitchen it's best to read the entire recipe and make either mental or written notes to have handy while you execute it. This helps you visualize what you are about to do. Your experience will tell you what will be easy and what might present a problem.

Another useful trick, if you are easily distracted (as I often am), is to prepare all of the ingredients in the form needed for the recipe. If the recipe calls for one cup of chopped onions, you might do that and set it aside. Then, providing the ingredients are not in large quantities, place all of them on a baking sheet or a serving tray and arrange them in the order in which you are going to use them. Whenever possible, I put the cooking utensils on the tray. The theory here is that if you have everything you need, you will be less likely to mistake amounts, or, as I often have done, simply forget to add something. When you check your tray, you will know whether you left out an ingredient.

You will find this system very effective in helping you picture how and when all the ingredients are to go into the dish. It also has the advantage of putting everything at hand, preventing such a situation as when the meat burns and you lose time by fumbling around for a fork or some tongs.

Probably the most important characteristic of my recipes is that they are un-complicated. They reflect the kind of cooking in this book. Quite often you will see the letters *q.b.* in the recipes. *Q.b.* means *quanto basta*, "enough" or "the amount that is needed." When you read directions that tell you to fry onions in oil, q.b., it means you should take into consideration the size of your frying pan. If it is too big for the amount of onions to be fried, you have two options: to use a predetermined amount of oil that might be insufficient to cover the bottom of your pan and therefore cause the onions to burn, or to add oil, q.b., and have no problems whatsoever. These options apply to such ingredients as salt, butter, flour, water, and wine. You will find that using the q.b. system will sharpen your instincts for cooking because you will be smelling, looking, thinking, and making judgments. Nero Wolf, one of the world's greatest detectives (and my idol because he hates crime and loves to eat) always said to his factotum, Archie, that he, Archie, could always be trusted to act for Wolf because he had been taught to use judgment based on experience. The same can and should be true of you in your kitchen with my recipes. Above all, have fun and enjoy the experience of cooking.

PIZZE E PANE

Pizzas
and Breads

Bread is indispensable in the Italian diet. It is appreciated plain or topped with a few morsels of piquant condiments to make it zestier (perhaps ensuring that those tag ends of good food, insufficient in quantity to make a dish, do not go to waste but decorate and flavor the bread). While much bread is bought in bakeries, many Italians still enjoy making their own. The same is true of pizzas.

Making your own bread is not only easy but it is very satisfying and with a little practice will become part of your everyday routine. Bread is one of the few dishes left on earth that you can make and fully control from start to finish with the technique and pride of an artisan.

Garlic Bread (*Bruschetta*) cries out to be made with homemade bread. The stuffed breads in this section are special and I doubt that, apart from Pizza and Calzone, you would be able to buy them anywhere. They can, with the addition of a side dish or two, or some salad, comprise a meal. After making such recipes as Pizza, Lanciano Style, assorted Focaccias and Calzones, to say nothing of the Sicilian Bread Roll, Old Style (perhaps my favorite), there is a feeling of triumph and fulfillment. Eating the delicious results is a reward of another sort.

⅔ cup warm water, not over 100° F

1½ teaspoons yeast, dry or fresh

¾ teaspoon salt

2 cups bread flour

DOUGH FOR PIZZA AND FOCACCIA

Add 3 tablespoons virgin olive oil to the warm water when you make bread dough. NOTE: You can easily double or triple this recipe.

Put the warm water in a large mixing bowl. If the bowl is cold, warm it first by rinsing with hot water. Crumble the fresh yeast into the water or sprinkle the dry yeast over the surface. Let it sit for 3 or 4 minutes and then gently whisk the water around to mix in the yeast. Add the salt and mix again. Add the flour, mix with the liquid, and start kneading. When the dough is soft and sticky but pulls away from the sides of the bowl with fair regularity, dump it out onto a wood surface and continue to knead it for about 12 minutes. If you are using an electric mixer, beat the dough on medium speed for about 7 minutes. The dough should have as much water in it as it will hold and still be somewhat manageable. Even if it is very sticky, do not add flour until you are convinced that further kneading and contact with more air will not dry it. Only then start adding an occasional small veil of flour as you continue working the dough.

When the dough is well kneaded, shiny, and smooth, clean the mixing bowl, put a little flour in the bottom of the bowl, and put the dough back in. Cover it with a clean kitchen towel, cover that with a thick, folded bath towel, and put the bowl in a warm place (about 80° F) to proof for at least 2 hours. The dough should be at least twice the original volume. When it is, punch it down and put the covers back on, and let rise again for another 2 or 3 hours. The longer and slower the proofing, the better the bread will taste.

You could even make your bread dough late at night and, providing you do not have a super-hot kitchen, proof the dough through the night. In the morning you could shape your loaves and then bake the bread after it proofs again. Many professional bakers prepare their dough this way.

When the dough has risen the second time, take it out of the bowl and shape it into loaves. I prefer *pane casereccio*, or *pagnotta*, homemade rustic loaves. The shape is round and a little bit flat. Make two 20-ounce loaves using 2½ recipes of dough if that suits you. You could make one large loaf, which is fun and dramatic if you have a crowd to feed. Little rolls of about 3 ounces are also nice to make. You can also make the bread into two football-shaped loaves or even larger and thinner shapes.

If you are in a hurry, you can form the bread into loaves after the first rising, proof them, and bake them with good results.

If you plan to bake the loaves on a preheated *plaque au four*, let the loaves rise in a warm place on a floured kitchen towel or cookie sheet, covered with another towel, until they are plump and firm, about an hour.

Basic Bread Dough for Making Homemade Italian-Style Bread, Pizza, and Focaccia

MAKES 1 POUND OF BREAD DOUGH

Making good homemade Italian-style bread eludes most people. Part of the problem is that homemade loaves are always compared to the kind bought at a bakery. Homemade bread, too, can possess the features of professional bread, including those large holes so characteristic of Italian bread (they emerge during a long, slow proofing).

The recipe that follows will serve you well if you want large round country loaves (*pagnotta*), baguette- or baton-shaped ones, or small rolls. You can also use it to make *pizze* or *focacce* by adding some olive oil while you are mixing it, or even beating it in later. It is a virtually indestructible and eminently versatile dough.

Basic Bread Dough
(*Pasta di Pane*)

YEAST: Fresh and dry yeast produce equally good results. Measure yeast by weight, and use the same quantity of fresh or dry yeast. To insure freshness, buy yeast frequently and in small amounts.

WATER: Yeast dies a quick death in water over 110° F. I use water the same temperature as my wrist. When I pour water over the inside of my wrist and cannot feel a change of temperature, I know the water is the right temperature.

FLOUR: Use bread flour if possible. All-purpose flour will also make a good loaf. You may add up to 20 percent whole wheat flour for a tastier, darker, and more Italian-type loaf. You could add up to 50 percent fancy durum flour to produce a firm, yellow-tinged loaf.

EQUIPMENT: Bake bread on a *plaque au four* (page 35). This works better than anything else I have tried, including unglazed tiles.

Pizza

The word *pizza* usually conjures the image of a round red object with the thinnest crust possible and the thickest topping possible. This is not really what pizza is all about. Many forms of flavored dough are called pizza in Italy. They range from the sumptuous Pizza, Lanciano Style, a square creation consisting of bread dough with a cured-meat and cheese filling and a sheet of pasta on top to the most unassuming, such as Roman (or Easter) pizza, a sheet of dough infused with lemon zest and eggs, and eaten as a bread with salami, salad, and cheese. What follows is a tour of the different kinds of pizzas the inventive southern Italians have created. They are irresistible, easy to make, and good in any setting, casual or elegant.

Assorted Pizzas
Pizze Diverse

Here are different toppings to put on pizzas. I have selected just a few to show the range and character of this wonderful, earthy, flat bread.

The portions are for 4 pizzas using 1½ recipes of Basic Bread Dough made with olive oil. The rest of the ingredients are *q.b.*, or to taste, unless I know the correct amount, in which case I certainly share them with you.

WINE: Etna Rosso (page 308), Marino (page 306), Greco di Tufo (page 302), Cannonau di Sardegna (page 307), or Corvo Rosso (page 308)

If you prefer, you can dust the unheated *plaque au four* heavily with flour and place the loaves on it to rise in a warm place, covered with a towel.

Half an hour before you are ready to bake the bread, preheat the oven to 475° F. Put a heavy veil of flour on the tops of the loaves. With a straight razor or a very sharp knife, slash the tops to permit expansion in the oven, so that the loaves don't split or collapse. If you are using a preheated *plaque au four*, put it on the lower rack of the oven while it is heating. For a loaf with a thick crust, put a shallow pan of hot water in the oven at the same time. Put the water as close as possible to the source of heat and leave it there the entire baking time. If the water evaporates, replenish it with boiling water.

Carefully place the loaves on a well-floured rimless cookie sheet or baker's peel and immediately shake and shimmy them onto the plaque. If the loaves have risen on a baking sheet, place it on top of the *plaque au four*. If you have placed the shaped loaves on a well-floured *plaque au four* to rise, simply put the *plaque au four* in the oven.

After 10 minutes, reduce the oven temperature to 400° F and bake the bread for about 40 minutes. To test for doneness, take the bread out of the oven, using mitts or a kitchen towel, and knock it on the bottom. If it sounds really hollow, it is done. If the knocking sound is halfhearted, put the loaf in to bake for another 10 minutes and check again. Bake rolls the same way, but check for doneness every 5 minutes. They should be golden and done in about 15 minutes.

Take the loaves out of the oven and place on a rack to cool. If you put the loaves down on a flat surface, steam will be trapped and make that part of the bread soggy. You can also stack the loaves on their sides against something solid to cool. The loaves should not be eaten hot unless you plan to make *pan i ogghiu*. If you do, cut a loaf of hot bread in half horizontally. Lay the two steaming halves out on a board and drizzle them with a lot of extra virgin olive oil. For a 20-ounce long loaf I would use about ⅔ cup oil. Then, grind evenly on each half loaf about ¾ teaspoon very fresh, coarsely ground black pepper. Put the top half on the bottom half and, using all your weight, press them together. Let them rest for about 2 minutes. Then cut large slices and eat them, accompanied by a large glass of red wine. Raw onions could be eaten also, as could dead ripe vine tomatoes.

Homemade bread will remain fresh, out of the refrigerator and wrapped in plastic, for about 4 or 5 days.

Pizza Margherita

1½ recipes Basic Bread Dough (page 47) with olive oil, once risen

Semolina or all-purpose flour for dusting the peel

6 large tomatoes, cored and sliced about ⅛ inch thick

1 pound Mozzarella, thinly sliced

About 20 large fresh basil leaves, coarsely chopped

Salt to taste

½ cup virgin olive oil, or q.b.

Place the sliced tomatoes into a low-sided dish that is easy to reach into, and spread the Mozzarella out on a large plate for easy reach. (If you pile it up too high, it sticks and slows you up.) Put the basil leaves in a bowl, and have the salt and olive oil handy.

Line the bottom of your oven with tiles or use the plaque as low down as you can get it. Preheat the oven to as high as it will go (but not to broil) for about 25 minutes before you bake the pizza.

Cut the bread dough into 4 pieces, and roll them into circles about 9 inches around. The dough should be a little less than ⅛ of an inch thick. Lay them aside on a lightly floured cloth for later use, but do not stack them or they will stick.

After the pizzas are rolled out, liberally sprinkle the peel with some semolina (which I prefer) or flour. Put one of the pizzas on the peel, and work quickly to put the topping on. (If you do not work quickly you could moisten the dough, which will stick, and you may never get it off in one piece. If you use a cookie sheet and the dough sticks, it is not such a problem; just put the cookie sheet with the stuck pizza on it in the oven, and it will cook very well and slide off when the dough is cooked.)

Put ¼ of the tomatoes on in concentric circles about ¼ inch away from the edge of the pizza. Cover the tomatoes with ¼ of the Mozzarella, scatter on ¼ of the basil leaves, and sprinkle the surface with salt. Drizzle at random all over the pizza 2 tablespoons or so of olive oil.

Open the oven door, and with a jerking motion of the arms, shake the pizza onto the hot plaque or tile. See that it is properly placed, and then close the door. The pizza should be done in about 7 minutes. Check the edges; if they seem brown, lift up the pizza with the edge of the peel, and check if the bottom is brown also. It will be spotty. That is normal. The top should be hot and bubbly.

Remove the pizza from the oven with the peel, put it on a heated plate, and eat it immediately. You can cut it into 6 or 8 pieces with a large knife or a pizza cutter, if you wish, before serving it. Repeat procedure with the 3 remaining pizzas.

This is my favorite pizza because of its simplicity. The ingredients, therefore, must be of the highest quality, so it is best to wait for summertime for fresh, ripe tomatoes, and until your wallet is full in order to buy the best imported Mozzarella. Fortunately, best-quality virgin oils are actually within most people's budgets. To tell the truth, I also make this pizza in the winter with canned tomatoes.

Another version of this pizza is called *Margherita bianca* (white), which means you leave off the tomatoes. This pizza is equally tasty, a good choice if you want tomatoes somewhere else in your menu.

MENU SUGGESTIONS: This is a terrific antipasto for a sit-down dinner if you make little individual pizzas. For a buffet you could make bigger pizzas and cut them into whatever size pieces you like, but in no case make them too dainty. A large platter of assorted *contorni*, such as Green Beans in Olive Oil and Lemon Juice (page 237) or Almond Peppers (page 249) would be good with the pizza or after it. You could also add a separate dish of Mussels with Saffron (page 103) to the meal.

WINE: Ravello Rosso (page 303)

Pizza alla Romana

Roman-Style Pizza

The Romans like their pizza even thinner than the Neapolitans do. You might well get 5 pizzas out of the Basic Bread Dough recipe (page 47).

1½ recipes Basic Bread Dough (page 47), made with olive oil, once risen

12 anchovy filets, whole or broken up

Make a Pizza Margherita (page 49) either with tomato or without (*bianca*). Arrange the anchovies in any design you like and proceed with the recipe.

¾ pound, or q.b., fresh porcini mushrooms, or 1½ ounces dried

About 3 tablespoons virgin olive oil for frying, or q.b.

Salt to taste

Freshly ground black pepper, q.b.

Big pinch finely chopped parsley

1½ recipes Basic Bread Dough (page 47), made with olive oil, once risen

Pizza con Funghi

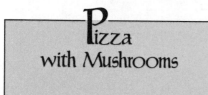
Pizza with Mushrooms

Slice the *porcini* about ⅛ inch thick and then cut them up into pieces about the size of a quarter. If you are using the dried, soak them in water in a deep, medium-sized bowl for about 1 hour. (Be sure there is enough water to enable the mushrooms to float. This allows any sand, which is heavy, to drop to the bottom of the bowl.) After an hour, scoop up the mushrooms floating on the surface and squeeze as much water out of them as you can. Strain the water through a cheesecloth and save the water for use in soups or sauces later. (The water is highly flavored with the mushroom taste, and it would be a pity to waste it.)

Heat about 3 tablespoons of olive oil in a frying pan, and add the mushrooms. Fry them over high heat for 3 to 4 minutes, or until they become slightly golden at the edges. Sprinkle on some salt and pepper, and throw on the chopped parsley. Stir the mixture, and let it cook for about 1 minute longer. Put the mushroom mixture into a bowl and let it cool until you are ready to use it on the pizza.

Spread the pizza dough out, and spread the mushrooms equally on it. Drizzle on a few threads of fresh virgin olive oil and bake as directed. No cheese, please. Bake according to directions for Pizza Margherita (page 49).

Virgin olive oil, q.b.

3 garlic cloves, peeled and well crushed

1½ pounds tomatoes, cored, peeled, and very well crushed

3 pounds Cherrystone clams, or 2 pounds Manila clams, in the shell

1½ recipes Basic Bread Dough (page 47), made with olive oil, once risen

Salt to taste

Plenty of freshly ground black pepper

1 tablespoon oregano, dried or q.b.

Pizza alle Vongole

Pizza with Clams

Heat 2 tablespoons of olive oil in a frying pan, add the garlic, and brown it, being careful not to burn it. Add the tomatoes, and let them cook over high heat for 15 minutes or until they become slightly dense (because the juice will evaporate). Remove the pan from the heat, and set the tomatoes aside to cool.

Scrub the clams to eliminate as much sand and debris as possible. Put ¼ cup of water into a pan with a lid, add the clams, bring the water to a boil over high heat, and steam the clams open. Do not overcook them; when they are open they should be done. Remove the pan from the heat, and remove the clams to a bowl to cool. (Reserve the broth to drink, or use it in a fish dish later.)

In Italy clams are served out of their shells, although recently it has become a novelty to serve them in their shells right on the pizza. If you are going to serve them out of their shells, shell the clams as soon as you can handle them, put them into a clean bowl, and drizzle on just a bit of virgin olive oil. Set aside for later use. If you are going to serve them in their shells, simply drizzle on a bit of olive oil, and set aside for later use.

Prepare Basic Bread Dough with olive oil, once risen, as directed on page 47. Spread the cooled tomato sauce evenly over the surface of the pizza, and sprinkle on a bit of salt and plenty of pepper. Drizzle on threads of virgin olive oil, and then sprinkle on the oregano. Put the pizzas into a preheated 500° F oven to bake. When they are about 3 or 4 minutes from being done, quickly remove them from the oven, and scatter on the clams, with or without the shells. Put the pizzas back into the oven for 3 to 4 minutes more. Serve the pizzas piping hot. No cheese, please.

Pizza Lancianese

Pizza, Lanciano Style

MAKES
1 14 × 15-INCH
OBLONG PIZZA

1½ recipes Basic Bread Dough (page 47), made with olive oil, once risen

5 ounces thinly sliced prosciutto

1 pound shredded Mozzarella, or use domestic Provolone

3½ ounces very thinly sliced salami

4 tablespoons drained capers, chopped

4 ounces very thinly sliced, large mortadella, cut in half and then in julienne strips

⅔ cup Parmesan, cut into little pieces

12 or 14 big grindings of fresh black pepper

4 large eggs, beaten

3 ounces very soft unsalted butter

5 ounces fresh, uncooked Pasta Dough for Lasagna (page 123), in 2 very thin sheets to match the size and shape of the baking pan

2 tablespoons virgin olive oil, and q.b. for brushing the pasta dough

This pizza is by far the most unusual I encountered in Italy. It has bread dough on the bottom, *mortadella*, salami, prosciutto, Mozzarella, and Parmesan in the middle, and a pasta dough on top. It is a pizza grand enough to serve at your most important party. The recipe was given to me by Augusto Chiavara, one of my food mentors.

MENU SUGGESTIONS: With Mushrooms Roasted with Pine Nuts (page 239) as an antipasto and *contorni* of Deviled Broccoli (page 217) and Roasted Onions (page 233), this becomes an earthy and satisfying meal. Chocolate Ice (page 291) or Spumoni (page 296) would make a nice finish to the meal.

WINE: Lacryma Christi del Vesuvio Rosso (page 305)

Push the bread dough into the baking pan so that it fits the bottom and goes up the sides comfortably. (Take your time, as the dough, when stretched, will resist and might spring back a lot. Persevere.) When the dough is stretched out, lay the *prosciutto* evenly on the bottom. Scatter on the shredded Mozzarella, and the capers. Lay the salami in a single layer over the cheese and scatter on the *mortadella*, the Parmesan, and the black pepper. Drizzle the beaten egg all over the surface and dot the surface evenly with the soft butter. Cover the surface with one sheet of the uncooked pasta, and brush it liberally with about 1 tablespoon of the oil. Place the other sheet of uncooked pasta on and tuck the pasta between the filling and the Basic Bread Dough to make a neat appearance and to anchor it. Then go around the edge of the pan, and pull the bread dough up over the edge of the pasta sheets by about ¾ of an inch. When the bread dough shows, pinch it down on the fresh pasta to make a neat border and to secure it as well. Brush the entire surface liberally with another tablespoon of olive oil. (If you cannot roll a thin sheet of pasta as large as the baking pan, you can barely overlap several sheets. Be sure to paint the edges that touch each other with beaten egg to make a sort of glue to hold the sheets together while the pizza bakes.)

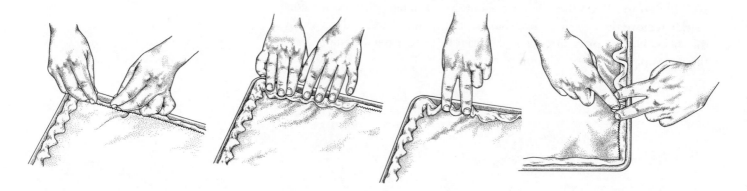

Prick the pasta top all over with a fork about every inch, as you would prick the bottom of a pie shell. Let the pizza rise a bit in a warm spot for about 15 minutes and then bake it in a preheated 375° F oven for about 45 minutes, or until the bottom crust is a deep gold and looks well cooked. You can check this by sticking a knife or fork down the side of the pan and lifting up a corner of the pizza so that you can see it. Remove the pizza from the oven and let it rest for about 10 minutes. Remove it from the pan, and lay it onto a board on which you can cut it.

The pizza can be eaten hot or cold. I find it is best at just warmer than room temperature. It can be made the morning of the evening you want to serve it. It is best if not refrigerated, unless you have so much that it cannot be eaten at one time. In this case, wrap it in plastic wrap after it cools and refrigerate it. When you want to eat some, let it come to room temperature first. If you want it warmer, wrap it in foil, reheat it in a preheated 375° F oven for about 15 minutes, then unwrap it and leave it in the oven for about 3 minutes more.

NOTE: As a lunch dish with salad this pizza will easily serve 12. A non-Italian use for the pizza would be to use it at a cocktail party. Serve it slightly warm, cut into 1½-inch squares. This should produce about 90 pieces.

2 large onions, peeled and diced about ¼ inch square

6 tablespoons virgin olive oil for frying and drizzling

1 pound tomatoes, cored, peeled, and well crushed

1½ recipes Basic Bread Dough (page 47), made with olive oil, once risen

Salt to taste

Plenty of freshly ground black pepper

About 1⅓ cups grated pecorino cheese, or q.b.

Pizza alla Cipolla

Pizza with Onions

Fry the onions in 2 tablespoons olive oil until they just begin to turn golden. Set them aside in a medium-sized bowl.

Put 2 tablespoons of olive oil and the tomatoes into a clean frying pan to cook over high heat for 15 minutes, or until they are slightly dense. Remove them from the heat, and add them to the onions. Let the mixture cool, and reserve it for later use.

Make the Basic Bread Dough as directed on page 47. Spread on the onion and tomato mixture, and salt and pepper to taste. Scatter on the grated *pecorino* cheese, drizzle on plenty of olive oil, and bake the pizza in a preheated 500° F oven for 7 minutes.

Pizza di Scarola

Christmas Eve
Pizza, Campanian Style

About 20 Gaeta olives, or use
Calamata, pitted and coarsely
chopped

4 tablespoons pine nuts, or q.b.

4 teaspoons small black or white
raisins, coarsely chopped

2 tablespoons capers, coarsely
chopped

1 medium head chicory or curly
endive, well washed

Virgin olive oil for frying and
drizzling

8 anchovy filets, chopped in pieces

1½ recipes Basic Bread Dough (page
47), made with olive oil, once
risen

Salt and pepper to taste

Put the chopped olives in a medium-sized bowl. Brown the pine nuts in a
frying pan with no oil, being careful not to burn them, and add them to the
bowl with the olives. Add the raisins and the capers to the olive and pine
nut mixture, mix everything together, and reserve it for later use.

Cut the chicory into 8 parts lengthwise. Put it into a sauce pan with
about 1 cup of water, and boil it for 5 minutes, or until it is very tender.
Drain the chicory well, reserving the water, and spread it out on a plate to
cool. When it is cool, wrap it in heavy kitchen towels, and squeeze as much
water out as you can. (The water in which the chicory was cooked tastes
delicious in homemade soup; or, drink it with some salt, pepper, and a drop
of olive oil added; or dispose of it.)

Cook the anchovies in about 2 tablespoons of olive oil in a frying pan
over medium heat, mixing the pieces of anchovy all around. Add the drained
and squeezed chicory, and mix it well. Add a bit more oil if it looks a little
dry. Gently cook this mixture for about 5 minutes, stirring often. Cool the
mixture, and set it aside for later use.

Make the Basic Bread Dough, with olive oil, once risen, as directed on
page 47. Spread the olive and pine nut mixture over the surface of the dough,
and then drizzle on a few threads of olive oil. Spread the anchovy and chicory
mixture over the surface evenly, and sprinkle on a bit of salt and plenty of
freshly ground pepper. Drizzle on quite a few threads of olive oil, crisscrossing
the whole surface of the pizza. Bake in a preheated 500° F oven for about 7
minutes. Eat the pizza piping hot.

2 medium bell peppers, red or green

1 large garlic clove, peeled and
   finely chopped

1 tablespoon fresh Italian parsley,
   finely chopped

   Salt to taste

4 or 5 grindings of fresh black
   pepper

Virgin olive oil for drizzling, q.b.

1½ recipes Basic Bread Dough (page
    47), made with olive oil, once
    risen, or q.b.

About ¼ pound fresh anchovies,
cleaned and beheaded (canned in
oil will do if fresh ones are not
available)

Burn the skin of the peppers over an open gas flame or in a broiler, turning
them frequently (see page 104). Brush the charred skin off them. Remove
the core and the seeds, and cut them into slices smaller than ¼ inch. Put
the peppers in a bowl and sprinkle on the garlic, the parsley, and some salt
and pepper. Drizzle on about 1½ tablespoons of olive oil and let the mixture
marinate for about 1 hour.

Preheat the oven to 375° F.

Take half of the bread dough and spread it out as for pizza, about ⅛
inch thick. Lay the slices of pepper all around the pizza in concentric circles,
leaving enough space between each circle to place ½ an anchovy (if you are
using fresh anchovies, they need no pre-cooking, since the heat of the oven
will cook them). Scrape the bowl the peppers were in to get all the oil and
the bits of garlic and parsley onto the surface of the pizza. Sprinkle on more
salt and pepper, and drizzle on about 2 tablespoons of olive oil. Spread out
the remaining half of the dough as for pizza and cover the first pizza. Pinch
the edges really well to make a secure closure.

Bake on a dark metal sheet or a baking stone in the oven until the top
and bottom are golden, about 30 minutes. (You could use a dark metal cake
pan, and the resulting pizza will be softer and thicker. If you have a brick
bread or pizza oven, it would be ideal. The usual woods for burning in it are
olive or bay.) Let the pizza rest for about 10 minutes and then eat it. It is
good hot or at room temperature.

Pizza dei Morti

Pizza
of the Spirits

FOR 2 TO 4 PERSONS

The following recipe, which is traditionally eaten on All Souls' Day, November
2, was given to me by my lawyer friends
Augusto Chiavara and Luigi Russo in the
Abruzzo. It is among the best dishes they
taught me—a kind of pizza sandwich with
fire-roasted bell peppers in between two
layers of pizza.

MENU SUGGESTIONS: Pizza is generally
the main part of the meal unless you intend
to have many courses. With this pizza I
would have Sweet-and-Sour Baby Onions
(page 234), Mushrooms Roasted with Pine
Nuts (page 239), followed by Orange and
Lemon Salad (page 242). Dessert is not
really called for.

WINE: Ravello Rosso (page 303)

Pizza Pasquale (o alla Romanesca)

Easter (or Roman) Pizza

MAKES 1 11-INCH
ROUND OR 9×12-INCH
RECTANGULAR PIZZA

No one is quite sure why this pizza must be made by starting with bread dough and then adding egg yolks and other ingredients. Everyone asks, "Why can't you add the eggs when you make the dough?" I have tried it both ways, and there is a difference, albeit a small one. Adding egg yolks while making the bread dough makes the pizza appear a little like a *brioche* but does not substantially change or improve it enough to warrant doing it. Besides, it would no longer be an authentic *pizza alla Romanesca*. This last point is the one I consider the worthiest.

Essentially, this is an egg-flavored, lemon-infused flat bread that is wonderful with most anything at any time. It used to be made only at Easter, but like so many things nowadays, it is found more and more at other times of the year.

MENU SUGGESTIONS: Use *pizza alla Romanesca* whenever you would use bread. It is very good with salads or accompanied by salami and cheese. It is also delicious toasted, although this is not the typical way to eat it.

WINE: Frascati Superiore (page 305) or Etna Bianco (page 308)

3 tablespoons lard
  All-purpose flour for dusting the work table and preparing the pan
1 recipe Basic Bread Dough (page 47), once risen
3 ounces fried pork cracklings (9 ounces before frying)
3 large egg yolks
  Big pinch of salt
  Zest from 1 lemon

Grease a 9 × 12-inch rectangular pan or an 11-inch round one well, using ½ tablespoon of the lard and dusting it with some flour. Set aside.

Dust a small amount of flour on a work surface and knead the dough for 2 to 3 minutes, or until it is very soft and elastic. Incorporate each remaining ingredient in the order listed into the dough. (This could take 15 to 20 minutes and is a little messy when you get to the egg yolks. But persist. You could use an electric mixer with a dough hook at medium speed.) If the dough looks too wet and sticky at this point, add *small amounts* of flour by the teaspoonful.

Let the dough rest, covered with a kitchen towel, for about 15 minutes and then gently push and stretch it by hand into the greased baking pan. It will be very resistant and elastic, but you will win out. Don't give up. When the dough is very nicely in place in the pan, cover it with a kitchen towel and put it in a medium-warm spot to rise for 4 to 5 hours. If it rises rapidly, the place is too warm, in which case move it somewhere cooler. During this long rising time the pizza develops its characteristic taste and forms little air pockets inside.

When it is time to bake the pizza, preheat the oven to 350° F and put the pizza on a rack in the middle of the oven. Bake for 45 minutes, or until the bottom and sides are a deep gold color. You can check this by lifting one edge up with a sharp knife and looking.

Eat the pizza lukewarm or cold. It keeps well wrapped in clear plastic and stored out of the refrigerator.

Sfinciuni (Sicilian name) are generally known to have a top and a bottom, the ultimate deep-dish pizza. Some, however are more like a thick pizza. In either case the dough must ultimately be the most important ingredient in the dish. The savory fillings or toppings are almost limitless but only in variety, not quantity. Use bread dough made with olive oil, risen only once, for these dishes. Here are 2 recipes for focaccia, one with a dough top and one without.

Sfinciuni o Focaccia (Focaccia Savory Pizza Bread)

⅓ cup virgin olive oil

⅔ cup onion fine chopped

1½ recipes Basic Bread Dough made with olive oil (page 47) and juice from ½ lemon

8 ounces Caciocavallo cheese, finely chopped

3 ounces salami sliced very thin and julienned

¼ teaspoon fresh ground black pepper

⅔ cup Marinara Sauce (page 78)

Optional: *Use 6 anchovies packed in oil cut into 5ths instead of the salami.*

Heat 1½ tablespoons oil in a small frying pan and fry the onion until translucent. Reserve for later use. Preheat the oven to 400° F. Knead the bread dough for 1 or 2 minutes and incorporate the lemon juice. Be sure it is well mixed. Sprinkle on a bit of flour if the dough is too sticky to work with. Lightly oil a 9-inch cake pan or any round pan and spread half the bread dough in it. Scatter on the onion, cheese, salami, and black pepper and then drizzle the marinara all over. Spread or roll the second piece of dough out to a circle and put it down on top of the filling and push the edges together as best you can. Drizzle or brush the top of the dough with the rest of the oil. Bake in the lower third of the oven for 25 to 35 minutes or until the crust is deep gold all over. Invert the pan onto a serving dish and serve the focaccia immediately. If you leave it in the pan it will get soggy from the steam. If you plan to eat it at room temperature place it on a cooling rack.

Sfinciuni di San Vito

Saint Vitus Focaccia

MAKES 1 9-INCH PIE

WINE: Etna Rosato (page 308) or Girò di Cagliari (page 307)

Focacce Capriciose

Capricious Focaccias

MAKES 1 11 × 17-
INCH FOCACCIA

These are called capricious because there is no hard and fast rule about toppings. This happens to be a selection of ingredients most of you will have on hand. The ingredients are approximate but you will soon get the idea of how to make delicious focacce.

WINE: Torre Ercolana (page 306), Torre Quarto Rosso (page 301), Solopaca (page 304), Trebbiano di Aprilia (page 306), or Ravello Bianco (page 303)

⅓ cup or more virgin olive oil

1½ recipes Basic Bread Dough made with olive oil (page 47)

Preheat the oven to 400° F. Grease the pan with about 1½ tablespoons oil and push the dough in to fit. Scatter on any of the ingredients listed or combinations, but remember this is a savory bread, do not overdo it. Make deep indentations all over the surface of the focaccia and push the ingredients into the dough with your fingers pointed out stiffly. It is essential to drizzle on more oil just before putting the focaccia in the oven. Use the remaining oil or even more. Bake the focaccia for about 30 minutes or until it is puffed and the top and bottom are a golden color. Serve hot or at room temperature. These focaccias can be used as savory bread for almost any meal. You can also make sandwiches of them, the best known one being a Muffaletto that always includes thin sliced mortadella.

Options:
1. 1 tablespoon fresh rosemary fine chopped
   ½ teaspoon salt
   ½ teaspoon fresh ground black pepper
   Drizzle on oil
2. 1½ cups yellow onion, peeled and fine chopped sautéd in oil
   ¼ teaspoon fresh ground black pepper
   Drizzle on oil
3. 1 cup raisins, black or white
   2 teaspoons fresh rosemary leaves fine chopped
   Drizzle on oil
4. 1½ cups marinara sauce brushed on
   1½ teaspoons dry oregano scattered on
   ½ teaspoon salt
   ½ teaspoon fresh ground black pepper
   ½ cup grated pecorino cheese
   Drizzle on oil
5. 2 bunches scallions, about 14, white and green part cleaned and cut into
   ¼ inch pieces
   ½ teaspoon salt
   ½ teaspoon fresh ground black pepper
   Drizzle on oil

EVEN THOUGH CALZONE MAY HAVE started out as pizzas and then gotten folded over by accident (one theory that has some merit), history shows us that there may have been a good reason for the name *calzone*, meaning "pant leg."

In the very old days calzone were made square. The filling was put on one half of the dough, just as it is done today, and the other half was placed over the stuffing. If you imagine this shape, you see that it resembles a pant leg. In modern renditions, calzone are shaped like turnovers, but the original name remains.

You can experiment with different fillings, but a few rules will help you out. The fillings should not be too moist, because moisture creates steam, causing the crust to be soggy. Commercial pizza makers have developed a clever technique of making a small slash in the top of the calzone after they are closed. Then they put a thin slice of cheese and a dab of tomato sauce over it. When the calzone cook and begin to puff, the little vent pushes up to let steam out. After the calzone are baked, the top settles down on the filling. The little camouflage for the steam vent becomes a delicious added attraction. The fillings should be in reasonably small pieces to make eating the calzone easier. If you let them rise or proof too much, they can become doughy, although additional risings before or after they are filled are called for in a few very old recipes.

All the recipes call for Basic Bread Dough (page 47) made with olive oil, once risen. Unless otherwise directed, divide the dough into 4 pieces and roll each piece into a round. To make larger calzone, use half the dough for each one. The method of handling the dough described in the first recipe (Calzone, Neapolitan Style, page 60) is the same no matter what size the calzone are, or whether they are baked or fried.

Calzone Diverse
(Varied Calzone)

Calzone al Forno alla Napolitana

WINE: Rosso del Salento (page 301) or Marino (page 306)

FOR THE FILLING

1 pound *Mozzarella, shredded or cut into little pieces*

2 ounces *salami, sliced very thin and julienned, or use equal amount of prosciutto*

6 ounces *of best quality Ricotta*

¼ cup *finely chopped parsley*

8 or 10 *leaves fresh basil, coarsely chopped*

Salt *to taste*

Plenty *of freshly ground black pepper*

1 cup *grated Parmesan*

Optional: *2 ripe tomatoes, cored and chopped into pieces about* ⅛ *inch square*

1½ *recipes Basic Bread Dough (page 47), made with olive oil, once risen*

Mix all the filling ingredients together in a bowl. Roll as many rounds of dough as you want and divide the filling equally. Put the filling on one half of the circle of dough. Then pick up the other half of the dough *without stretching it* and fold it over the filling so you end up with a giant turnover. Be sure not to overfill the calzone. If you stretch the dough over the filling, it may break during baking. Pinch the edges of the dough together to seal them. Then fold the edges up and over by about an inch to make a sort of border. Press the folded edges firmly with your fingers and make little indentations all around. You could use a fork to do this if you wish. If you are artistic, you could make any design you like.

The oven temperature is the same as for pizza. Turn the oven up as high as it goes; try to get it close to 500° F. Preheat for at least 20 minutes. If you are using a *plaque au four*, put it in the middle of the oven before preheating.

Transfer the calzone carefully to a peel (well sprinkled with semolina or flour) and shake them onto the *plaque au four* just as you would do with pizzas. Or make the calzone on a cookie sheet placed right on the *plaque au four*. Bake the calzone for 20 to 25 minutes. They should look deep gold top and bottom. They could even have little burned spots on them here and there. This is normal and very attractive. Serve piping hot.

1½ recipes Basic Bread Dough (page 47), made with olive oil, once risen

FOR THE FILLING

1¼ pounds of onions, peeled and sliced about ⅛ inch thick

¼ cup virgin olive oil, or q.b.

4 ounces Gaeta olives or Calamata, pitted and coarsely chopped

1½ pounds fresh tomatoes, cored and coarsely chopped

4 anchovy filets, cut in pieces

⅓ cup finely chopped parsley

1⅓ cups grated pecorino

Salt to taste

Additional virgin olive oil for brushing the dough

Calzone Pugliese

MAKES 2 LARGE
CALZONE

WINE: Castel de Monte Bianco (page 299), Colli Albani (page 304), or Faro Rosso (page 309)

Divide the dough into two portions, one being 60 percent, the other 40 percent. Cut each piece in half. With the larger amounts of dough, line two 9-inch cake pans or springform molds, letting some of the dough come up the sides by about 1½ inches or so. Put a towel over the pans and let the dough rise in a warm spot.

Push or roll the smaller remaining pieces of dough into circles large enough to make a cover for the pans later on. Place them on floured towels, and put another towel on top of them. Put the tops in a warm place to rise along with the dough in the pans, about 1 hour or until it has risen to 10 or 15 percent beyond its original size.

Meanwhile fry the onions in the olive oil over medium heat until they are transparent. Add the olives and mix everything very well. Add the tomatoes and stir the mixture well. Cook over medium heat until the tomatoes lose their liquid and the mixture becomes slightly thick. Add the anchovy and parsley, and cook the filling for a few more minutes. Remove the pan from the heat and add the cheese. Mix thoroughly, and correct it for salt, if necessary. Let cool.

When the dough in the pans has risen to about half again its original volume and the filling has cooled, assemble the calzone for baking. Spread half the filling on the dough in the pans, cover it with the tops, and pinch the 2 edges of the top and bottom doughs together. (You can use an eating fork to make a crimp design all around the sides if you wish.) Using a pastry brush, coat the tops with plenty of olive oil.

Put the 2 calzone on a *plaque au four* in the middle of a very hot oven, 500° F, and let them bake for about 25 minutes or until the sides and bottoms are soft and golden. The top will be more cooked and may be darker. You can check the sides by taking one of the calzone out of the oven and sliding a knife along the side of the pan to see the color. This calzone should be eaten piping hot.

Calzone Fritti

Fried Calzone

MAKES 6 OR 8
CALZONE

In Sicily many ovens are fired by wood so baking calzone is expensive and inconvenient. Frying calzone in virgin olive oil produces a fluffier texture than baked calzone have. The oil lends an earthy perfume all its own.

MENU SUGGESTIONS: Follow Calzone with Artichokes in Embers (page 224) and a nice big Orange and Lemon Salad (page 242).

WINE: Favonio Cabernet Franc (page 299)

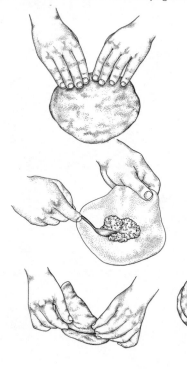

1½ recipes Basic Bread Dough (page 47), made with olive oil, once risen

1 pound Ricotta

2 or 3 tablespoons virgin olive oil

Freshly ground pepper to taste

1 cup plain olive oil for frying

Optional (but often done): ½ teaspoon dry oregano added to the Ricotta mixture

Cut the bread dough into 8 pieces. Roll them into little balls. Cover them with a towel and set them aside for later.

In a small bowl mix the Ricotta, the virgin olive oil, the ground pepper, and, if you wish, the oregano, and set it aside for later use.

Flatten out a piece of the bread dough with your fingers to a round shape, about 5 inches across. (If you find it easier, use a rolling pin to gently flatten it out.) At first the dough will be very elastic, and you will find that it is not working so well. Continue working the dough for 1 to 2 minutes and it will begin to hold its shape. Make it about ⅛ inch thick. Place the appropriate amount of filling (equally divided by the number of pieces of dough) on half of the dough and turn over the other half to cover the filling, forming a turnover shape. Do not use so much filling that you have to stretch the dough to cover it. The stretched dough may break while cooking. Press the edges firmly closed with your fingers. Lay each calzone on a floured cloth or on a floured cookie sheet as you complete it. Repeat the procedure with the remaining pieces of dough and the filling.

Heat the oil to 350° F in a frying pan large enough to hold 2 of the calzone at a time. Fry the calzone gently for 5 to 6 minutes, or until they are a deep golden color, turning them once during cooking. (The oil should not be hotter than 350° F in order that the dough become dark and luscious, and you can get that color only if the oil is not too hot. Above 350° F, the dough burns. If the oil were much lower, there is a chance that the calzone would become oil soaked and inedible.) Drain the calzone on a napkin for a moment or two, and serve them hot. Eat them out-of-hand or on a plate. They are good when they have cooled off, but like so many Italian dishes, they should not be eaten ice-cold. Calzone eaten at room temperature or warmer are fine, and they make very good picnic fare.

NOTE: You can vary the filling by adding some cooked, cooled, and drained spinach to the Ricotta mixture. This combination is very popular in all of southern Italy and is pretty as well. Or, add some finely chopped salami instead, or make a different filling altogether, such as fried onions and Swiss chard that has been boiled, cooled, and strained dry very well. You could even use what would normally go on top of a pizza. Just be sure you don't fill it to bursting.

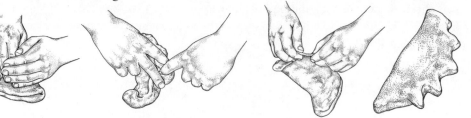

| 2 cups all-purpose flour (see note) | 1 teaspoon salt |
| 1 cup semolina | 1¼ cups warm water (approximately) |

In a bowl, mix together the flour, the semolina, and the salt. Gradually add the water until you have a smooth dough that is very easy to shape, not sticky, and not stretchy or glutinous. You might need as little as a cup of water—it all depends on the flour and the weather.

Place a *plaque au four* (see Kitchen Equipment, page 35) on the rack close to the bottom of the oven, and preheat the oven to 400° F for at least 20 minutes. If you are using two *plaques*, place one on the top rack and rotate the bread from one *plaque au four* to the other once during baking to ensure even baking and coloring.

While the oven is preheating, divide the dough into 10 small balls (or more if you want to make smaller sheets of bread or, conversely, fewer if you want to make larger ones). Cover them with a towel and let them rest for about 15 minutes. If you do not care to roll them out at this point, put the little balls of dough on a lightly floured cloth and then cover them with another cloth, also lightly floured. Put a large piece of plastic wrap on top of that. Put them somewhere cool, leave them for several hours. If you roll and bake them the next day, store them covered in the refrigerator.

On a floured surface, roll each ball to a thickness just under ¹⁄₁₆ of an inch. Put each round onto a heavily floured peel and slide onto the hot *plaque au four* in the oven. Bake for 2½ minutes on one side.

When the bread surfaces begin to bubble, watch the bread constantly, as they can readily burn. Turn the rounds over and bake another 2½ minutes. When one is a very light gold with dark highlights, remove it to a rack to cool. Continue to do this until all the rounds are finished. After the *pane* cool, you can stack them to save space.

Sardinian Parchment Bread will keep in perfect condition for at least 2 or 3 weeks if you keep them stored in a cool, very dry place. Put them into plastic bags, and keep them in your garage or back porch. If they are not tender and crunchy, you can "revive" them by putting them on a rack in a preheated 375° F oven for 2 to 3 minutes and then letting them cool. They should be as good as fresh.

NOTE: You can use all-purpose flour and no semolina, or all bread flour to make Sardinian Parchment Bread. Without the semolina it will not be as *friabile*, that is, crumbly, crunchy, tender, and very good.

Pane Carasau (Carta Musica)

Sardinian Parchment Bread

MAKES ABOUT 10
10-INCH ROUNDS

Surely this bread has its roots in the very ancient past. It resembles, to some degree, Armenian cracker bread, but cracker bread is thicker and flakier. *Pane carasau* is very thin and when held up to the light is translucent and looks quite fragile. This was the bread the Sardinian shepherds took along while guiding their flocks on grazing forays. It has a rather mottled, bubbly beige surface with lots of golden areas and little dark brown or burned spots here and there.

MENU SUGGESTIONS: Use with Roasted Tomatoes (page 99) or Mixed Vegetable Stew (page 232). Sardinian Parchment Bread is a perfect palette for spreading your favorite pâtés or for laying on slices of semisoft cheeses. It is also a good nibbling food—tasty, healthy, satisfying, and low in calories.

WINE: Monica di Sardegna (page 307) or Colli Albani (page 304)

'Nfigghiulata Antica

Sicilian Bread Roll, in the Old Style

This bread roll may predate calzone, pita, and empañadas. Its shape may date from the time of the Saracen occupation, in ninth-century Sicily, because the crescent is important in Oriental culture. The filling ingredients vary, but as long as you learn the taste and method of this particular recipe, you can improvise. Cauliflower may have been a more recent addition, and you can substitute spinach for the Swiss chard. Bread rolls can even be made without meat by adding more of the vegetables or different kinds, and perhaps some Ricotta.

MENU SUGGESTIONS: 'Nfigghiulata can be eaten as a meal in itself with salad and some wine. Or use thinner slices of it as a first course followed by Mussels with Saffron (page 103) or Braised Rabbit Sardinian Style (page 198).

WINE: Rosso del Salento (page 301)

2 recipes Basic Bread Dough (page 47), once risen

5 or 6 tablespoons virgin olive oil, or q.b.

½ pound ground veal

½ pound ground pork

1 yellow onion, peeled and diced coarsely

1 bunch green Swiss chard, well washed

1 small head cauliflower, washed and broken into small flowerettes about ¾ inch all around

4 scallions, chopped coarsely (more if you like)

¼ pound Sicilian black oil-cured olives, pitted and coarsely chopped

6 thin slices of salami, cut into julienne strips

½ pound Provolone, cut into small dice (more if you like)

Plenty of salt and pepper

Put about 1 tablespoon of oil into a large frying pan, and gently sauté the veal and pork, being careful not to overcook the meat. As soon as it loses color, it is done. Set aside the meat and its pan juices in a small bowl to cool.

In the same pan sauté the onion in another tablespoon of olive oil until it is soft and transparent. Add it to the bowl with the meat, and let it cool also.

Cut the Swiss chard crosswise into 1-inch-wide pieces either before or after washing. It does not matter. Put the pieces into a pan with a lid and cook them using just the water clinging to the leaves for 5 to 6 minutes, or until they are tender but not overcooked. Drain them very well, gently squeeze them dry. Set the Swiss chard aside in a small bowl.

The cauliflower should be cooked in lightly salted water for 4 or 5 minutes. Drain it well, cool, and reserve in a small bowl to use later.

In individual bowls or dishes, put the chopped scallions, pitted chopped olives, julienned salami, and the diced Provolone.

Grease an 11 × 16-inch jelly-roll pan with 2 tablespoons of the oil, spreading it all around. Set this aside. Preheat the oven to 350° F.

On a lightly floured surface pound and push the dough into an oval shape. (Use a rolling pin if it helps.) The dough should be ¼ inch thick and quite large, perhaps bigger than the size of the jelly-roll pan. Drizzle on a few teaspoons of the olive oil, and then scatter on all the rest of the ingredients. (I usually do this by scattering all of one ingredient to within an inch of the borders all around. You could also mix all of the ingredients together, once they are cool, and scatter that on just as well.) Carefully roll the dough and filling up, lengthwise, to resemble a giant sausage, being sure that the filling is compact and the roll tight. (Do not stretch the dough, because it could easily rip.) You do not want to end up with a roll that is loose with lots of air spaces. After the rolling, pinch the ends hard so that no filling leaks out.

Transfer the *'nfigghiulata* to the oiled jelly-roll pan. Try using a cookie sheet with no borders as a giant spatula. Oil the cookie sheet and very gently slide it under the roll. Tilt the cookie sheet alongside the jelly-roll pan and gently ease the *'nfigghiulata* off the cookie sheet and onto the pan. Be sure that the seam side of the roll is down and gently push the *'nfigghiulata* into a curved shape like a wide-open horse shoe or a crescent. Brush it all over with any remaining olive oil, or use more if you need to. Put the *'nfigghiulata* into the preheated oven to bake.

After 15 minutes, brush the roll again with more oil. If there is a lot of oil in the pan, use it to brush onto the roll. The *'nfigghiulata* should bake for about 1½ hours. Continue to brush the surface with oil every 15 minutes. If it browns too fast, lower the temperature to 325° F.

Let the *'nfigghiulata* cool in the jelly-roll pan for about 20 minutes before cutting it. Remove it later to a wooden board, and cut it into slices 1½ to 2 inches wide.

Pizza Rustica

Neapolitan Country Pie

MAKES ENOUGH
DOUGH FOR 1 9-INCH
SPRINGFORM MOLD

The name *pizza rustica* is deceptive. First, most of the pizzas that carry the name "rustic" are anything but that. Second, the name is attached to so many dishes that it is very difficult finding one that fully defines a true *pizza rustica*.

The dough for this pizza is essentially Tender Pastry (page 258) but without so much sugar. There are some Italians who prefer a more heavily sugared version. The recipe that follows is the version most Neapolitans would accept as the real thing. It is a very rich pie, equally good hot or cold. It is the sort of savory that can be successfully reheated in some lightweight foil. It lasts in the refrigerator for at least 5 days.

MENU SUGGESTIONS: Cut into small pieces, the *pizza rustica* makes a good antipasto, cold or warm. Eaten with Artichokes, Stuffed Agrigento Style (page 226), and some Almond Peppers (page 249), it could be a fine meal.

WINE: Montepulciano d'Abruzzo (page 298)

2 cups all-purpose flour

4 ounces very cold butter, cut into ¼-inch squares

2 large eggs

½ teaspoon salt

1 tablespoon sugar

22 ounces of the best Ricotta you can find

1 cup Provolone, cut into ¼-inch dice

1 cup Mozzarella, cut into ¼-inch dice

4 ounces prosciutto, sliced thin and chopped into small bits

¼ teaspoon freshly ground black pepper

6 large eggs

5 ounces grated Parmesan cheese

¼ cup finely chopped parsley

TO MAKE THE DOUGH

If you are making the dough by hand, mix the flour, salt, *and sugar* on a work surface. Add the butter and, using the tips of your fingers, mix it with the flour and salt until the pieces of butter are the size of peas. (If you are using an electric mixer, use the paddle or flat beater attachment to get the same result.) Add the eggs quickly, and the moment the dough just barely holds together, stop mixing. The dough will be very sticky and hard to handle. Gather it together, and wrap it tightly in plastic wrap. Put it in the refrigerator for at least 6 hours; overnight is better.

TO MAKE THE FILLING

Mix all the remaining ingredients together in a bowl, and reserve the mixture in the refrigerator until you are ready to use it. It is best to make the filling several hours before using it.

Preheat the oven to 400° F. Unwrap the cold dough and cut it into two pieces, one being 65 percent, and the other 35, approximately. Lightly flour a work surface and roll out the larger piece of dough to about ⅛ inch thick. (It is wise to use a ruler to give you an idea of just how thick this is.)

Line a 9-inch springform mold with the dough, which should hang over the edge by about 2 inches or more. Spread the filling into the mold. Roll out the smaller piece of dough to about ⅛ inch thick and cover the filling and dough in the springform pan with it. It also should overhang the sides of the mold by about 2 inches. Pinch the two overhanging doughs together and then neatly trim them all around the mold to about a 1-inch overhang. Fold this edge of double dough to form a border just inside the top of the mold. Make it as fancy as you like. (After making this fold, I simply pinch the dough up around the edges to make a little scallop design.)

Cut a large square cross, about 3 inches by 3 inches, with a small sharp knife in the center of the top piece of dough. Place the *pizza rustica* in the middle part of the oven on a *plaque au four*. After 20 minutes check to see

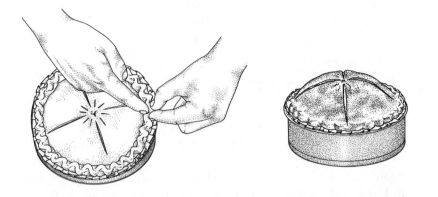

that the top is starting to puff up. (The square cross allows the cheese to push up but not break the dough.)

Reduce the heat to 375° F for about another hour. The cooking time varies according to the oven, but it should take a total of 1½ hours. The top should be a deep golden color and puffed up in the shape of a dome. When it is done, remove the *pizza rustica* from the oven, and put it on a rack to cool for about 1½ hours before removing it from the springform mold. It will still be quite warm, so be careful not to burn yourself or damage the pizza.

After removing the pizza from the oven, the top will remain very high. This will eventually collapse. Using a towel to protect your hands, occasionally and gently push the points of the square cross into the bulging filling to help it collapse evenly while it is cooling. Sometimes the collapse is severe and can leave a large cave-in at the center. This does not affect the taste or texture and actually can lend an interesting effect.

Taralli col Pepe

Taralli with Black Pepper

MAKES
APPROXIMATELY
60 TARALLI

Taralli could be called Italian pretzels. Some types even have coarse salt all over them. They are smooth and crunchy on the outside and flaky on the inside. The shapes vary, but the most common are round and resemble small doughnuts. *Taralli* are good to much on between meals. They are also wonderful with wine or whiskey or even with a plate of antipasti. In Italy, *taralli* are often given as gifts to friends and relatives. Tightly covered, they will last more than a month.

MENU SUGGESTIONS: Use *taralli* whenever you would like a tasty, highly flavored cracker. They are good with beer and with very cold white wine.

WINE: Ravello Bianco (page 303) or Frascati (page 305)

½ cup water
¼ cup dry Marsala
1 teaspoon yeast
1 cup bread flour
1 cup all-purpose flour
1 tablespoon freshly ground black pepper
1 teaspoon salt
3 tablespoons lard

Put the water, Marsala, and yeast into a medium-sized bowl, and let it all rest in a warm place until the top of the liquid just begins to froth.

Put the flours, pepper, salt, and lard in another bowl, and rub the mixture thoroughly with your hands to make a pebbly texture. Combine the ingredients of both bowls and work them into a dough. (You can use an electric mixer with the dough hook if you wish.) When you have a dough that holds together, dump it out on a wooden surface and knead it for about 7 minutes, or until the dough is firm, supple, and glossy. Put the dough back into the bowl and cover it with a kitchen towel. Place a bath towel, folded in half, over that and let the dough rise in a warm place for about 1 hour.

Cut the risen dough into 4 pieces. Roll each piece into a rope as long as you can make it, about ⅜ inch across. Cut the rope into 4-inch pieces, more or less, and form each into a little circle by tying the beginning of a knot, or else just pinch the ends together. Lay the *taralli* out on a lightly floured cloth. When you have finished, cover the *taralli* with another clean cloth and let them rise for about 1 hour.

When you are ready to cook the *taralli,* fill a skillet half full of water and bring to boil. Grease a cookie sheet lightly with lard. Preheat the oven to 375° F. When the water is boiling, put the *taralli* in, 3 or 4 at a time. After about 1 minute, take them out, drain them momentarily on a cloth, and line them up on the greased cookie sheet. Place the *taralli* in the middle of the oven and let them bake for about 15 minutes, watching carefully so that they do not overcook. The *taralli* should be just golden. Take them off the cookie sheet, and let them cool on a rack. When they are completely cool, store them in glass jars or in plastic containers.

Because of their long shelf life, *taralli* make good gifts at holiday time.

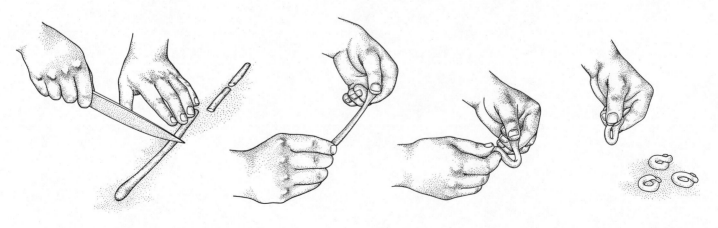

SALSE

Sauces

Sauces, as such, are not a substantial part of Italian cooking. For the most part, anything resembling a sauce is the result of pan juices spooned onto the food. These sauces are about as concentrated and delicious as anything I can think of, and unique to the dish. You can see from the recipes in this book that the basic ingredients are so importantly fresh and of prime quality that reliance on a sauce to enhance them or even make them palatable is not necessary. This could well describe Italian food in general.

The sauces given here are for specific use in certain dishes but I have noted variations that make them useful and tasty in other applications. Marinara Sauce, for example, should become part of your cooking repertory, giving you a fast and easy route to a quick dish of pasta, or the base, with a little white or red wine, for fish, fowl, and meat dishes that would profit from a zesty tomato sauce.

2 cups milk

3 tablespoons unsalted butter

3 tablespoons all-purpose flour

Salt and pepper to taste

Optional: *grating of nutmeg, slice of onion, garlic clove, bay leaf*

Besciamella
Béchamel or White Sauce

MAKES ABOUT
2½ CUPS

Heat the milk in a saucepan and infuse it with any or all of the optional flavorings (or none, if you want a bland-tasting sauce) by simply dropping in the herbs and spices. Do not let the milk boil, but keep it hot.

In another saucepan melt the butter over medium heat. When it is bubbling, add the flour all at once, stirring constantly with a whisk. Let the mixture cook for about 3 minutes, being careful not to let it burn or scorch. Remove the pan from the heat, add the hot milk, straining it all at once through a small sieve and stirring the whole time. Add the salt and pepper. Put the sauce back on the heat, and stir constantly until it begins to boil. Lower the heat and cook the sauce, stirring, until it is thick and glossy. Use immediately.

You can make the sauce thinner or thicker simply by adding more or less of the liquid or solid ingredients. If the sauce is too thick, add a little hot milk, and mix well, returning it to the heat for a bit, if necessary. If the sauce is too thin, cook it longer over slow heat, being careful not to let it scorch.

NOTE: If you do not wish to use this sauce right away, butter a piece of parchment or wax paper, and push it, butter side down, onto the surface of the sauce, pressing the paper tightly against the sides of the pan to keep all of the air off the surface. Buttered plastic wrap works very well also, and if it touches the sides of the hot pan, it will not burn or melt. You can store the sauce like this for several days in the refrigerator, and it will not "skin over" because it has been protected from the air. When you are ready to use it, simply remove the paper, place the sauce on the heat, and stir until it is hot and glossy.

Everyone knows that the Italians had *béchamel*, or as they call it, *balsamella* (commonly called *besciamella* these days), before the French did. Some very beautiful illuminated Italian recipes dated from around the year 1400 give good enough directions for making some of this sauce in your own kitchen today. The French Marquis Louis de Béchameil, who gave his name to the sauce, was appointed Lord Steward in the household of Louis XIV from 1648 to 1653. That gives the Italians at least a 150-year lead. All this leads me to ponder why the Neapolitans use a good deal of *besciamella*. Perhaps the Renaissance made a stop at Naples.

Ragù d'Agnello

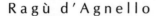

Abruzzese
Lamb Sauce

MAKES 2 QUARTS

Some Abruzzese claim that this *ragù* has *peperoncino rosso*, red pepper flakes, while others insist it has bell peppers cut into little pieces. Apparently it never has both.

Here is a straightforward recipe for *ragù d'agnello* that is delicious, easily made, and authentic.

4 tablespoons virgin olive oil

3 large garlic cloves, peeled and well crushed

1 pound coarsely ground lamb meat, preferably shoulder

1 large bay leaf, torn in half

1 4-inch branch fresh rosemary, or 1 teaspoon dry

3 pounds fresh tomatoes, cored, peeled, and well crushed, or approximately the same amount canned

1 cup dry white wine

1½ teaspoons salt

¾ teaspoon freshly ground black pepper

Optional: *2 bell peppers (about 6 ounces total), cored, seeded, and cut into ¼-inch dice, or 1 teaspoon red pepper flakes*

In a saucepan large enough to hold all the ingredients, heat the oil over high heat. When it is hot, add the garlic, and fry it until it is deep brown but not burnt. Add the meat, and fry it until it just begins to get gilded on the edges. Add the rosemary and the bay leaf, stir the mixture, and continue to cook the sauce over low heat for about 10 minutes. Add the tomatoes, stir everything, and cook the sauce for about 10 more minutes. Add the wine, and stir again. Add the salt, pepper, and the optional bell peppers or red pepper flakes, and stir again. Cook the *ragù* over low heat for about 2 hours, stirring frequently, or until it is thick and heavily coats the back of a spoon or is reduced to 2 quarts. Use the sauce on Strummed Macaroni (page 136) or on other pasta dishes.

2 *pounds beef rump or bottom round, or 2 pounds veal shoulder in one piece*

3 *tablespoons lard*

1 *large yellow onion, finely chopped*

3 *ounces* prosciutto, *cut into tiny pieces*

3 *garlic cloves, finely chopped*

1 *cup water*

3½ *pounds tomatoes, cored, peeled, and finely chopped, or use same amount canned*

1 *cup dry red wine*

4 *tablespoons tomato paste*

Sprig of fresh oregano, or 1 teaspoon dried

Salt to taste

Freshly ground black pepper to taste

Wipe the meat dry. Heat the lard in a deep, heavy pot. When the lard is hot but not smoking, add the meat, and fry it over medium heat, turning it often until it is quite brown all over. Add the finely chopped onion, and let it fry until it is transparent. If it is cooking too fast, turn down the heat. Add the *prosciutto,* gently fry it for about 5 minutes, add the garlic, and let it brown but do not let it burn.

Slowly add the water, a few spoonsful at a time, stirring the ingredients frequently, until all the water is incorporated and begins to look and smell like a deep-flavored broth. Add the tomatoes, and stir again. Combine the red wine and tomato paste in a glass, stir it well to dissolve the tomato paste, and add it to the sauce. Add the oregano, and salt and pepper to taste, and stir the sauce very well. Let it barely simmer, uncovered, for about 3 hours over low heat, stirring about every 20 minutes.

When the sauce is done, correct it for salt and pepper, and make any necessary additions. It should be thick and highly flavored. Remove the piece of meat, scraping off any sauce. Put it aside to be eaten in the meal, or save it for another use.

Ragù napolitana is used primarily on big stubby pasta and in baked pasta dishes.

Ragù Napolitana

Neapolitan Tomato Sauce with Meat

MAKES ABOUT
2 ½ QUARTS

Ragù certainly implies something with substance. This sauce has as its base Traditional Tomato Sauce (page 78), with the addition of *prosciutto* and a nice big piece of veal or beef, browned first. In the old days it was lard and salt pork that was used in place of *prosciutto*.

An interesting thing about this dish is that the meat, after cooking, is never used in or on the dish of pasta to be anointed with the sauce. It is always used separately, either in a different meal, or in the same meal but as another course. This way of eating resembles the dish Macaroni and Roast in Natural Juices, made with roast meat and pasta, separately served.

Sugo di Carne

Meat Sauce

MAKES ABOUT
1 QUART

This really should not be called a meat sauce. It is actually a braised dish in which the cooked meat is eaten for its own sake, and the juices, well strained, are then saved for use in other dishes. You can follow suit and make the recipe, eat the meat, and have a very tasty and thick sauce for flavoring other dishes such as Vermicelli, Prince of Naples Style (page 150). In Campania this dish is also known as *carne alla glassa* reminiscent of the French cooking term *glacé*, where the stock is reduced, but the meat is not meant to be eaten.

3 *tablespoons lard*

2 *pounds top sirloin, in one piece*

4 *ounces* prosciutto, *cut into tiny pieces*

1 *large yellow onion, with the skin on, washed, and cut into eighths*

2 *carrots, scraped and cut into 1-inch pieces*

1 *celery branch, washed and cut into 6 pieces*

1 *cup of parsley, including stems, coarsely chopped*

   Salt to taste

5 *or 6 grindings of freshly ground black pepper*

2 *tablespoons tomato paste*

2 *cups dry white wine*

2 *quarts of water*

Heat the lard in a large fireproof casserole dish until it melts and gets hot. Dry the beef well with paper towels and brown in the lard, turning it often. Be sure it is very brown all over. Add the *prosciutto* and the onion, and cook them over fairly high heat but be careful not to burn anything. Add the carrots and celery and continue to cook everything until all the ingredients are dark brown.

Lower the heat and add the parsley, some salt to taste, and pepper, and the tomato paste. Pour the wine in, about ⅓ cup at a time, until it is all incorporated. Add the water slowly. Cook the meat slowly for about 2 hours, basting as often as possible and turning it once in a while. When the meat is done, remove it from the casserole and serve it sliced, or put it away for use in another dish like Neapolitan Ravioli (page 144) or Cannelloni (page 207). When the juices have reduced by half, the sauce should be done. It should be very highly flavored with depth and body. Put the juices and solids into a food mill and puree them. Extract every drop of sauce that will come out. If the sauce needs to reduce a bit more let it simmer another half hour or so. The sauce should coat the back of a metal spoon well and be glossy. Use it as needed. If you keep it refrigerated, boil it for about 5 minutes every three days, or it will spoil. Otherwise, it would be best to pack the sauce in very small containers and freeze it.

Mock
Meat Sauce

MAKES
APPROXIMATELY
1½ QUARTS

4 *ounces* prosciutto *fat, cut into small pieces*

1 *small yellow onion, finely chopped*

1 *carrot, scraped and finely chopped*

1 *celery branch, washed and finely chopped*

2 *pounds fresh tomatoes, cored, peeled, and well crushed, or use the same amount canned*

2 *tablespoons finely chopped Italian parsley*

1 *cup dry white wine*

1 *cup veal or beef broth, well seasoned*

Salt to taste

4 *big grindings of fresh black pepper*

In a deep, heavy saucepan melt the *prosciutto* fat over medium heat, add the onion, carrot, and celery, and gently fry them until they become transparent. Add the tomatoes and parsley, and let the mixture simmer for about 10 minutes. Add the white wine, the broth, the salt, and the pepper, and stir it all well. Let the sauce gently simmer for about 30 to 40 minutes, stirring occasionally.

Use this sauce on anything calling for tomato sauce. It will keep, covered, in the refrigerator, for 5 days, or it can be frozen indefinitely.

If you want a meatless sauce with that particular meat flavor, do as the Romans do and make *sugo finto*. By using *prosciutto* fat, you get the pungent and tasty notion that meat really is in the sauce. If you add a ladleful or so of meat broth, so much the better. There are those who think that you can dispense with the broth. Others insist on it. This is a good sauce for pasta or rice or to use as a base to braise meat. It is indispensable in Roman-Style Omelette in Strips (page 85).

Salsa alla Marinara

Marinara Sauce

MAKES
APPROXIMATELY
1½ QUARTS

There can be no simpler sauce that tastes as good as this one. It is fast, easy, and goes with so many other ingredients that it should be a staple in your cooking repertory.

The idea behind the name is that the sailors used to make this sauce in a hurry, because they had work to do and could not spend the day steeping and stirring it.

1 *large yellow onion, finely chopped*
½ *cup virgin olive oil*
3 *medium-sized garlic cloves, finely chopped*
3½ *pounds fresh tomatoes, cored, peeled, and well crushed, or use same amount canned*
2 *large sprigs fresh oregano, or 1 teaspoon dried*
4 *basil leaves, finely chopped*
  Salt to taste
  Freshly ground black pepper to taste
  Optional: *pinch crushed red pepper*

Put the chopped onion in a wide, heavy pan, add the olive oil, and fry it over medium heat until it is transparent. Add the garlic, and fry the mixture for about 3 minutes more. Add all the other ingredients, and cook the sauce on a brisk flame for about 15 minutes, stirring occasionally. Add the optional crushed red pepper now if you are going to use it. The fast cooking will help reduce the sauce and make it thick, but be careful not to burn the bottom.

NOTE: The same base can be used in making fish stew. Add ⅓ cup of dry white or dry red wine to every cup of *salsa alla marinara*. Simply put the fish into the sauce, and cook it for just a few minutes.

Salsa di Pomodoro

Traditional Tomato Sauce

MAKES 1½ QUARTS

This straightforward sauce is the one most people associate with Italian cooking.

4 *tablespoons virgin olive oil*
1 *large yellow onion, finely chopped*
3 *garlic cloves, peeled and finely chopped*
3½ *pounds fresh tomatoes, cored, peeled, and well crushed, or 6 cups canned*
2 *cups water*
1 *cup dry red wine*
4 *tablespoons tomato paste*
  Sprig of fresh oregano, or 1 teaspoon dried
1 *teaspoon salt*
½ *teaspoon of fresh black pepper*

Heat the oil in a wide, heavy pan, and fry the onion until it is soft and transparent. Add the garlic, and fry it until it is golden. Add all the other ingredients, and simmer the sauce, uncovered, over very low heat for 3 hours, stirring occasionally. Use on baked pasta or on big stubby boiled pasta.

This sauce can be stored in a covered jar, in the refrigerator, for about 5 days. Frozen, it will keep several months. If you do freeze it, divide the sauce into portions, so that you will not have to defrost the whole amount if you want just some of it.

Eggs

While eggs are used as a matter of course in many dishes, they take on a special quality when they are eaten as a main ingredient. Then, the condiments or presentation of the egg serves as a medium for the character and ingenuity of the cook. The succulent Egg "Meatballs" are sheer eating enjoyment; the Roman-Style Omelette in Strips provides whimsy and fun as well as nourishment and delicious taste.

These egg dishes are attractive and easy to execute as part of a meal such as an intermezzo or, served in larger portions, constitute light lunches and suppers. Of course, they are best used as a separate course in a meal. They deserve that place. Chickens are still considered choice and expensive in Italy, but eggs, cheaper and more abundant, are no less highly regarded. Eggs are revered by Italians to the point where, as in this volume, they are given their own place in the menu. They are not mere afterthoughts or convenience food in the wrong sense.

Frittata di Menta

12 *large mint leaves, washed, dried, and coarsely chopped*

½ *cup Italian parsley, washed, dried, and coarsely chopped*

6 *large eggs*

2 *tablespoons bread crumbs*

⅔ *cup grated* pecorino

About 3 tablespoons virgin olive oil for frying

In a medium-sized bowl, mix well the mint, parsley, eggs, bread crumbs, and cheese. Let the mixture set for about 5 minutes to let all the flavors come together.

Heat the olive oil in a 9-inch frying pan over medium heat so that it is quite hot, but nowhere near smoking, gently pour in the egg mixture, and lower the heat. When the bottom has set, pull back one edge of the *frittata* with a fork, and tilt the pan so that the uncooked, runny egg slides onto the hot pan. Do this once or twice, and let the *frittata* get golden on the bottom. Check this by simply lifting up an edge and looking at it. When it is golden, either flip the *frittata* up in the air to turn it over, or, if you are afraid to do this, put a dinner plate over the pan, and carefully turn the pan over so that the *frittata* falls onto the plate. Slide the *frittata* back into the pan, and let it cook for a moment or so longer, or until the bottom is golden.

Most Italian *frittati* are well cooked and, to some people, a bit dry. In this case, the *frittata di menta* should be moist and soft in the middle. It is good hot or at room temperature.

If you have ever wondered what to do with all that mint in your yard, besides making mint juleps, here is the solution.

Mint smooths out when it is cooked and does not have the rather biting quality it has when fresh. The aroma lingers after cooking, and it will entice anyone who is near to eat the *frittata* with gusto.

The mint signifies Southern Territory. On a balmy summer evening in one of the thousands of outdoor Roman restaurants, a *frittata di menta* could be one of many courses in a light but earthy dinner.

MENU SUGGESTIONS: At room temperature the *frittata* would be nice as an antipasto. It could also be used as a small course somewhere in between more robust dishes. Hot, it could be used as a first or *primo piatto*. In any case, *frittata alla menta* complements Chicken, Potenza Style (page 179); Mussel or Oyster Soup, Taranto Style (page 117); or Lamb Chops, Calabrian Style (page 162).

WINE: Greco di Tufo (page 302) with the omelette; Fiorano Rosso (page 305) with the lamb chops

Polpette d'Uovo
Egg "Meatballs"

MAKES 20 TO 25 BALLS

An inventive dish of exotic flavors, these egg "meatballs" are as scrumptious as they are unusual. While chicken is relatively rare in southern Italian dishes, eggs are used abundantly. These morsels of goodness are wonderful to serve to the ever growing number of vegetarians in our ranks. Made smaller, they are a tasty and elegant first course.

MENU SUGGESTIONS: These are excellent as a hot antipasto. You could follow them with Tuna and Fennel Seeds (page 201). A *contorno* on the side of String Bean Bundles (page 235) would be a good choice. Walnut Cakes (pages 276–277) would make a tasty finish to this light and flavorful meal.

WINE: Vesuvio Bianco (page 304)

FOR THE EGG "MEATBALLS"

¼ cup white raisins, finely chopped

½ cup pine nuts

6 slices fresh Italian-style bread, soaked in water just covering for about 5 minutes

3 large eggs

1 cup grated Parmesan cheese

¼ cup parsley, finely chopped

6 fresh basil leaves, finely chopped

½ cup olive oil for frying the "meatballs," q.b.

FOR THE SAUCE

2 tablespoons virgin olive oil

1 medium yellow onion, peeled and very finely chopped

Salt to taste

6 grindings of fresh black pepper

1½ pounds fresh tomatoes, cored, peeled, and well crushed, or use the same amount canned

TO PREPARE THE MEATBALLS

Raisins in Italy are small and flavorful. In the United States they are larger and much more sugary but have less depth of flavor. That is the reason for chopping them rather small. After you have chopped them, put them into a medium-sized bowl.

Toast the pine nuts in a small frying pan over low heat with no oil, shaking the pan often. Do not leave them for even a moment, for they burn instantaneously. The moment they become an even dark gold, quickly remove them from the pan and put them into the bowl with the raisins. (If you were to leave them in the frying pan, off the heat, they would continue to cook and eventually burn.)

Remove the bread from the water and squeeze it as hard as you can to extrude as much water as possible. You may even want to wrap the ball of bread in a kitchen towel and squeeze it again. Tear the bread into tiny pieces and put them into the bowl with the raisins and pine nuts. Break the eggs into the bowl, and mix everything together. Add the Parmesan, and mix everything again. Add the parsley and half of the chopped basil, and mix once again, reserving the other half of the basil for later use. Try forming a small ball. If the dough is too soft to shape into balls, add some bread crumbs. If it seems very stiff, add a bit more egg. (You can make this mixture up to 1 day ahead. Store it, covered, in the refrigerator.)

TO PREPARE THE SAUCE

Heat the olive oil in a low-sided frying pan over medium heat, add the chopped onions, and fry them until they are transparent but not colored. Add some salt and pepper and the crushed tomatoes. Cook the sauce for about 10 minutes, or until it just begins to tighten and reduce a bit. (You can make the sauce up to 2 days ahead. Store it, covered, in the refrigerator.)

TO FRY THE "MEATBALLS"

Meanwhile, shape the bread mixture into balls about the size of a golf ball. Roll them between your palms to make the shape, or use a small sherbet scoop. Lay them, as you finish them, on a sheet of wax paper or on a dish.

Put the olive oil into a frying pan about 8 inches across. Heat the oil to about 360° F, but do not let it smoke. Fry the little "meatballs" until they are a beautiful golden color and set them on an absorbent towel to drain. Place the "meatballs" into the tomato sauce, and let them simmer for about 10 minutes. Serve the *polpette d'uovo* hot and sprinkle on the rest of the chopped basil.

6 *large eggs*

2 *tablespoons of finely chopped Italian parsley*

2 *leaves fresh mint, finely chopped*
 Salt to taste

4 *or 5 grindings of fresh black pepper*

3 *or 4 tablespoons virgin olive oil for frying*

1½ *cups Mock Meat Sauce (page 77)*

⅓ *cup grated* pecorino *cheese*

Beat eggs until they are just frothy. Add the parsley, mint, salt, and pepper, and mix well.

Heat the oil in a 12-inch frying pan (or use two smaller ones) until it is very hot but not smoking. Lower the heat, pour the egg mixture in, and let it set on the bottom. The *frittata* should be about ⅛ inch thick. When the bottom has set, pull back one edge of the *frittata* with a fork, and tilt the pan so that the uncooked runny egg slides onto the hot pan. Do this once or twice, and then let the *frittata* get golden on the bottom. Simply lift up an edge and check it. When it is golden, either flip the *frittata* up in the air to turn it over or put a dinner plate over the pan, and carefully turn the pan over so that the *frittata* falls onto the plate. Slide the *frittata* back into the pan, and let it cook for a minute longer, or until the bottom is golden. Slide the *frittata* onto a plate, and let it cool.

Cut the *frittata* into thin strips to simulate tripe. Gently roll up the *frittata* like a jelly roll and, using a long knife, cut it into little rounds, and then unroll them.

Butter a low-sided casserole dish that can double as a serving dish at the table. Alternate the strips of *trippa* with some of the Mock Meat Sauce in the casserole, ending with sauce on the top. Sprinkle on the cheese. Put the *uova in trippa* in a preheated 375° F oven for 15 minutes, or until it is very hot. Serve immediately.

U o v a i n T r i p p a

Roman-Style Omelette in Strips

S E R V E S 4 T O 6

Here is a cheese-and-herb omelette cut into strips after it is cooked and then finished in the oven with a mock meat sauce. This amusingly named dish shows to what extent Romans love tripe, to create a dish that merely resembles it. *Uova in Trippa* is beautiful on the plate, and an elegant meatless meal for a large breakfast or light lunch.

MENU SUGGESTIONS: This is a good *primo piatto* followed by Braised Rabbit, Sardinian Style (page 198). Almond Tart (page 270) or Spumoni (page 296) would be good choices for dessert.

WINE: Faro Rosso (page 309)

Uova in Purgatorio

Poached Eggs
in Tomato Purgatory

SERVES 6

3 *cups Marinara Sauce (page 78) with extra chopped basil or some parsley in it*

12 *fresh large eggs*

6 *or 8 grindings fresh black pepper*

4 *tablespoons grated Parmesan cheese, or q.b.*

Uova in Purgatorio are traditionally served in a sauce made of lard, onions, crushed tomato, and a lot of basil or parsley, finely chopped. I have taken the easy road and used marinara sauce, which I usually have on hand. You can use the aforementioned ingredients and make your own sauce following the method for Marinara Sauce (page 78), or you can simply add more basil, or add a healthy fistful of parsley to your own marinara.

MENU SUGGESTIONS: For a first course you could serve 1 egg instead of 2. This is an ideal dish for brunch or a buffet lunch because the eggs will stay hot in the sauce while people serve themselves. You could serve room temperature Pizza, Lanciano Style (page 52), cut into small pieces, and perhaps some Stuffed Pasta Dumplings (page 139) in a basket. A bowl of Sweet-and-Sour Baby Onions (page 234) or a platter of Roasted Onions (page 233) offer a refreshing balance. A large shallow platter of Pears in Chocolate (page 285) would not only be pretty but welcome after such a meal.

WINE: Monica di Sardegna (page 307)

Preheat the oven to 375° F. Put the Marinara Sauce into a low-sided ovenproof casserole dish that will hold all the eggs. Put the casserole in the oven, and let the sauce within get hot enough to simmer. Working close to the surface of the sauce, break the eggs carefully into the hot sauce so that the yolk remains intact and there is a little space between each one. Grind on the black pepper. Put the casserole back into the upper third of the oven. (If the rack was previously lower, remove it and put it as high as you can in the oven.) Bake the *uova in purgatorio* for about 6 minutes or until the tops of the eggs are white, with a yellow center showing through. The yolks must be very soft on the inside. Remove the casserole from the oven and sprinkle on the grated Parmesan. Serve the *uova in purgatorio* immediately. Crusty homemade bread is called for here.

ANTIPASTI

Before the Meal

This is almost a mystery course because no one can tell whether the antipasto will determine the breadth and scope of the meal or play a minor or major role in it. If you have hearty dishes as first and second courses, you might want a very light and refreshing antipasto such as Garlic Bread, Roman Style, or if the meal is to be a celebration calling for a banquet, you might want the *antipasti* to be elaborate and numerous, such as "Phone-Wire" Rice Croquettes, Mussels with Saffron, Eggplant "Sandwiches," and Cauliflower Salad.

The *antipasti* in this section were chosen as mere examples of the kind and character to be used to open a meal. Luckily, these *antipasti* can easily be multiplied by using *contorni* (side dishes) interchangeably. It would take another book at least as big as this one to provide examples of just the categories of *antipasti*.

Because *antipasti* are so diverse, they make a perfect *assàggio* meal, "a meal of tastes." A meal comprised of several *antipasti* not only rewards the palate, but also educates, letting the eater savor more or less of many different dishes. In any event, *antipasti* are always enjoyed as a kind of warmup to the rest of the meal and need not be more complicated than Chick-peas in Olive Oil. So, include two or three of them when you have a small simple supper, to give it more stature, and also when you want to celebrate and eat more for a longer period of time.

6 slices *Italian bread, cut ½ inch thick*
2 large *raw garlic cloves, peeled*
2 tablespoons *virgin olive oil*

The ingredients are approximate and should all be *quanto basta*, or q.b. Toast the bread over an open fire or on a hot iron or stone surface until it is golden but still soft on the inside. Rub it well on one side with the raw garlic, and drizzle on the olive oil.

Bruschetta

Garlic Bread

This is garlic bread in its original form. More than once I've offered it to guests who thought I'd forgotten all the cheeses, herbs, paprika, and, of course, the obligatory cup of raw garlic. The Italian hand is restrained in matters of love and garlic, both to good effect. My guests liked eating the real thing.

LAZIO

Bruschetta alla Romana

Garlic Bread, Roman Style

Slices of *Italian bread, cut about ½ inch thick*	Fresh *tomatoes, chopped into small dice*
Raw *garlic cloves, peeled*	Fresh *sweet basil, chopped coarsely*
Virgin *olive oil*	Salt *and freshly ground pepper to taste*

Toast the bread, preferably over an open fire or on a hot iron or stone surface until it is golden but still soft on the inside. Rub it well on one side with raw garlic. Drizzle on the olive oil, and add the tomatoes, basil, salt, and pepper.

Eat *bruschetta* as antipasto or as a snack with red wine. *Bruschetta* does not have to be warm, but it should be freshly made. *Bocconcini* or slices of *pecorino morbido pepato* could be eaten as a side dish.

This bread is a perfect pick-me-up on the kind of day when you want to indulge yourself. Making *bruschetta* is a wise and scrumptious way to use up some of the bread you make at home, or to use bought bread that has lost its "bloom" after only one day.

As a guide, you will need 1 large clove of garlic, about 3 tablespoons of oil, 1 large tomato, and about 8 large leaves of sweet basil for 4 big slices of bread.

WINE: Frascati (page 305) or Montepulciano d'Abruzzo (page 298)

Crostini al Pomodoro

Tomato Toasts

1 medium yellow onion, peeled and very finely chopped

2 tablespoons extra virgin olive oil for sautéing the onion, or q.b.

3 large tomatoes, peeled, seeded, and very finely chopped

½ teaspoon salt, or to taste

¼ teaspoon freshly ground pepper, or to taste

1 large egg yolk

4 tablespoons freshly grated Parmesan or Romano cheese, or q.b.

1 teaspoon red wine vinegar

4 slices Italian-style bread

These *crostini* are unusual and always well received. They are particularly good for putting a real edge on the appetite. Of course, the very best ingredients would include vine-ripened tomatoes that are picked at just the right moment of maturity and that give this dish its characteristic flavor. On the other hand, you can also use tomatoes that are not so interesting in their normal state. By accenting the savory ingredients you can make a very delicious meal opener with these little treats.

MENU SUGGESTIONS: Start your meal with Tomato Toasts and some very tender yellow branches of celery and some Eggplant "Sandwiches" (page 98). Follow this with Chicken Infused with Bay Leaves (page 161).

WINE: Fiorano Bianco (page 305)

Cook the onion in the olive oil in a medium-sized frying pan over very low heat until it is golden and very soft. Add the tomatoes, the salt, and the pepper, and cook the mixture over the same low heat for 15 to 20 minutes, or until all the moisture has evaporated and you have a very thick mixture. Be careful not to burn the tomatoes. You also have to be sure that you do not make the mixture so dark that the tomatoes begin to caramelize, because then you lose the fresh flavor which is so characteristic of this dish.

When the mixture is dense and smooth, remove it from the heat and set it aside, stirring it now and then to cool it. When the mixture is cool, stir in the egg yolk, cheese, and the red wine vinegar. (You can do all of this up to a day ahead of time and store the mixture in the refrigerator.)

Toast the slices of bread on both sides. Either leave them whole or cut them into squares or triangles. Preheat the broiler, or use the highest part of a very hot oven (500° F). Divide the tomato mixture among the pieces of bread, and heat them in the broiler or oven for a few minutes, or until they are bubbly. Serve the *crostini* hot.

If using these as antipasto, use small cuts of bread. As a first course, use whole slices of crusty Italian bread, and serve them on a heated plate decorated with something green like parsley or watercress or small spinach leaves.

METHOD #1 ROASTED SPIEDINI

1 pound best Mozzarella (or soft
  Monterey Jack), sliced about ¼
  inch thick

12 slices Italian-type bread

Salt and pepper to taste

12 tablespoons unsalted butter, plus
   more for greasing the roasting pan

7 anchovy filets

Assemble first a layer of bread, then a layer of cheese ending with a layer of bread on top so that each *spiedino* has 3 pieces of bread and 2 pieces of cheese. Trim the edges, and cut each assembled stack of bread and cheese into 4 square portions. Skewer the 4 portions as in *brochettes*, using long Japanese-type bamboo sticks.

Rub plenty of room-temperature butter all over the bottom of a small roasting pan with sides. Place all of the *spiedini* on the buttered surface, leaving some space around each one. Roast them in a very hot oven (500° F) until the bread begins to color and the cheese is very soft.

While the *spiedini* are cooking, finely mince the anchovies, mix them with the butter, and set the mixture aside for later use. When the *spiedini* are done, remove them from the roasting pan and put them on a heated plate. Quickly put the anchovy butter mixture into the hot roasting pan, and with a spoon swirl everything all around. The butter should melt immediately. If you are serving the *spiedini* on individual plates, divide the anchovy mixture equally onto the *spiedini* before serving.

METHOD #2 FRIED SPIEDINI

1 pound best Mozzarella (or soft
  Monterey Jack), sliced about ¼
  inch thick

12 slices firm but soft Italian-type
   bread

3 large eggs

1 cup plain olive oil for frying

1 cup strong chicken stock

7 anchovy filets

Salt and pepper to taste

Prepare the bread and cheese as in Method #1 and skewer them. Beat the eggs in a dish long enough to hold the skewers lengthwise, and dip the skewers in the beaten eggs. Be sure that all of the bread and cheese is well coated and the egg begins to seep into the bread. Shake well to keep from dripping.

Heat the oil in a frying pan over high heat to 350° F, and fry the *spiedini* in the hot oil, turning them at least once to be sure that they are properly cooked on all sides and until they are golden all over. Place them on a dish as they are finished. If you are frying a lot of *spiedini*, keep the finished ones in a warm oven with the door slightly ajar. The *spiedini* should be fried just before serving, but if you carefully prepare everything in advance, including soaking them in egg, this is not at all difficult. If you have an electric frying pan, preset the temperature for the oil. While your guests are being seated, the *spiedini* could be well on their way to completion.

Serve the *spiedini* very hot with the following sauce spooned over:

Heat the chicken stock in a small saucepan to a simmer. Chop the anchovies coarsely, and add them to the chicken broth. To blend flavors, simmer gently for about 5 to 6 minutes. Add freshly ground pepper to taste.

Spiedini alla Romana

Bread
and Cheese Skewers,
Roman Style

SERVES 6

Spiedini alla Romana is one of the most popular *antipasti* in the world and everyone seems to have a different way of preparing it, including myself. I have provided two versions, one roasted, the other fried. Both are scrumptious.

MENU SUGGESTIONS: Prepared either way, the *spiedini* would be good followed by Rabbit, Ischian Style (page 182), with a salad of Cousin Mary's Eggplant (page 241). Perhaps a plate of Dessert Ravioli, Teramo Style (page 283), and some sweet wine such as Malvasia delle Lipari (page 309) or Anghelu Ruju (page 306) would be an elegant close to this meal.

Panzanella

Savory
Bread Salad

SERVES 6

In Rome during springtime, getting on to summer, when the tomatoes are ripening and the basil is up, this is a characteristic salad enjoyed by many people eating *al fresco*. It is cool, refreshing, and uncommonly tasty. *Panzanella* would be an excellent dish to make if you want to use up homemade bread that has seen better days. You will find that this form of "no waste" makes good sense and good eating.

MENU SUGGESTIONS: *Panzanella* for antipasto followed by Fried Codfish, Roman Style (page 190), would be very good. For a cold supper or lunch Chicken Infused with Bay Leaves (page 161) seems perfect. Pears in Chocolate (page 285) would be a fine dessert.

WINE: Ravello Rosso (page 303)

6 *large, thick slices of hard, dry Italian bread (homemade preferred, but bought will do; no sourdough, please)*

2 *large, ripe unpeeled tomatoes, cored and chopped into ¼-inch dice*

2 *tablespoons red or white wine vinegar, depending on its strength, or q.b.*

Plenty of salt

⅓ *cup virgin olive oil, or q.b.*

8 *large fresh basil leaves, coarsely chopped, or to taste*

Freshly ground black pepper to taste

Plunge the bread into a bowl of cold water, and leave it there until it soaks up enough water to wet it thoroughly. Let the bread drain in a colander for about 15 minutes, and squeeze it as dry as you can with your hands. (It also helps to wrap the bread in a kitchen towel and roll it tightly to get rid of any excess water.) With your hands tear the bread into pieces about the size of a marble, and put them into a salad bowl from which you will serve. Add all the other ingredients, and mix everything together. Let the whole mass set for about an hour in the refrigerator. The juices should all be absorbed into the bread.

Ordinarily *panzanella* is served alone on a plate, but it is also very good heaped up on a leaf of butter lettuce or on the yellow inner leaves of Romaine.

½ pound dry chick-peas or 1½ pounds
  canned

¼ cup virgin olive oil

2 large yellow onions, peeled and cut
  into tiny dice

3 large garlic cloves, peeled and finely
  minced

Salt to taste

Plenty of freshly ground black
pepper

Extra virgin olive oil for drizzling

Ceci all'Olio

Chick-peas in
Olive Oil

SERVES 6

Soak the chick-peas overnight in a bowl of cold water to cover by 4 inches.
When you are ready to cook them, discard the soaking water. Put the *ceci*
in a pan large enough to hold them easily after they expand during cooking,
and cover them with about 2 quarts of water. Cook them over a low heat,
uncovered, for about 3 hours, or until they are tender. If the water level gets
too low, add boiling water to barely cover them. When the *ceci* are done,
remove them from the heat, and let them rest for about ½ hour in the pot
in the water. Drain the *ceci*, and reserve about ½ cup of the cooking water.
Discard the rest.

Heat the olive oil in a large frying pan, and sauté the diced onions until
they are just tender and slightly gilded. Add the chopped garlic, and fry that
until it, too, is gilded. Combine the *ceci* with the onion and garlic and cook
the mixture together for about ten minutes. Add a good big pinch of salt.
Add the reserved cooking water and stir everything well. Serve the *ceci* piping
hot in a rimmed soup dish. At the table grind on plenty of fresh black pepper
and drizzle on plenty of extra virgin olive oil.

In all parts of Calabria these delicious morsels are eaten at Christmastime. There is something about the sweet softness of the *ceci* that counters, yet balances, the browned garlic and pepper that completes the dish. Dried *ceci* will last almost forever on your shelf, and when you want some, you simply soak them overnight in water and then proceed to use them. Some argue that the canned peas are a lot less work. You can use canned *ceci*, but there really is no work involved in soaking the dried ones overnight. Dried chick-peas generally triple in weight when they are soaked and cooked.

MENU SUGGESTIONS: This is an excellent antipasto that I love to serve hot, but it is good at room temperature. When it is room temperature, add fresh, sliced tomatoes and some fresh basil and make a wonderful salad.

WINE: Regaleali Bianco (page 310)

Supplì al Telefono

"Phone-Wire" Rice Croquettes

MAKES ABOUT
30 SUPPLÌ

These rice croquettes, so charmingly named, are eaten all over Lazio but are considered a Roman specialty. To eat the *supplì*, pull them apart first, not only because they are just big enough that you cannot get them into your mouth in one bite, but because the Mozzarella cheese cooked into the middle stretches between each half to resemble a mass of phone wires. The visual effect of this is as important as the taste and texture. This, surely, is one food that is both fun to play with and delicious to eat.

MENU SUGGESTIONS: *Supplì* would be good as an antipasto eaten hot, followed by Snails in Tomato Sauce (page 172) or Mussels with Saffron (page 103) or Braised Oxtails, Roman Style (page 187). For dessert Walnut Cake #2 (page 277) would be a nice finish.

WINE: Cirò Rosso (page 302)

1 medium yellow onion, peeled and chopped fine

3 cups olive oil (or other vegetable oil)

2 cups uncooked Arborio or Vialone rice

1 quart water (or use chicken stock)

1 teaspoon salt, or to taste

¼ teaspoon pepper

1½ cups tomato sauce

½ cup grated pecorino cheese

4 large eggs

10 ounces Mozzarella, or q.b., cut into generous ½-inch cubes. Allow about ¼ ounce per supplì.

1½ cups plain, fine bread crumbs

Sauté the onion in a large frying pan with a tablespoon of olive oil until it is soft and transparent. Add the rice, and stir it all around to coat each grain. Sauté the rice for about 2 minutes, but do not let it get brown.

Meanwhile, in a large saucepan with a lid, bring the water (or chicken stock), salt, and pepper to a boil over high heat. Lower the heat, add the onion and rice mixture all at once, and stir for a moment. Replace the lid on the pan, and simmer the rice for about 16 minutes, or until it is tender but *al dente*. (If the liquid is not thoroughly absorbed, continue to cook the rice over medium heat, with the lid off, until the rice is sticky but not wet.)

When the rice is done, remove it from the heat, add the tomato sauce and the grated cheese, and mix it well. Set it aside in the pan to cool for about 2 hours. (You may refrigerate it, well covered, after this if you wish, and continue the rest of the recipe the next day.)

When the rice mixture is cool, add 2 of the eggs and mix well. There are two ways to form the *supplì*. The traditional method is to pat out 2 tablespoons of the mixture to cover the palm of one hand, place a cube of Mozzarella in the center of the rice, and gently close your hand to envelop the cheese. Using both hands. shape the mass into an oval about the size and shape of a large chicken egg. Lay the finished "egg" on a cookie sheet or a large piece of wax paper and continue until you have used up all the ingredients.

I find it faster and more convenient to scoop up about 1½ tablespoons of the rice mixture in a small ice cream scoop, push my finger to make a small opening, and put in the cheese. Flip it out of the scoop and finish shaping it by hand.

Beat the remaining 2 eggs in a medium-sized bowl. Spread the bread crumbs in a low-sided dish. Dip the *supplì* into the egg mixture, making sure they are well covered, then roll them all around in the bread crumbs. Obviously you will have bread crumbs left over. Either sift out any lumps and reuse, or discard. Set the *supplì* on a cookie sheet or wax paper.

Heat the oil in a large pan to about 350° F, and put in as many *supplì* as will fit comfortably. Fry them until they are a deep golden color. Remove each one with a slotted spoon, and lay it on absorbent material.

Supplì can be very successfully frozen after you form them (*before* you add eggs and bread crumbs). One day before you are ready to use them, thaw them out overnight in the refrigerator, and then proceed to finish them as directed. You can also completely finish them, including deep frying and cooling, and then freeze them. When you want one, put it unwrapped and still frozen into a preheated 325° F oven for about 30 minutes.

Insalata di Cavolfiore

Cauliflower Salad

SERVES 6

1 *large head cauliflower, washed, trimmed, and cut into small pieces*

Salt for cooking water

8 *anchovy filets, coarsely chopped*

¼ *cup parsley, finely chopped*

3 *tablespoons capers*

12 *Gaeta olives, pitted and coarsely chopped*

Plenty of freshly ground black pepper

⅓ *cup extra virgin olive oil*

Big pinch of red pepper flakes

Boil plenty of salted water in a large pan. Add the cauliflower, and cook it for about 5 minutes, or until it is just tender; they should not be crunchy, but not overcooked either. Drain them, and quickly spread them out on a large platter to cool.

Put the cooled pieces of cauliflower into a large salad bowl. Add the rest of the ingredients, and carefully but thoroughly mix the salad. Serve it cool but not cold. Good crusty Garlic Bread, Roman Style (page 91), is ideal to serve with *insalata di cavolfiore*.

Southern Italians really like vegetables, and they are inventive in preparing them. This salad is an example. The sweet, mild flavor of the cauliflower is enhanced yet contrasted by the anchovies and black olives. This dish makes a good antipasto as well as a tasty *contorno* to roast chicken, pork, or grilled fish.

MENU SUGGESTIONS: Cauliflower Salad and Pizza Margherita (page 49) would be nice starters. Rabbit, Ischian Style (page 182), and a *contorno* of Eggplant Dumplings (page 247) followed by a dessert of Spumoni (page 296) would make a good meal.

WINE: Per'e Palummo (page 303)

Fette di Melanzane Ripiene

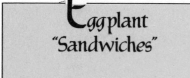

Eggplant "Sandwiches"

MAKES ABOUT 7 EGGPLANT ''SANDWICHES''

If you absolutely hate eggplant, this dish is for you. Even though I prepare many complicated dishes, probably none is more requested than this simple one. Be careful not to pile in loads of *mortadella* and cheese. You want just a hint. If you overdo the stuffing, you will lose the idea and charm of this extraordinary little sandwich. If your family and friends love eggplant, you may well be attacked when you bring the *fette di melanzane ripiene* forth.

MENU SUGGESTIONS: I would use these eggplant sandwiches in every conceivable meal, even having a plateful for lunch with some crusty bread. They are so good it would be hard to choose a meal in which to include them. They are perfect no matter how you use them.

WINE: Brindisi Rosso (page 298)

1 *eggplant, approximately 1 to 1¼ pounds, with firm, tight skin and no blemishes*

1½ *ounces* mortadella *sliced ¹⁄₃₀ inch thick, cut or torn into pieces about 3½ × 3½ inches*

2 *to 2½ ounces Provolone cheese sliced ¹⁄₃₀ inch thick, cut or torn into pieces about 3½ × 3½ inches*

2 *large eggs*

⅓ *cup fine, dry bread crumbs*

⅓ *cup grated Parmesan cheese*

2 *tablespoons minced Italian parsley*

Olive oil for drizzling on "sandwiches"

Slice the eggplant crosswise about ⅜ inch thick. If the flesh is cream colored and the seeds are not easily visible, there will be no need to salt the eggplant to draw out the bitter juices. If the eggplant is more mature, salt the slices lightly, let them drain in a colander under a 2-pound weight for an hour, and pat them dry with paper towels.

Tear the *mortadella* to fit in a single layer between each 2 slices of eggplant. Do the same with the Provolone, placing it over the *mortadella* in each of the "sandwiches." Put the other slice of eggplant on and press down on each sandwich so that the filling clings to the eggplant. Beat the eggs in a low-sided dish. Mix together the bread crumbs, grated Parmesan, and parsley in a low-sided dish. Dip the sandwiches first into the beaten egg, coating them evenly and well, then into the plate of mixed crumbs, cheese, and parsley, being sure to blanket the edges of the sandwiches as well as the tops and bottoms with the crumb mixture. Drizzle on about 1 teaspoon of extra virgin olive oil over the top and bottom of each sandwich. Arrange them on a baking sheet, and place in a preheated 375° F oven for 35 minutes or until they are golden brown and crisp-crumbed. Turn them once during the cooking cycle.

The eggplant sandwiches are delicious cut into wedges and served with drinks at cocktail time. They are good hot or at room temperature.

Pomodori Arrostiti

Roasted Tomatoes

SERVES 6

6 medium, vine-ripened tomatoes, well washed

⅓ cup extra virgin olive oil

1 teaspoon red pepper flakes, or q.b.

6 large slices crusty homemade bread (or more)

Cook the whole tomatoes on the grill over medium heat, turning them carefully once or twice. The skins will split and they will ooze a bit. When they are quite soft, carefully remove them from the grill, put them into a low-sided serving dish, and while the tomatoes are still quite hot, mash them coarsely with a fork. Add the olive oil and the red pepper flakes, and mix the tomatoes well. Slice the bread just when you are ready to serve the tomatoes. For an added treat, use Garlic Bread (page 91). Spread some of the tomatoes on the bread with a spoon, and eat it out of hand.

For those who love to grill on wood fires and like to eat their vegetables in different interpretations, this is a marvelous dish. Unless you grow your own or have friends that will supply you with vine-ripened tomatoes, it is best to wait for the heat of summer, when you can find good ones in the markets. The skins on the homegrown kind are very thin, tender, and edible. As long as the tomatoes are well washed, you can and should eat everything, including the core.

MENU SUGGESTIONS: Roasted Tomatoes make an excellent antipasto, followed by Fried Codfish, Roman Style (page 190), as a *secondo* with a *contorno* of Artichokes in Embers (page 224). Slices of Golden Christmas Bread (page 280) are a fitting dessert.

WINE: Regaleali Bianco (page 310)

Zucchini a Scapici

Marinated Zucchini

SERVES 6

6 to 8 zucchini, fresh and firm (roughly 1½ pounds)

½ cup or so extra virgin olive oil, or q.b.

1 medium yellow onion, sliced ⅛ inch thick

3 or 4 garlic cloves, finely chopped

2 leaves fresh sage, torn into small pieces, or 1 teaspoon dry, whole leaves

Pinch of salt

⅔ cup good wine vinegar, red or white

Scapici is the Sicilian equivalent of *escabeche*, known as the Spanish method of "cooking" fish in lime or lemon juice. In Mexico it is called *ceviche*. There is some debate as to how this name came to be, as it is used all over Southern Italy. Some think it derives from *ex Apicius*, which is hard to ponder because it means the "former Apicius." He was the Roman who wrote the first cookbook about two thousand years ago. Some Sicilians think it comes from a word meaning "askew" or "akimbo," because a sharp acid is added to make the zucchini piquant. Probably the first fish prepared this way was cooked and then put down in vinegar. Whatever the reality, *scapici* dishes are justifiably popular all over the South of Italy.

MENU SUGGESTIONS: *Zucchini a scapici* is delicious as part of an antipasto dish that includes some crunchy raw vegetables for a contrast in texture as well as some Sardinian Parchment Bread (page 63). A perfect *primo piatto* would be Penne with *Porcini* in a Hot Tomato Sauce (page 143); that is what Maria Guarnaschelli chooses to have with the zucchini. You could follow this with Homemade Sicilian Sausage (page 188) or Breaded Lamb Chops (page 186).

WINE: Cesanese del Piglio (page 304)

Wash the zucchini well under cold running water, or soak them in cold water for about 10 minutes. Be sure to get all of the sand off. If they are not perfect, cut or scrape any blemishes. Dry with towels, and cut the tops and the ends off, and discard them. Slice the zucchini lengthwise about ¼ inch or a little less.

Heat 3 tablespoons of the olive oil in a large frying pan and fry the slices, a few at a time, over high heat until they have deep golden crisp areas on them but are not too limp. (Use as little oil as possible; do not let them become oil soaked! Add oil only as needed. Depending on the zucchini and the pan itself, you may find that you do not have to use all the oil.) As the zucchini slices are done, set them into a deep platter or casserole dish. They should have just enough of the cooking oil on them to make them very tasty. If you made an error and let them get a little too oily, blot them for a moment or two on paper towels. Continue until you have cooked all of the zucchini.

In the same frying pan, replenish the oil, if needed, heat it, and brown the onions. Add the garlic, sage, and salt. When the garlic is just golden, add the vinegar all at once, bring it to a boil, and boil the mixture for 2 to 3 minutes, or until there is very little liquid left. It becomes a sort of dressing for the onions. Pour the mixture over the zucchini, and carefully and gently mix all the ingredients together so that they flavor each other.

Zucchini a scapici may be eaten warm right away or later, cooled to room temperature. It's even better left for a day in the marinade, but it should always be up to room temperature when served; never ice cold!

⅓ cup virgin olive oil, or q.b. for
frying

3 large garlic cloves, peeled and well
crushed

1 pound pumpkin or banana squash,
seeded, peeled, and cut into ¼-inch
slices

Salt to taste

Freshly ground black pepper to
taste

About 30 mint leaves, 15 washed
and coarsely chopped, the rest used
as garnish

FOR BREADED PUMPKIN

2 large eggs, beaten

Bread crumbs, q.b.

Optional: ½ pound fresh
Mozzarella cheese, thinly sliced

TO PREPARE FRIED PUMPKIN

Heat the oil in a large low frying pan until it is hot but not smoking. Add
the garlic, and gently fry it over low heat until it is deep gold in color and
smells aromatic and pungent. Remove the garlic from the pan, and either eat
it, save it for later use, or discard it. Fry the slices of pumpkin in the hot oil
for 1 to 2 minutes, or until they begin to get little dark brown blisters on
the bottom, being careful not to let them burn. If the heat is too high, lower
it. Use a spatula to carefully turn them, and fry on the other side. When
they are slightly brown, sprinkle the slices generously with salt and pepper.
Set on an absorbent towel to drain. Sprinkle them with the chopped mint,
and use the whole leaves for garnish. Serve either hot or at room temperature.
Drizzle on additional virgin olive oil when you serve them, if you wish.

TO PREPARE THE BREADED PUMPKIN

Beat the eggs in a low-sided dish, add the uncooked pumpkin slices, and turn
them around and around. Spread the bread crumbs in a low-sided dish. Shake
off any excess egg from the pumpkin slices, and coat them with the bread
crumbs, patting the crumbs on well with your hand. Repeat the procedure
once more. This should provide sufficient coating for the pumpkin. (If you
find that this method troubles you, simply dip the slices into all-purpose flour
before the egg dip, but this should not be necessary.) Follow the recipe as
previously described. If you are going to add the Mozzarella cheese, simply
place some thin slices on top of the *zucca* as it finishes cooking. The heat
should be sufficient to melt the cheese a little; if not, put the fried slices of
zucca on a cookie sheet, and put them into a hot oven (500° F) for 5 minutes,
or until the cheese is melted.

Zucca Dorata

olden
Fried Pumpkin
(or Banana Squash)

SERVES 6

Pumpkin is certainly the vegetable of choice
for this unusual dish. But, if you cannot
get it, banana squash or Hubbard squash,
as it is sometimes called, will be delicious.
Zucca dorata is versatile and equally good
as an antipasto or a *contorno* for roast fowl,
lamb, or pork. Sometimes *zucca dorata* is
made with bread crumbs. You can also
add some thinly sliced Mozzarella cheese
on top of the breaded *zucca* and have a
more elaborate and scrumptious rendition.

MENU SUGGESTIONS: You could make
an entire meal of *antipasti* by adding Savory Bread Salad (page 94), Roasted Peppers with Italian-Style Tuna and Clams (page
104), Roasted Tomatoes (page 99), "Phone-
Wire" Rice Croquettes (page 96), and
an Italian Potato Pancake (page 246).
"Drowned" Ice Cream (page 293) for dessert would be perfect with a few cookies.

WINE: Trebbiano d'Abruzzo (page 298)

Insalata di
Baccalà

Codfish
Salad

SERVES 6

This simple salad makes a wonderful antipasto. The combination of *baccalà* and cauliflower seems unlikely, but you will truly enjoy the taste contrasts. The dressing calls for the very best extra virgin olive oil and wine vinegar.

MENU SUGGESTIONS: Codfish Salad and Hot Devil Potatoes (page 243) make a nice antipasto. Breaded Lamb Chops (page 186) with a *contorno* of String Beans in Tomato Sauce (page 236) make a good meal. Finish it with Saint Joseph's Day Fritters (page 289) filled with Pastry Cream (page 260).

WINE: Cesanese del Piglio (page 304) or Castel del Monte Rosso (page 299)

1½ *pounds soaked* baccalà *(see Fried Codfish recipe for method, page 190)*
1 *large head cauliflower, washed and cut into small pieces*
⅓ *cup finely chopped parsley*

White wine vinegar, q.b.
Several grindings of freshly ground black pepper
Extra virgin olive oil, q.b.

Put the *baccalà* into 2 quarts of simmering water and cook for 20 minutes. Remove it with a slotted spoon and set aside to cool.

Boil plenty of salted water in a large pan, add the cauliflower, and cook it for about 5 minutes, or until it is just tender; not crunchy but not overcooked either. Drain the cauliflower and spread the pieces on a large platter to cool.

When the cauliflower is cool, put it into a large salad bowl. Break the cooked *baccalà* into small pieces. A fork is handy to tear off little bits. Mix them with the cauliflower, and add the parsley. Sprinkle on the vinegar, not too much, and some freshly ground black pepper. (You can judge the correct amount of vinegar by tasting only.) Mix the ingredients again, and then drizzle on plenty of extra virgin olive oil. Serve the salad cool but not cold.

Cozze
al Zafferano

SERVES 8

2 pounds plump fresh mussels

1 yellow onion, peeled and finely chopped

2 or 3 parsley sprigs

1 cup dry white wine

1 branch fresh thyme, or ⅛ teaspoon dry

1 small bay leaf

4 big grindings of freshly ground black pepper

1 pinch whole saffron threads, chopped fine and dissolved in ¼ cup dry white wine

2 tablespoons virgin olive oil

Wash the mussels in cold water, and pull off their beards if they have any. Put all the ingredients into a large sauté pan. Turn the heat on as high as it will go, and cook the mixture, uncovered, shaking the pan often, until the mussels have opened. Remove the pan from the heat, and immediately remove the mussels from the pan with tongs, leaving the juices in the sauté pan. Discard any unopened mussels. Put the mussels into a bowl that will hold them all.

When they are cool enough to handle, remove one shell from each mussel and discard it. Leave the cooked mussels in the other half of their shells, and place on a serving platter. Put them into the refrigerator to chill. Be sure to save any juices that are in the bowl or that come from the mussels as you do this part of the preparation and add to the sauté pan.

Strain the pan juices through cheesecloth into the bowl that contained the mussels to remove any sand. Rinse the sauté pan with warm water to rid it of residual sand that may have been in the juices. Put the juices back into the sauté pan.

Reduce the pan juices over high heat by about two thirds. Remove the pan from the heat, and set it aside. You should have a very small amount of intensely flavored juice, just enough to barely coat the mussels. When the liquid is fairly cool, drizzle it over the mussels. Continue to chill the mussels in the refrigerator for at least 2 hours. When everything is quite cold, serve the mussels as a solitary antipasto or as part of a more elaborate scheme.

If ever a dish represented a marriage of the sea and the mountains, it is this one. Very few people know that Abruzzo is the only region in Italy that produces saffron, even though it is not a fundamental ingredient in that region's cooking, probably because the populace found it too expensive. Other regions of Italy, however, find it indispensable in such dishes as Sicilian Rice Dumplings (*arancini*), some fish stews, and *risotto Milanese*, which cannot be made without it. It is believed that the seeds for the *crocus sativus* (the flower that produces the stamens that are, in fact, saffron) were brought to Navelli in the Abruzzo by a Dominican monk who had visited the Orient.

Cozze al Zafferano is one of the rare uses of saffron in Abruzzese cooking (it might be the only one), and in this case it works wonders.

MENU SUGGESTIONS: Tuna and Fennel Seeds (page 201) would be a good first course, as would Clay-Cooked Prawns (page 196) or Fried Codfish, Roman Style (page 190). *Contorni* of Italian Potato Pancake (page 246) and some Roasted Onions (page 233) would be my choices. Cream Puffs (page 256) to finish the meal should satisfy the eaters very well.

WINE: Corvo Bianco (page 308) or Five Roses (page 300)

Peperoni col Tonno e Vongole

Roasted Peppers with Italian-Style Tuna and Clams

SERVES 6

The success of this tasty dish depends on charring the skins off the peppers.

MENU SUGGESTIONS: This dish makes a good antipasto or a light lunch, if you serve more to each person. A nice big Pizza Margherita (page 49) would be a good complement.

WINE: Salice Salentino (page 301)

2 *large red bell peppers (use green if red is not available)*

1 *tablespoon extra virgin olive oil*

½ *teaspoon salt*
   Plenty of freshly ground black pepper

1 *6-ounce can best Italian tuna (tonno) in olive oil; do not drain the oil*

2 *pounds fresh Cherrystone or Manila clams cooked until just tender, cooled and chopped (or use 6- or 7-ounce can chopped clams)*

¼ *cup chopped parsley*
   Juice of 1 lemon

1 *medium garlic clove, minced*
   Optional: pinch of coarse red chili pepper

Roast the whole peppers on a high gas flame (or throw them into a roaring fire or barbecue). If you do not have a gas flame, cut the peppers into quarters and push them down a bit to flatten them. Place the skin side as close as you can under the preheated element of an electric broiler. Proceed for gas and electric as follows: When the skins of the peppers are completely black and charred, but the flesh is still firm, using tongs, remove the peppers from the flame or broiler, and place them in a paper bag. When the peppers are cool enough to handle, rub off the burnt skin with your fingers and scrape any stubborn areas with a knife. (Don't worry if a few small burnt spots don't come off, as they will add to the flavor and the appearance of the dish.) Remove the stems and seeds of the peppers, and discard them. Cut the peppers into thirds (or quarters if they are bigger). Sprinkle on the garlic and then drizzle on some of the olive oil. Add the salt and freshly ground black pepper. Set the peppers aside.

TO PREPARE THE CLAMS

Using a brush, scrub the clams under cold water. Place them in a pan with a lid and add ¼ cup of water. Cover and turn the heat on high. When the clams open (in about 5 minutes), reduce the heat and cook for another 5 minutes. Remove from the heat. Uncover the pan and allow the clams to cool in their own juice. When they are cool, remove the shells and discard them. Reserve the juice for another dish or drink it. Chop the clams coarsely.

In a large bowl, mix well the tuna with its oil, the clams, parsley, lemon juice, salt, pepper, and the rest of the olive oil (also the red chili pepper, if you are using it). Let it all rest, and then blend it with a fork until it is a loose but integrated mass.

Arrange the peppers with the inside up on a serving platter and divide the tuna-clam mixture among the pieces. Garnish the platter with lemon wedges. Serve the peppers with crusty Italian bread.

MINESTRE

*S*oups

A good soup is as challenging to make as any dish I know. Here, the balance of flavor is nothing short of critical. The soup must be delicious and the smell of it, before you eat even a spoonful, should immediately calm and satisfy you. The elegant Miniature Meatball Soup, the heroic Three Virtues Soup, and the bountiful Calabrian Celery Soup (imagine a bountiful soup made with a base of hot water!) are a tribute to soup making at its best. In selecting these dishes I wanted to show not only the diversity of soup concepts in the South of Italy but how, in most cases, minimal ingredients produce soul-satisfying results and how, in the Three Virtues Soup, the same result is achieved by using what amounts to a veritable catalog of fresh, cured, and dried foods. In Italy most soups do not have a recipe per se, but are intuitive assemblages of bits and pieces of food from other meals added to the normal stores one keeps in the house, such as onions and celery and carrots; an example of how frugality in its best sense can have an epicurean result.

The soups in this section are authentic recipes from the South of Italy and were chosen because of their uniqueness. It is better to make them as directed and leave other, more spontaneous soups for those intuitive times we all should cultivate.

1 3-pound stewing hen or chicken dressed and washed

1 medium yellow onion with the peel on, cut in quarters

1 carrot, scraped and cut into 4 pieces

1 celery branch, washed and cut into 6 pieces

1 small tomato, washed and crushed only enough to burst open the skin

3 large fresh parsley sprigs

1 bay leaf, torn in half

1 large garlic clove, peeled and well crushed

4 whole peppercorns

1 whole clove

3 quarts cold water, or enough to cover the chicken well

Brodo di Pollo

Homemade Chicken Broth

MAKES ABOUT 2 QUARTS

Remove the liver from the chicken, and reserve it for something else. Cut the chicken into 18 or 20 pieces. Be sure that you cut through the back to expose the marrow. Be sure to cut across the breast bone and wing, leg, and thigh bones for the same reason.

Cover the chicken parts, the vegetables, the herbs, and the spices (in other words, all the ingredients) in an 8-quart stock pot (nonaluminum preferred) with cold water. Bring the water to a simmer over medium heat, and then lower the heat as far as possible to allow just the faintest simmer. Skim and discard the froth often. (If you do not do this the broth will be cloudy.) Let the broth simmer, uncovered, for at least 2½ hours.

When the broth is done, let it set for about 2 hours to cool off. Strain the broth through a fine sieve, removing first the chicken parts and the vegetables. Reserve the meat for another use. (See **note.**) When it is quite cool and there is no steam whatsoever coming off the top, put it into a glass or plastic container and refrigerate it uncovered. When the broth is very cold (and not before), cover it. If you keep it in the refrigerator for several days, you must sterilize it every 3 days by bringing the broth to a simmer and cooking it for about 10 minutes. Then cool and store it as described.

Before using the broth, you may want to discard most of the fat that will have solidified on the top. Do not take all of it off, because it brings some flavor to the dish and is desirable in small amounts. The broth will need salt before it can be used.

NOTE: If you have simmered the broth very slowly and carefully, the chicken parts, while not prime eating, make a delicious light dish. At home we used to pull the meat off the bones and skin it while it was still quite warm and drizzle on extra virgin olive oil, lots of cracked pepper, a pinch of salt, and some dried oregano. With toasted homemade bread it was a tasty meal, indeed.

Home cooks tend to speak of "broth" and chefs of "stock." To me broth is more comforting and "homemade." The word derives from "brew." Any way you refer to it is correct, and the results must be judged by taste and color.

Most Italian recipes ask you to use a *gallina*, specifically, a hen. It is not so easy to find stewing, or brewing, hens. These are mature birds over two years old that have stopped laying. Their flavor is more pronounced than that of younger birds. If you can find chickens, no matter what you are going to use them for, try to get ones with the head and feet still on. In large ethnic markets you may be able to get them.

The feet and heads impart a depth of flavor that really enhances the broth. The feet, in particular, are desirable because they are mostly cartilage, which softens as it cooks and becomes gelatin. Even when the broth is hot you can see the difference with this natural gelatin; it is glossy and thicker. *Brodo di pollo* is indispensable. Make large quantities and freeze it in small batches so that you can use it as you need it.

Pallottoline in Brodo

Miniature Meatball Soup

MAKES 4 TO 6
SERVINGS

With a good homemade broth these Lil-liputian meatballs are utterly delicious. I would call this soup earthy and soothing. Yet it can also be quite glamorous. How-ever you present it, *pallottoline in brodo* ranks with the best soups in the world. The broth wants to be light in color, yet very flavorful, but not powerful. It should be smooth-tasting and reduced enough, in volume, to have a concentrated meat and vegetable taste. I've given you recipes for broth made with beef and with chicken, but they really are not "recipes" after all; they are just guides.

½ pound veal, finely chopped (or beef)

3 tablespoons grated Parmesan cheese

4 tablespoons bread crumbs

1 large egg

1½ tablespoons parsley, chopped
Salt and pepper to taste

1 quart broth, veal, chicken, or light beef

Optional: *Add* tiny *amount of garlic to meatballs; add precooked and drained tiny pasta such as* acini pepe *or* lingue di cardinale *to the broth and meatballs just before serving.*

In a medium-sized bowl, mix all the ingredients, *except the broth*, together, and form mixture into small meatballs about the size of a small marble. Set them aside on a plate big enough so that they don't touch.

In a large pot, bring the broth to a gentle boil over medium heat. Add the meatballs slowly, a few at a time. Lower the heat and simmer them gently for 6 to 7 minutes, or until the meatballs float to the top. Gently ladle some of the meatballs and the broth into warm soup dishes. Serve the *pallottoline in brodo* very hot and pass more grated Parmesan cheese separately at the table.

Brodo di Carne

Meat Broth

MAKES ABOUT
2½ QUARTS

2 pounds rump roast with a little fat left on, or chuck roast

2 pounds beef bones, from the legs if possible

2 celery branches

1 large ripe tomato, skin and core left on, cut into ⅛-inch dice

2 large yellow onions with skin left on, cut into ⅛-inch dice

1 bay leaf
Salt

Freshly ground pepper, about 3 good cranks of the mill

Fresh, clear, cold water (clean collected rainwater would be good)

Have the butcher crack the bones, or slice them, using a saw, into small pieces. Put all the ingredients into a large, heavy pot, preferably nonaluminum. Cover the ingredients to twice their depth with the water. Bring the water to a simmer over a very low heat. (This could take an hour or so.) When it begins to simmer you will notice froth coming to the top. With a large, flat spoon or a ladle, skim off as much froth as you can and discard it. Continue to do this the whole time it is simmering. Cook the broth for another 2 hours, skimming whenever necessary. At that point you can remove the meat from the broth. Slice the meat and serve it hot or cold with virgin olive oil and lemon juice or chop it up and use it in other recipes, such as Cannelloni (page 207). I do not subscribe to the idea that the meat is tasteless and worthless after having been cooked so long. Some of the most magnificent *bollito misto* dishes I have ever eaten were made with a variety of meat and poultry cuts that stewed that length of time. It depends on the quality of meat as much as anything.

When the broth is done, let it rest for about a half hour, then carefully strain it through moistened cheesecloth. Correct the broth for salt. When it tastes deep and satisfying and is relatively clear, let it cool in an open, airy place. When it is completely cooled, put it into a glass or clean plastic container, and store it in the refrigerator. Remove any fat that congeals on the top. If you do not use the broth within 3 days, simmer it in a pan for at least 15 minutes. (Otherwise, it may turn sour or start to grow harmful bacteria.) Repeat this procedure as often as you like, but for long-term storage, it is best to freeze whatever broth you don't use.

Brodo di Pollo: Follow directions on page 109.

Stracciatella alla
Romana

SERVES 4

1 quart *Homemade Chicken Broth
(page 109) or light veal broth*

3 *large eggs*
Salt *to taste*

3 *big scrapings fresh nutmeg*

1 *tablespoon semolina*

4 *tablespoons grated Parmesan cheese
(the best you can afford)*

Reserve ¼ cup of cold broth. Bring the remaining broth to a very low simmer over low heat. Meanwhile, break the eggs in a small bowl, and add a pinch of salt and the nutmeg, and mix well. Add the semolina and the cheese, and mix again. Add the ¼ cup of cold broth, and mix again.

When the soup is at the simmer, gently drizzle in the egg mixture. Paddle the broth back and forth slowly with a wooden spoon, almost languidly, so that the egg mixture stays intact but in flowing little raglike conformations. Simmer the soup for 1 minute longer. Serve it piping hot.

While this soup is known as a Roman specialty, there are versions of it in many parts of southern Italy. Eggs mixed with a little semolina and grated cheese are added to chicken broth at the last minute and then swirled. The effect is like little rags floating in water. It is a very pretty soup, but more important it is delicious, especially if you make your own chicken broth. A light meat broth could be used instead.

MENU SUGGESTIONS: After a bowl of *stracciatella*, a dish of Linguine with Clams (page 134) would be good followed by Swordfish, Stuffed Sicilian Style (page 199). Sicilian Cassata (page 266) or a Semi-freddo (page 286) would be just the right ending to this meal.

WINE: Trebbiano di Aprilia (page 306)

Scrippelle 'Mbusse

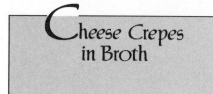

Cheese Crepes in Broth

SERVES 5 OR 6;
MAKES 12 TO 14
SCRIPPELLE OF
APPROXIMATELY
6-INCH DIAMETER

These crepes can be made as large as 6 inches across or as small as 3 inches across, depending on how they are going to be used.

Some of the old books counsel you not to sprinkle grated cheese on *scrippelle* before rolling them up like good cigars, their traditional shape. Other books insist that you not only do that, but that you add some grated cheese to the batter. The *scrippelle* must be very thin and tender, and the broth must show that you were extravagant in the use of chicken. Homemade Chicken Broth (page 109) is called for.

A handy feature of this dish is that the *brodo* can be made ahead as can the *scrippelle*. You can even freeze them, before sprinkling on the cheese, with a sheet of wax paper between them. Warm them in a preheated 350° F oven for about 5 minutes before using them.

MENU SUGGESTIONS: There is no need for antipasto. A *secondo* of Mussels and Sausage (page 194) seems ideal with a *contorno* of String Bean Bundles (page 235). A Hazelnut Semifreddo (page 289) would be a perfect finish to this meal.

WINE: Fiano di Avellino (page 302) or Castel del Monte Rosso (page 299)

5 *large eggs*
1¼ *cups whole milk*
¼ *teaspoon salt*
2 *tablespoons finely chopped parsley*
¾ *cup grated* pecorino *cheese*
4 *tablespoons all-purpose flour*
3 *big scrapings fresh nutmeg*
    Lard or fresh fatback for greasing the crepe pan
2 *quarts Homemade Chicken Broth (brodo di pollo, page 109)*

Beat the eggs in a bowl or a deep dish. When they begin to get frothy, add the milk, salt, parsley, cheese, flour, and nutmeg. Beat the mixture some more and then set it aside for about 20 minutes to allow the gluten to form. The consistency should be like heavy cream. If too thick, add water, 1 teaspoon at a time, gently mixing to the desired consistency. If too watery, add flour, ½ teaspoon at a time, gently mixing to the desired consistency.

Heat a 6-inch crepe pan or a light-weight steel or iron omelette pan over high heat. When it is quite hot, rub the surface with some lard smeared on a paper towel, or use a pure bristle pastry brush. The surface of the hot pan should just glisten; it should not be oily in any way.

Using a tablespoon or small ladle, put in enough batter just to cover the bottom of the pan. It should be liquid enough to quickly spread over the bottom surface. If it is not, take the pan off the fire to keep it from burning, and add more water to the batter. When the batter is the correct consistency, resume making the crepes. The crepes should be as thin as you can make them and still hold together. (Generally, the first crepe is a test, so it is all right to throw it away if it is not perfect. The second one will be.)

Continue making the crepes, and gently stack them on each other. If you do not plan to use them immediately, cover them with plastic wrap or a damp kitchen towel until you are ready for them. (There is no need to refrigerate them if they are going to be used the same day they are made.)

When you are ready to serve the *scrippelle*, bring the broth to a gentle boil over medium heat in a medium-sized pot, being sure not to boil it so long that froth is raised. If you do, reduce the heat, and skim the surface. The *brodo* must be very clean, wholesome-looking and -smelling, and certainly delicious.

While the broth is heating, lay the *scrippelle* out on a table, and sprinkle them on one side only with 1 tablespoon of grated *pecorino* cheese to make a very light layer. Roll the *scrippelle* up very tightly so that they look like good cigars.

Heat soup plates or bowls large enough to comfortably hold the length of the *scrippelle*, lay 2 *scrippelle* in the dish side by side, ladle about 1½ cups of hot *brodo* over them, and serve them at once. (I like to bring the *scrippelle* in the hot dishes to the table, along with a tureen of boiling hot *brodo*. I have each person pass his dish so that I can fill it with *brodo*.)

Zuppa di Accia

SERVES 6

1 *pound celery, washed and cut into*
¼-inch slices

1½ *quarts water*

1½ *teaspoons salt*

2 *tablespoons extra virgin olive oil*

6 *slices homemade bread, toasted*
and cut into 4 pieces each

3 *large hard-boiled eggs, peeled and*
quartered

3 *ounces thinly sliced* soppressata,
cut into julienne strips

4 *ounces fresh pork sausage without*
fennel, skinned and broken into
tiny pieces

3 *ounces Caciocavallo cheese, thinly*
sliced and cut into julienne strips

¾ *cup grated* pecorino *cheese*
Freshly ground black pepper to
taste

Cover the celery in a small stock pot with the water, bring to a simmer, and add enough salt so it is tasty, but not too salty, because you will be adding more salty ingredients later. Add the olive oil, and simmer the soup over low heat for 15 minutes, or until the celery is tender but not soft.

Meanwhile, put the pieces of bread all over the bottom of a heated soup tureen and, at random, scatter on all of the other ingredients, except the grated *pecorino* and the black pepper. Bring the soup to a rolling boil, and quickly ladle it onto the ingredients in the tureen. The boiling soup should cook the sausage bits quickly because they are so small. The other ingredients do not need cooking, only heating and melting. Sprinkle on the *pecorino* cheese and then, very gently, mix the soup with a large spoon, using folding motions, for about 30 seconds. Grind on plenty of fresh black pepper, and serve the soup immediately in hot soup plates.

In the Pugliese dialect, the word *accia* (pronounced *ah-cha*) means celery. This is the same word Sicilians use for celery. In Italian the word is *sedano*. This soup is very hearty, the kind I would tend to have as a whole meal with a salad. A small bowl makes a very good soup in a bigger meal, or a big bowl in a meal where there will be little else to follow.

Soppressata, a Southern Italian cured meat specialty, is generally available in good Italian delicatessens. It is made by packing large chunks of highly spiced meat into a casing, and cured much like *salame*. When you slice it you can see the pattern of the chunks of meat. If you cannot get it, you could substitute mild *capocollo* or a very moist, highly flavored *salame*.

MENU SUGGESTIONS: After the Celery Soup some Tuna, Calabrian Style (page 200), would be good, with a *contorno* of Spinach, Roman Style (page 245). Spumoni (page 296) or Lemon Ice (page 291) with some Bitter Almond Cookies (page 278) would be a good dessert.

WINE: Favonio Cabernet Franc (page 299)

LE VIRTÙ

Three Virtues Soup

SERVES ABOUT 12

Le virtù is truly a big soup of virtues, traditionally eaten on May 3. Teramo is most passionate about this soup. However, in L'Aquila they get just as excited about it.

The ingredients go through a sort of seasonal itinerary. The dried legumes are holdovers from winter stores, as is the cured meat. The fresh meat and the enormous array of fresh vegetables signal spring and rebirth. A riot of pasta shapes rounds out the bountiful ingredients.

Le virtù is slightly complicated, but once you realize what must be done, you can easily tackle the job and do it well. This is an ideal one-dish meal and, surprisingly, Italians often eat it cold as well as hot.

Make this dish when you want to feed large numbers of people; it's especially good for an open house. Somehow *le virtù* loses something when it is made in small amounts.

MENU SUGGESTIONS: I would let this soup be a one-dish meal for a festive party. Choose a tureen that comes with very large soup bowls and let people serve themselves. Heaping dishes of cheese should be on the table near *le virtù*. For a dessert offer Almond Tart (page 270).

WINE: Trebbiano d'Abruzzo (page 298)

¾ pound mixed dried legumes, such as beans, navy, or cannellini, chick-peas, peas (green and/or yellow), fava, and lentils, all in equal amounts, if possible

¼ pound prosciutto, in one piece, if possible

1 fresh pig's foot, washed well

1½ ounces salt pork

½ pound fresh pork skin, well scraped of any fat

3 large garlic cloves, peeled and well crushed

1½ pounds mixed fresh vegetables, such as carrots, bulb fennel, spinach, Swiss chard, and chicory, all washed, trimmed, and cut into bite-sized pieces

1 large yellow onion, peeled and finely chopped

3 large whole tomatoes, peeled, cored, and well crushed, or use an equal amount canned

4 sprigs fresh parsley, finely chopped

4 fresh mint leaves

3 whole cloves

⅛ teaspoon fresh ground nutmeg
Salt to taste

6 or 8 grindings of fresh black pepper

½ pound assorted dried pasta in as many shapes as you can find

3 ounces handmade pasta, maltagliati, poorly cut or random cut (as your fantasy allows) (page 127)

½ pound freshly grated pecorino cheese, or q.b.

The day before you make *le virtù*, cover the legumes with cold water to twice their height in a large stock pot, and soak them overnight. The following day drain the water and discard it. Cover the legumes to half again their height with slightly salted water. Bring to the boil, turn down the heat, and half-cook them at a very low simmer. Leave them in the cooking water (about 40 minutes) and set them aside.

Meanwhile, put the *prosciutto*, the pork skin, and pig's foot into another stock pot, and cover them well with water. Bring to a boil, turn down heat, and simmer them gently for about 3 hours, skimming the surface well of any froth and as much fat as you can. When the meats are tender, remove them from the liquid, and pick any meat off the bones. Discard the bones. Cut all the meat into ¼-inch dice and set it aside. Skim the cooking water of any remaining froth or fat, and set the water aside also. Don't be surprised to find that some of the cooked meats are translucent and sticky. They taste wonderful and lend the soup an incomparable texture.

Melt the salt pork in another large stock pot over medium heat, add the garlic, and brown it, being careful not to burn it. Add the carrots, and cook them until they begin to soften. Add the onion, and cook it until it is transparent. Add the tomatoes, fennel, herbs, and spices, and stir, coating everything well in the salt pork fat, so the flavors begin to mingle. Add salt and pepper to taste.

Drain the legumes, reserving the cooking water, and add them to the stock pot with the tomato mixture, stirring. Add the chopped meats to the tomato and legume mixture, and pour on the water in which the meat was cooked to cover the vegetables well. Add some of the legume cooking water if the meat water is insufficient. If even that is not enough, add boiling water. Add additional boiling water at any time during the cooking if you think there is not enough liquid to make a good thick soup.

When the legumes are tender, add the leafy vegetables, i.e., the spinach, Swiss chard, and chicory. Add the various pasta, and cook everything for 5 to 7 minutes, or until the pasta is almost *al dente*. At this point add the *maltagliati*. Correct for salt and pepper. When the *maltagliati* are *al dente*, serve *le virtù* in hot bowls. Sprinkle on loads of freshly grated *pecorino* cheese. Any *le virtù* left over can be eaten the next day, cold or reheated.

NOTE: This recipe can be doubled easily.

Pane Fritto

Fried Bread

MAKES 12 SLICES

12 *slices Italian-style bread, ¼ inch thick*
Olive oil for frying

In a heavy frying pan put 1 tablespoon of olive oil for each slice of bread, heat the oil until it is hot but nowhere near smoking, and carefully fry the slices of bread in the oil for 1 to 2 minutes, or until they are browned. Turn them over and brown the other side. If the bread has absorbed all of the oil, replenish it, and finish the frying.

Serve the fried bread hot, straight from the pan. When you serve it, do not cover it with a napkin, or it will get soggy immediately.

MENU SUGGESTIONS: You could use Garlic Bread in place of the Fried Bread. Macaroni and Roast in Natural Juices (page 212) would be a good *secondo* followed by Orange and Lemon Salad (page 242).

WINE: Sangiovese di Aprilia (page 306) or Etna Bianco (page 308)

Zuppa di Asparagi

Sicilian Asparagus Soup

SERVES 6

In Sicily this soup would be made with wild asparagus, which is very long and as slender as a pencil. Almost everywhere in the foothills in early summer, you can gather fistfuls of asparagus and use them with abandon, as you see in this recipe.

While you get a slightly different flavor using domestic asparagus, I highly recommend this soup. It will not be as "grassy" tasting as the wild version and perhaps not as naturally sweet. The real test is that Sicilians who know this dish declare the domestic version not only edible but delicious. The asparagus flavor backed up with the natural tang of the cheese and a hint of garlic combine to make a soup that can be used for rustic *al fresco* lunches or can become quite elegant if served for dinner in your best dishes and with your best silver. In either case, I always serve Fried Bread (page 115) or Garlic Bread (page 91) with it.

1 *pound fresh asparagus*

2 *tablespoons olive oil*

1 *large garlic clove, crushed*

1 *generous quart chicken, veal, or beef broth, preferably homemade (pages 109, 110)*

Salt and pepper to taste

4 *large eggs*

6 *tablespoons grated* pecorino *cheese*

1 *tablespoon chopped parsley*

Trim the asparagus so that only the top green tender parts remain. Boil them in a small amount of lightly salted water (enough to just cover them) for about 4 minutes. Remove them from the boiling water, and drain them well, reserving the water for later use. When they are cool enough to handle, cut them into 1-inch pieces. Set them aside for later use. Save the water in which the asparagus was cooked for later use in the soup.

Heat the oil over low heat in a small frying pan that will hold all of the pieces of asparagus, and add the garlic. When the garlic is brown, remove and discard it. Add the asparagus, and fry it for about 2 minutes. Remove the asparagus from the frying pan and set it aside.

In the meantime, combine the cooking water from the asparagus and the broth in a medium-sized pot, and bring it to a boil. The moment it reaches the boiling point, reduce the heat so that it simmers.

Beat the eggs in a small bowl, and add the cheese and parsley. Stir the mixture well, add the asparagus pieces, and pour all of these ingredients into the simmering broth. As soon as the eggs begin to curdle, stir vigorously with a spoon to mix it well. Salt and pepper to taste.

Serve the *zuppa di asparagi* very hot with Fried Bread or Garlic Bread.

Zuppa di Cozze o
Ostriche alla
Tarantina

Mussel or Oyster Soup, Taranto Style

SERVES 4

¼ cup virgin olive oil

¼ cup finely chopped yellow onion

2 large garlic cloves, peeled and well crushed

4 pounds mussels, well cleaned and bearded, or 48 small oysters, well scrubbed

¼ cup finely chopped parsley

1¼ cups dry white wine

8 large slices homemade or Italian-style bread, toasted and rubbed with raw garlic (see Garlic Bread, page 91)

Heat the olive oil over medium heat in a frying pan large enough to eventually hold all the mussels or oysters (use a roasting pan if you do not have a big enough frying pan), add the onions, and cook them until they are just transparent. Add the crushed garlic, and brown it, being careful not to burn it. Add the mussels or the oysters to the pan, and shake them around well. The minute the first mussel or oyster begins to open, add the parsley and the white wine. The wine must cook long enough to lose its alcoholic content (about 4 minutes), and the shellfish must all open. Do not overcook them. Discard the shellfish that have not opened.

While the shellfish are cooking, toast the bread, and rub it with raw garlic. Put the bread in large warm soup plates. When the shellfish have all opened, portion them out among the soup plates, on top of the toasted bread, and pour on the pan juices. Serve the *zuppa* hot, immediately.

This mussel soup is simple and fast to make. It is easily used as a starter course, in smaller portions, or it can be a main dish, if the portions are as shown below. The use of oysters as an option is really fascinating. It is the one and only recipe I have found that uses cooked oysters. In Taranto, where the oysters are exceptional, they are eaten raw. I have not found cooked oysters used in dishes from other parts of Italy.

MENU SUGGESTIONS: Fried Caciocavallo Cheese, Silversmith Style (page 151), would be a very good antipasto. A dish of Fiery Macaroni (page 138) would be a perfect *primo piatto* followed by a *secondo* of the mussels or oysters. Walnut Cake #2 (page 277) would be a mild and tasty dessert, served just plain.

WINE: Marino (page 306)

Pane Frattau

Bread and Cheese Soup

SERVES 6

This dish is hardly a soup but it certainly qualifies as a *primo piatto*, at least. *Frattau* is Sardinian dialect for "grated." *Pane frattau* started out as Sardinian Parchment Bread (page 63) with grated cheese sprinkled on it and a ladleful of hot broth. Now it has evolved to include eggs, marinara sauce, and other ingredients. It is a handsome dish, as tasty as it looks. It takes a little bit of juggling to get it all together, but it is not difficult.

MENU SUGGESTIONS: Bread and Cheese Soup as a *primo* followed by Trout Vernaccia (page 177) would give you a good start for a Sardinian meal. A *contorno* of Artichokes Stuffed with Ricotta and Salami (page 227) would be excellent either with the trout or just after. A dish of Bitter Almond Cookies (page 278) would be a nice finish to the meal.

WINE: Bianco Alcamo (page 308)

1½ cups strong chicken or meat stock (pages 109, 110)

3 cups Marinara Sauce (page 78)

4 tablespoons white wine vinegar

6 large eggs

6 disks Sardinian Parchment Bread (page 63), about 5 inches across

1 cup grated pecorino Sardo cheese

Heat the stock in a wide, low frying pan, and keep it hot. Heat the Marinara Sauce in a small pan, and keep it at a simmer. Heat 2 quarts of water in a low-sided nonaluminum pan, such as a skillet, and add the vinegar. Heat 6 rimmed soup plates, and keep them handy.

Break the eggs into small saucers, and slide them gently into the simmering water and vinegar. Poach the eggs for no longer than 4 minutes. The yolks should be runny.

Meanwhile, dip the Sardinian Parchment Bread discs into the hot stock to soften them. This will happen almost immediately when they hit the hot stock. Carefully lift them out of the stock with a wide slotted spoon or spatula, and put each one into a warm soup plate. Spoon enough hot stock on each piece of bread. It should not be floating but there should be enough to distinguish that there is some liquid in the dish. Spread about ½ cup of hot Marinara Sauce on each disc of bread, and place 1 poached egg on each pool of Marinara Sauce. Divide the cheese evenly among the plates, and sprinkle it all over the sauce and the egg. (You should not need salt because the *pecorino* Sardo is quite salty. However, correct the dish for salt before serving it.) Serve the *pane frattau* very hot.

NOTE: In Sardegna, sometimes salted water is used in place of chicken or meat stock for dipping the bread. This could be a matter of either economy or convenience.

First Courses

First dishes are not first for nothing. These dishes are the ones that probably are the most memorable in a meal whether they are preceded by *antipasti* or not. The ones listed here reinforce what is almost a rule: that first dishes are essentially pasta dishes, at least in the South of Italy. There is something about eating a first dish that makes an important impression on the eater; not the least because surely another equally important dish will follow. A first dish is a larger portion than what may have preceded it, and is a dish that will determine your appetite for the remainder of the meal. If you eat Baked Semolina Gnocchi or Sardinian Ravioli, you may be sated and leisurely eat small amounts of following dishes. Or if you eat Fiery Macaroni, for instance, your taste buds may be so stimulated that you will eat with gusto the other offerings set before you. When Italians want to eat smaller meals, they leave out dishes, but the chances are very good that *the* dish to be eaten in such a meal is a *primo piatto*.

IN SOUTHERN ITALY MOST HANDMADE pasta is used largely for *lasagne, orecchiette, fregnacce, cannelloni*, and so forth.

With the aid of the hand-operated rolling machines, there is no reason not to have fresh pasta daily with little effort. The rolling takes care of some of the handling and kneading of the dough, and the results can be admirable. Most people make their machine-rolled pasta too moist, and it becomes very fragile with no body. Since the machine is doing the work, you might as well get a better product and save your strength for other jobs. (Let me quickly point out that if you are making ravioli, your dough should be moist and soft or it will tear when you mold the pasta around the filling. If the pasta dough is too dry it will not adhere to itself well enough to make a good closure for the filling.)

½ pound (about 2 cups) unbleached
    all-purpose flour
½ pound (about 1½ cups) fancy
    durum flour
4 large eggs, q.b.

I would not bother to attempt to make this very strong dough by hand. I would use an electric mixer or a food processor with these cautions. The dough may become stiffer and drier than with all-purpose flour alone. In this case, add some more egg a little at a time. It is very difficult to do this because egg is so stringy. Put the egg in a large spoon and let some dribble into the dough. Use a kitchen scissors to cut the string of egg. It may seem silly to do this, but when you are making small amounts of dough, it may be necessary. When you make, as I often do, 30 or 40 pounds of pasta at a time, the additional amounts are not so critical and much easier to handle. I think you will find this a good pasta dough for general use.

Pasta per
Lasagne, Fregnacce,
Cannelloni, e
Fettuccine

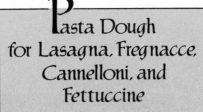

Pasta Dough for Lasagna, Fregnacce, Cannelloni, and Fettuccine

MAKES ABOUT 1½
POUNDS

FIRST COURSES
123

Pasta Dough for Ravioli (Makes about 1 pound 10 ounces)

If you are going to make ravioli, for which you need a softer dough, use the following formula:

> 1 *pound (about 4 cups) unbleached*
> *all-purpose flour*
>
> 5 *large eggs, at room temperature*

MIXING THE DOUGH IN AN ELECTRIC MIXER OR FOOD PROCESSOR

In an electric mixer: Put the flour into the bowl, attach the paddle or flat beater, and start the motor on low. Add the eggs one at a time and do not be in a hurry. Let the dough mix for about 2 or 3 minutes between each addition of egg. The resulting dough will be lumpy. This does not matter. When the flour and eggs are well incorporated, stop the motor and remove the bowl from the machine. Dump the ingredients out onto a work surface and finish kneading the dough by hand for about 2 minutes. The dough should be firm, pliable, and shiny. If it is too soft and sticky add a bit more flour and knead it well for at least 2 minutes before attempting to add any more. If, on the other hand, the dough is too stiff and not moist enough, wet your hands with some warm water and knead the dough a bit longer. There should be enough water on your hands to take care of the dryness of the dough. If not, wet your hands again and continue. Wrap the pasta dough in plastic or foil and set it aside for about ½ hour. Do not refrigerate it.

In a food processor, it will take no time at all to make the dough. You must be careful not to make it too moist, though. The mixing blade is so efficient that you could easily make a wet, soggy mess. First put the flour in the bowl, start the motor, and add 3 of the eggs. Do not put in the fourth egg until you stop the food processor and firmly pinch the grainlike mixture. It should hold together very well with no effort. If it does not, add the last egg and process for a minute more. It should just begin to ball up in the bowl. The moment it does, stop the machine and remove the dough. Knead it by hand for about 2 minutes. If the dough is too wet or too dry, refer to the directions at the end of "In an electric mixer:" Wrap the dough in plastic or foil and set it aside for about ½ hour. Do not refrigerate it.

ROLLING THE DOUGH WITH A PASTA MACHINE

The method is the same for both formulas. Cut the mass of dough into 3 parts. Cover 2 parts with plastic wrap. Put 1 part of the pasta through the widest setting of the rollers on the machine. When it comes out, fold it into thirds to make a neat shape. Close the opening of the rollers 1 notch and put the dough through again. Keep closing the rollers 1 notch and sending the dough through until you have reached the desired thickness. If the dough becomes a little sticky, sprinkle it with a bit of flour. When the pasta is rolled out as thin as you want it, lay it on a floured board to dry for 10 minutes (unless you are making ravioli). Turn it over and let it dry for a few more minutes, when it should be ready to cut, either by hand or using the cutters built into the machine. If you are making fettuccine, do not make the sheets of pasta longer than 11 inches. If you do, the fettuccine will be difficult to cook, serve, and eat.

MIXING THE DOUGH BY HAND

Heap the flour on a wooden or other work surface. Make a well in the center of it by using two fingers held together and swirling them, starting in the center of the mass, in ever widening circles. You should end up with something that looks like a moon crater.

Break the eggs into the center of the crater. Get all of the egg white out of the shells by scraping them clean with your fingers. If you use cold eggs, much of the white will stick to the sides of the eggs, and you will lose yield. (If your eggs are cold and you are in a hurry, simply place them in a bowl of very hot tap water for about 5 minutes, dry them, and proceed with the recipe.)

Scramble the eggs with a fork, and using a circular motion, pull in some of the flour from the inner wall of the crater, being careful not to break the wall while the eggs are very liquid, or they will run out. As soon as the egg begins to form a soft dough, start using your fingers to pull in more of the flour. Incorporate all the flour into the eggs, and knead the resulting dough vigorously for about 6 to 8 minutes, or until the dough is firm, pliable, and shiny. If it is too soft and sticky, add a bit more flour, and knead it well for at least 2 minutes before adding any more. If, on the other hand, the dough is too stiff and not moist enough, wet your hands with some warm water, and knead the dough a bit longer. There should be enough water on your hands to take care of the dryness of the dough. If not, wet your hands again, and knead again. Wrap the pasta dough in plastic or foil, and set it aside for about 30 minutes. Do not refrigerate it. (You can make the dough, up to this point, several hours before rolling it. You could even make it the day before you use it, but I do not see the value of doing so.)

ROLLING THE DOUGH BY HAND

Use the dough made with only all-purpose flour when rolling it out by hand. You will need a *matterello*, or rolling pin. They can be bought at most well-stocked gourmet cooking stores or at an Italian hardware store. (See Kitchen Equipment, page 36).

Dust the work surface with some flour. Flatten the ball of dough so that it looks like a giant lozenge by pushing down with your palms, or hit the dough with the rolling pin. Put the rolling pin in the center of the lozenge, and start to roll the dough away from you. Continue doing that while rotating the dough by quarters or thirds to maintain a circular shape. Do not be compulsive. If the shape looks a little like the state of Texas, it may take some remedying, but otherwise the dough should resemble a circle.

Keep in mind that you do not want to compress the dough, you want to stretch it. Continue to roll the dough until it is as thin as you can make it without tearing it. It should be less than 1/16 inch thick.

When you have reached this stage, the fun part begins—stretching the dough. It is much more difficult to explain than to do. You must have good coordination, so if you can rub your belly and pat your head at the same time, you should have no trouble. Don't take more than 10 minutes to roll the dough, for it will dry out, lose its pliability, and be impossible to thin.

Be sure that the pasta is lightly but completely floured. Place the *matterello* at the top of the circle of dough, pull up the top edge of the dough around the *matterello*, and roll up about 1/4 of the dough sheet. You should be rolling the *matterello* toward you. Put both your hands on top of the dough in the center of the *matterello*, and very quickly slide your hands across the dough, firmly pressing and thinning the dough. Your fingers should be straight out. Both hands should be just touching when you begin, then they should separate and slide firmly toward the opposite ends of the *matterello*. Do this several times, using quite a bit of strength. Roll another 1/4 of the dough on top of the amount you have already rolled, and repeat the same steps. Stop, unfurl the dough, and turn it completely around, so that the bottom is now the top. Repeat steps 1 and 2. Continue to do the entire operation no less than 3 or 4 times. The pasta should be perfect.

If you are going to make ravioli with a *raviolatrice*, stop at this point and immediately proceed with the ravioli recipe.

Place the completed circle of pasta onto a lightly floured cloth. I find an old bedsheet saved just for this purpose works perfectly. If you have limited space, you could lay the bedsheet on your bed, flour the sheet lightly, and lay the circle of dough on it. Let the dough air-dry for about 10 minutes. Turn it over. Using the *matterello*, carefully roll the dough and then be sure that the side that was down is up. Lay the dough back on the bedsheet and let it air-dry for another 10 minutes. The dough should feel like a piece of beautiful chamois cloth, soft and supple, yet strong and not sticky. If the day is particularly humid, you may have to allow more drying time. Without this drying time the pasta will stick together hopelessly.

If you want to cut the pasta by hand, you can do so after the dough has dried. You could use the cutters on a pasta machine as well.

You can successfully store freshly made pasta by putting it into a low, flat dish, in a very thin layer, and covering it with plastic wrap. It will keep in the refrigerator for about 2 days maximum. I do not recommend doing this, but if it is necessary, you can get away with it. I would rather store the dough in a ball, let it come to room temperature, and then complete the recipe.

COMMERCIAL PASTA IS PROBABLY THE most natural and the most healthful processed food you can eat. It is, simply, the best semolina (hard winter wheat, called durum) and water; nothing else is needed or wanted in this product. Pasta has a long shelf life without the aid of preservatives. The only reason for the package is to identify the manufacturer and to keep the dust off of the pasta.

When you think of Southern Italian pasta dishes, you should immediately picture dry pasta in exotic shapes that have been bought either in packages or by weight in bulk. Pasta in this form has been used for a very long time. It certainly is not a "trend," as the taste for this product is firmly entrenched in the psyche of Southern Italians. While pasta is still made by hand, that product is less used than commercially manufactured pasta. Such things as *strascinati* ("dragged"), pasta sometimes called *orecchie* ("ears") made from semolina or fancy durum flour and hot water and then stretched and cajoled into shape by a peculiar little tool known as a *rasaul*, are still made in the home by women who will not give up their traditions for any price. Their families help out in this regard in that they won't eat any other form of this pasta. Of course, cannelloni and ravioli are still made by hand.

Too much emphasis has been put on homemade pastas, such as fettuccine, which certainly deserve the credit they get. It is unfortunate, though, that the commercial pastas have had to take a backseat to the pastas variously described as "feather soft," "tender," and "light." After almost 50 years of living on pasta, I have never eaten any that fits those descriptions, if it was made and cooked properly. The term *al dente* has become part of the American language. It means "to the teeth," meaning chewy and chewable.

I believe commercial pasta became a part of the everyday life of Southern Italians because of its low cost and it was easier to buy, store, and have available at a moment's notice. For them pasta was the very stuff of life. It still is, but more from choice than by rigid economic constraints. Southerners eat their pasta more *al dente* than their northern neighbors.

The riot of pasta shapes is available only by the extruded method of making pasta, that is, the dough is pushed, under enormous pressure, through a brass plate with openings in it. The openings determine the size and shape of the pasta.

Southern Italians love short, stubby pastas with openings in them, such as *rigatoni* and *penne* and *bucatini*. Spaghetti probably heads the list of all-time favorites, though, and it is used with almost any sauce you can name. There are literally hundreds of shapes available. Trying to track them down and describe them is probably a lifelong exercise. Just when you think you have seen them all, one more shape shows up.

Cooking pasta is quite easy, after you have cooked enough of it to forget the clock. Throw it away. You have no need for it. After a few hundred cookings of pasta, you will "know" when it is done. Generally, when you think it needs just a bit more cooking, it is actually perfect. Give in and drain it and eat it. If you find that it was not just right, adjust the timing next time you cook it; not by the clock but by your intuition.

Here are a few rules about cooking that you should never forget. Following them will take the mystery out of cooking pasta and give you results that will make you an expert in the art of cooking pasta.

Always allow at least 4 or 5 quarts of water per pound of pasta. More water never hurts. Salt it to the ratio of about 1 teaspoon per quart of water. A little more will not hurt, but be aware that if you use a salty sauce, you could end up with a bit too much of a salty flavor. Even if you are going to rinse the pasta (a rare occurrence, which will be discussed further), add salt to the water, as it does affect the flavor.

The pasta cooking water must be at a rolling boil. Add the pasta a little at a time to keep the boil. Do not worry that the pasta does not all go in at the same time. Nature has a way of taking care that it will all be just fine when it finishes cooking. If you simply dump all the pasta in at once, you cool the water sufficiently that it could take as much as 2 minutes for the water to return to the boil. This can adversely affect the final texture of the pasta.

Never, never rinse pasta that is to be eaten hot. The best method for cooking pasta is to use that ingenious pot that comes with a large, deep colander, almost the same size of the pot itself. When the pasta is done, carefully and slowly lift the colander part straight up, and the water drains back into the pot. When you use this method, some of the cooking water remains with the pasta, which is desirable. If you drain every drop out of the pasta, it can become sticky easily, and the pasta, which will continue to absorb liquid, will soak up the sauce and cause dryness in the dish. Some like to pour the cooked pasta and the water into a colander in the sink. This method is fine, if you like it. Others fish around in the water with a skimmer and keep dredging up pieces of pasta. This method, too, is all right, but be aware that it could take minutes to find all the pasta before you can pull it out, and thereby overcook it.

If you must rinse pasta in preparation for a salad or for making *lasagne* (page 204), it is all right to do so. This is the only time when you may rinse pasta. This is done to either wash any excess starch off the surface of it, thereby helping prevent its sticking to itself, or to cool the pasta to prevent further cooking. Always salt the water when cooking pasta for such preparations. Even though the rinsing washes most of the salt out, there will be enough that has penetrated the pasta itself to make a taste difference.

I always use salt unless there is a medical reason not to. In such a case there are lots of recipes that are delicious and safe for the diet. I prefer specific dishes that are meant to be made without salt rather than adjusting dishes that have traditionally had salt. The elimination of salt so alters these dishes as to render them impotent and, therefore, of little satisfaction to anyone.

Cooking times for pasta are simply not worth mentioning. So many conditions come into play when you discuss timing that it is futile to make any rules. Suffice it to say that the larger, stubby pastas that are quite dense will need more cooking time than do ones that are smaller and thinner. Only trial and error will enable you to learn to cook pasta.

Everything must bow to pasta cooking: the sauce, the table setting, the guests, the service. Everything. When the pasta hits the water, there must be peace, tranquillity, patience, and the anticipation of enjoyment. This rule cannot and must not be broken or even bent. Pasta waits for no one under any circumstances. When a concert or a ballet or even a movie starts, you are there, or else.

The plates must be heated so that the pasta reaches the eaters in good condition. Do not stand on ceremony. When the pasta arrives at your place, eat it. I dislike serving pasta in large bowls unless it is baked or is a short, stubby pasta like *penne*. Spaghetti in a large bowl to be served at the table is a mess and it is very awkward, indeed, to do a good job. You end up splattering everyone near you as well. It is better to plate individual dishes in the kitchen and send them out immediately.

Saucing pasta is a sore spot with me. In America you get too much sauce. One reason I am sore is that I feel forced (an unusual situation for me as far as cooking goes) to give more sauce than I myself eat. I have a morbid fear that my family and guests will not get enough to eat. I also know that if a sauce is good, people will work diligently to get every last drop. There should be enough sauce on the pasta so that none is left by the time you have finished the pasta itself. Putting on the right amount of sauce, like timing the pasta cooking, takes experience and wisdom, but remember you are serving pasta with sauce on it, and not serving sauce with pasta as the excuse for eating it.

Culingiones

Sardinian Ravioli

MAKES ABOUT 100
RAVIOLI MADE WITH
A RAVIOLATRICE

In Oliena these ravioli are called *angiul-lotus*; in Nuoro, just a stone's throw away, they are referred to as *culurjones*; in most other parts of Sardegna the ravioli are known as *culingiones*. What distinguishes Sardinian ravioli is that fancy durum flour, oil, water, and salt are used to make the dough. This makes them very chewy indeed. Most recipes I have seen tell you to use plain flour and eggs. The secret to making *culingiones* really good and a bit more tender to the bite is to roll the dough out very thin and to be fanatic about not letting it dry out in the least while you make them. Another thing is that Swiss chard instead of spinach is mostly used in Sardegna. If you do not have Swiss chard handy, by all means use spinach, but the taste will be considerably different. Swiss chard is sweeter and smoother and is a better counterbalance to the *pecorino*, which is critical to *culingiones*.

The sauces are optional. You can use a plain tomato sauce or one with meat in it. I think plain tomato sauce would be the most authentic.

FOR THE DOUGH (SEE PAGE 124)

1 *pound (about 3½ cups) fancy durum flour*

5 *large eggs*

2 *tablespoons virgin olive oil*
   Pinch of salt

FOR THE FILLING

1 *pound soft, fresh* pecorino *cheese*

1 *pound Swiss chard, washed and cut into 2-inch pieces*

3 *large eggs*
   Pinch of saffron, in powder or pulverize the threads

8 *big scrapings fresh nutmeg*
   Salt to taste
   Freshly ground black pepper to taste

FOR THE SAUCE

MAKES ABOUT
1½ QUARTS

1 *large yellow onion, finely chopped*

½ *cup virgin olive oil*

3½ *pounds fresh tomatoes, cored, peeled, and well crushed, or use same amount canned*

8 *leaves basil, finely chopped*
   Salt to taste
   Freshly ground black pepper to taste

TO FINISH

1¼ *cups grated* pecorino Sardo

PREPARE THE SAUCE

Make the sauce up to 3 days ahead, in which case store it in the refrigerator in a glass jar. Put the chopped onion in a wide, heavy pan, add the olive oil, fry it over medium heat until it is transparent, and then cook it for 3 minutes more. Add all the other ingredients, and cook the sauce over high heat for about 15 minutes, stirring occasionally. The fast cooking will help to reduce the sauce and make it thick, but be careful that it does not burn on the bottom.

After you have made the pasta dough and it is resting, make the filling, and put it aside for later use.

PREPARE THE FILLING

If you cannot find fresh *pecorino* Sardo, use Cacio Bianco, a fresh Sardinian sheep's cheese. Or use a combination of ⅔ Caciocavallo cheese and ⅓ grated *pecorino* Sardo, which will also be used later to dust onto the finished dish. Shred the fresh *pecorino* cheese. Put all the filling ingredients into a large bowl, and mix them very well.

PREPARE THE RAVIOLI

Roll out the pasta dough into 2 very thin long sheets, about $\frac{1}{32}$ inch thick. (You could make 4 shorter sheets if space is a problem or you are having a problem handling the length of dough.) Put tablespoon-sized dollops or so of the filling onto the bottom sheet, spacing them about 2 inches apart. Continue until you have filled the bottom sheet. (You may have filling left over. It is very hard to judge just how to make everything come out even.) Brush the spaces between the mounds of filling with some beaten egg. Carefully lay the other sheet of pasta down on top of the filling. Push the top dough down all around into the spaces between the mounds. Cut the ravioli with a crimp cutter, which will not only separate them, but also seal them. Lay them on a floured kitchen towel or cookie sheet in one layer only. If you are not going to cook them immediately, cover them with plastic wrap and put them in the refrigerator. Be sure that they do not overlap each other or they will stick badly. You probably will not get as many ravioli with this method as you would if you use the *raviolatrice* (see Kitchen Equipment, page 38), which I prefer.

Heat the sauce in a medium-sized saucepan over low heat to a simmer, stirring occasionally.

Boil a large amount of salted water in a big pan. Put the *culingiones* into the water, a few at a time, and boil them for 4 minutes, stirring them often. Try one to test the doneness. I prefer them *al dente* but you may want to cook them longer. When the *culingiones* are done, scoop them out of the water with a slotted spoon or drain them through a colander, leaving just a touch of water with them. Put them onto heated plates, and spoon on some of the hot tomato sauce. Sprinkle lots of grated *pecorino* cheese on the *culingiones*. Serve them as hot as possible.

MENU SUGGESTIONS: A hot antipasto of Mushrooms in Parchment (page 240) would be a good starter, or a *minestra* of Miniature Meatball Soup (page 110). Following the *culingiones* a nice mild dish such as Chicken Infused with Bay Leaves (page 161) would be unusual and quite delicate, especially for a late-night meal or an early Sunday supper. A plate of Saint Agatha's Nipples (page 273) would be a delicious ending to this meal.

WINE: Corvo Bianco (page 308) or Colli Albani (page 304)

Fettuccine alla Romana

Fettuccine Roman Style

FOR 6 VERY LARGE
PORTIONS

You probably know this dish as *Fettuccine all'Alfredo*. So far I have never found a person who has not eaten every last length of noodle and spooned up every last drop of sauce in this dish. Of course, the quality of the ingredients takes this dish from the range of delicious to epicurean. Fresh sweet butter, dairy cream that has not been over-errefined, and the real McCoy, *Parmigiano-Reggiano*, would put this dish into the latter category. The ultimate would be to have a large bottle of Roman water sent over so that you could cook the fettuccine in it.

The amounts listed below are only a guide as to quantity. I never measure when making this dish and would find it offensive to have to. This is a matter of instinctive cooking, and if you cook this dish a few times, you will see how well your instincts have developed.

MENU SUGGESTIONS: You could follow with Chicken Roasted with Rosemary (page 178) or Pomegranate Quail as *secondi* (page 181). A few Bitter Almond Cookies (page 278) and coffee would be a light finish to this meal.

WINE: Taurasi (page 304) or Torre Ercolana (page 306)

Salt to taste

6 to 8 ounces sweet butter, at room temperature

1¾ cups heavy cream, at room temperature

2 cups grated Parmesan cheese

1½ pounds fresh or commercial fettuccine (pages 123, 127)

4 to 5 scrapings nutmeg

Freshly ground pepper to taste

Boil a large amount of water in a big pan and add some salt. While the water is violently boiling, place the butter in a large, heavy frying pan or similar vessel, and put it near the boiling water or in a *very warm* place or even over very low heat to melt but not to cook. Heat your serving dishes, and keep the cream and cheese handy.

Gently place medium amounts of the pasta into the water, and stir frequently. Cook the pasta until it is *al dente*, tender but chewy (and not soft and mushy!). Drain the pasta but don't shake all of the water out, just most of it. Immediately put the drained pasta into the frying pan with the butter, and toss it all around to coat it. Add the heavy cream, then the grated cheese, and gently toss it all around. Every strand of fettuccine should be glossy and coated with the sauce. Add 4 or 5 vigorous scrapings of fresh nutmeg and plenty of ground pepper, and toss the pasta once again. Serve the pasta on the heated plates, and rush it to the table. Do not let anything detain you. Pass more cheese at the table.

NOTE: If the pasta looks a little too wet, don't worry unless it is excessive. The pasta, as it sits in the dish, will take up quite a bit of the liquid. If the pasta looks perfectly creamy when you first serve it, it may become dry on the plate. If the pasta still looks too wet, the only remedy is to put more grated Parmesan on it.

1 quart milk
1 teaspoon salt
1½ cups semolina
2 large egg yolks

6 ounces (10 tablespoons) sweet butter, very soft
2 cups grated Parmesan cheese, plus more for passing at the table

Heat the milk and salt in a heavy saucepan, preferably nonaluminum, over medium heat until it begins to simmer. Lower the heat, and drizzle in the semolina while you vigorously stir the milk, in one direction only, with a whisk. The semolina will begin to thicken almost immediately. Watch that the bottom does not burn. Adjust the heat so that the mixture maintains a simmer, and stir constantly for 5 minutes. Stir occasionally for another 5 minutes, or until the mass is very thick and it is smooth and glossy. Remove the mixture from the heat and let it "cook" for about 10 minutes. Add the egg yolks, 1 ounce (2 tablespoons) of the soft butter, and 1 cup of cheese, stirring the whole time.

Rinse with cold water a baking sheet with sides, 10 × 15 inches (approximately), such as a jelly-roll pan. Do not dry it. Tap it on its side once to remove any droplets of water. Pour the cheese and semolina mixture onto the baking sheet, scraping it all out of the saucepan with a rubber spatula. Using a flexible metal spatula or palette knife, spread the mixture all around to about ½-inch thickness. Wet the spatula with water frequently to facilitate this part of the job. Let the mixture firm up in the jelly-roll pan for 1 hour or more. If you do not plan to use it immediately, refrigerate it, covered with plastic wrap. Meanwhile, using 2 ounces (about 4 tablespoons) of the butter, grease a low-sided, ovenproof baking dish that can double as a serving dish.

When the *gnocchi* mixture is firm, using a biscuit cutter or a glass with a 2½-inch diameter, cut out rounds, and lay them down on the buttered surface *a cavallo*. In other words, lay one row down, then slightly overlap the next row on top of that. Continue until you have used up all of the rounds. Preheat the oven to 400° F. (You can make the *gnocchi* up to this point a day in advance. Cover them with plastic wrap, and store in the refrigerator. Proceed with the recipe when you are ready.)

The little odd shapes that result from cutting rounds can be put into soup at the last minute, or simply thrown into another small baking pan to make additional *gnocchi* pieces.

Spread the *gnocchi* with the remaining 3 ounces (6 tablespoons) of butter, grind on plenty of black pepper, and sprinkle on ⅔ cup of the grated cheese evenly.

Put the *gnocchi* on the rack in the upper third of the oven. Bake for about 20 minutes, or until they are hot and sizzling, and the cheese is a golden hue all over. You could use a broiler to get a good, deep color, but the heat should be moderate because the *gnocchi* must be very hot all the way through. Sprinkle on the remaining ⅓ cup of grated cheese. Serve the *gnocchi caldissimo!* (Hot!) Pass more grated Parmesan cheese at the table.

NOTE: You can make nontraditional, "no waste" *gnocchi* by simply cutting them into diamonds or squares.

Gnocchi
di Semolella

Baked Semolina Gnocchi

MAKES ENOUGH FOR
4 TO 6 SERVINGS

These morsels are so good that your family and guests will want to eat 3 helpings and forget the rest of the dinner. The dialect word for semolina is *semolella*. It is the same product from which the best commercial pasta is made.

The cooking procedure here is the same as cooking polenta (see Polenta, page 30) except it takes less time. If you have leftover polenta, you can use it in this recipe but be sure to call the dish *gnocchi di polenta all 'uso Romano*. Authentic *gnocchi di semolella* are made only with semolina.

MENU SUGGESTIONS: These make a wonderful midnight supper. They are also very good followed by Trout Vernaccia (page 177). Walnut Cake #1 (page 276) or Pears in Chocolate (page 285) would be a good ending.

WINE: Aglianico del Vulture (page 301)

36 *Littleneck or Cherrystone clams, or 48 Manila clams, or use 2 3½-ounce cans chopped clams in their own juice*

½ *cup virgin olive oil*

2 *or 3 very large garlic cloves, finely chopped*

4 *tablespoons chopped parsley (Italian preferred), or to taste*

Salt to taste

Plenty of freshly ground black pepper

1 *pound linguine*

Big pinch crushed red pepper flakes

Linguine alla Vongole

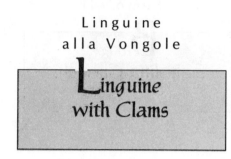

Linguine with Clams

SERVES 4

There are two versions of this dish, *bianco* (white), and *rosso* (red) or *al pomodoro*, with tomato. Both recipes are fabulous and featured here. The versions below are the kind made in home kitchens. Wine would be considered essential if they were made in a restaurant.

MENU SUGGESTIONS: Marinated Zucchini (page 100) and some Chick-peas in Olive Oil (page 95) would be good *antipasti*. After the *linguine alla vongole*, a dish of Chicken, Potenza Style (page 179), would be very good, accompanied by some String Bean Bundles (page 235). Saint Joseph's Day Fritters (page 289) would be a very tasty end to this meal. Provolone and bread could replace the sweet dessert.

WINE: Rapitalà (page 308)

NOTE: If you want to make this dish *rosso* ("with tomatoes"), you will need 2 large, ripe tomatoes, peeled, cored, and chopped into small pieces, or the same amount canned, without the juice.

Wash the clams well by scrubbing them with a brush under cold running water but do not let them stand in the cold water for even a short period of time as they might open. (If they do, they might well disgorge themselves of any sand, but they will also surely eject their natural water and lose some flavor.) Place the washed clams in a frying pan that is large enough to hold them all comfortably and can also hold the cooked pasta. Pour on half of the olive oil, cover the pan, and cook the clams over high heat for 6 minutes or until they open, shaking the pan occasionally. Remove the pan from the heat, and set it aside, uncovered.

When the clams are cool enough to handle, remove them from their shells (if they are the tiny Manila clams, leave them as they are) over a bowl so that any disgorged liquid is caught there. If the clams are very large, chop them in pieces, otherwise halving them is good enough. Strain the liquid through a sieve or cheesecloth to remove any sand. Reserve the clams and the strained liquid in a small bowl. Save the shells for decorating the serving plate, if you like, or discard them.

If you are using canned clams, simply open them, and then add them, with their juices, to the dish as is described below.

Put the remaining olive oil into the empty frying pan, and heat it to just under the smoking point. Add the chopped garlic, and quickly stir it around, until it is golden brown and very aromatic. Remove pan from the heat, and add the clams, the reserved juices, the parsley, and salt and pepper to taste. Be careful of steam when you add the liquid, and of hot oil splashing out of the pan. The residual heat from the hot oil and pan will be sufficient to do any cooking necessary. Set the sauce aside until the pasta is done.

(This part of the dish can be done up to a day ahead of time. Store the sauce in a glass jar, well covered, in the refrigerator. Gently reheat it when it is time to use it. Making this sauce ahead should be done only if there is no other alternative to making it just before using it.)

Boil the pasta in plenty of salted water until it is very *al dente*. Meanwhile, gently reheat the sauce over low heat in the frying pan. When the pasta is done, drain it, but leave in a few spoonsful of the cooking water, perhaps a scant half cup. This helps the flavor and makes the sauce easier to mix into the pasta. If you are unable to judge the amount of water to remain in the cooked pasta, scoop some of it out with a heatproof measuring cup before straining the pasta. When the pasta is well drained, add the reserved hot pasta water.

Put the pasta into the frying pan with the clam sauce, and mix it well for at least one minute and maybe a moment or so longer. This helps develop the flavor more and keeps everything hot. Serve immediately on hot plates, and sprinkle on a good pinch of crushed red pepper flakes. If you are going to garnish the dish with the discarded shells, do so now. If you are using the Manila clams, they will remain with their shells on, as they are so small and very pretty. No cheese on this dish—please!

To make this dish *rosso*, with tomatoes, add them to the frying pan after you have browned the garlic as described above. Cook the tomatoes for about five minutes over medium heat, and then proceed with the recipe as described. And no cheese on this version either!

Maccheroni alla Maniera di Andria

Macaroni with Arugula and Fresh Tomatoes, Andrian Style

SERVES 6

¼ cup virgin olive oil

1 small yellow onion, peeled and very finely chopped

2 garlic cloves, peeled and well crushed

2 pounds fresh tomatoes, cored, peeled, and well crushed

1 bunch (approximately 2 cups) arugula, washed and cut into 4-inch pieces

1 pound short pasta such as penne, small rigatoni, fusilli, etc.

1⅓ cups grated pecorino cheese

Heat the olive oil in a large frying pan until it is quite hot, add the onion, and cook it until it is just transparent. Add the garlic, and fry it until it is golden and fragrant. Add the tomatoes, and stir the mixture well. Cook the tomato sauce for about 30 minutes or so.

Boil about 6 quarts of salted water in a large pot. Add the pasta, and after about 2 minutes, add the arugula. When the pasta is *al dente*, pour it through a colander. Put the pasta and arugula mixture on hot plates, and ladle on some tomato sauce. Sprinkle plenty of the grated *pecorino* cheese on the pasta, and serve it immediately, very hot.

Of all the unusual but tasty pasta dishes I encountered in Puglia, this one with arugula seemed to be the least eaten, even though many people knew it.

MENU SUGGESTIONS: There is no need for antipasto if you have, as your *secondo piatto*, some Homemade Sicilian Sausage (page 188) or some Chicken Roasted with Rosemary (page 178). Chocolate Bread (page 284) would make a nice dessert for such a meal.

WINE: Torre Quarto Rosso (page 301)

Maccheroni alla Chitarra

Strummed Macaroni

SERVES 6

1 pound (about 3½ cups) fancy durum flour (not semolina)

1 tablespoon virgin olive oil

Big pinch of salt

4 large eggs

All-purpose flour for dusting

Of all the Abruzzese dishes, this one surely is the most renowned. Although it is hand-made, it calls for *farina di grano duro*, or hardwheat flour, a flour that, if ground coarser, would be semolina.

Northern handmade pastas are made with softer flour. The Abruzzese add eggs and salt and produce a very yellow, beautiful pasta that is quite firm and, for most Americans, a hard-to-manage dough, if it is made totally by hand. With a hand-cranked pasta machine the rolling out of the pasta becomes easy and enjoyable.

The trick to cutting this *maccheroni* is the *chitarra*. It is an oblong, wooden frame made of birch, about 12 × 16 inches or so. On each end is a series of tiny iron or brass nails perfectly spaced. In and around each of these nails is strung a very long, thin wire, much like piano wire, which is stretched taut. There is a space about 1 inch high underneath the wires where the pasta falls after it is cut.

The idea is to place the rolled sheet of pasta on top of the wires and then, with a rolling pin, roll back and forth length-wise on top of the wires. The wires cut the pasta into thin strips and they begin to drop below the wires, but not completely. Then comes the part that probably named this dish. You strum the strings with your thumb, just like you would do if you were playing a guitar. This sends the little strips of pasta

If you are using a food processor, put in the flour, olive oil, and salt, and pulse on and off several times. Add 1 egg at a time, pulsing on and off several times, until the last one. Judge whether the dough is too dry or too wet, and put in the fourth egg, or a part of it, or not at all.

If you are mixing the dough by hand, you will find that it is more difficult to work than most doughs, but just stay with it. If you find that after using all the ingredients it is still too stiff or too hard to handle, you can sprinkle on a *few drops of water* and continue to knead.

After the dough is kneaded, wrap it in plastic and let it rest for about a half hour. Roll it out to the desired thickness, and cut it on the *chitarra*, or by hand. Scatter the pasta on a lightly floured board or kitchen towel, and let it dry for a few minutes. When you are ready to cook it, bring a large pot of water to the boil and add salt. Cook the pasta really *al dente*. If it was made correctly, it should cook only 2 minutes in the water. Sauce it as you like, but one of the favorite ways is to use Abruzzese Lamb Sauce (page 74).

flying under the wires, ready for you to scoop up and get ready for boiling.

If you have a *chitarra* with wider spacing, you will want to use a sheet of pasta that is the same thickness as fettuccine (see the recipe for Pasta, page 123). Proceed exactly as described above.

MENU SUGGESTIONS: For an antipasto, Marinated Zucchini (page 100) would be good. A good second dish would be Pomegranate Quail (page 181) followed by some Mushrooms Roasted with Pine Nuts (page 239). Chocolate Bread (page 284) would be a good finish to this meal.

WINE: Rosso del Salento (page 301)

CALABRIA

Maccheroni alla Pastora

SERVES 6

8 *ounces fresh pork sausage, pan fried and cut into small pieces*

1 *pound* penne, rigatoni, ziti, *or* bucatini, *broken up*

1 *pound best-quality Ricotta*

Plenty of freshly ground black pepper

2 *teaspoons red pepper flakes, or q.b.*

1 *cup grated* pecorino *cheese*

Put the sausage into a frying pan with a few spoons of water, cover the pan with a lid, and cook the sausage over medium heat for about 6 minutes. Remove the lid, and continue to cook until the water evaporates and the sausage is quite brown. Remove it from the pan to paper towels to absorb any excess fat. When the sausage is cool, rough chop it into small pieces. Set aside.

Boil plenty of well-salted water, and put the *maccheroni* in to cook until they are *al dente*. Meantime, heat a casserole dish large enough to hold all the pasta later. When the pasta is almost done, put the Ricotta in the casserole, add about ½ cup of the pasta water, and gently stir. This will loosen the Ricotta and make it blend and mix better. Add the sausage and mix again. Add freshly ground black pepper and the red pepper flakes, and stir again. The mixture should be quite loose and easily spreadable.

When the *maccheroni* is done, drain it, and reserve some of the cooking water. Add the *maccheroni* to the casserole, and toss it well with the other ingredients. If the mixture seems too thick, add some of the reserved pasta water, up to half a cup or even more. The dish should look glossy and appetizing. If it is too dry, it will not be good to eat. Serve the *maccheroni* on heated plates, and put plenty of grated *pecorino* on top. If you have more *pecorino*, pass it at the table.

Break the budget if necessary to buy the best-quality Ricotta and enjoy this rustic and satisfying dish. If I have a choice Ricotta, I leave the sausage for another time.

MENU SUGGESTIONS: You could start the meal with the *maccheroni alla pastora*. Trout Vernaccia (page 177) would be a good *secondo* with *contorni* on the side of String Bean Bundles (page 235) and some Mushrooms Roasted with Pine Nuts (page 239).

WINE: Brindisi Rosato (page 298) or Fiano di Avellino (page 302)

Maccheroni di Fuoco

Fiery Macaroni

SERVES 6

½ cup extra virgin olive oil, or q.b.

5 garlic cloves, peeled

6 dried whole red peppers, about 1½ inches long

1 teaspoon salt, and to taste

14 ounces perciatelli, bucatini, or spaghetti

Your entire body will react when you eat this dish of *maccheroni* and crushed red peppers. It makes the American South and Southwest hot dishes mere embers compared to roaring flames.

I would suggest a large bottle of rough red wine and a large bottle of mineral water be at the ready when you serve or eat this dish. Some soothing vegetables should also be kept on hand, such as tepid boiled artichokes and some fried cauliflower and perhaps a dish of Spinach, Roman Style (page 245). Bites of these *contorni* interspersed with bites of *maccheroni di fuoco* should enable you to get through the meal in relatively good shape. This is not the way a Southern Italian from Basilicata would do it, but then they are used to inner warmth.

MENU SUGGESTIONS: An antipasto of Roasted Peppers with Italian-Style Tuna and Clams (page 104) and Mint Omelette (page 83) would be good starters followed by this dish. Codfish Salad (page 102) would be a good *intermèzzo* followed by Chicken Roasted with Rosemary (page 178). Sicilian Cannoli (page 261) would be a nice finish to an earthy meal.

WINE: Primitivo di Manduria (page 300) or Faro Rosso (page 309)

Heat about 2 ounces of olive oil (about 4 tablespoons) in a frying pan over medium heat, and add 3 cloves of garlic. Move the garlic around to be sure you do not burn it. Do not let the oil get too hot. Add the whole red peppers, and stir them around. When the garlic is a deep golden color, put it, the red peppers, and the oil into a mortar and mash them all together with the pestle with about one teaspoon of salt to get a paste. Set it aside.

Bring plenty of salted water to a boil, and add the pasta. When the pasta is half cooked, put about 2 more ounces of olive oil into the frying pan, and get it hot. Add the remaining 2 cloves of garlic, and fry them until they are golden. The moment that happens, remove the pan from the heat, and add the paste from the mortar, stirring everything well. If the mixture seems too thick and dry, add more of the olive oil. (Perhaps you will not use all of the oil.)

When the pasta is done, drain it, leaving some of the water in it. Put the pasta into a warm bowl or back into the cooking pot, and add a tablespoon or so of olive oil to it. Toss it well.

Dish up the pasta on hot plates, and put some of the red pepper "sauce" on top. Rush it to the table, and let everyone mix the pasta and "sauce" on their plate and commence to eat immediately. *Maccheroni di fuoco* neither needs nor gets cheese on it.

FOR THE FILLING

- 4 *ounces sweet butter, at room temperature*
- 4 *ounces fresh small peas, shelled, or use frozen tiny peas*

  Salt to taste
- 5 *or 6 grindings fresh black pepper*
- 4 *ounces* prosciutto, *thinly sliced and coarsely chopped*
- 1⅔ *cups Mozzarella, shredded*

FOR THE REST OF THE RECIPE

- 20 *ounces fresh or commercial* tagliolini *(page 127)*
- 1 *recipe* Béchamel *Sauce, cooled (page 73)*
- 1⅔ *cups grated Parmesan*
- ⅓ *cup finely chopped parsley*
- 3 *large eggs*

  Olive oil or peanut oil for frying, q.b.

  Plenty of bread crumbs, fresh or dry

TO PREPARE THE FILLING

Put the ingredients for the filling into a bowl, and mix them all together well. Add ½ cup of *béchamel*, and mix thoroughly once again. Set aside.

TO PREPARE THE DUMPLINGS

Cook the *tagliolini* in plenty of salted water for about 1 minute, drain them well, and put into a large bowl or back into the cooking pot. While they are still warm, add 1½ cups of the *béchamel*, the grated Parmesan cheese, and the parsley, and mix it together very well. Let the mixture cool for a few minutes, carefully stirring it 2 or 3 times to keep it from sticking. In a separate bowl slightly beat the eggs with a fork, and pour them, about ⅓ at a time, in with the pasta, stirring and mixing well the whole time.

Take a handful of the pasta mixture, and mold it into a pancake shape in the palm of your hand. Put a big spoonful of the filling into the center of the pasta, and form the pasta into a ball around the filling. You will not be able to roll it around. Cup both hands, and press very hard to make the shape. Lay the balls as they are finished on a piece of wax paper. Continue until you finish all the dumplings.

When you have finished, put enough oil into a wide, low frying pan to come up 1½ inches on the sides. Let the oil get hot but not smoking; 350° F would be ideal. Spread the bread crumbs in a low-sided dish, and gently roll the finished *palle* in them. (You do not need flour or eggs, just bread crumbs; enough of them will stick to make a covering.) Fry the breaded *palle*, turning them in the hot oil until they are deep golden. Remove them with a slotted spoon, and place on a kitchen towel to drain for 1 to 2 minutes. If you are making a lot of *palle*, put them into a roasting pan lined with kitchen towels, and keep them in a hot oven, with the door open, until you finish. Serve the *palle* piping hot on heated plates.

NOTE: You could make the *palle* a day ahead, to the point of rolling them in bread crumbs. If you have refrigerated the *palle*, you must let them come up to room temperature for at least 2 hours before breading and frying them. The dumplings are very tasty at room temperature.

Palle di Tagliolini

Stuffed Pasta Dumplings

MAKES ABOUT 16 DUMPLINGS

These balls of fresh pasta envelop a mixture of butter, peas, *prosciutto*, and Mozzarella, with *salsa Besciamella* binding it all. Fried and eaten hot, they are so good that they could constitute a meal in themselves.

This recipe shows the sophisticated cooking of Campagnia, the home of lasagna and cannelloni and pastries and desserts. Every time I go there, I become more convinced that the cooks Catherine de' Medici took to France were Neapolitan.

The pasta here should be fresh, and cut like a very skinny fettuccine; actually *tagliolini* are about ¹⁄₁₆ inch wide. If you buy commercial pasta, you might not find *tagliolini*, in which case get *fedelini*, which are the same; sometimes *tagliolini* are sold by the name of *tagliarini*.

MENU SUGGESTIONS: *Palle di tagliolini* would be excellent to have in a *fritto misto*, a mixed fry. You could add Fried Codfish, Roman Style (page 190), Spinach and Cheese Croquettes (page 154), and some Fried Calzone (page 62). A *contorno* of Almond Peppers (page 249) or Orange and Lemon Salad (page 242) or Cousin Mary's Eggplant (page 241) would be good as well.

WINE: Montepulciano d'Abruzzo (page 298)

Orecchiette con Braccioletti

Pasta Cushions with Meat Rolls

SERVES 6

In Andria and Bari, and other places as well, *orecchiette* are also known as *strascinati*, the Italian for "dragged." This is because you drag them on the work surface with the *rasaul*, the tool used to make the pasta (it resembles a very strong putty knife). These little *paste* are also known as *chiangarelle* and *stacchiodde*. If the pasta is "dragged" a little too energetically, and, as a result, closes a little more, it becomes known as *cavatiedde*.

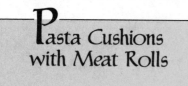

Orecchiette are made with only semolina, a little normal flour to help hold them together, salt, and warm water. When you eat them with *ragù* you make them smaller; when you eat them with greens, you make them bigger. This is a recipe of pure judgment. Trial and error is the only method for mastering it.

FOR THE ORECCHIETTE

3 cups semolina

¼ cup all-purpose flour

¼ teaspoon salt

1 cup very warm water, or q.b.

FOR THE MEAT ROLLS

1½ pounds sirloin, or similar meat, cut into 6 thin slices

3 garlic cloves, peeled and puréed

Salt to taste

Plenty of freshly ground black pepper

½ cup finely chopped parsley

6 thin slices pancetta

2 cups pecorino cheese, 1 cup in little pieces, 1 cup grated

¼ cup virgin olive oil, or q.b.

2 pounds tomatoes, cored, peeled, and well crushed

1 small yellow onion, peeled and very finely chopped

TO PREPARE THE ORECCHIETTE

Mix the semolina, the flour, and the salt together on a work surface, and form the semolina into a "well." Pour some of the warm water in the well, start gathering the semolina into the well from the inner well walls, and mix it with the water. Keep doing this until you have incorporated all of the semolina. You may use all of the water and perhaps you may not; it is even possible you may have to add more water. You should end up with a dough that is soft, supple, and smooth, but not sticky. Knead the dough for about 10 minutes. If it dries, add a little more warm water, and continue to knead it. It should feel like a soft dough, but it should not be stretchy. If it is, it is probably too dry. Cover the dough with plastic wrap, and let it rest for about 10 minutes.

Pull off a piece of the dough about the size of a lemon, and roll it into a long rope about ½ inch thick. (If you want to make the *orecchiette* bigger, you may do so by making the rope about ¾ inch thick.) Cut the dough into little round slices about ⅛ inch thick. Lay each slice down on a work surface, and with a *rasaul* or a table knife, push down on the little piece of dough as though you were buttering bread. Use more force than if you were buttering bread, but the action is the same. The dough should curl up on the edges to look like a tiny pizza. Of course, the shape will not be perfect, and the result, then, may look more like an ear: Hence the name. It is difficult to get it right the first time, and you may wonder why you are doing it, but once you get the hang of it, you can go surprisingly fast. (At the home of a friend, his mother made these in 15 minutes, from start to finish.)

If the dough is not too stiff, you should learn the movements fairly readily. If the dough is too soft, you will simply smear the dough. If that happens, incorporate some more semolina, knead it, let the dough rest for a few more minutes, and then proceed to make *orecchiette*. (I have always thought this pasta would be perfect for children with reasonably long interest spans to make.)

TO PREPARE THE MEAT ROLLS

Pound the slices of meat with a meat bat until they are quite thin, and season them with salt and pepper. Spread the garlic purée on them equally. Sprinkle on the parsley equally among the slices of meat. Cut each slice of *pancetta* into 2 or even 3 pieces, divide the pieces among the 6 sirloin slices, and lay them out flat on each slice of sirloin. Scatter the small pieces of *pecorino* cheese evenly on the 6 slices of sirloin. Make little packages out of the meat by taking the left and right ends of each slice and folding them over about ¼ of the way. Then take the top and bottom ends, and fold them over each other lengthwise. Either tie the little bundles with string, or secure them with wooden or metal picks to be removed before serving the *braccioletti*.

Heat the olive oil in a pan large enough to hold the tomatoes later and brown the meat bundles over medium heat all over, turning them several times. Remove from pan temporarily. Add the onions and sauté until they are transparent and add the tomatoes and some salt and pepper. Put the meat bundles back in to the sauce and cook for about 30 to 40 minutes, or until the sauce thickens and the *braccioletti* are tender, about 30 minutes.

Cook the *orecchiette* in plenty of boiling water for about 5 minutes, or until they are tender but *al dente*. Meanwhile take the *braccioletti* out of the sauce, and remove the string or wooden or metal picks from them. Put them back into the sauce to keep hot.

When the *orecchiette* are done, drain them, and divide them among heated plates. Spoon some of the sauce over them, and put plenty of grated cheese on them. Serve them very hot. Reserve the *braccioletti* for the *secondo piatto*.

MENU SUGGESTIONS: For an antipasto I would serve Artichokes Stuffed with Ricotta and Salami (page 227). The pasta and the *braccioletti* would be the *primo* and *secondo* dishes. A plate of Rose Wheels (page 264) would be a fine way to end this meal.

WINE: Brindisi Rosso (page 298)

Pasta Ammudicata

Pasta with Red Pepper Flakes and Toasted Bread Crumbs

SERVES 6

Several Southern Italian regions feature pasta dishes with bread crumbs. Some are eaten on feast days, such as Saint Joseph's Day, and some are just marvelous, every-day family fare. The version below adds anchovy for a saltier and livelier taste. Some dishes with the same name do not call for anchovy. It is a matter of local custom or momentary mood. In either case, you cannot go wrong.

MENU SUGGESTIONS: Mushrooms in Parchment (page 240) for antipasto would be good followed by the *pasta ammudicata*. Then you could have Grilled Sword-fish (page 197) or Swordfish, Stuffed Sicilian Style (page 199), with a *contorno* of Spin-ach, Roman Style (page 245), or Broccoli and Cheese Casserole, Sicilian Style (page 220). Sicilian Cannoli (page 261) or Spu-moni (page 296) are good endings.

WINE: Greco di Tufo (page 302)

½ cup virgin olive oil

1 tablespoon red pepper flakes

9 whole anchovy filets, finely chopped or ground in a mortar

1½ cups freshly ground bread crumbs

Salt to taste

1 pound any pasta, but perciatelli or bucatini, *broken into small pieces before cooking, are typical*

Heat half of the olive oil in a frying pan over medium flame. Add the red pepper flakes, and fry them, being careful not to let them burn. Add the anchovy, stir everything well, remove the pan from the flame, and set it aside.

Heat the remaining oil in another frying pan over medium flame, add the bread crumbs, and cook them, stirring with a wooden spoon, until they become golden and smell wonderful. Remove the bread crumbs from the heat immediately, or they will burn.

Meanwhile cook the pasta in plenty of salted water until it is *al dente*. When the pasta is done, drain it, but leave some of the water with it, and put it in a large bowl or back into the cooking pot. Mix the anchovy and red peppers into the pasta, then add the bread crumbs. Mix the pasta well, and serve it on heated plates.

NOTE: This pasta is not really dry, but it is not sauced in the conventional sense. That is why it is important to leave some of the pasta cooking water in with it or it becomes too dry to enjoy. *Pasta ammudicata* never gets cheese on it.

1 *tablespoon virgin olive oil*

½ *pound* pancetta, *cut into small dice (see* Pancetta, The Italian Pantry, *page 28)*

3 *large garlic cloves, peeled and well crushed*

4 *ounces (8 tablespoons) butter*

¾ *pound fresh* porcini *mushrooms, cut into* ½*-inch dice, or use 1 ounce dry* porcini, *rehydrated in water (see* Mushrooms, The Italian Pantry, *page 26)*

1 *pound fresh tomatoes, cored, peeled, and crushed in small pieces, including the juice, or use the same amount canned*

8 *or 10 large basil leaves, coarsely chopped, or 1 tablespoon dried (see* Basil, The Italian Pantry, *page 21)*

Salt to taste

5 *or 6 grindings of fresh black pepper*

1 *teaspoon red pepper flakes, or to taste*

1 *cup grated* pecorino *cheese*

Penne Arrabbiata

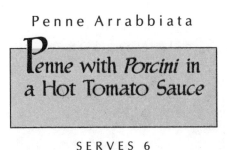

Penne with *Porcini* in a Hot Tomato Sauce

SERVES 6

This version of *penne arrabbiata* includes *porcini* and butter, an unusual but utterly delicious variation (not mine) of a classic dish.

Here pen-shaped pasta are bathed in tomato sauce with *porcini* mushrooms, *pancetta*, basil, and lots of red pepper flakes. *Penne arrabbiata* is one of the best *primo* dishes I know. It is good as a whole meal, or a very effective "appetite opener."

The spelling of this dish sometimes has one *b* or two *b*s. No one seems to agree. All agree on the two *r*s, which precludes its having anything to do with the Arabs. *Arrabbiata* means "rage," "fury," or "anger," since a mouthful might well make you get up and dance around the table. The name, like so many Italian names, is more whimsical than descriptive. The little jolts of hot only stimulate your taste buds.

MENU SUGGESTIONS: The *penne* would be a wonderful *primo* to have before Lamb Chops, Calabrian Style (page 162). Sicilian Cannoli (page 261) or "Drowned" Ice Cream (page 293) would be a perfect way to end this meal.

WINE: Primitivo di Manduria (page 300)

Heat the olive oil in a large frying pan, add the *pancetta*, and cook it over high heat until it is crisp and golden. Remove the *pancetta* with a slotted spoon, and set it aside. Pour out all but 2 tablespoons of the remaining fat, if there is any, and put in the garlic. (The fat from the *pancetta* imparts a very characteristic flavor, which is essential to the dish.) If you find that there is not enough fat, add more olive oil. Brown the garlic well over medium heat, but do not burn it, and discard it after it is brown. Add 1 ounce (about 2 tablespoons) of the butter to the pan, heat it, and add the *porcini*. Cook them for 5 minutes, or until they are slightly brown. Add the fried *pancetta*, tomatoes, basil, salt, black pepper, and red pepper flakes. Cook the mixture over medium heat for about 15 minutes, stirring often.

Meanwhile, in a large pot bring to a rolling boil 1 gallon of water with 5 teaspoons of salt, and add the *penne*, stirring the whole time. Cook them for 7 minutes, or until they are really *al dente*. Drain the *penne* in a colander, but do not shake out all of the water, allowing about ⅓ cup to remain in the pasta. The water is absorbed into the pasta instead of the sauce and produces a more succulent dish. If you are not sure you have the right amount of water, simply scoop out some of the boiling water before draining the pasta with a metal or glass measuring cup, and add it after draining the pasta. Arrange the pasta on a large heated serving platter, pour on the sauce, and mix everything well. Sprinkle on most of the cheese, leaving some to be passed at the table, and dot the hot pasta with the remaining 3 ounces of butter. Serve the pasta hot.

Ravioli
alla Napolitana

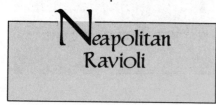

Neapolitan Ravioli

MAKES ABOUT 110
RAVIOLI

After lasagna, ravioli must be the best-known Italian dish in America. They are quite easy to make. Like all pasta dishes, they should be made often. It is the only way to keep the skill honed so you can just dash them off.

I use a *raviolatrice di legno* to make ravioli. It is a thick, round rolling pin with little windows cut into the wood in even rows. The windows are connected by long thin strips of very flat wood that make dividers between the rows. Once you are comfortable using the ''ravioli maker'' (see Kitchen Equipment, page 38) you will not use any other implement. The whole idea behind this tool is to eliminate so much of the time and effort of making each individual square.

The dough must be made with all-purpose flour if you are going to have an easy time handling it. Semolina or fancy durum flour will produce a brittle dough.

MENU SUGGESTIONS: You could have Artichokes, Stuffed Agrigento Style (page 226), and some Marinated Zucchini (page 100) as *antipasti*. After the ravioli, if you are still hungry, you could have Skewered Pork Rolls (page 210). Chocolate Ice (page 291) with some Bitter Almond Cookies (page 278) would be a good dessert.

WINE: Colli Albani (page 304) or Solopaca Rosso (page 304)

1   recipe Pasta, made with all-purpose flour *(page 124)*
1¼ pounds Ricotta cheese
1¾ cups grated Parmesan cheese
4   ounces prosciutto, *thinly sliced and finely chopped*
⅓   cup finely chopped parsley
1   large egg
½   teaspoon salt, *or to taste*
6   grindings fresh black pepper
Sauce *(see note page 145)*

Make the pasta as directed on page 125. While it is resting, combine well the remaining ingredients, and set the filling aside.

TO PREPARE THE RAVIOLI WITH A
RAVIOLATRICE

Put a large sheet of pasta down on a large work surface. A handmade circle of pasta as described on page 125 is ideal, but you can use strips made with the pasta machine. The pasta sheets should be about ¹⁄₃₂ inch thick. If there are any delays in making the ravioli, cover the dough with plastic wrap. Spread the filling all over half of the circle of dough to about 1 inch of the edges. Fold the other half of the dough over onto the filling, and press the edges closed. It should now look like a giant turnover.

Place the folded, straight edge of the dough so that it is on your left and you have a straight line in front of you and the curved, semicircular edges on your right. The width of the dough, at this point, must not be wider than your *raviolatrice*.

Line up the left edge of the dough with the farthest left window divider of the *raviolatrice*. Slowly and pressing hard, roll the pin over the dough. Little pillows appear in the wake of the rolling. Continue rolling until you have reached the other end of the dough. Some of the ravioli on the very edges and some on the curve are not well formed. These you simply cook and eat as a snack or discard. (I do not like to be wasteful, but when you see some 100 or so ravioli made in 2 minutes, you can afford to throw a little out.) Ravioli made with a *raviolatrice* are flatter and less filled than the ones below. Cut the ravioli apart by running the pastry cutter into the spaces between the pillows.

TO PREPARE THE RAVIOLI WITH A
CRIMP CUTTER

Roll the dough out into strips as wide as your pasta machine makes them. Lay about 1½ teaspoons of filling in neat rows about 1 inch apart on one sheet of dough. Lay another sheet of dough on top of the filling. Gently push the top dough all around the filling, and then press firmly to make sure the dough sticks together. If there is any doubt, brush some water or beaten egg around each mound of filling with a pastry brush or with your finger, and then put the top sheet of dough on, and proceed as directed. Push the top dough down to make a good seal and use a crimp cutter to cut between the mounds of filling and separate the ravioli. You will not get as much yield with this method, because you use a lot more dough to make each pillow than you do using the *raviolatrice*.

TO COOK THE RAVIOLI

Do not pile up the ravioli or they will stick. Use a spatula to pick them up by the row, and put them on a floured kitchen cloth on a cookie sheet. Cover them with a clean kitchen cloth until you are ready to cook them. If you are not going to cook them immediately, you should refrigerate them.

Boil plenty of water in the largest pot you have. You should put in 1 teaspoon of salt per quart of water. It is best to cook only up to 3 dozen at one time. Use another pot if you are cooking more. Drop the ravioli into the rapidly boiling water, a few at a time. Do not be in a hurry. Stir the ravioli frequently with a long wooden spoon. It is hard to say how long ravioli take to cook, but I estimate that it will be somewhere from 4 to 6 minutes, depending on how you made the pasta and how thin or thick it is. Drain the ravioli well in a colander, and serve them on heated plates with some sauce covering. Serve them very hot with grated Parmesan cheese passed at the table.

Ravioli can be successfully frozen if you put the finished pillows on a lightly floured cookie sheet (no cloth), and put them into the freezer, uncovered. In about 1 to 2 hours the ravioli will be frozen, and you can then put as many as you want in plastic bags or in plastic containers. When you want to cook them, take out as many ravioli as you want, and plunge them into boiling water while they are still frozen. If you let them defrost, they will become soggy and unmanageable. Allow 1 minute more of cooking time to compensate for the frozen state.

NOTE: These ravioli are usually served with Neapolitan Tomato Sauce with Meat (page 75). Allow ⅔ cup of sauce for each person. This is approximate, and it depends on how many ravioli people eat. Generally, for a large serving I give about 15 ravioli.

Another good way to serve these ravioli is to drizzle lots of melted butter over them as soon as they are taken out of the boiling water, then shower them with grated *pecorino* or Parmesan cheese.

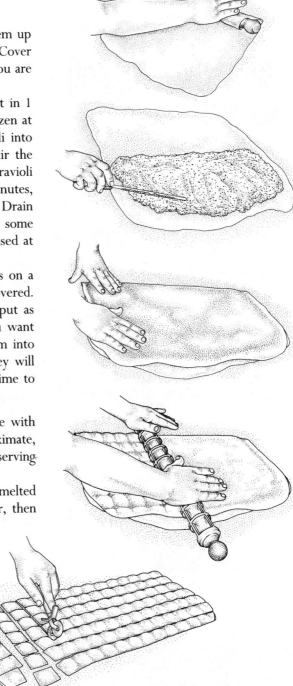

Penne con gli Asparagi

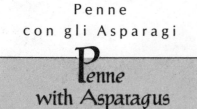

Penne with Asparagus

SERVES 6

The Italians love their pasta *al dente*; but they do not appreciate the crunchiness of vegetables cooked this way. This dish is an exception, but keep in mind that vegetables that are not overcooked are not exactly crunchy. The asparagus here should be tender and juicy and slide down the throat with ease.

Penne con gli asparagi really calls for wild asparagus, a pencil-thin grass that is unbelievably delicious. Nothing I have encountered on the commercial market comes close. You can get a nice result by using the pencil asparagus available in the spring.

MENU SUGGESTIONS: Miniature Meatball Soup (page 110) would be a good *minestra*. After the *penne con gli asparagi*, a small helping of Braised Beef, Roman Style (page 184), or Braised Oxtails, Roman Style (page 187), would be satisfying. Saint Joseph's Day Fritters (page 289) would be a festive finish to this meal.

WINE: Aglianico del Vulture (page 301) or Etna Rosso (page 308)

¼ cup virgin olive oil

2 large garlic cloves, peeled and well crushed

1½ pounds tomatoes, or q.b., cored, peeled, and well crushed

14 pounces penne

1 pound thin, tender, and fresh asparagus, well washed, trimmed, and cut into 2-inch pieces

1 cup grated pecorino *cheese, plus more for the table*

2 large eggs

Salt to taste

Plenty of freshly ground black pepper

Cook the asparagus in boiling salted water for 4 minutes. Drain and reserve for later.

Heat the olive oil in a large frying pan over a medium flame, add the garlic, and fry it until it is deep gold. Add the tomatoes, and stir all the ingredients well. Cook the sauce for about 10 minutes, and keep it hot but not simmering.

Meanwhile boil plenty of water in a large pot and add salt. Cook the *penne* really *al dente*. You should be able to actually chew them. When the *penne* are done, drain them, leaving in just a bit of the cooking water.

Mix together in a large, heated casserole dish the *penne* and the asparagus. Add the cup of cheese, and mix everything again. Break the eggs into a small dish, beat them lightly, add them to the *penne* and the asparagus, and mix once more. (Adding the cheese before the eggs creates a kind of insulation to keep the eggs from becoming too hot and accidentally curdling.) When you have a nice, glossy, well-coated mass of *penne*, asparagus, cheese, and eggs, add the tomato sauce, and stir everything until it is well blended. Add salt and pepper to taste.

Serve the *penne* on heated plates immediately. Pass a bit more grated *pecorino* cheese at the table.

Spaghetti con le Cozze

Spaghetti with Mussels

MAKES 4 SERVINGS

Salt to taste

12 ounces spaghetti

2½ cups, or q.b., Marinara Sauce (page 78)

3 tablespoons virgin olive oil

2 pounds mussels, scrubbed and bearded

¼ cup finely chopped parsley

Freshly ground black pepper to taste

Put 5 quarts or more of water in a large pan, add salt, bring it to a boil, and add the spaghetti, stirring. Put the sauce into a small pan, and heat it until it just simmers. Keep it at a simmer.

Heat the oil over high heat in a frying pan large enough to hold all of the mussels until it is quite hot but not smoking. Put the mussels into the hot oil, and shake the pan. Keep the heat on high until the first mussels begin to open. Add the chopped parsley, lower the heat, and continue to shake the pan. When all of the mussels are open, pour on the hot Marinara Sauce, mix it well with the mussels, and add salt and pepper to taste. Turn the heat off, and let the mussels and the sauce set until the spaghetti is *al dente*.

Drain the spaghetti, leaving a little of the cooking water on it. Return the spaghetti to the pan, and set aside for a moment. Divide the mussels equally among heated serving plates, removing them from the sauce with tongs or with a slotted spoon. Finish opening any mussels that are only half-opened. Arrange the mussels all around the edge of the plate to make a border. (Work very quickly or the pasta will get overcooked and stick together.) Divide the pasta equally among the plates, putting it in the center of the mussel border. Put the sauce on the pasta, and serve the dishes immediately. No cheese on this dish, please.

When I left Puglia, the battle was still raging between two old men I had met in a restaurant there about whether it is necessary to remove the shells from the mussels of *spaghetti con le cozze* or not. One felt the shells look unsightly on the plate, and no host or hostess who wanted to make a *bella figura* ("look good") would do such a thing. The other man maintained you get more flavor with the shells left on, and if your hosts were really considerate, they would let you pick them up and suck on them to get every last drop of sauce. It really depends on the host and guests, whether to shell the mussels or not. Me? I never take the shells off.

The discussion about whether the parsley should be cooked in the sauce along with the mussels or simply strewn on top of the finished dish would be too lengthy to present here.

MENU SUGGESTIONS: I like a complete fish dinner sometimes. A cold antipasto of Roasted Peppers with Italian-Style Tuna and Clams (page 104) would be a good starter. Then the Spaghetti with Mussels could be followed by Trout Vernaccia (page 177) with a *contorno* of Fava Beans and Chicory (page 238). A plate of Dessert Ravioli, Teramo Style (page 283), would be a nice ending to this meal.

WINE: Merlot di Aprilia (page 306)

Spaghetti o Vermicelli alla Sangiovanello

Spaghetti (or Vermicelli) for St. John's Eve

SERVES 4

¼ cup virgin olive oil

3 large garlic cloves, peeled and well crushed

3 whole anchovies

1 pound tomatoes, or q.b., peeled, cored, and well crushed

1 tablespoon capers, finely chopped

Big pinch of red pepper flakes

Salt to taste

12 ounces spaghetti or vermicelli

In typical Italian fashion this dish, traditionally eaten on June 24, especially around Brindisi, often features different ingredients depending on who serves it to you. Sometimes it calls for black olives. In most cases it has capers, but in one recipe, from a distinguished son of Puglia, there is neither olives nor capers; only olive oil, garlic, anchovy, and tomatoes. There seems to be unanimous agreement that the dish must have garlic and anchovy and tomato. The use of a large amount of garlic is unusual because Pugliese cooking is elegant, refined, and by no means garlicky. This sauce has been compared to the Campanian *puttanesca* sauce that has red pepper flakes in it. This dish is frequently made with vermicelli instead of spaghetti.

MENU SUGGESTIONS: A dish of Bread and Cheese Soup (page 118) would be a good *minestra* followed by the Spaghetti for Saint John's Eve. Then a dish of Fried Squid (page 174) or Stuffed Squid (page 175) with a *contorno* of Almond Peppers (page 249) would be good. A slice of Chocolate Bread (page 284) or some Roman Cheesecake (page 271) would be a good finish to this meal.

WINE: Cirò Rosso (page 302)

Heat the olive oil in a large frying pan over medium heat, add the garlic, and when it is a very dark gold, mash it with a fork, and spread it around the pan. Add the anchovies and mash them with a fork. Add the tomatoes, and cook the sauce for about 15 minutes. Add the capers and the red pepper flakes, and stir again. The sauce is now ready for use. You may use it immediately or store it for later use.

Boil plenty of water in a large pot, and add some salt. Add the pasta, and cook it *al dente*. (If the sauce needs heating, do it now.) When the pasta is done, drain it, leaving just a bit of the cooking water with it. Put the pasta on heated dishes, and spoon on some of the sauce. Serve the pasta very hot. This dish neither needs nor wants cheese on it.

1 2-pound, live Dungeness or Rock crab (use more if you like)

¼ cup virgin olive oil, or q.b.

2 large garlic cloves, peeled and well crushed

2½ pounds fresh tomatoes, cored, peeled, and very finely chopped to make almost a purée

¼ cup finely chopped parsley

Salt to taste

Plenty of freshly ground black pepper

1 pound spaghetti or vermicelli

Spaghetti o Vermicelli al Sugo di Granchio

Spaghetti (or Vermicelli) with Crab Sauce

MAKES 6 SERVINGS

Lay the crab on its back in a pan of cold water to cover by at least 4 inches. Put a heavy lid on the pan, and put it over very high heat. When the water begins to simmer, lower the heat, and let the crab cook for about 4 minutes. Turn the heat off, and let the crab set in the hot water for about 12 minutes. (If the crab is smaller than 2 pounds, let it set in the hot water for 10 minutes.)

Begin cleaning the crab by breaking the legs off at the body and setting them aside. Pull the large back shell off. Clean all the debris out of the center of the body, and discard it. Pull out the air sacs, known as "dead man's fingers," and discard them as well. Break the body into small segments. Crack the legs and claws with a heavy, blunt instrument. Remove the meat from the body segments and the legs with a small fork or a crab pick, and put it into a bowl for later use.

Heat the olive oil in a large, wide pan and brown the garlic in it. Add the tomatoes, the parsley, and salt and pepper to taste. Let the tomatoes cook for about 20 minutes, add the parsley and the crabmeat to the tomato sauce, and simmer the sauce for about 5 minutes.

Meanwhile, bring 6 quarts of salted water to a boil, add the pasta, and boil it until it is *al dente*. Drain it, and arrange it on heated plates. Spoon some of the crab sauce on each portion of pasta, and serve it very hot. Do not put any cheese on this dish!

NOTE: If you wanted to have crab in two ways in the same meal, you could cook more crab, preparing it as described. You could put a small amount into the sauce and have a dish of pasta as a *primo*, and then have the remaining crab, either hot or cold, as a *secondo* with lemon juice, parsley, and olive oil on it.

For those lucky enough to get live crab, this dish comes highly recommended. You could use fresh boiled crab from the fishmonger, but it will not be as highly flavored or as sweet.

Plunging crabs in boiling water makes the flesh tough. I've provided a method I learned from a Neapolitan waiter. The result is unbelievably moist, tender, and delicious crabmeat. You could eat the crab without a condiment of any kind. Lobster can be done in the same way.

MENU SUGGESTIONS: An antipasto of Golden Fried Pumpkin (page 101) and some Chick-peas in Olive Oil (page 95) would be good starters. Chicken Roasted with Rosemary (page 178) as a *secondo piatto* with some Mushrooms Roasted in Pine Nuts (page 239) as *contorno* could follow. Walnut Cake #1 (page 276) would be a nice dessert for this meal.

WINE: Greco di Tufo (page 302) and Rosato del Salento (page 300)

Vermicelli alla Principe di Napoli

Vermicelli,
Prince of Naples
Style

SERVES 6

This is another treasure from my friend Dottore Manzon. He has an unfailing sense of what is good and worthwhile. The flavors of the vermicelli, butter, meat sauce, and cheese alone make the pasta irresistible.

MENU SUGGESTIONS: An antipasto of Golden Fried Pumpkin (page 101) or Mushrooms in Parchment (page 240) would be a wonderful way to start the meal. After the *vermicelli alla principe di Napoli*, I would have Lamb Chops, Calabrian Style (page 162). For such a festive menu I would finish with Almond Tart (page 270) or Spumoni (page 296).

WINE: Regaleali (page 310) with the vermicelli; Cannonau di Sardegna Riserva (page 307) with the lamb chops

8 ounces vermicelli

½ cup thick Meat Sauce (page 76) or use demi-glacé

5 ounces (10 tablespoons) butter, plus more for greasing a casserole

⅔ cup grated Parmesan cheese

Meat from ¼ roast chicken, cut in thin julienne strips, or torn into small pieces (use white or dark meat or both)

About 3 ounces boiled fresh beef tongue, cut into thin julienne strips

1½ ounces of prosciutto, *thinly sliced and finely chopped*

½ cup fresh peas, or use frozen petit peas

Salt and freshly ground pepper to taste

Virgin olive oil for frying, q.b.

2 medium tomatoes, cored, peeled, seeded, and chopped into fine dice

8 ounces imported Mozzarella, sliced thin

Optional: *Allow 1 cup more Meat Sauce if you plan to pass more sauce at the table.*

Heavily butter an ovenproof casserole dish that can be used on the stove as well as in the oven. Cook the vermicelli in plenty of boiling, salted water for about 2 minutes, or until they are really *al dente*. Drain them well by pouring the cooking water through a colander. Immediately, return the pasta to the pan in which it was cooked, add the ½ cup of meat sauce, and mix the pasta well. Add about 4 ounces (or 8 tablespoons) of the butter to the pasta and sauce, and mix again. Add the Parmesan cheese, and mix again. Before the pasta cools too much, twirl some around a large cooking fork to make a kind of bird's nest shape. You should get 12 such nests. As you finish, put each nest into the buttered casserole, leaving a little space between each one. Continue until you have used all the pasta. (You can prepare the dish to this point up to 1 day in advance, but I would prefer that you not do that.)

Divide the chicken meat, including the skin if it is well cooked, among the nests of vermicelli. Do the same with the cooked tongue. (Some people do not like tongue. The dish really calls for it, but if one ingredient had to be absent once, it might be the tongue.)

Heat 1 ounce (or 2 tablespoons) of the butter in a small pan with the *prosciutto* over medium heat, add the peas, and cook the peas for only a minute or so, being careful not to overcook them. Salt and pepper to taste. When the peas are done, divide the mixture equally among the pasta nests.

Put a few teaspoons of olive oil into a small frying pan over high heat. When the oil is hot, add the tomatoes, and toss them around for only 1 minute. Put a pinch of salt and pepper on them, and remove the pan from the heat. After 2 minutes, spoon equal amounts of the tomatoes onto the pasta nests. Meanwhile, preheat the oven to 375° F, and move the rack to the upper third of the oven.

Put the Mozzarella slices on top of the nests. Put the casserole on a burner over a medium heat to just heat the bottom of the casserole. When the butter begins to sizzle, lower the heat just a bit, and leave the casserole to heat for 1 minute more, being careful not to burn the bottoms of the nests. Put the casserole in the oven, and let it bake for about 12 minutes, or until the pasta is hot and the cheese has melted down the slopes of the nests. Serve the vermicelli on heated plates.

Caciu all'Argentiere
o
Caciocavallo Fritto all'Argentiere

Fried Caciocavallo Cheese, Silversmith Style

SERVES 6

⅓ cup extra virgin olive oil for frying, or q.b.

3 large fresh garlic cloves, peeled and well crushed

1¼ pounds Caciocavallo or whole-milk Mozzarella cheese, cut into ½-inch-thick slices

⅓ cup red wine vinegar

Salt to taste

4 or 5 big grindings of fresh black pepper

1 teaspoon dried, crushed oregano

Heat serving plates until they are fairly hot, and set them aside in a very warm spot for later use.

Heat the oil in a large, wide sauté pan, add the garlic, and fry it until it is light brown all over and is very aromatic. Push the garlic aside, and add the slices of cheese. Fry them over high heat until they just begin to take on a golden hue and become a little soft and runny here and there. Turn the slices of cheese over and fry them on the other side. Do not let them melt or they will be hard to serve later. Splash on the red wine vinegar, and shake the pan a bit. Scatter on the salt, pepper, and the oregano, and turn the heat off. Wait 1 minute, and then serve the cheese immediately on the heated plates; otherwise it will begin to harden. The cheese should be loose, succulent, stringy, and very hot to be enjoyed.

See Italian Pantry (page 21) for a description of Caciocavallo cheese.

MENU SUGGESTIONS: Use the *caciu* for a hot antipasto with chunks of crusty homemade bread. You could add an additional cold antipasto of Roasted Peppers with Italian-Style Tuna and Clams (page 104), and have a dish of Macaroni with Arugula and Fresh Tomatoes, Andrian Style (page 135). Lamb Chops, Calabrian Style (page 162), would be a substantial *secondo piatto*. After this meal, I would have a basket of seasonal fruit along with some Moscato di Trani (page 300) for dessert.

WINE: Lacryma Christi del Vesuvio (page 305)

Arancini

MAKES 12 ARANCINI

Pronounced "ah-ron-chee-nee," this word translates literally into "little oranges" because of the way these golden-fried rice balls appear. They are a favorite Sicilian street food, eaten out-of-hand at *rosticer-rie*. They are also a favorite at the dinner table accompanied by a large salad. They are usually eaten warm as opposed to hot, and the filling, for the most part, is chopped pork and onions, or chopped chicken and peas cooked in tomato sauce. Often you will find them loaded with soft Mozzarella cheese in the middle.

WINE: Corvo Rosso (page 308), Fiorano Bianco (page 305), or Rapitalà (page 308)

1 quart water or Homemade Chicken Broth (page 109)

1 teaspoon salt, or to taste

¼ teaspoon pepper

½ teaspoon saffron threads, finely chopped, or ⅛ teaspoon ground saffron

2 cups Arborio or Vialone rice

2½ cups Marinara Sauce (page 78)

½ cup grated pecorino cheese

8 ounces uncooked chicken meat, boned, or the same amount pork, or a combination of them both

Lard for browning meat, q.b.

1 medium yellow onion, finely chopped

½ cup fresh or frozen tiny peas

4 large eggs

1½ cups plain, fine bread crumbs (you will have lots left over)

3 cups olive oil or other vegetable oil

Optional: *Use Mozzarella, Teleme, or Monterey Jack cheese instead of the chicken mixture as a stuffing. Allow about ½ ounce per rice ball. Make the arancini as directed below.*

Place the water or chicken broth, salt, pepper, and saffron in a medium-sized saucepan with a lid, bring it to a boil over high heat, and then lower the heat. Add the rice all at once, and stir for a moment. Replace the lid on the pan, and simmer the rice for about 16 minutes, or until it is tender but *al dente*. The liquid should be thoroughly absorbed. If you find it is not, continue to cook the rice on medium heat with the lid off until the rice is sticky but not wet. When the rice is done, remove it from the heat, and add the tomato sauce and the grated cheese, and mix it well. Set it aside in the pan to cool for about 2 hours. (You may refrigerate it, well covered, after 2 hours if you wish, and continue the rest of the recipe the next day.)

TO PREPARE THE MEAT FILLING

Cut the meat into large chunks, and in a frying pan brown them in some olive oil or lard over medium heat. When the meat is brown, add the onion, and gently brown that also, but do not make it too dark. Add 1 cup of marinara sauce, and cook the mixture slowly for about an hour. Add fresh or frozen peas and cook it for 5 minutes longer.

Remove the meat from the sauce with a slotted spoon, let it cool until you can just handle it, and using your fingers and perhaps a fork, shred all the meat into fairly small pieces. Return the meat to the pan.

When the rice and tomato mixture is cool, add 2 of the eggs, and mix well. Take about one twelfth of the mixture, and pat it out on the palm of one hand so that it looks like a thick crepe. Place about 2 tablespoonsful of the meat mixture into the center of the rice crepe, and gently close your hand so that you envelop the meat. Do the same thing if you are using the

optional cheese. Shape the mass into a round ball using both hands, gently circulating one against the other. Lay the finished ball on a cookie sheet or on a large piece of wax paper, and continue until you have used up all the ingredients.

TO FRY THE ARANCINI

Beat two eggs lightly in a low-sided dish. Spread the bread crumbs in a low-sided dish. Roll the *arancini* in the egg mixture, making sure they are well covered, and then roll them all around in the bread crumbs. As you finish each one, set it on a cookie sheet or on some wax paper.

Heat the oil to about 350° F in a deep fryer, put in as many *arancini* as will fit comfortably into the pan, and fry them until they are a deep golden color. Remove them with a slotted spoon, and lay them on absorbent paper or on a clean kitchen towel. If you have a lot of them, store them in a warm oven as you make them. Keep the oven door ajar so that they will stay hot but with air circulating around them.

Arancini can be very successfully frozen after forming them into balls. See details in "Phone-Wire" Rice Croquettes recipe (page 96).

Arancini are perfect for lunch accompanied by a large green salad, or they make a delicious first course followed by roast lamb or large slices of roasted fish such as sea bass.

Crocchetti di Spinaci

Spinach and Cheese Croquettes

SERVES 4

These morsels of spinach combined with Ricotta and Parmesan cheeses depend for their goodness on the freshest spinach obtainable. Friends have pointed out that this dish is northern in origin. They are partially correct. The fact that they are fried, but not deep-fried, especially in olive oil, makes them southern.

MENU SUGGESTIONS: These are a delicious hot antipasto or a wonderful *contorno* to Breaded Lamp Chops (page 186) or Fried Codfish, Roman Style (page 190). Italians will often have several fried things in a menu, either in courses or all together.

WINE: Faro Rosso (page 309)

2 *pounds spinach, carefully washed (see Spinach, Roman Style, for details on washing spinach, page 245)*

2 *ounces (4 tablespoons) soft, sweet butter*

8 *ounces Ricotta*

1½ *cups grated Parmesan cheese*

4 *big scrapings of nutmeg*

Salt to taste

All-purpose flour for dredging

2 *large eggs*

⅓ *cup virgin olive oil for frying, or q.b.*

Put the spinach in plenty of salted water to cook for about 3 to 4 minutes or until it is limp. Drain the spinach very well in a colander, and gently squeeze out as much water as you can. Put the hot, drained spinach in a medium-sized bowl, add the butter, and mix well. Set the spinach and butter aside to completely cool.

When the spinach is cool, add the Ricotta, Parmesan cheese, nutmeg, and salt to taste, and mix it all thoroughly. Spread the flour evenly in a low-sided dish. Beat the eggs lightly in a low-sided dish. Form dollops of the cheese and spinach mixture into ovals about the size of a chicken egg, and roll them in the flour. They will be very hard to handle because they are very soft, so you must work carefully. Use a fork or a large spoon to handle them after you have formed them and while you are attempting to flour and egg-wash them. Dip the floured *crocchetti* in the beaten egg, shaking them well to get rid of any excess.

Heat the oil in a frying pan to 375° F, add the *crocchetti*, 1 or 2 at a time, and fry them until they are golden, carefully turning them once or twice. Remove them from the hot oil with a slotted spoon, and put them on an absorbent towel to drain. Serve the *crocchetti* very hot.

SECONDI PIATTI

Second or Main Courses

The dishes presented here stand on their own merits. Delicious and relatively un-complicated, if they are eaten after practically any one of the *primi piatti*, they develop taste and character that become more important and resolute than when they stand alone. They are part of a bigger picture and become a link in a chain of eating that brings satisfaction and balance to a meal; they reinforce the rule that each course is equal but different, to be enjoyed on its own, neither taking precedence over nor submitting to the other dishes in the meal. By now you can see that a so-called "continental" plate of food with several items on it cannot compare with eating single dishes in multicourse meals. Rolled Steak, Stuffed Sicilian Style, surely requires a buildup of at least a first-course dish such as *Penne Arrabbiata*. The dishes included here were chosen not only because many of them have not seen the printed page before, at least not in America, but because they are so good to eat and easily executed by most home cooks. They illustrate the diversity of taste and cooking techniques the Southern Italians have enjoyed for so long.

2 *large eggs*
1 *tablespoon olive oil*
1 *cup milk*
½ *cup all-purpose flour*

¼ *teaspoon salt*
Tiny amounts of vegetable oil or butter for greasing crepe pan

Beat all the ingredients together in a medium-sized bowl, except the oil or butter for greasing the pan, to make a batter. Let it stand for an hour, or until it is the consistency of whipping cream. The batter should coat the back of a spoon well, but it should be liquid enough to slide into shapes easily so as to conform to the shape of the crepe pan. If the batter becomes too thick to pour easily, add a little water, and beat it again until it is the right consistency.

Coat an 8-inch heavy crepe or frying pan with a tiny amount of oil or butter. Use a paper towel all bunched up like a pad to do this job. Get the pan hot, but not smoking, and pour in about 3 tablespoons of batter, or a bit more. Tip the pan all around to spread the batter and make a thin pancake. Brown the *crespella* on one side. Turn it over with a spatula, and cook it for 1 minute or even less. As the *crespelle* are done, stack them on a plate until you are ready to use them. You should grease the pan after each *crespella* is made, but if your pan is in excellent condition, it may not be necessary after the first 3 or 4 are done.

If you are going to use the *crespelle* later on the same day you make them, you can simply refrigerate them, covered with wax paper or clear wrap. If you are going to use them perhaps a day later, put a small piece of wax paper or clear wrap between each one, then cover them with additional clear wrap, and store them in the refrigerator for up to 3 days.

The *crespelle* freeze very well. Put wax paper or clear wrap between each one, as previously described, cover them well with more clear wrap, and freeze. Packed this way, you can retrieve whatever amount you want without having to defrost the whole stack.

Use *crespelle* for savory as well as sweet dishes. They are also excellent filled with leftover meats or fowl and baked in the oven, much as you would do cannelloni (page 207).

Crespelle

Crepes

MAKES ABOUT 16
8-INCH CRESPELLE

In Southern Italy, crepes are used in soups as in the Abruzzese speciality Cheese Crepes in Broth (page 112) and in Crepes Filled with Ricotta and Prosciutto (page 160) done by the Romans. The following basic crepe recipe is easy and reliable.

Crespelle di Ricotta e Prosciutto

Crepes Filled with Ricotta and Prosciutto

MAKES 8
CRESPELLE

If ever a dish cried out for the best Roman Ricotta obtainable, this is the one. When the Ricotta mixture is tucked into the tender, golden *crespelle* and then drizzled with butter and baked until it begins to puff, you have a dish fit for a king. The words "light" and "feathery" describe this dish perfectly.

MENU SUGGESTIONS: Roasted Tomatoes (page 99) would be a good antipasto with the *crespelle*, making a good *intermezzo* dish. A good *secondo* would be Pan-Simmered Baby Trout (page 176) with a *contorno* of Mushrooms Roasted with Pine Nuts (page 239). White Meringues (page 279) make a light dessert.

WINE: Bianco Alcamo (page 308) with the *crespelle*; Marsala Superiore (page 309) with dessert

2 cups Ricotta
1½ ounces finely chopped prosciutto
About ¼ cup heavy cream for softening the Ricotta
Salt to taste
4 big grindings of fresh black pepper

½ recipe Crepes (page 159)
4 ounces (8 tablespoons) unsalted butter, or q.b.
½ cup grated Parmesan cheese (or more)

Mix the Ricotta, *prosciutto*, cream, salt, and pepper in a large bowl. When the mixture is well combined, set it aside.

Heavily butter a casserole dish large enough to hold all the *crespelle* with some of the butter. Place 4 or 5 tablespoons of the cheese and *prosciutto* mixture on each of the *crespelle*, roll the *crespelle* up like cannelloni or like a giant cigar, and put them into the prepared casserole dish. Dot them very generously with the rest of the butter, and sprinkle the grated Parmesan cheese all over them. Bake the *crespelle* in a preheated 400° F oven for 10 to 12 minutes, or until they are hot and have little golden burnt spots all over them. Serve them from the casserole immediately.

NOTE: You can serve the *crespelle* hot as an antipasto or as a light lunch dish.

TOP RIGHT: Pizza, Lanciano Style (Abruzzo) (page 52) · MIDDLE LEFT: Fried Calzone (Sicily) (page 62) · BOTTOM RIGHT: Neapolitan Country Pie (Campania) (page 66)

TOP: Mussels and Sausage (Campania) (page 194) · BOTTOM RIGHT: Roasted Tomatoes (Calabria) (page 99) on Garlic Bread (Lazio) (page 91) · BOTTOM LEFT: Mussels with Saffron (Abruzzo) (page 103)

TOP: Clay-Cooked Prawns (Lazio) (page 196)   ·   BOTTOM RIGHT: Calabrian Celery Soup
(page 113)   ·   BOTTOM LEFT: String Bean Bundles (Sicily) (page 235)

TOP RIGHT: Stuffed Pasta Dumplings (Campania) (page 139) · TOP LEFT: Penne with *Porcini* in a Hot Tomato Sauce (Lazio) (page 143) · BOTTOM RIGHT: Macaroni with Arugula and Fresh Tomatoes, Andrian Style (Apulia) (page 135) · BOTTOM LEFT: Stuffed Beef Bagatelles (Abruzzo) (page 205)

TOP LEFT: Polenta on a Board (Abruzzo) (page 203)   ·   TOP RIGHT: Sicilian Rice Dumplings
(page 152)   ·   BOTTOM: Chicken Infused with Bay Leaves (Sardinia) (page 161)

TOP RIGHT: Fiery Macaroni (Basilicata) (page 138) · MIDDLE LEFT: Braised Rabbit, Sardinian Style (page 198) · BOTTOM RIGHT: Vermicelli, Prince of Naples Style (Campania) (page 150)

TOP RIGHT: Stuffed Squid (Sardinia) (page 173) · TOP LEFT: Cousin Mary's Eggplant (Calabria) (page 241) · BOTTOM: Homemade Sicilian Sausage (page 188)

TOP: Tuna and Fennel Seeds (Sicily) (page 201) · BOTTOM: Orange and Lemon Salad (Sicily) (page 242)

Pomegranate Quail (Sicily) (page 181)

TOP RIGHT: Cauliflower Salad (Calabria) (page 97) · BOTTOM LEFT: Lamb Chops, Calabrian Style (page 162)

TOP: Signora Bonanno's Artichokes (Sicily) (page 225) · BOTTOM: Sicilian Bread Roll, in the Old Style (page 64)

TOP: Mixed Vegetable Stew (Basilicata) (page 232) · BOTTOM RIGHT ON GRILL: Garlic Bread (Lazio) (page 91) · BOTTOM LEFT ON GRILL: Skewered Pork Rolls (Calabria) (page 210)

TOP: Sardinian Parchment Bread (page 63) · BOTTOM: Lamb Stew with Wild Mushrooms (Basilicata) (page 164)

TOP: Eggplant Dumplings (Calabria) (page 247)   ·   BOTTOM RIGHT: Italian Potato Pancake (Lazio) (page 246)   ·   BOTTOM LEFT: Golden Fried Pumpkin (Sicily) (page 101)

TOP LEFT: Golden Christmas Bread (Lazio) (page 280) · MIDDLE RIGHT: Rose Wheels (Apulia) (page 264); · BOTTOM LEFT: Spumoni (Campania) (page 296)

TOP RIGHT: White Meringues (Sardinia) (page 279) · MIDDLE LEFT: Almond Tart (Abruzzo) (page 270) · BOTTOM RIGHT: Sicilian Cassata (page 266)

1 *large yellow onion, peeled and cut into ⅛-inch slices*

1 *large carrot, washed and cut into 1-inch pieces*

1 *branch celery, leaves left on, washed, and cut into 1-inch pieces*

5 *sprigs parsley*

Salt to taste

1 *3-pound whole chicken, dressed for cooking*

6 *quarts cold water*

60 *myrtle or bay leaves, or q.b., for lining a platter*

Pollo al Mirto

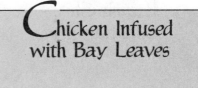

Chicken Infused with Bay Leaves

SERVES 6

If you can imagine the tastes of vanilla, nutmeg, mint, and lemon, you might come close to guessing the flavor of bay leaves. The intriguing aroma produced here is subtle and no salt or pepper is called for. If ever a chicken dish represented simple elegance, this is it. In Sardinia, this chicken is made with myrtle, abundantly available on that island. California Laurel or plain bay leaves are good substitutes.

MENU SUGGESTIONS: Potato Croquettes (page 231) would be a good hot antipasto, along with some "Phone-Wire" Rice Croquettes (page 96). The chicken could be a *secondo* served with or without bread, with a *contorno* of Almond Peppers (page 249). White Meringues (page 279) and some Bitter Almond Cookies (page 278) would be a good dessert, along with some Moscato di Trani (page 300) or Marsala Superiore (page 309).

WINE: Lacryma Christi del Vesuvio (page 305), Trebbiano di Aprilia (page 306), or Corvo Bianco (page 308).

Put the vegetables, except the bay leaves, into an 8-quart pot. Add 6 quarts of cold water and bring it to the boil. Add the chicken, and when the water comes back to the boil, reduce the heat and simmer the chicken until it is done, about 45 minutes. While the chicken is cooking, line a small platter with myrtle or bay leaves, covering the entire bottom, but reserving enough leaves to cover the bird later. When the chicken is done, remove it from the water with a slotted spoon (to keep from piercing it, thereby letting valuable juices escape), and shake it to remove any excess moisture. Lay it on the bed of leaves, and while it is still very hot, place the rest of the myrtle or bay leaves all over the top of it. Put a bowl large enough to just cover the platter and the chicken over them. This traps the steam from the chicken and also permeates the meat with the flavor and aroma of the leaves. Let the chicken cool for about 2 hours, and then refrigerate it, still covered by the bowl. The chicken should be served cold the next day. Carve it as you like, either in large pieces or in thin slices.

NOTE: Small game birds such as partridge, large quail, and small pheasant can be done the same way. Use the same method, but take into account the ingredients for the difference in the size of the bird used.

If you do not have an abundance of bay leaves or find them too costly where you live, eliminate the ones for the bottom (40 percent). The flavor will be slightly fainter. You could save even more by fine-chopping 6 or 7 bay leaves and adding them to the water in which you put the chicken.

Costolettine di Agnello alla Calabrese

Lamb Chops, Calabrian Style

SERVES 4

Lamb chops made this way are beautiful because the rib bone is left so long. When the chops have been properly pounded, the rib eye will be about 3½ inches around. Each one resembles a flag with a curved pole. This dish is marvelous for large parties because you can set up a heated serving platter with all the garnishes on it and, at the last moment, fry the lamb chops, which you have previously prepared.

MENU SUGGESTIONS: You could begin your meal with Potato Croquettes (page 231) or with Stuffed Pasta Dumplings (page 139). There would be no need for an antipasto. Cream Puffs (page 256) would be a good dessert for this meal.

WINE: Montepulciano d'Abruzzo (page 298), Corvo Rosso (page 308), or Brindisi Rosso (page 298)

2 *large red bell peppers (use green if red not available)*
1 *large garlic clove, minced*
  About ½ cup virgin olive oil
2 *large, juicy lemons*
8 *baby artichokes, washed and trimmed*
1 *teaspoon salt and to taste*
  Freshly ground black pepper to taste
½ *pound mushrooms*
8 *rib lamb chops with long bone left in*
2 *tablespoons capers*
8 *anchovy filets*

Wash the bell peppers, and dry them. Put them on the burner plate over a high gas flame and let the flames lick up around them. After one side has become charred and very black, turn the pepper around with tongs and burn the skin on the other side. When they are totally black, set them aside to cool on a dish. (It is not necessary to put them into a bag unless you want to cook them a bit, as the bag, when you seal it, becomes a little oven when you put the hot peppers in it.)

When the peppers are cool enough to handle, lay them down on a board or on the edge of your sink, and scrape the blackened skin off of them. (It should slip right off.) Cut the peppers open, scrape out and discard the seeds, and remove and discard the core. Cut the peppers into slices about ¼-inch thick, and put them on a plate. Scatter the garlic all over them, drizzle on about 2 tablespoons of virgin olive oil, and squeeze on the juice of ¼ of a lemon. Set the peppers aside for later use. (For more details about burning the skin off peppers, see Roasted Peppers with Italian-Style Tuna and Clams, page 104.)

Soak the baby artichokes in cold water to clean them, and in another large bowl prepare 3 quarts of acidulated water by adding 3 tablespoons of white vinegar or lemon juice. Peel off the outer tough leaves of the artichokes until the inner, yellow leaves appear, dipping the artichoke you are working on in the acidulated water occasionally to keep it from turning black. Leave each soaking in the acidulated water. When you have finished this part of the job, remove each one from the water, and, with a sharp paring knife, trim the bottom so that it looks clean and neat. The bottom is edible and choice, so don't take off any more than is necessary. Cut about 25 percent of the top off, and cut each artichoke into quarters lengthwise.

Place the artichokes in a small saucepan, cover them with cold water and add 3 slices of lemon, skin and all, 1 teaspoon of salt, 4 grindings of fresh black pepper, and 2 tablespoons of olive oil. Turn the heat to medium, bring the artichokes to a simmer, and cook them for 10 minutes, or until they are tender. The liquid should be evaporated, except for the oil, which should remain to coat them. If the artichokes are done and there is too much liquid, quickly remove them from the water with a slotted spoon, and put them temporarily into a dish. Reduce the liquid over high heat until only the oil remains. Remove the lemon slices, and discard them. Put the artichokes back into the oil, and stir them all around. Set them aside for later use.

Wipe the mushrooms clean with a paper or kitchen towel. If they are large, cut them into quarters. In a frying pan that will just hold the mushrooms, heat 2 tablespoons of olive oil over high heat, add the mushrooms, and stir them. Sauté them for 5 minutes, or until they become golden. Do not overcook them. Squeeze on the juice of ½ lemon, and with the heat still high, swirl and stir everything around to evaporate the lemon juice. If there is any liquid left, remove the mushrooms from the frying pan with a slotted spoon, put them into a bowl or dish to cool, and reduce the pan juice over high heat until it is thick and there is very little of it. Pour this remaining juice on the mushrooms. Set them aside until later.

Gently pound the meat with a meat bat to less than ¼-inch thickness. Add salt and pepper to taste. Heat 1 tablespoon olive oil in a large frying pan to almost smoking, quickly fry the chops for about 1 minute on each side, and put them aside on a heated plate. They should be well browned outside but pink inside, not raw or even blood rare, just pink.

Assemble the chops attractively on a serving platter. They are very pretty if you place the bones pointing toward the middle of the platter or toward the outside of the platter. In between the bones, where there is plenty of space, carefully put in some of the bell peppers, artichoke pieces, and some mushrooms in little heaps. Scatter a few capers on top of these vegetables, and then, either on top of the vegetables or off to the side, place the anchovies. (The vegetables do not need to be hot, but the meat does. The vegetables are more like garnishes in this dish, as opposed to a regular portion.)

NOTE: Ask your butcher to cut the lamb rib bones so that they are about 6 inches long. Take the chine bone (the chine is the part of the back bone to which the ribs are attached and is usually left on chop cuts) off the ribs using a heavy cleaver, or carefully dissect it off. Or have the butcher do it. (Leave the rib bone on. It looks nice and makes it easy to pick the meat up with the fingers.)

Agnello con
Funghi Salvatici

Lamb Stew
with Wild Mushrooms

SERVES 6

Even though *cardoncelli* (*Lactarius deliciosus*) are used in Basilicata, you can reproduce this divine stew with fresh *porcini*, chanterelles, or tree-oyster mushrooms. Use a combination of commercial mushrooms with an ounce of rehydrated dried *porcini* (see Italian Pantry, page 26) if the others are not available where you live.

MENU SUGGESTIONS: Bread and Cheese Skewers, Roman Style (page 93), would make a splendid antipasto. After the *agnello* a nice *contorno* of Orange and Lemon Salad (page 242) would be perfect. "Drowned" Ice Cream (page 293) made with vanilla ice cream, a bit of coarsely ground, toasted hazelnuts, and Scotch whisky would be my choice for dessert.

WINE: Castel del Monte (page 299), Salice Salentino (page 301), or Aglianico del Vulture (page 301)

2 *pounds lamb, from the shoulder or leg*

1½ *pounds fresh* porcini, *chanterelles, or tree-oyster mushrooms. Or 1¼ pounds commercial mushrooms and 1 ounce dried* porcini

¼ *cup virgin olive oil, or q.b.*

Salt to taste

2 *teaspoons red pepper flakes (more if you like)*

Cut the lamb into 2-inch-square pieces, or have the butcher do it for you, leaving a bit of fat here and there, or you will get no flavor, and the meat will not be as tender. You can use the shoulder if it is not too fat or cartilaginous; otherwise use the leg. Put the pieces of lamb into an ovenproof casserole dish large enough to hold all the ingredients.

Clean the mushrooms with a soft brush, or wipe them clean with a paper or kitchen towel. Do not wash them. (If you are using commercial mushrooms, this also applies. If you are using the dried *porcini*, prepare them as directed in the Italian Pantry section, page 26). Cut the mushrooms into large pieces and add them to the lamb. Add the olive oil, making sure everything gets anointed with it, sprinkle on some salt and then the red pepper flakes, and mix everything again.

Meanwhile preheat the oven to 325° F. Put the casserole in the center of the oven, and let it bake for 1¼ hours, or until the meat is well done and the mushrooms thoroughly cooked, stirring everything around every 10 minutes or so. Be sure all the juices blend, and all the ingredients have a chance to be enhanced by each other. Serve the *agnello* hot with plenty of crusty homemade bread.

About 3½ pounds russet or baking potatoes (about 5 large potatoes), rinsed well

Lard, q.b.

Unsalted butter, q.b.

2 cups grated Parmesan cheese, or q.b.

Bread crumbs, q.b.

2 cups heavy cream, or q.b.

Salt to taste

Plenty of freshly ground pepper

2 large raw eggs

4 hard-boiled large eggs, peeled and quartered

4 ounces mortadella, sliced very thin and torn into pieces

Sformato di Patate di la Cugina Maria

Cousin Mary's Potato Pudding

SERVES 6

My cousin Mary practices the kind of cooking that calls for "a pinch of that and a handful of this." Mary's magic is evident in this simple dish that shows some signs of modern times: First, the use of potatoes is not typical of Calabrian dishes, and second, there are signs of affluence in the use of cream, which is usually reserved for sweets. Mary prepared the *sformato* for me in a trice and it was eaten almost as fast because it is so delicious.

MENU SUGGESTIONS: *Antipasti* consisting of Roasted Tomatoes (page 99) and some Cauliflower Salad (page 97) would be good starters. The Potato Pudding could be a middle dish in a bigger meal followed or preceded by Skewered Pork Rolls (page 210) or Chicken, Potenza Style (page 179), or Chicken, Roman Style (page 180). Hazelnut Semifreddo (page 289) or a Lemon Ice (page 291) would be very nice choices for dessert.

WINE: Cacc 'e Mmitte di Lucera (page 299)

Boil the potatoes, unpeeled and quartered, in a pan with plenty of salted water, for 40 minutes, or until they are done but not soggy. Meanwhile, grease well a casserole dish about 9 or 10 inches around and about 3 inches high. Coat the bottom and sides with plenty of lard and some butter. Then coat the bottom and sides with the Parmesan and some bread crumbs, and set it aside for later use. Preheat the oven to 375° F, and place the rack in the middle of the oven.

When the potatoes are done, drain them well, let them cool until you can handle them, and peel them. Purée the potatoes in a food mill until they are very smooth, and put them into a bowl. Add the heavy cream, a little at a time, mixing well after every addition. Add some salt, pepper, and the 2 raw eggs, and mix the ingredients well with wet hands. This keeps the mixture from sticking to your fingers.

Spread about half of the mixture in a layer on the bottom of the casserole dish, and put some of the mixture up the sides as well so that you have a sort of "casing" of potato mixture in the casserole dish. Arrange the quartered hard-boiled eggs in concentric circles on the layer of potato mixture, scatter on the pieces of *mortadella* at random, most of the remaining Parmesan, and all of the Provolone or Mozzarella. Add a bit more salt and pepper if you think it needs it. With wet hands apply the rest of the potato mixture in a layer over the other ingredients, smoothing it out but not tamping it down. Sprinkle on the remaining Parmesan and some more bread crumbs.

Bake the casserole for 1½ hours, or until it is hot and bubbly and has a golden crust on top. Take it out of the oven and let it cool for about 15 minutes before serving it. It can be served hot or at room temperature. Most people like it hot, but it should not be served so hot that it is too difficult to eat.

Farsumagru

Rolled Steak, Stuffed Sicilian Style

SERVES 6

The Sicilian name of this dish means "false lean," the idea being that when the meat is rolled up, it looks like a lean roast. Inside is an abundance of items you might have on hand, plus a few that make the dish authentic, such as hard-boiled eggs. Beef in Sicily is rare enough; to have it stuffed with so many delicious condiments means that there is a feast lurking, probably a saint's day. In our house, a gathering of close friends is occasion enough to set this tasty dish before them.

MENU SUGGESTIONS: This special dish should be preceded by Garlic Bread, Roman Style (page 91) and Mushrooms in Parchment (page 240) as *antipasti*. Then a big dish of Spinach and Cheese Croquettes (page 154) could be an *intermezzo*, followed by a dish of Penne with *Porcini* in a Hot Tomato Sauce (page 143). The *farsumagru* could be in the company of Hot Devil Potatoes (page 243). You could have a simple salad now or go straight on to a platter full of Sicilian Cannoli (page 261) with some Moscato di Pantelleria (page 309). This is by no means a simple supper for two but rather a meal to have when you are in an expansive mood.

WINE: Monica di Sardegna (page 307)

About ½ cup cooked spinach or Swiss chard, well drained but not dried

1 small yellow onion, peeled and finely diced

About 3½ ounces extra virgin olive oil

2 pounds round steak, or similar cut of beef, cut into a single slice not more than ½ inch thick

¼ cup grated pecorino cheese

¼ cup bread crumbs

Scant ¼ pound ground veal, beef, or pork

¼ cup chopped Italian parsley

2 large raw eggs to bind mixture

Salt and pepper to taste

3 hard-boiled large eggs, peeled

Equal amounts of various cold cuts and cheeses: salami, prosciutto, Provolone or Caciocavallo cheeses in medium dice or in julienne strips, to total 1 pound or so

½ cup fresh or frozen peas

2 or 3 ounces pork fat, finely chopped

1 cup (or more if needed) dry red wine

1 cup (or more if needed) veal, beef, or chicken broth, homemade preferred (page 109)

2 tablespoons tomato paste

Wash and pick over the spinach or Swiss chard to clean it well, and put it into a medium-sized pan with a lid with just the wash water clinging to the leaves. Gently cook the spinach or Swiss chard over medium heat for about 10 minutes, or until it is tender, remove the pan from the heat, and let the spinach or Swiss chard cool. When it is cool, drain and squeeze it to remove as much water as possible. (Use the water in soup, or discard it, as you wish.)

Sauté the onions in about 3 tablespoons of the olive oil until they are just golden. Remove them from the heat, and put them into a bowl large enough to hold all of the filling later on. Keep the sauté pan handy for later use.

Have the butcher "butterfly" the slice of steak to facilitate pounding it out. Pound out the slice of meat gently to ¼ inch thick with a mallet or the flat side of a heavy cleaver, being careful not to tear it. (Sometimes the butcher cannot get a large enough slice of meat in one piece. If not, get 2 slices of equal weight, and proceed as described. You will end up with 2 smaller rolls of meat. This is perfectly acceptable.)

Mix the grated *pecorino* cheese, bread crumbs, chopped meat, and the parsley in the bowl with the sautéed onions. Add salt and pepper to taste. Add the raw eggs, and mix again. Spread the mixture evenly on the pounded meat. Lay the hard-boiled eggs lengthwise, in a row, on the meat mixture. Scatter the cold cuts, cheeses, peas, chopped pork fat, and the spinach (or Swiss chard) evenly on top of the ground-meat mixture and the hard-boiled eggs. Roll the meat tightly over the stuffing into the shape of a log, and tie it with a string in several places to secure it during the cooking period.

Brown the meat roll in a large skillet in 4 tablespoons of the olive oil, turning it often. When the meat is browned, put it into a flameproof casserole dish, and pour on the wine and the broth. Add the tomato paste, and stir the liquids well to disperse the paste. Bring the liquid to a boil, and then immediately reduce it to a simmer. Finish cooking the *farsumagru* on top of the stove at a simmer, or in the oven at 350° F for 1½ to 2 hours, turning the meat often to baste it with the liquid. There should be about 1 cup of liquid left in the pan when the meat, which is used as the sauce in the dish, is done. Remove the meat from the casserole, let it rest in a warm place for about 10 minutes, and then remove the string. Serve the *farsumagru* in slices about ¼ inch thick, on heated plates, and spoon on the remaining pan juices.

LAZIO

Baccalà al Pomodoro

Cured Cod in Tomato Sauce

SERVES 6

2 pounds dried salt cod (or stockfish)

⅓ cup extra virgin olive oil, or q.b.

2 medium yellow onions, peeled and sliced about ⅛ inch thick

2 garlic cloves, finely chopped

1 pound peeled, cored, and chopped tomatoes, or use the same amount canned

½ cup dry white wine

½ cup freshly collected rainwater (if possible) or tap water

½ teaspoon salt, or to taste

6 big grindings fresh black pepper, or to taste

Big pinch of oregano

1 teaspoon capers

2 tablespoons finely chopped parsley

See Fried Codfish, Roman Style (page 190), for details of the preparation of *baccalà*. When the fish is plump and well hydrated, cut it into pieces about 3 × 4 inches, removing bone and skin. Dry the pieces of *baccalà* with a paper towel. Set the pieces of fish aside for later use.

Heat the oil in a large frying pan, add the onions, and sauté them until they are soft but not brown. Add the garlic, and sauté it until it is golden, and add the tomatoes, white wine, water, the salt, and pepper, stirring. Be careful of the amount of salt, as the fish, which you will add soon, may still be a bit salty. Add the oregano and the capers, and cook the mixture for 15 to 20 minutes, or until it is tasty and medium thick. Add the parsley and the pieces of fish, and simmer them for about 20 minutes, or until the fish is tender and a bit flaky. Serve immediately.

This is the most popular of all *baccalà* preparations offered in homes and restaurants. *Baccalà al pomodoro* is the kind of dish to be served with chunks of crusty homemade bread, but it is equally tasty with polenta or with large chunks of boiled potatoes.

MENU SUGGESTIONS: An antipasto of Roasted Peppers with Italian-Style Tuna and Clams (page 104) would be a good start, perhaps with some Chick-peas in Olive Oil (page 95). A dish of Pasta with Red Pepper Flakes and Toasted Bread Crumbs (page 142) is a good prelude to the *baccalà*. Serve a *contorno* of Cauliflower in a Basket (page 229) and a dessert of Lucanian Fritters (page 282).

WINE: San Severo Bianco (page 301)

Cozze a Raganati

Mussels
in Bread Crumbs

SERVES 4

Raganati is surely a dialect word. It is spelled so many ways that I took the one with the fewest letters. The root is *gratinato*, in Italian, and/or *gratin*, in French. Simply put, it refers to the fact that the food is slightly burnt. Bread crumbs are often used on "*a Raganati*" dishes not only to hold in juices, but to make a little covering that holds in steam, aroma, and flavor. Bread crumbs also brown readily, easily providing baked or broiled foods with color.

This recipe is almost exactly like those I found in Sicily, except the Sicilian recipes call for chopped basil. I am sure that the variations are limited. You can see why. After doing what is described to them, it would be hard to change any ingredient, and, I am sure, the dish would taste no better. Obviously, the freshest mussels obtainable make the dish what it should be.

MENU SUGGESTIONS: A dish of Fiery Macaroni (page 138) would be a good *primo piatto* with the *cozze* being a *secondo piatto*. You could have *contorni* of Mixed Vegetable Stew (page 232) and Fried Celery (page 248). Roman Cheesecake (page 271) would be a nice dessert with this meal.

WINE: Colli Albani (page 304) with the pasta; Favonio Cabernet Franc (page 299) with the mussels

4   pounds mussels, washed and
    bearded
1⅓ cups fresh fine bread crumbs,
    lightly browned in a frying pan
    without any oil
1   teaspoon dried oregano, or to taste
    Plenty of freshly ground black
    pepper

½   cup finely chopped parsley
⅓   cup virgin olive oil
1   cup tomatoes, cored, peeled, and
    very finely chopped
½   cup dry white wine

Open the mussels by heating them in a large pan with a lid, without any liquid, over high heat, shaking the pan continuously until the mussels open. Their own juices will create steam. Lower the heat if you see signs of the mussels or the juice beginning to burn. Remove them from the heat when the shells begin to open, and cool the mussels until you can handle them. Peel off one shell on each mussel, and discard it. Put the mussels in the remaining shells in a single layer in a baking pan. If there is any mussel juice, collect it from the pan and reserve it for later use. You may want to strain it through damp cheesecloth or a paper towel to be sure to eliminate any sand that may have been disgorged by the mussels.

Preheat the oven to 450° F and move the rack to the upper third of it. Scatter on the bread crumbs, oregano, pepper, and parsley, and then drizzle on most of the olive oil. Put the mussels into the upper third of the oven, and roast them for about 5 minutes. Carefully remove the pan from the oven, and quickly scatter on the reserved mussel juice, tomatoes, and the wine. Drizzle on the remaining olive oil, and send the pan back into the oven for another 5 minutes or so. Serve the *cozze a raganati* very hot with crusty homemade bread.

NOTE: Sometimes the tomato is left out. If tomatoes are on the menu elsewhere and you do not want to repeat them, this would be a good way to prepare the dish.

L'Impepata di Cozze

Pepper-Sprinkled Mussels

MAKES 4 SERVINGS

4 pounds mussels

⅓ cup virgin olive oil

4 garlic cloves, peeled and finely chopped

⅓ cup finely chopped Italian parsley

About 1 tablespoon freshly ground black pepper, or to taste

Big pinch of salt, or to taste

4 lemons, washed, and each cut into 6 wedges

Wash the mussels in cold water and pull off their beards, if they have any. The best way to do this is to take a damp cloth and use it between your thumb and forefinger to do the pulling. This not only saves your fingers, but it gets most of the beard out because it does not slip away.

Put the olive oil into a frying pan large enough to hold the mussels, or use a roasting pan. (Roasting pans do not have suitable handles for grasping as normal frying pans have, so be sure to use fireproof potholders to move and shake the pan, if you need to.) Heat the oil, but not so it smokes, add the garlic and the mussels, and shake the pan back and forth. Stir the mussels around so that they heat evenly and all open at about the same time. The minute the mussels are open, scatter on the parsley, the black pepper, and the salt. After a moment or two, stir the mussels again to blend all the flavors. Have heated dishes or a large heated serving platter ready.

When all the mussels have opened and the flavors have blended, divide the mussels among the dishes, and pour on the pan juices. Be sure to scrape the pan well, leaving nothing behind. Arrange the lemon wedges around the mussels. There should be 1 lemon per person.

The mussels should be served piping hot with lots of crusty homemade bread. The lemon juice should be liberally squeezed on just before eating the mussels.

NOTE: There are about 20 mussels in 1 pound. That is just the right amount for 1 person for a substantial course in the meal. If the meal is light, serve even more.

This is another of Cousin Mary's dishes. In this recipe the flavors are few and very simple, each one distinguished and distinguishable. It is the kind of a dish Mary would prepare, making it seem as if she had left the dining room for only a few minutes. No fuss, no folderol, just profound simplicity. "Q.b." (*quanto basta*) is the key here, although I try to give you amounts to work with. Just close your eyes, and let the concept seep in; then let your instincts take over, but read the recipe carefully.

MENU SUGGESTIONS: If you use *l'impepata di cozze* as an antipasto, you could easily get double the yield from the recipe. Stuffed Beef Bagatelles (page 205) would be a good *pietanza* ("dish") with a *contorno* of Artichokes, Stuffed Agrigento Style (page 226), served after it. Lemon Ice (page 291) for dessert would repeat the lemon, but in a totally different treatment, which, I think, is a nice way to show the various characters of one ingredient.

WINE: Est! Est!! Est!!! (page 304) and Cesanese del Piglio (page 304)

Teglia Barese

Casserole Barese

SERVES 4 OR 6

A casserole made with vegetables, rice, mussels, and potatoes sounds a little bit as if it could be a distant cousin to *paella*. It may have common origins, if you consider that the Arabs so greatly influenced Spain and Italy. The *teglia*, which means casserole, is found in other parts of Puglia, but nowhere is it more required as part of the meal than in Bari, which rightfully claims to make the best. It is offered in almost every restaurant as an antipasto or as a *primo*.

MENU SUGGESTIONS: I would start the meal with the *teglia* and then follow with Grilled Swordfish (page 197), or Tuna and Fennel Seeds (page 201). Mixed Vegetable Stew (page 232) and/or Fried Celery (page 248) would be a good *contorno*. Lucanian Fritters (page 282) make a soothing end to the meal.

WINE: Locorotondo (page 300)

2 pounds or more fresh mussels

4 medium tomatoes, peeled, cored, and chopped medium fine

2 stalks tender celery, finely chopped

⅔ cup parsley (Italian preferred), chopped medium

2 large garlic cloves, finely chopped

⅓ cup virgin olive oil, or q.b.

4 ounces or so grated pecorino cheese

1 pound potatoes, peeled and sliced about ⅛ inch thick

12 ounces Arborio, Vialone or other plump rice, washed

Salt and pepper to taste

About 3 cups water plus the mussel juices

½ cup bread crumbs, or q.b.

Put the mussels and about ¼ cup of water in a frying pan with a lid, and cook them over high heat, covered, for 2 minutes, or until the shells have just parted. Immediately take the pan off the heat, remove the lid, and let the mussels cool. When they are cool enough to handle, remove one shell from each mussel, and discard it. Reserve the mussels in the other half of their shells and the juices in the pan for use later. Strain the juices with cheesecloth to eliminate any sand.

In a 3-quart casserole dish, arrange ⅓ of the tomatoes, celery, parsley, and garlic in an even layer, and drizzle on ⅓ of the olive oil. Sprinkle on ⅓ of the cheese, and layer on ⅓ of the potatoes. Layer on the mussels in their remaining half shell, faceup. Sprinkle on all of the rice. On top of the rice, layer another ⅓ of the tomatoes, celery, parsley, and garlic, drizzle on another ⅓ of the oil, spread another ⅓ of the cheese, and salt and pepper to taste. Layer on the remaining potatoes, then the remaining vegetables and the remaining oil. Pour the water and the reserved mussel juice evenly over the top, and sprinkle on the bread crumbs and the remaining cheese, and salt and pepper again. Depending on the exact size of your casserole, you may find that the liquid comes over the top of the potato. This is normal.

Bake the *teglia* in the top third of a preheated 375° F oven for about 1 hour and 15 minutes. If the casserole gets a little dry, add a bit of *boiling* water. This is important because if you add water that is not hot, you will stop the cooking process and, worse yet, if the water is cold, you could shatter the casserole dish. The texture of this casserole should be moist but neither dry nor runny. When it is done, let it rest for about 45 minutes. This dish should be eaten warm, not hot.

Lumache all'Origano

Snails with Oregano

SERVES 6

6 dozen large snails ready for cooking
Extra virgin olive oil, q.b.

6 garlic cloves, peeled and very finely chopped

4 leaves fresh mint, finely chopped

1 tablespoon dried oregano, or use 12 or more branches of fresh, or q.b.

Salt to taste

Plenty of freshly ground black pepper

Heat a little olive oil in a fireproof casserole dish over moderate heat, and fry the garlic. The moment the garlic is a deep gold and very fragrant, add the mint and the snails, and toss everything well. Add some salt and plenty of pepper, and then add the oregano. Cook the snails for 10 to 12 minutes, letting them get well anointed with all the flavors, over very low heat. You should end up with a slight, very highly flavored pan sauce. Serve the snails on heated plates with plenty of garlic bread (page 91) and lots of red wine.

In our home we usually prepared snails, in true southern style, in tomato sauce laced with red wine and garlic. This Pugliese recipe uses no tomato and it is excellent. You might even like it as much as the classic French preparation.

MENU SUGGESTIONS: Tomato Toasts (page 92) as an antipasto would be very nice followed by a dish of Penne with *Porcini* in a Hot Tomato Sauce (page 143). The snails could be an *intermezzo* before some Breaded Lamb Chops (page 186) or some Homemade Sicilian Sausage (page 188). A good *contorno* would be Spinach, Roman Style (page 245), and some String Bean Bundles (page 235). My choice for dessert would be a "Drowned" Ice Cream (page 293).

WINE: Cirò Rosso (page 302)

Pecorelle in Salsa

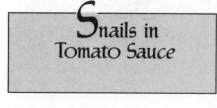

Snails in
Tomato Sauce

SERVES 6

In Basilicata, where snails are referred to as *pecorelle* ("little sheep"), these are a favorite. Although it can be eaten any time, this dish is usually part of a large, festive meal. You can serve *pecorelle* at the beginning as an opener, or as a major dish. In either case, *pecorelle* call for lots of crusty homemade bread and crocks of red wine.

MENU SUGGESTIONS: Antipasto of Mushrooms in Parchment (page 240) would be a good starter. Tuna and Fennel Seeds (page 201) and the snails could be two *secondi* with *contorni* of Sweet-and-Sour Baby Onions (page 234) and some String Bean Bundles (page 235). Walnut Cake #1 (page 276) and some Marsala Vergine (page 309) would be a good ending to this meal.

WINE: Cirò Rosso (page 302)

6 dozen snails ready for cooking

⅓ cup virgin olive oil

3 large garlic cloves, peeled and crushed until almost a purée

2 pounds tomatoes, cored, peeled, and well crushed by hand

Salt to taste

1 teaspoon dried oregano

1 tablespoon red pepper flakes

Put the prepared snails in a bowl ready for later use. Be sure to provide picks or oyster forks if you serve the snails in their shells.

Heat the olive oil in a large frying pan over medium heat and when it is hot, fry the garlic until it is deep gold. Add the tomatoes, stir the mixture well, and cook them for about 15 minutes. Add some salt, the oregano, and the red pepper flakes, and stir the sauce well. Add the snails, and cook them for about 15 minutes, or until they are tender.

Serve the snails very hot in heated shallow soup plates, with plenty of crusty homemade bread.

CLEANING SQUID

Cleaning squid is easy and, once you are organized, you can finish the job in minutes. If the squid are fresh, put them into very cold water to wash them. If they are frozen, defrost them slowly by placing them in a bowl and refrigerating them for at least 24 hours. If you thaw them too fast, their texture is not as tender. When the squid are soft and pliable, you can proceed to clean them.

There are two very large eyes in the head, behind which is a large ink sac. (Some cooks save this ink and put it into pasta sauces or in *risotto Nero*, "black rice.")

Lay the squid down on a cutting board and with a sharp knife, cut the tentacles off just below the eyes. Discard the eyes, unless you are going to save the ink, in which case have a little glass handy to collect it. If the ink sac is not broken, pierce it with the tip of the knife or a cooking needle, and gently squeeze the ink into the glass. Discard the eyes. Save the ink for later use by covering it well with clear plastic wrap and freezing it, or use it immediately. It will not keep well, just refrigerated, for more than 2 days. Put the bodies, or sacs, in a bowl of cold water.

Pick up the tentacles, and squeeze the top firmly. This will expel a round marble-like object that is the mouth. It has a very sharp little beak like a rose thorn in it, and it is not good eating. Discard. Put the tentacles into a separate bowl of cold water. If you mix tentacles and sacs, the sacs will turn purple from the color on the surface of the tentacles.

Line up the sacs, which are yet to be cleaned, in neat rows. Get a heavy cook's knife. Lay one sac down, with the open end to your right, on a cutting board, and hold the pointed tip of the squid down very tightly with your left thumb or forefinger (whichever is strongest). Place the blunt side of the knife (opposite the cutting edge) down just next to your finger and using very heavy pressure, slide the knife along the length of the squid. This should expel all the innards, including the long clear cuttle bone that looks like a feather. If this action does not expel the cuttle bone, simply ease it out with the point of the knife, or reach in with your finger and pull it out. This action also loosens and pretty much removes the dark gray skin of the squid. (It is perfectly all right to eat the skin but some people think it makes the dish look messy because it fragments during cooking. It also has a dye that can color the juices.) Leave the little fins on the squid, as they are just as good as the sac, and it is wasteful to not use them. They should remain attached, but if they don't, simply add them to your dish at cooking time. Place all of the cleaned sacs in the bowl with fresh cold water.

When you have finished cleaning all of the squid, wash the tentacles and sacs again, separately, in very cold water. The squid are now ready to use any way you like.

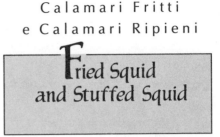

Fried Squid and Stuffed Squid

Squid has recently become popular in America, especially in California. Of course, it has been a staple in the Mediterranean diet for millennia, and it is treated in many different ways. The following recipes display the diversity of taste and texture of squid.

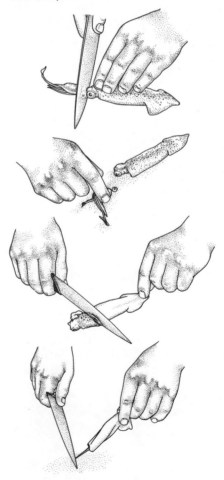

Calamari Fritti

Fried Squid

SERVES 4 TO 6

12 *large squid*

2 *cups all-purpose flour for dredging (you will have some left over), q.b.*

Salt and pepper to taste

½ *cup chopped parsley*

3 *lemons, each cut into 12 wedges, for juice and decoration*

About 2 cups oil for frying (vegetable or olive)

Clean and wash the squid thoroughly (see page 173). Dry and cut them into pieces of any shape or size you like. Most people cut the bodies crosswise, making little circles. The tentacles are left whole, unless they are too big, in which case cut them in half or thirds, lengthwise (not across).

Mix together the flour, salt, and pepper in a paper or plastic bag. Add several pieces of squid (not too many), and shake the bag vigorously. Remove the *calamari* from the bag, shaking any loose flour off them.

Heat the oil in a deep frying pan to 360° F, and fry the squid in the hot oil until they are golden. Remove them from the oil with a slotted spoon, and drain them on absorbent towels. Do this until all the *calamari* are fried. Place them on a heated platter, put the lemon wedges among the *calamari*, and toss them all together. Sprinkle them generously with chopped parsley. Serve the *calamari* hot.

NOTE: Do not flour the *calamari* too far in advance of frying or they will become sticky and doughy. Some people like to dredge *calamari* in flour, place them in a beaten egg, and then roll them in finely chopped fresh bread crumbs. Proceed as above.

18 *medium squid, about 2 pounds*
    total, or a bit more
    Virgin olive oil, q.b.

2 *lemons*

3 *whole salted anchovies, washed and*
   bones removed, or use 5 anchovy
   filets packed in olive oil

1 *or 2 large garlic cloves, peeled and*
   well crushed

⅓ *cup finely chopped parsley*

⅓ *cup freshly ground bread crumbs*

1 *large egg*
   Salt to taste

5 *or 6 grindings of fresh black*
   pepper

Calamari Ripieni

Stuffed Squid

SERVES 6

Prepare the squid for cooking (see Fried Squid and Stuffed Squid, page 173, for method). Put the bodies in a separate bowl, and set them aside in the refrigerator for later use. Put the tentacles into a small frying pan with some olive oil, and cook them over medium heat for about 2 minutes. When they are done, sprinkle them with the juice from ¼ lemon, remove them with a slotted spoon, chop them into tiny bits, and put them into a bowl. Finely chop the anchovy and the garlic, and add them to the bowl. Add the parsley and the bread crumbs, and drizzle on about 1 tablespoon of olive oil. Add the egg, some salt, and black pepper, and mix all the ingredients well.

Preheat the oven to 375° F. Stuff the squid bodies with equal amounts of the tentacle and bread crumb mixture, securing the openings of the squid with a toothpick or a metal skewer. Brush the stuffed *calamari* well with olive oil, and put them into an ovenproof casserole dish. Sprinkle on some salt and freshly ground black pepper. Roast the squid for 15 minutes, or until they have turned white and firm, basting them often with the casserole juices, and drizzle on a bit more olive oil. When the stuffed squid are done, sprinkle on the juice of ½ lemon, and serve them hot. Pass more lemon at the table.

If you are going to cook the stuffed squid on an open fire, brush them liberally with olive oil, and cook them on the medium hot part of a grill for about 5 minutes, basting them often with fresh olive oil, and turning them often. When they have turned white with brown grill marks on them, they are done. Put them on a heated tray, sprinkle on the juice of ½ lemon, and serve them hot. Pass more lemon at the table.

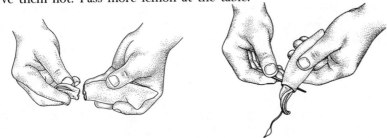

NOTE: You can make the squid even more beautiful if you save the tentacles and add a bit more stuffing. Place the tentacles back into the openings so that they look as they originally did. Secure them with toothpicks, and proceed as directed. When you serve the *calamari*, either leave the toothpicks in or remove them before bringing the *calamari* to the table.

Throughout all the regions of Southern Italy, there is a local rendition of stuffed squid. From being stewed, in tomatoes to being braised in a pan with mushrooms and wine, the ingenuity is endless. This Sardinian version is versatile because you can cook the squid either in the oven or on an open wood fire. The anchovies add a certain piquancy. Be careful not to overcook the squid because that piquancy will lose its original character.

MENU SUGGESTIONS: An antipasto of Chick-peas in Olive Oil (page 95), some Tomato Toasts (page 92), and Marinated Zucchini (page 100) would be good. The *calamari* could have a *contorno* of Artichokes Stuffed with Ricotta and Salami (page 227). A Semifreddo (page 286) with some kind of nuts would be a welcome dessert at such a meal.

WINE: Vesuvio Bianco (page 304)

Trotelle al Pomodoro

Pan-Simmered Baby Trout

SERVES 6

The River Sangro in the Abruzzo gives up some of the world's best trout. The icy mountain water is perfect for the fish, and they are in such abundance that the tiny ones are often used to flavor tomato sauce and then discarded! This is the rarest display of waste I ever saw in Italy. Paolo Scipioni, the owner of the wonderful restaurant Tre Marie, in L'Aquila, was sheepish when he told me this. Maybe that explains why the sauce here is known locally as *senza parlare*, which means "don't talk." Although there are many delicious trout preparations in the Abruzzo, this way is not only the most characteristic but the most flavorful.

MENU SUGGESTIONS: A dish of Chickpeas in Olive Oil (page 95) and some Marinated Zucchini (page 100) would be good as *antipasti*. I would like two *pietanze* or *secondi piatti*. The trout could be followed by another second dish of Macaroni and Roast in Natural Juices (page 212). This would be a big meal but an unusual one for the American palate. The Italians would find such a meal normal. Chocolate Bread (page 284) is an appropriately simple dessert.

WINE: Salice Salentino (page 301)

¼ cup virgin olive oil

2 large garlic cloves, peeled and well crushed

1½ pounds tomatoes, cored, peeled, and well crushed, or use same amount of canned

Big pinch of salt

5 grindings of fresh black pepper

¼ cup finely chopped parsley

6 6-ounce trout, cleaned and dressed for cooking (optional: with heads and tails left on)

Heat the oil in a large frying pan or other wide-bottomed pan large enough to hold all the fish later until it is hot but not smoking. Add the garlic, and turn the heat down immediately. When the garlic is brown but not burned, add the tomatoes, salt, pepper, and parsley. Stir everything well, and simmer the sauce for 15 minutes, or until it becomes slightly dense. When this happens, push the trout into the sauce so that they are slightly covered with it. If the sauce does not seem sufficient, spoon some over the trout to try to cover them. Cook the trout for 6 to 8 minutes, or until the flesh flakes when tested with a fork. Serve the trout on heated plates, and spoon some sauce on each one. Crusty homemade bread should accompany this dish of simple trout.

NOTE: Another marvelous way of serving trout, which they do at Tre Marie, is to lay some thinly sliced potatoes on the bottom of a clay casserole and drizzle them with some olive oil, then scatter on salt and pepper and a few cured black olives, and roast the potatoes in the oven until done. Place the trout, which has been cleaned of any little bones and quickly roasted in a very hot oven or even on a grill, splayed out over the potatoes. Cover the casserole with parchment paper and return to the oven for a short time. The trout finishes cooking by the vapors from the potatoes and gives off its own contribution in juices.

⅓ cup virgin olive oil

2 garlic cloves, peeled and well crushed

1 large carrot, scraped and chopped into tiny pieces

1 large yellow onion, peeled and finely chopped

2 branches celery, washed and finely chopped

½ teaspoon dried oregano

1 lemon, cut into thin slices

⅓ cup coarsely chopped parsley

1 large fresh tomato, cored, peeled, and well crushed

Salt to taste

6 big grindings of fresh black pepper, or q.b.

1 peach or apricot kernel (optional, see headnote)

6 8-ounce trout, cleaned and ready for cooking

2 cups, or q.b., Vernaccia di Oristano wine (see the headnote for an alternative)

In a deep frying pan large enough to hold all the ingredients, heat the olive oil over moderately high heat. When the oil is quite hot, fry the crushed garlic until it is a deep gold and very aromatic. Add all the other ingredients, except the trout and the wine, stirring all the ingredients well and making sure they are lightly coated with the garlic-flavored oil. Fry the ingredients until the slightest gold color develops on the major vegetables. Reduce the heat, and stir again.

Spread the ingredients evenly over the bottom of the pan and lay the trout on them. Pour on the wine, using more or less enough to cover the vegetables and come halfway up the trout. Let the trout cook for about 5 minutes on one side, carefully turn them over, and cook them on the other side for another 5 minutes, or until the flesh just flakes when tested with a fork. Carefully remove the trout with a slotted spoon or spatula, and put them on a heated platter. Cover them with aluminum foil or another heated platter, and set them aside in a warm spot. Strain the vegetable mixture through a sieve into a bowl, pushing down hard on the solids with a wooden spoon to get all the juices and flavor out. Discard the solids. Put the liquid back into the frying pan, and reduce it over high heat until there is just enough left to make a bit of sauce for each trout, perhaps 1 cup total.

Serve the trout on heated plates, and spoon some of the juices over them.

Trota alla Vernaccia

Trout Vernaccia

SERVES 6

Vernaccia di Oristano from Sardegna may not be available in American wine shops. (Vernaccia di Oristano has nothing to do with Vernaccia di San Gemignano, a Tuscan wine, by the way.) My friend Darrell Corti, a wine scholar, gave me a recipe for a good substitute. Mix 3 parts California Golden Sherry from a maker such as Christian Brothers, with 1 part dry white vermouth, such as Cinzano or Martini and Rossi. The vermouth has a higher alcohol content than a dry white wine and therefore is more in keeping with the spirit of Vernaccia di Oristano. For that essential characteristic undertaste of bitterness, add 1 kernel, well crushed, from the pit of a peach or apricot. This adds just enough of that *amaro* ("bitter") taste, providing zesty body to the finished flavor of the dish.

MENU SUGGESTIONS: Start out with a dish of Vermicelli, Prince of Naples Style (page 150), followed by the Trout Vernaccia with *contorni* of String Bean Bundles (page 235) and Italian Potato Pancake (page 246). A nice piece of Sicilian Cassata (page 266) would be a fine finish to this meal.

WINE: Corvo Bianco (page 308) or Vernaccia di Oristano (page 308) for the trout; Girò di Cagliari Liquoroso (page 307) with the cassata

Pollo Arrosto con Rosmarino

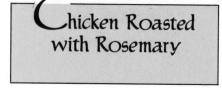

Chicken Roasted with Rosemary

SERVES 6

Chicken is not used in the South as much as it is used in the North of Italy. This dish is reserved for special times. It is heaven and utterly simple to make.

MENU SUGGSTIONS: Serve the chicken with Mushrooms in Parchment (page 240) and follow with a bowl of fresh fruit.

WINE: Monica di Sardegna (page 307)

1 *roasting chicken (about 3½ pounds), washed and carefully dried*

3 *medium-sized garlic cloves, peeled and crushed*

1 *medium carrot, washed and cut into small pieces*

1 *stalk celery, washed and cut into small pieces*

Half a medium-sized onion, peeled and cut into quarters

Salt and pepper to taste

About ¼ cup virgin olive oil

5 *4-inch-long sprigs of fresh rosemary*

1 *lemon, cut in half*

Preheat the oven to 375° F. Put the garlic, carrot, celery, and onion into the cavity of the chicken with salt and pepper, 1 tablespoon of olive oil, and 3 springs of rosemary. Place the rest on the bird later. Truss the bird for appearance so that it looks neat and tidy. Rub the chicken all over with 2 tablespoons of the oil. Add more salt, and massage the bird again very well. Tuck one of the remaining 2 sprigs of rosemary into each wing, so that they are close to the body. These outside sprigs may well burn up during the roasting if they are too exposed, so tuck them almost under the wings. But in any case, do not worry because even burned they will give that characteristic rosemary flavor to the chicken.

Add about 1 tablespoon of oil to the roasting pan and spread it around. Then lay the chicken on its side to roast for the first 15 minutes. Turn it over to cook on the other side for 15 minutes. Then turn it on its back, which will mean the breast is up, for about 1 hour more. Every time you turn it, baste the chicken with the oil and pan juices. A turkey baster works very well for this job or else just use a large metal spoon. Continue to roast the chicken until it is cooked, basting as often as you can. When it is done it should have an internal temperature of 165° F at the thickest part of the thigh meat. In Italy chickens are cooked longer and as a result they can be dry. You can cook yours longer if you like, but do not overcook too much because then you won't enjoy the taste and juiciness of the chicken. As soon as the chicken is out of the oven, squeeze the lemon juice all over it.

Let the chicken rest in its juices for about 10 minutes and then remove it to a heated dish and keep it in a warm place. Skim off and discard most of the fat from the top of the liquid remaining in the roasting pan. Thoroughly scrape the pan of any bits of skin and pour them, along with any other pan juices, into a frying pan. Cook the juices on high heat for about 2 minutes to reduce them a bit and then strain them through a sieve into a hot gravy boat. By the time you have done this, the chicken will have rested a total of 20 minutes, which is just about right. If you serve chicken too hot or try to carve it too hot, your results neither taste nor look as good. Carve the chicken and serve it on warm plates. Spoon on the pan juices. Some people like to eat the vegetables that were in the cavity. They are delicious and soaked with juices.

1 2½-pound chicken cut into 8 pieces

1 tablespoon lard for frying

1 tablespoon olive oil for frying
   Virgin olive oil, q.b., for rubbing on the potatoes

1 large yellow onion, peeled and cut into thin slices

½ teaspoon, q.b., red pepper flakes

1 cup dry white wine

2 large tomatoes, cored, peeled, and well crushed

¼ cup finely chopped parsley

12 large leaves fresh basil, coarsely chopped

   Salt to taste

2 large peeled roasting potatoes cut into eighths the long way

Pollo alla Potentina

Chicken, Potenza Style

SERVES 4

Wipe the chicken well to be sure it is dry and cut it into halves, then into fourths, and then into eighths. Heat the lard and the oil over a medium flame in a heavy frying pan that will hold all the chicken. When the fat is hot, add the pieces of chicken, a few at a time, and brown them well. Turn them once or twice. Rub olive oil on the potatoes and roast in a preheated 400° F oven. The pieces may overlap—flip them to brown.

As the chicken begins to brown add the onion and brown it also. Add the red pepper flakes and stir everything well. When you see the ingredients in the pan taking on a red blush from the pepper flakes, add the wine, ¼ cup at a time. Shake the pan vigorously after each addition of wine. When the wine has evaporated, add the crushed tomatoes, parsley, basil, and salt. Lower the heat a bit and cook all the ingredients for another 20 minutes or so or until the tomatoes have tightened up a bit and the chicken is just finishing cooking. Add the oven-roasted browned potatoes to the chicken and carefully spoon the tomatoes and pan juices all over them. This is a succulent not wet dish that yields a light coating of thick pan juices.

NOTE: Sometimes plain sautéed mushrooms are served, on the side, as a *contorno* to this dish.

Lard and olive oil for frying, and red pepper flakes in abundance for a rousing taste, tempered by soothing potatoes, meld this dish into a trademark of Potenza.

MENU SUGGESTIONS: A cold antipasto of Mussels with Saffron (page 103) would be wonderful before. The chicken is especially good with sautéed mushrooms. Pears in Chocolate (page 285) would be an elegant ending.

WINE: Corvo Bianco (page 308) with the mussels; Torre Quarto Rosso (page 301) or Sangiovese di Aprilia (page 306), served slightly chilled, with the chicken

Pollo alla Romana

Chicken, Roman Style

SERVES 4

The farther south you go, the fewer chicken dishes you see because the meats of choice and availability are lamb and pork. *Pollo alla Romana* is probably in the category of *cacciatore*, which means "hunter style," and as a result gives one license to have a rather free-form recipe.

MENU SUGGESTIONS: "Phone-Wire" Rice Croquettes (page 96) are a natural choice as an antipasto. Green Beans in Olive Oil and Lemon Juice (page 237) or Mushrooms Roasted with Pine Nuts (page 239) would be excellent *contorni*. For dessert a Semifreddo (page 286) or "Drowned" Ice Cream (page 293) is a good choice.

WINE: Etna Rosso (page 308)

1 *frying chicken, about 2½ pounds ready for cooking, cut into 8 pieces*

1½ *tablespoons lard for frying*

3 *ounces* prosciutto, *thinly sliced and julienned*

2 *large garlic cloves, peeled and well crushed*

3 *large tomatoes, cored, peeled, and well crushed*

⅔ *cup dry white wine*

1½ *tablespoons fresh marjoram or 1 teaspoon dried*

Salt to taste

5 *grindings of fresh black pepper*

Optional: *1 large green or red bell pepper, cored and seeded and cut into scant ¼-inch-thick slices*

Cut the chicken into halves, then into quarters and then into eighths. Heat the frying pan and add the lard. When the lard begins to sizzle, add the chicken pieces and fry them until they are a deep gold. Turn them once during cooking. If you are going to use bell pepper, add it now and let it soften just a little. Add the *prosciutto* and the garlic. When the garlic is well browned and smells pungent, add the tomatoes and carefully stir everything around. Add the wine slowly. Cook the chicken at simmer for about 5 minutes and then add the marjoram and the salt and pepper. Stir again. Gently simmer for about 20 minutes more or until the chicken is done. Serve the chicken very hot and have plenty of crusty homemade bread to go with it.

If you have a clay pot that can go on a flame on top of the stove, you could use it and then take it to the table and serve from it. That would be my choice.

Pomegranate
Quail

SERVES 6

1 *large pomegranate*

2 *medium-sized mint leaves, finely
chopped*

Dry Marsala wine to taste

Salt and pepper to taste

6 *quail, dressed*

6 *thin slices* pancetta

2 *navel oranges*

*About 5 ounces (about 10
tablespoons) sweet butter, or q.b.*

*About 10 or 12 whole fresh sage
leaves*

Remove the seeds from the pomegranate, place them in a small bowl with the chopped mint leaves, and just barely cover them with some Marsala. Let them sit for about an hour or even longer.

Salt and pepper the quail well, and truss them, wrapping each one in a slice of *pancetta* and securing the *pancetta* by tucking it in under the wings after the final wrapping. If the *pancetta* seems loose, hold it in place with toothpicks, but be sure to remove them before serving the quail. Set the quail aside.

Carefully peel the oranges so that they do not have any pith (white membrane just under the skin), and slice them crosswise ¼ inch thick. Set them aside.

Strain the pomegranate seeds and mint in a colander, reserving the Marsala, and stuff the quail with them. If there are any seeds left over, add them to the dish later.

In an ovenproof skillet sauté the quail wrapped in the *pancetta* in about 1 ounce (2 tablespoons) of butter over high heat until they are very brown. Add the whole sage leaves and any remaining pomegranate seeds, splash on some of the reserved Marsala, and finish cooking the quail in a preheated 375° F oven for about 10 minutes. Midway during the oven cooking, add the rest of the Marsala and 2 ounces (4 tablespoons) butter to the quail. Mix all of the pan juices around, and be sure the butter melts and coats everything. Do not overcook the quail. They should be rare and nice and pink.

Meantime, in a separate frying pan, gently sauté the orange slices in about 2 ounces (about 4 tablespoons) butter over low heat, being careful not to break them up. After about 5 minutes, remove them and arrange them in the center of a heated platter. When the quail are done, remove them from the oven, and arrange them on the sautéed orange slices. Spoon onto the quail any pomegranate seeds that were in the roasting pan, and drizzle on the pan juices. Serve immediately.

This is a baronial eighteenth-century dish from Sicily, from the period when the aristocratic families wielded great power and ate well. I think it ranks with any I have tasted in the grand restaurants of France and America. There is even a French connection here. In the great houses, the *capo cuoco*, or "chef," was called by the Sicilian aristocracy the highest name they could give someone who was not of their own ranks; that is, *monzu*, a corruption of *monsieur*, meaning "master" or "gentleman." That name still is used today in a house or two, though the fact is very well hidden. In the *piazze* the "*monzus*" would join each other in an evening stroll or a chat. They would stand apart from other less highly regarded cooks who did not have a similar title, and certainly away from everyone else who they thought might overhear their secret talks about recipes and the eating habits of their masters.

MENU SUGGESTIONS: Tomato Toasts (page 92) would be a good starter course. Potato Croquettes (page 231) would be delicious as a side dish or just preceding the quail. This dish calls for a festive dessert; Sicilian Cassata (page 266) would be a fine choice.

WINE: Taurasi (page 304), Aglianico del Vulture (page 301), or Montepulciano d'Abruzzo (page 298)

Coniglio all'Ischitana

Rabbit, Ischian Style

SERVES 4

This scrumptious dish is from my friend Domenico Manzon. Although there are many variations of it, he tells me this one is the most authentic.

MENU SUGGESTIONS: A steaming hot bowl of Bread and Cheese Soup (page 118) would be a good soup before the rabbit. After, you could have Artichokes Stuffed with Ricotta and Salami (page 227) as a *contorno*. After such a meal, which is quite substantial, I think a Semifreddo (page 286) would be ideal.

WINE: Merlot di Aprilia (page 306) or Torre Ercolana (page 306)

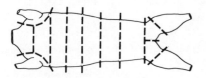

1 *2½-pound rabbit, dressed for cooking and cut into pieces*
   All-purpose flour for dredging

3 *tablespoons virgin olive oil*

4 *ounces* pancetta, *cut into very small pieces*

1 *4-inch branch fresh rosemary (if you must, use 1 level tablespoon dried)*

3 *big fresh sage leaves (if necessary, use dried whole leaves; see Italian Pantry, page 32)*
   Salt to taste
   Plenty of freshly ground black pepper

2 *pounds tomatoes, cored, peeled, and well crushed*

⅔ *cup dry white wine*

⅔ *cup boiling water, or q.b.*

Cut the rabbit into 10 pieces. Cut off the back legs and thighs, leaving them attached to the backbone, then cleave the backbone in half, separating the back legs. These are the two biggest pieces that the rabbit yields. Cut off the front legs where they attach to the body. You should now have a long sausagelike body left. Cut it crosswise into about 6 pieces approximately 2 inches wide. (Some people like to cut the belly off up to the end of the ribs, but this is so insignificant a portion that I simply leave it attached to the ribs.)

Spread the flour in a low-sided dish, and dredge the rabbit pieces in it. Heat the oil in a large fireproof casserole dish over moderately high heat, and fry the rabbit pieces until they are golden. Set them aside in a bowl. Fry the *pancetta* in the hot oil until it is light gold in color. Add the rosemary, sage, some salt, and pepper, and stir everything very well, being careful not to let anything burn. Add the tomatoes all at once, stirring, let them heat up until they simmer, then lower the heat, and let the resulting sauce simmer for about 10 minutes. Add the pieces of rabbit, 1 or 2 at a time, pushing them into the sauce. Pour the wine on, and continue to simmer the sauce, but over higher heat. After about 20 minutes, when the sauce has gotten fairly dense, add the boiling water, and gently mix everything to blend the flavors. Cook the rabbit until the sauce becomes slightly dense. Remove the casserole from the heat, and let the rabbit rest for about 10 minutes. Serve it very hot with crusty bread.

NOTE: Some Ischians do not dredge the rabbit in flour before browning it; some add basil instead of sage; and some put in red pepper flakes instead of black pepper. Some others add a bay leaf, and still others add some carrot and celery to the tomatoes, but first they fry them in a little oil.

You could do as the Italians do: Cook a batch of pasta, any kind you like, while the rabbit is resting, and use the rabbit sauce on it as a first dish. Then you could have the rabbit meat, kept aside warm, as your second dish.

2 *generous pounds beef in slices about*
    ⅜ inch thick

¼ *cup virgin olive oil, or q.b.*
    Plenty of salt
    Plenty of freshly ground black
    pepper

4 *garlic cloves, peeled and well*
    crushed

5 *or 6 large ripe tomatoes, cored,*
    peeled, and well crushed

About 1½ teaspoons dry oregano,
or 6 4-inch sprigs fresh

Optional: About ½ cup dry white
wine

Bistecca alla
Pizzaiola

SERVES 6

Flatten the meat with the meat pounder of your choice to a little less than ¼ inch thick, being careful not to break the meat. Cut it into pieces about 3 by 4 inches, or whatever size you like.

Heat the oil in a heavy frying pan large enough to hold all the ingredients. A fireproof casserole dish is ideal. When the oil is quite hot, add the meat, brown one side over high heat, and turn it over to brown the other side. This is only to sear it and should not take more than a minute or two to do. Add the garlic, and let it turn gold. Salt and pepper to taste, making sure it is enough to make a difference.

Scatter on the tomatoes and the oregano. If it is in sprigs, pull the leaves off as best you can, and scatter them all around. I throw the twigs in as well. If you are using the optional wine, add it now. Reduce the heat, and let the meat cook. If it is crossrib, it will only take a few minutes. If it is top round, it will take about 10 to 12 minutes. (This meat is never rare unless you use very thick cuts of rib. Although this is sometimes done in Italy, it is not common. I would save such a cut for grilling over a live fire.)

When the meat is tender and done, serve it on heated plates, and spoon on some of the sauce from the pan. If you have thicker slices of meat, you can do as some Neapolitans do: Cook some spaghetti or *penne*, timed to be drained when the meat is done. Hold the meat back in a warm place, spoon the tomato sauce from the meat on it, and have that as your first dish. Serve the meat separately as your second dish.

The most important element in this dish is *origano selvatico*, wild oregano, which is hard to come by, at least locally. You can use imported dried Italian or Greek oregano with very good results. In many parts of Italy where this dish is appreciated, but none more than Naples, you often get veal rib, which assures a more tender rendition of the dish. When selecting the beef, buy the type that is tasty and will cook relatively fast. Use a slice of top round or, if you have bought a large cross-rib roast, cut a large slice from it and make a mighty fine *bistecca alla pizzaiola*.

MENU SUGGESTIONS: You could have Mushrooms in Parchment (page 240) for an antipasto, followed by a dish of "Phone-Wire" Rice Croquettes (page 96). After you have the Beefsteak Pizzaiola, a big glass of "Drowned" Ice Cream (page 293) would seem perfect.

WINE: Aglianico del Vulture (page 301) or Fiorano Rosso (page 305)

Manzo Garofolato

Braised Beef, Roman Style

SERVES 6

3 ounces hard, firm fatback, in one piece

2 garlic cloves, peeled and pounded into a paste

6 whole cloves

3 pounds beef top round, or similar cut, in one piece

2 ounces prosciutto *fat*, or 4 tablespoons butter

Salt to taste

Freshly ground pepper to taste

3 tablespoons parsley, finely chopped

2 big scrapings of nutmeg

3 cups dry red wine

1 cup fresh tomatoes, cored, peeled and finely chopped (or use same amount of Marinara Sauce, page 78)

Optional (and often done):

1 yellow onion, finely chopped

1 carrot, scraped and very finely chopped

1 stalk celery, finely chopped

Obviously this dish is not everyday fare in Southern Italy, as beef is a scarce item. That does not mean it does not exist at all. With the exception of the Chianina beef, so highly prized by the Tuscans, the meat used here has fat marbled in the tissue and it is at its best eaten braised. *Manzo Garofolato* therefore calls for larding, which means inserting fat into the tissue with a special needle prior to cooking it, because it carries flavor and juiciness to the mass of muscle itself. The fat is the flavor carrier of the garlic and the cloves as well as giving a moister taste and texture to the beef. It is traditional in southern Italy to eat meats, braised or sometimes roasted, as a second dish with the majority of their juices reserved for saucing a first dish of pasta or risotto or polenta.

MENU SUGGESTIONS: Sweet-and-Sour Baby Onions (page 234) would be a good antipasto followed by a dish of spaghetti, or *fusilli*, or better yet, *bucatini* (see Dry Packaged Pasta, page 127) with the braising sauce on it, and then a slice of Golden Christmas Bread (page 280) for dessert.

WINE: Aglianico del Vulture (page 301) or Rosso del Salento (page 301)

Make sure the fatback is very cold and firm. Put it into the freezer for half an hour so it will be easier to slice. With a thin knife cut the fat into as many 3/16-inch-square batons as you can, depending on the shape of it. Try to get the batons about 4 inches long. Put them into a small bowl, and set them aside for the moment.

Purée the garlic in a mortar and pestle. If you do not have one, put the peeled garlic clove down on a board, and sprinkle a tiny bit of salt on it. Scrape and mash it with a stiff steel table knife until the garlic is disintegrated and like a purée. You may continue to mash it this way for a moment or two longer. Put the puréed garlic and the whole cloves into the bowl with the lard batons, and mix them gently so that the batons are well covered with them. Let the batons marinate for at least 2 hours. (Even longer is better. This step could be done the day before, and the batons stored in the refrigerator overnight.)

Wipe any moisture off the meat. Determine which direction the grain of the meat is going.

The modern larding needle has a little serrated hinged clamp on the end of it. Scrape the garlic off the lard baton. Pull open the clamp, put the tip of the lard baton into it, and close it. This grasps the baton and holds it firmly. Some larding needles have a flared, fluted, and slit opening at one end into which you jam the baton of lard. The pressure of the meat, as you put the needle through it, holds the baton secured on the flared end until you pull the needle through and release it.

The baton should now look like a giant white thread at the rear end of the needle. Be sure the fat and the needle are long enough to go through the meat so that at least the sharp tip of the needle can be pulled through to complete the threading of the lard baton. Push the needle into the meat and gently start pulling the tip of it out the moment it appears at the opposite side. When the clamp is exposed, open it, and the lard will be released to remain in the meat. Continue until you have inserted all the batons in an arc into the meat. Push the 6 whole cloves at random into any of the needle holes, but being sure to stud the meat evenly. Reserve the garlic purée for later use.

Heat a heavy casserole dish that can later double as a braising pan, and heat the *prosciutto* fat in it over low heat. When the fat is melted, turn the heat up, and let the fat get very hot. Put the roast into the pan, and brown it well on both ends and all around.

If you plan to use the optional vegetable ingredients, remove the browned meat, lower the heat, and put them in the pan. Cook them for 12 minutes, or until they are just transparent. Put the meat back into the pan, and proceed with the recipe.

Mix the salt, pepper, chopped parsley, and the nutmeg, plus any remaining garlic purée, with the wine and tomatoes in a large bowl, and pour the mixture all over the meat. It should come up the sides of the meat two thirds of the way. Put a lid on the braising pan (casserole dish), and gently simmer it over low heat for about 2 hours. (However, I prefer braising in the oven because the heat is more even and gentle. It also prevents burning the bottom of the pan, which can easily happen on top of the stove. If you choose to do this, preheat the oven to 325° F before putting the pan in. Braise it for the same amount of time.)

Test the doneness of the meat by piercing it with a fork. The fork should withdraw with no effort. If it does not, let the meat cook another half hour or so. Approximately half the liquid should have evaporated. If there seems to be too much liquid when you are ready to serve, remove the meat to a warm place, and reduce the pan juices over high heat until you have approximately half the original amount.

When you are ready to serve the meat, cut it across the grain in ¼-inch slices, and serve it hot with very little of the resulting juices from the cooking.

Braccioletti d'Abbacchio Panate

Breaded Lamb Chops

SERVES 6

Italians like their lamb slightly rare and this recipe preserves the character of the meat superbly. Don't be fooled by the simplicity of this dish. A platter of *braccioletti* will disappear in seconds. You should serve them at a special event. A birthday, anniversary, or a holiday would all be good excuses for making them.

MENU SUGGESTIONS: Roasted Peppers with Italian-Style Tuna and Clams (page 104) would be good for an antipasto. A *contorno* of Artichokes Stuffed with Ricotta and Salami (page 227) and/or Hot Devil Potatoes (page 243) for the *braccioletti* is ideal. "Drowned" Ice Cream (page 293) is a good choice for dessert.

WINE: Taurasi (page 304) or Cirò Rosso (page 302)

18 *rib chops from a very young lamb (leave the bones rather long)*

Salt to taste

Plenty of freshly ground black pepper

3 *large eggs, beaten*

Plenty of bread crumbs

½ *cup virgin olive oil*

Pound the lamb chops with a meat bat or the flat side of a heavy meat cleaver as flat as you can without breaking them. Lay them out in a single layer, and salt and pepper them well. Beat the eggs in a low-sided dish. Spread the bread crumbs in another low-sided dish. Dip each chop into the beaten eggs, and then dredge it in the bread crumbs. Make sure the bread crumbs stick.

Heat a large, heavy frying pan, and add the oil. The oil must be hot but not excessively hot; 360° F would be ideal. Fry the lamb chops, a few at a time, for about 1 minute on each side. As they are finished, put them on an absorbent towel to drain. Keep the chops as hot as possible by putting them onto a heated platter and into a 375° F oven, keeping the door ajar so as not to cook them further. This also keeps the chops from getting steamy, because air circulates around them. Serve the *braccioletti* on a heated platter, and rush them to the table.

4 *pounds oxtails, cut into sections*

2 *ounces* prosciutto *fat (or use boiled salt pork or lard)*

2 *large garlic cloves, peeled and well crushed*

2 *carrots, scraped and finely chopped*

2 *branches celery, washed and finely chopped*

1 *large yellow onion, peeled and finely chopped*

1 *bay leaf, torn in half*

1 *cup dry white wine*

12 *ounces fresh tomatoes, peeled, cored, and crushed, or use same amount canned*

⅓ *cup finely chopped parsley*

Salt to taste

Plenty of freshly ground black pepper

Coda alla Vaccinara

Braised Oxtails, Roman Style

SERVES 6

Wash the oxtails well in cold water, and let them soak for about an hour to release any blood or other impurities. Drain them well, and discard the water.

Boil about 3 quarts of fresh water in a stock pot. (Collected rain water would be good for this; see Water, The Italian Pantry, page 34.) When the water is at a rolling boil, plunge the oxtails in, 1 or 2 at a time, being sure the water always boils, until they are all in. Let the oxtails boil for about 10 minutes, lower the flame, and simmer them for about 1 hour, uncovered. The water should have evaporated some, and the level of it should be lower.

Meantime, slowly melt the *prosciutto* fat in a casserole dish large enough to hold all the ingredients, which can double as a serving dish at the table. When the fat is hot, add the garlic, and fry it until it is lightly browned and very aromatic. Add the carrots, celery, and onion, and lightly brown them. Add the bay leaf, the wine, the tomatoes, parsley, some salt, and pepper, and stir. Be sure to be generous with these last 2 items. They are essential to good flavor. Simmer the sauce for about ½ hour.

Remove the meat from the simmering water with a slotted spoon, a few pieces at a time, and nest them into the sauce in the casserole. Reserve the water for use in the dish later.

The pieces of meat should be just barely covered with liquid. If this is not the case, ladle in some of the oxtail cooking water. Put a lid on the casserole, and simmer it for about 3 hours. From time to time add some more of the oxtail cooking water to keep the level of liquid up. When the oxtails seem very tender and done, remove the lid from the casserole, and let them cook another 30 to 40 minutes to reduce the juices and to "finish" the dish. Correct for salt and pepper. If you find that there is far more liquid than you want, take the oxtails out, and raise the heat to medium, and reduce the liquids by about half. Return the oxtails to the casserole to heat them through.

Serve the *coda alla vaccinara* very hot in deep plates. Serve them with plain Garlic Bread (page 91).

Nowadays oxtails are really cows's or steer's tails. In times gone by the tails really did come from oxen. Also in those days, the dish always included one or more ox jowls. These imparted a deep flavor and a gelatinous dimension. In the recipe that follows, the directions call for "searing" the meat by plunging it into boiling water, but you may, if you like, brown the meat in fat. It is a matter of preference, but most Italians are used to having the meat surface sealed by the use of hot water.

Coda alla vaccinara is truly an ancient dish and is at the very foundations of Roman cooking. It is still enjoyed with gusto not only in homes but in restaurants. It should not be rushed in the cooking process, and is ideal for making ahead because it actually improves it. This also takes the stress out of cooking at the last minute during a dinner.

MENU SUGGESTIONS: Start out with some "Phone-Wire" Rice Croquettes (page 96) and some Chick-peas in Olive Oil (page 95) as part of an antipasto. A *contorno* of Green Beans in Olive Oil and Lemon Juice (page 237) would be excellent with the *coda*. Some fruit and Bitter Almond Cookies (page 278) would be a pleasant finish to this meal.

WINE: Solopaca Rosso (page 304)

Salsiccia alla Siciliana

Homemade Sicilian Sausage

MAKES ABOUT 20
4-INCH LINKS

This sausage is the one traditionally made in Agrigento, Sicily, where my father was born, and where he learned to make it. It was handed down to him, and he handed it down to me. If you follow the directions faithfully, you will turn out a sausage the people of Agrigento would applaud. The meat is *always* chopped very coarsely, and it must *always* have fennel in it. The best-tasting seeds are wild, but you can get very good ones from Italy at your Italian deli-catessen. For those who like their sausage hot, red pepper flakes are added. One of the most authentic and popular variations features Caciocavallo or *pecorino* cheese, with or without red pepper flakes.

This sausage must be chopped very coarsely because at one time it was called *salsiccia al punto del coltello*, which means "hacked sausage." The meat was pains-takingly cut into little bits, allowing all of the spices and flavoring to penetrate it on all surfaces. It also meant you could stuff a hog, sheep, or cow casing. It would be impossible to insert large chunks of meat. So, to keep the meat's true character, a coarse grind is the only one that will do.

Without fat, sausage would neither taste good nor have a good moist texture. Ideally, sausage meat should contain about 30 percent fat. If it does not, I recommend that you buy the best quality fatback and add it. Lean sausage of this type does not taste or feel good in the mouth. Fat dis-tributes the flavors, and it tenderizes. In

5 pounds fresh pork butt (shoulder) with plenty of fat on it, coarsely ground

5 teaspoons salt

1 cup minced Italian parsley

5 tablespoons fennel seeds

1 teaspoon freshly ground black pepper

1 cup dry white wine (or use cold water)

About ¼ pound salted hog casings

Optional (use 1 or both):

2 tablespoons red chili pepper flakes

1 cup coarsely shredded or chopped Caciocavallo cheese or pecorino cheese

Flush out the casings under running water by putting an open end onto the faucet, then soak them in a quart of cold water until you are ready to use them.

Make sure all the ingredients are ice cold, except the casings. Put them into the freezer if necessary, but don't allow them to freeze. If you are grinding your own meat, make sure all the metal parts of the grinder are also ice cold. You can put them into the freezer as well. This prevents what the sausage makers call "smearing"; that is, the fat and the red meat become indistinct from one another. This produces poor quality sausage in terms of texture and appearance. Smearing is controllable if you keep the ingredients very cold and do not overwork the meat and generate heat in the process.

Combine all of the ingredients in a large bowl, except the hog casings, and mix them well with your hands, being careful not to overmix or use too much force. (If you are using either of the optional ingredients, or both of them, add them now, and continue with the recipe.) Let the mixture rest in the refrigerator for a few hours, if possible, to develop flavor.

When you are ready to stuff the sausage, rinse out the casings thoroughly under cold running water, and keep them handy in a small bowl of cold water. Put one of the casings onto the "snake" (stuffing tube), leaving 2 inches dangling, empty, off the end. There is no need to, and in fact you should not, tie a knot in it. Put the sausage meat into the hopper, and start your machine, be it electric or manual (my favorite way). Carefully let the meat fill the casings, which should slide along the snake and feed itself. If it doesn't, gently push it along the snake with your fingers.

Do not overfill the casings. This is a common mistake. The sausage in the casing should feel quite soft and supple, and when you press it, it should maintain your finger marks. When you cook it, the meat expands, and the casing shrinks. If the sausage is too tight to begin with, you will have links that burst badly. Be sure that there are no air pockets in the sausage links; that, too, encourages bursting during cooking. Also, if the sausages are going to be stored for 3 or 4 days in the refrigerator, these air bubbles encourage the growth of bacteria, which accelerates spoilage.

An easy way to eliminate air pockets is to stuff carefully and use a large sewing needle, sailmaker's needle, or an upholstery needle. Get one as long as possible, and prick the places where the air bubbles are. You can do this as much as you like; nothing will happen to the casing. Trussing needles and eating forks make holes that are too large. If you make sausage often, have your knife vendor get you a sausage binding knife. It has a very short, very sharp, curved blade that is used to cut the links or casing. On the end of the handle are three very thin, very sharp needles. These are used to prick the air bubbles in the cased sausages. If you make cured sausages, such a knife is indispensable.

To make links, lay the length of sausage in front of you horizontally. Press down with a finger, making an indentation every 4 or 5 inches, depending on how large you want them. Then, starting either from the left or the right end, pick up the first link, twist it, rotating it towards you about 3 times, take the second link, and twist it in the opposite direction. Keep doing this until all the links are finished. There is no need to tie them. They will maintain their shape easily. You should end up with about 20 4-inch links of sausage with this recipe.

The best way to cook sausages is in the oven. Place the links in a cookie pan with low sides, and cook them in a preheated 350° F oven for about 35 minutes. You may gently prick them halfway through cooking, but don't get carried away; any fat you let escape this way also takes juices and flavor with it. I would use the same large sewing or sailmaker's needle as described above for this, or use the binding knife, if you have one.

If you wish to fry the links, start them in a little cold water, about ⅛ inch high, in a frying pan with the lid on it. Turn the heat on very low, and wait 5 to 6 minutes, or until the water comes to a simmer. Wait about another 5 minutes, remove the lid, and raise the heat to medium so that the water evaporates, if it has not done so by then. If, after another 5 minutes of cooking, the water still has not evaporated, discard it, holding the sausages back with a fork and pouring the water into a dish or down the drain. (You could also use red or white wine instead of water, which gives extra flavor and is quite delicious.) Put the pan back on the fire, and cook the sausages for about 15 to 20 minutes, to a wonderful dark brown color. Turn them once in a while.

If you want to cook the sausages over an open fire, start them out in the least hot spot on the grill or they will burst immediately. As they begin to cook and get a little firm, move them to a hotter spot, if you want. If you have a lot of them to barbecue, for instance for a party, either half-cook them in the oven or half-cook them by gently poaching them first, then put them over a live hot fire, and they will never burst. I use this method for large parties, and it has never failed. The taste is as good and fresh and succulent as can be.

Sausages freeze beautifully. Make a big batch, and freeze those you will not use immediately. Lay them out on a cookie sheet with lots of space between them, and put them into the freezer. When they are very firm, after about 2 to 3 hours, remove them from the freezer, with a knife or scissors separate each link, and then wrap them, or put them into plastic containers for storing in the freezer. This method allows you to defrost as few or as many links as you want. If you freeze them all bunched up, you have to defrost the whole lot to use them. When you want to cook them, place them, still frozen, in a roasting pan, and put them into the oven as described before, or in the frying pan with a bit of water. Just allow more cooking time. You can thoroughly defrost the sausages first, but I think they lose a little flavor and texture that way.

beef, you look for marbleized texture if you want prime quality and taste. In the old days, pork meat was more like modern marbleized beef. It was so good and juicy and tender. Now pork is grown so that there is more separation of meat and fat, so you have to adjust to this.

If you own a good electric mixer, you can make sausage by buying a special attachment. If you do not, you can buy small, table-attachable meat grinders that can be used for stuffing sausage. I prefer them, because it is all done by hand, providing control you cannot get with an electric machine.

You can buy hog casings from Italian or Chinese butchers who make their own sausages. If you are required to buy a large amount known as a "hank" (enough for about 300 pounds of sausage), share it with friends. If it is the kind of casing that is packed in salt, which is the best kind in my opinion, it will keep for at least 2 to 3 years in your refrigerator in a sealed jar. If, when you are making sausage, you find that you have a nice, long piece of leftover casing that has been hydrated, simply pat it dry, and rub it well with table salt. Put it back into your supply, cover it completely with more salt, and it will keep perfectly until the next use, even if that is a long time. Casings, salted or not, freeze extremely well. Be sure to parcel them out so that you do not have to defrost a huge mass just to make 5 pounds of sausage.

This sausage is marvelously versatile as a stuffing. In birds it is heavenly placed in the cavity or under the skin before roasting. You can also crumble it all up, fry it, and then add it to *lasagne* or other casserole dishes.

MENU SUGGESTIONS: There are so many that it would be easier to sum it up by saying that *salsiccia alla Siciliana* is perfect for any kind of meal imaginable, formal or *al fresco*. Spicy vegetables, potatoes, sliced tomatoes, and basil are all natural allies for the sausage. It can be used, out of its casing, as a stuffing for birds and veal.

WINE: Rosso del Salento (page 301), San Severo Rosso (page 301), or Cirò Rosso (page 302)

Baccalà Fritto

Fried Codfish,
Roman Style

SERVES 6

One of the best ways to eat *baccalà* is the recipe that follows. It is special.

MENU SUGGESTIONS: I would love a meal of Penne with *Porcini* in a Hot Tomato Sauce (page 143) followed by large platters of the following, all brought out at once so that you could make selections, but surely having some of them all: Fried Codfish, Roman Style; Artichokes in Embers (page 224); Mixed Vegetable Stew (page 232); Homemade Sicilian Sausage (page 188); and then a dessert of Sicilian Cannoli (page 261). This would make an excellent buffet supper for a party.

WINE: Locorotondo (page 300)

1½-pound piece of baccalà, *preferably boned and skinned (or get several smaller pieces, totaling 1½ pounds)*
All-purpose flour for dredging, q.b.
Olive oil for frying, q.b.

MARINADE

½ *cup virgin olive oil*
Juice of 2 lemons
4 *tablespoons Italian parsley, finely chopped*

Big pinch of salt
4 *grindings of black pepper*

PASTELLA (PASTE) (BATTER FOR FRYING)

4 *large eggs*
Big pinch of salt
3 *grindings of black pepper*
3 *tablespoons all-purpose flour*

NOTE: *Baccalà*, as far as I can ascertain, is invariably cod; invariably it is split in half, but without the head on it; is lightly salted; is thick, fleshy, and supple; comes from Canada; is often skinned; and needs to be soaked from one to three days. *Stoccafisso*, on the other hand, while invariably cod, is split in half, the head being removed, and then tied back together (*a cavallo*) after it has been cured; is heavily salted; always has skin; is dry, skinny, and thin; comes from Norway, and needs to be soaked as long as 10 days.

When you buy *baccalà*, it is very plump at the front end and very thin at the rear end. This creates problems in terms of cooking it and certainly in terms of its salt content at either end. When you soak the *baccalà* in cold water, the salt will leech out much faster from the thin end than from the plump end. You must use the plump end as your guide as to how many days to soak it to rid the salt from the flesh. The cooking is not such a problem; you simply cook the plumper, bigger pieces first, and then add the smaller, thinner ones later.

Soak the *baccalà* for 3 days in about 5 gallons of very cold water, changing the water no less than 3 times a day. If the *baccalà* is grossly divergent in thickness, you may want, after it has softened in the water for a day or so, to cut the thick parts in half horizontally. This exposes more of the flesh to the water and helps to eliminate the salt.

When the *baccalà* is very plump and supple, remove it from the water. Using gentle pressure, with your hands squeeze out as much moisture as you can. Let the fish drain in a colander until you are ready to use it. If you are not going to be using the *baccalà* within 2 or 3 hours of removing it from the water, refrigerate it. (It can be refrigerated, after soaking, for up to 2 days.)

Make the marinade by combining all the ingredients in a wide, shallow dish or bowl. Mix everything well.

When the *baccalà* is fairly dry, cut it into pieces roughly 3 by 4 inches. Soak the pieces in the marinade for 2 hours or more. Meanwhile, make the *pastella*. Beat the eggs in a low-sided dish until they are frothy, add the salt and pepper, and then beat in the flour, a spoonful at a time, until the ingredients just come together. Do not overbeat.

Put the olive oil in a wide, low frying pan so that the oil is about ¼ inch high, and heat it to about 360° F. Spread the flour in a low-sided dish. Take each piece of *baccalà* out of the marinade, shake it once or twice, but do not scrape off any of the parsley that clings to it, and dredge each piece of *baccalà* in the flour, gently tapping off any excess. Dip the dredged *baccalà* into the *pastella*, and then carefully place it in the hot oil to cook until it is a dark gold on one side. Turn the fish over and fry the other side until it, too, is a dark gold. Put in as many pieces as the pan will comfortably hold, being careful not to overcrowd or add the pieces too fast. This cools the oil and makes the fish soggy. Put the finished pieces on an absorbent towel to drain. Serve the *baccalà* hot with lots of crusty homemade bread.

NOTE: You could vary the recipe by simply taking the *baccalà* pieces out of the marinade, dredging them in flour, dipping them in the *pastella* ("batter"), and then rolling them in bread crumbs. Proceed as directed.

Baccalà in Guazzetto

Codfish Stew

SERVES 4 TO 6

This version of *baccalà* must surely have its roots in the Arab cuisine. (Romans would not like to hear that, especially when one of its ingredients is pine nuts, undoubtedly gathered from one of the very famous "Pines of Rome." Raisins, olive oil, and parsley give the feeling of antiquity. The tomatoes are modern, added after 1750 when the *pomodoro* ("golden apple") was finally eaten by some brave soul, who declared it indispensable to Italian cooking. Not just Southern Italian cooking either. The Northerners have red lips and a gleam in their eye, and it does not all come from heavy cream and veal.

MENU SUGGESTIONS: I would start out with Artichokes Stuffed with Ricotta and Salami (page 227). Then as a *contorno* I would have some Hot Devil Potatoes (page 243). A plateful of Dessert Ravioli, Teramo Style (page 283), and a bottle of Moscato di Trani (page 300) would be a good ending for this splendid meal.

WINE: Corvo Bianco (page 308)

2 pounds baccalà, *before soaking, cut into 3-inch pieces (see soaking method, page 190)*
All-purpose flour for dredging, q.b.
⅓ cup virgin olive oil for frying, q.b.
3 large garlic cloves, peeled and well crushed
1½ pounds fresh tomatoes, cored, peeled, and well crushed, or use same amount canned

Salt to taste
4 grindings of fresh black pepper
¼ cup finely chopped Italian parsley
2 tablespoons smallest white raisins available (chop them coarsely if necessary)
2 tablespoons pine nuts, toasted without oil until they are a dark gold

Dry the pieces of *baccalà* with a paper or kitchen towel. Spread the flour in a low-sided dish, and dredge the fish in it. Heat the olive oil in a large frying pan to 360° F, and fry the *baccalà* until it is golden on one side, turn it over carefully, and fry the other side until it, too, is golden. Set the fish aside on an absorbent towel to drain. When you have finished frying the *baccalà*, add the garlic to the pan, and fry it until it is a very dark gold. Leave it in the pan or discard it, as you like. Add the tomatoes, parsley, raisins, toasted pine nuts, salt, and pepper to the pan, and mix them well. Cook the mixture for about 15 minutes, and then gently place the pieces of fish into it. Simmer the mixture gently for about another 15 minutes. Serve the *baccalà in guazzetto* very hot with chunks of crusty homemade bread.

¼ cup virgin olive oil

1 large yellow onion, peeled and thinly sliced

10 to 12 ounces of fresh small peas, or use frozen tiny peas

⅔ cup dry white wine

2 large garlic cloves, peeled and well crushed

¼ cup finely chopped Italian parsley

2 pounds squid, washed, cleaned, and cut into ¼-inch-long strips

Salt to taste

3 or 4 grindings of fresh black pepper

Calamari con Piselli alla Romana

Squid and Peas

SERVES 4 TO 6

Heat about 2 tablespoons of the olive oil in a large frying pan, and over moderately low heat gently sauté the onions until they are soft with little flecks of brown on them here and there. Add the peas, and cook them for about 1 minute. Add the wine, raise the heat, and cook at a rolling boil for about 3 minutes to reduce the wine and evaporate the alcohol. Reserve the mixture in a bowl.

Wipe the frying pan clean, and put in the rest of the olive oil. When it is hot, add the crushed garlic, and fry it until it is a dark gold. Remove the garlic at this point if you want to, but I leave it in. Add the parsley and the strips of squid, and cook them for 2 minutes, or until they turn white. Add the onions and peas, and cook the mixture until everything is piping hot, but watch that you do not cook the squid more than 2 to 3 minutes more, or it will become quite tough. Add salt and pepper, and stir well.

The *calamari con piselli* should be quite liquid but not like a bowl of soup. Serve it in rimmed soup plates. Provide a spoon to be sure to get all the juices, which are very rich and concentrated. Serve large chunks of crusty homemade bread or Garlic Bread (page 91) with the *calamari con piselli*.

In Rome this dish is made with *seppie*, or cuttlefish. *Calamari* are a good substitute. Fresh garden peas are so sweet and flavorful that they are certainly the kind preferred in this dish. Be sure not to overcook them. Prepare the *calamari* or the *seppie* as described in the Fried Squid and Stuffed Squid recipe, page 173.

MENU SUGGESTIONS: For a *primo piatto* I would serve Stuffed Pasta Dumplings (page 139). As a *contorno* Hot Devil Potatoes (page 243) or Artichokes, Stuffed Agrigento Style (page 226), are very good. Chocolate Bread (page 284) would be a good closer to this meal, followed by some Moscato di Pantelleria (page 309).

WINE: San Severo Bianco (page 301)

Le Cozze con le Salsicce

Mussels and Sausage

SERVES 4 TO 6

When you taste the zesty, peppery sausages and the sweet smoothness of the mussels, you will see how much sense this unlikely combination makes. It probably will become a staple on your menus.

Even though it is considered a main dish, I would not hesitate to serve smaller portions of it as a starter. It could be part of a hot antipasto. This recipe is from my friend Dottore Domenico Manzon's book, *La Campania,* "Dove andare, Cosa comprare, Come Mangiare" (*Campania,* "Where to Go, What to Buy, How to Eat"), and it is a favorite dish of my wife, Lisa, as well as one of mine.

MENU SUGGESTIONS: A dish of Potato Croquettes (page 231) and some Artichokes, Stuffed Agrigento Style (page 226), would be great *antipasti*. A small dish of Penne with Asparagus (page 146) would be a good *primo piatto*, followed by the *cozze*. A bowl of assorted fresh fruit would probably be welcome after such a meal.

WINE: Salice Salentino (page 301) or Greco di Tufo (page 302)

⅓ cup virgin olive oil

5 small yellow onions, peeled and diced about ¼ inch square

Big pinch of red pepper flakes

1 pound fresh sausage made with plenty of black pepper (or use Homemade Sicilian Sausage, page 188, and add more black pepper to the dish), skin removed, and broken into bits

4 ounces very lean prosciutto, *cut into tiny pieces*

3 very large tomatoes, peeled, cored, seeded, and chopped coarsely

⅓ cup parsley, finely chopped

2 large garlic cloves, peeled and well crushed

2 small bay leaves

⅔ cup dry white wine

4 pounds mussels, well cleaned and bearded

In a frying pan with a lid and large enough to hold all the ingredients (a fireproof casserole dish would be good), heat the oil, and add the onions. Gently fry the onions until they are just transparent but not colored. Add the pinch of red pepper flakes, and stir everything well. Add the sausage meat, stir it well, and cook it gently until it just loses its red color. Add the *prosciutto,* and mix it in with the other ingredients. Add the tomatoes, garlic, and bay leaves. Make sure everything is well integrated. Add the white wine, ⅓ cup at a time, stirring well after each addition.

Scatter the mussels all over the surface of the hot mixture. Push them into the mixture if there are too many. You can have more than one layer of mussels if you need to. Sprinkle on the parsley. Put the lid on the pan, and let the mussels cook until they are all opened, but do not overcook them. (They get rubbery and tasteless.) The mussels should have a gray rather than orange look. Generally the orange look comes from overcooking. If any fail to open, try putting them in a really hot spot in the sauce. It could be that they are stubborn and will not open. If after trying that they still remain closed, you can assume they were dead when you put them into the pan, and that means they will never open. Discard those.

Serve the *cozze con le salsicce* in deep, rimmed soup dishes, and if you have not had a large dish of pasta preceding them, pass some crusty homemade bread, or make Garlic Bread (page 91).

Polenta con le Vongole

Polenta and Clams

SERVES 6

6 pounds Cherrystone clams or 4 pounds Manila clams

1 cup polenta (see Polenta on a Board, page 203)

⅓ cup virgin olive oil

3 large garlic cloves, peeled and finely chopped

3 pounds fresh tomatoes, peeled, cored, seeded, and finely chopped, including the juice, or use same amount canned

Salt to taste

5 grindings of fresh black pepper

2 teaspoons red pepper flakes, or q.b.

Carefully wash and scrub the clams to rid them of any sand. When the polenta is ready for serving, take a very large frying pan or low-sided stock pot with a lid, and heat the olive oil in it over high heat. Add the chopped garlic, and brown it, but do not burn it. Add the tomatoes, turn the heat down to medium, and let them cook for about 5 minutes. Add the clams, and cook them, covered, until they open. When they are opened, let them cook for another 5 to 6 minutes. Salt and pepper to taste.

Serve the polenta on heated plates, and spoon some of the tomato sauce on it. Divide the clams among the plates, and serve immediately. This dish gets no cheese. Sprinkle red pepper flakes all over it. Use about ½ teaspoon per plate.

This earthy polenta dish is highly regarded in the coastal areas of the Abruzzo. One way to make it work in a more formal dinner is to serve small portions of it as a first course. Polenta with sauce drizzled over it and surrounded by half-open clams is very glamorous.

MENU SUGGESTIONS: I would start the meal with a dish of Sweet-and-Sour Baby Onions (page 234) and sliced salami or *prosciutto*. I would have a *contorno* after the polenta of Orange and Lemon Salad (page 242). Almond Tart (page 270) would be perfect as a sweet with some Marsala Superiore (page 309).

WINE: Greco di Tufo (page 302) or Regaleali Rosso (page 310)

Mazzancolle al Coccio

Clay-Cooked Prawns

SERVES 4

16 *giant prawns*
All-purpose flour for dredging, q.b.
¼ *cup extra virgin olive oil, or q.b.*
⅓ *cup brandy*
⅔ *cup dry white wine*
Salt to taste

4 *grindings of fresh black pepper*
Juice of 1 lemon
Optional *(and often done): 2 tomatoes, cored, peeled, and well crushed*

Mazzancolle are not found in America. Giant prawns work well, and if you can find fresh ones with the heads still on, I recommend that you break the bank and get as many as you can. I never weigh the amount of prawns needed. I always count them out according to the number of guests. Four per person is enough if you have other courses of substance. The use of a clay pot really does make the difference in this extravagant dish.

MENU SUGGESTIONS: Fiery Macaroni (page 138) may seem like a volcanic start, but it certainly would wake up every nerve in your body. The mildness of the prawns with the bread would pave the way for some Fava Beans and Chicory (page 238). "Drowned" Ice Cream (page 293) is my definite choice for dessert, in this case soft vanilla ice cream topped with a big shot of Scotch whisky.

WINE: Five Roses (page 300) or Castel del Monte Bianco (page 299)

Wash the prawns in plenty of cold water, and drain them. If you are fortunate enough to have fresh ones, leave the heads and the tails on, removing only the armorlike shell on the body and the legs. With a sharp knife, carefully remove the alimentary canal, which is black and may be full of sand. If you have frozen prawns, remove the armor and the alimentary canal.

Spread the flour in a low-sided dish, and dredge the prawns in it. Heat the olive oil in the clay pot over medium heat. Add the prawns, and the minute they begin to turn orange on the bottom, turn them over. Add the brandy, being careful that it does not flare up. If you are using the tomatoes, add them now. Add the white wine, stirring, and cook the prawns for about 3 minutes more to be sure to burn off all of the alcohol in the wine. At the last moment add plenty of salt and pepper, and add lemon juice. Serve the prawns at the dining table from the clay pot. *Mazzancolle* cry out for large chunks of homemade bread.

Pesce Spada in
Graticola

Grilled
Swordfish

SERVES 6

12 *thin slices swordfish, about 2½ pounds*

About ¾ cup fresh ground bread crumbs, or q.b.

4 *garlic cloves, peeled and very finely chopped*

Virgin olive oil, q.b.

Dry oregano, q.b.

Salt to taste

Lay the slices of swordfish out on a board or on a plate. Sprinkle about 1 tablespoon of bread crumbs on each slice of fish. Divide the garlic equally among the slices of fish, and sprinkle it on at random. Drizzle about 1 teaspoon of olive oil on each slice, and then put a pinch of oregano on each slice. Salt to taste. Roll the fish so that it looks like a cigar, and secure it with a toothpick. Brush the rolls with a bit more of the olive oil. Roast the *pesce spada* over a medium-hot live fire of oak, olive, or fruit wood for about 8 minutes total cooking time. Serve the rolls hot.

Swordfish (*pesce spada*) is plentiful in the South and greatly loved. It is stewed, grilled, fried, baked, or roasted. It is a wonderful-tasting fish with firm flesh. This is a simple and scrumptious recipe for preparing it.

MENU SUGGESTIONS: A hot antipasto of Fried Caciocavallo Cheese, Silversmith Style (page 151), would be a good starter. After the swordfish, I would have a *contorno* of Italian Potato Pancake (page 246). A piece of Chocolate Bread (page 284) would be a good dessert.

WINE: Bianco Alcamo (page 308) or Cannonau di Sardegna (page 307)

Coniglio a Succhittu

Braised Rabbit, Sardinian Style

SERVES 4

This is one of the best ways I know to prepare rabbit. Its taste is sharp and assertive. Any leftover pieces are good cold with a salad and some bread.

MENU SUGGESTIONS: I would have a warm antipasto of Artichokes Stuffed with Ricotta and Salami (page 227). With the rabbit I would have Potato Croquettes (page 231) and Cauliflower *au Gratin* (page 230) as *contorni*. Flaming Chestnuts (page 281) with some Aleatico di Puglia (page 298) would make a very nice dessert for this meal.

WINE: Corvo Bianco (page 308) or Regaleali Rosso (page 310)

1 2½-pound rabbit, dressed for cooking, liver reserved and chopped

¼ cup virgin olive oil

1 large yellow onion, peeled and chopped into ¼-inch dice

2 large garlic cloves, peeled and well crushed

⅓ cup finely chopped parsley

½ cup white or red wine vinegar

½ cup water

Salt to taste

Freshly ground black pepper to taste

⅓ cup capers, drained

Wash the rabbit under cold running water, and dry it well with a kitchen towel. Remove the liver, cut it into about 6 pieces, and set it aside for later use. Cut the rabbit as described in the recipe Rabbit, Ischian Style, page 182. Heat the olive oil in a large frying pan, and brown the rabbit over moderately high heat. The color should be a deep gold and look very appetizing. Add the onion, stir the ingredients well, and fry the onions until they just barely begin to take on some color. Add the garlic, and mash it around the pan with a wooden spoon, being careful not to burn it. Add the parsley, and stir all the ingredients around. Add the vinegar and water all at once, then salt and pepper to taste. Add the chopped liver. When the liquid has reduced by about half, add the capers, and stir everything well. The rabbit should be done in about 30 minutes total cooking time. It might take a few minutes longer, but do not overcook it, or it will become dry and tough.

Remove the rabbit pieces from the pan to a heated serving platter. Remove all of the solids from the pan, and scatter them over the rabbit. If you have more than 1 cup of juice in the pan, reduce it over high heat. Drizzle it over the rabbit, and serve it hot.

Swordfish, Stuffed Sicilian Style

SERVES 6

¼ cup grated pecorino *or* Parmesan cheese

1 cup bread crumbs

2 tablespoons capers, coarsely chopped

¼ cup chopped parsley

8 Gaeta, Calamata, or sun-dried black olives, pitted and finely chopped

Plenty of freshly ground black pepper

5 to 6 tablespoons virgin olive oil

6 large slices of swordfish, crosscut about ¼ inch thick

All-purpose flour for dredging, q.b.

About 3 cups (1½ pints) Marinara Sauce (page 78)

Optional: ⅓ cup dry white wine added to the Marinara Sauce

Combine in a medium-sized bowl the cheese, bread crumbs, capers, parsley, olives, and ground black pepper. Lay the slices of fish out on a board or on wax paper. Spread the cheese mixture in equal portions evenly over the fish slices, and drizzle them with about 2 tablespoons of the olive oil. Roll each fish slice so that it resembles a cigar, and secure it with a toothpick or a skewer, or tie it with string.

Spread the flour in a low-sided dish, and dredge the rolls in the flour. In a frying pan large enough to hold all of the fish rolls comfortably, heat about 3 tablespoons of the olive oil until it is hot but not anywhere near smoking, and brown the rolls lightly, turning them once or twice. This should take about 2 to 3 minutes. Carefully pour the Marinara Sauce all over the fish rolls, and simmer the rolls gently, uncovered for 15 to 20 minutes, or until the flesh just flakes when tested with a fork. Turn them once during the cooking in the sauce. Do not overcook the fish, or it will be very dry and uninteresting.

NOTE: Some Sicilians like to add about 1 tablespoon of very small raisins to the Marinara Sauce before it is poured onto the fish rolls. In Italy raisins tend to be smaller and not so sugary but with a more profound grape taste. Currants would work well in this dish.

In the famous *Vucciria* market in Palermo, you see hundreds of *pesce spada* of varying sizes, their heads on with their long swordlike snouts. The market is so named because the vendors yell their lungs out to hawk their wares. In Sicilian the word meaning "to yell" is *jetta vucci* (*getta voce* in Italian), literally "throw the voice." Some think that the word is a corruption of the French word *boucher*, meaning butcher, and thus corrupted to *vucci*, and so on. But it is believed that the market had its name before the French occupation. Speaking Sicilian as I do, I am all for the first explanation.

Some of the very best swordfish in Italy come from the Strait of Messina, where they can grow to 15 or 16 feet long. If you cannot get swordfish, this recipe can be made with fresh tuna, as they are very similar in texture. Other fish would work well also; shark or large cuts of halibut would be fine.

MENU SUGGESTIONS: You could begin with some Sweet-and-Sour Baby Onions (page 234) as an antipasto and then have a plate of Penne with Asparagus (page 146). After that the swordfish could be served with some Garlic Bread (page 91). A dish of Dessert Ravioli, Teramo Style (page 283), and some Moscato di Pantelleria (page 309) would be a good end to this meal.

WINE: Greco di Tufo (page 302)

Tonno alla Calabrese

Tuna, Calabrian Style

SERVES 6

Tuna goes well with lots of ingredients. In this case, tomato provides the tasty extra.

MENU SUGGESTIONS: An antipasto of Pizza, Lanciano Style (page 52), Pizza with Mushrooms (page 50), or Fried Calzone (page 62) with some Sweet-and-Sour Baby Onions (page 234) would be excellent. A *contorno* of Artichokes in Embers (page 224) before the *secondo* of the *tonno* would be a good choice. Lemon Ice (page 291) would be a nice finish to this meal.

WINE: Etna Bianco (page 308) or Favonio Bianco (page 299)

3 tablespoons extra virgin olive oil

2 pounds fresh tuna, in 6 slices

½ cup fresh bread crumbs, or q.b., not too fine, slightly toasted

1 tablespoon red pepper flakes, or to taste

About ½ cup Marinara Sauce (page 78)

Salt to taste

Few grindings of fresh black pepper

Preheat the oven to 375° F. Put the oil in an ovenproof casserole dish. Put the slices of tuna into the casserole, and moisten one side with the olive oil. Turn the tuna slices over, and moisten the other side with the oil. Sprinkle on the bread crumbs and the red pepper flakes. Spoon some of the Marinara Sauce on each slice of tuna, but the fish should not be swimming in it; the sauce is a condiment rather than a cooking medium. Sprinkle on a bit of salt, and grind on some fresh black pepper. Bake the fish for about 20 minutes, or until it is cooked through but not dry. Test it by breaking open one of the pieces. The tuna should be juicy and hold together well, but it should have lost the very pink color of rawness. If it is flaky, it is overdone. Serve hot with crusty homemade bread.

NOTE: In parts of Calabria the preparation is more elaborate. Sliced onion is gently fried in olive oil, and then some crushed garlic is put in and browned. Crushed fresh tomatoes are added and cooked for about 15 minutes. Chopped anchovy is then added to the sauce, and it is cooked for another 10 minutes. The tuna is pushed into the sauce and baked as described.

Tonno in Padella

Tuna and Fennel Seeds

SERVES 4

1¼ pounds tuna, sliced about ½ inch thick

4 to 6 tablespoons extra virgin olive oil

4 tablespoons fennel seeds

½ teaspoon salt, or to taste

Several grindings of fresh black pepper

Optional: *splash of dry white wine*

Carefully dry the tuna slices. If they have skin, leave it on, as it hurts nothing and looks nice on the plate. Put the olive oil and the fennel seeds in a large frying pan over medium heat. When the seeds begin to sizzle, put the slices of tuna down on top of them, and sprinkle on some salt and a few grindings of pepper. In about 5 minutes, carefully turn the tuna slices over, and sprinkle on a bit more salt, and grind on more pepper. After about another 3 minutes the slices of tuna should be done. Do not overcook them, but be sure they are not raw in the middle.

Put the slices of tuna on a heated serving dish or on heated individual plates, as you like. Then, if you are using the optional wine, put it into the pan with the juices and the remaining seeds that have not clung to the fish. Cook the juices and wine over very high heat long enough to cook off the alcohol and to get a very quick reduction of the pan juices. Drizzle the juices on the pieces of fish, and serve them immediately. The fennel seeds are meant to remain in the dish. You will invariably eat some of them and leave others behind. This is characteristic of this dish, so it would be a pity to strain out the seeds; and very un-Italian.

If you are not going to use the optional wine, drizzle the pan juices and remaining seeds on the pieces of tuna.

NOTE: This dish is also very good made with 1 pound of shelled shrimp instead of the tuna. The recipe remains the same, as do the menu suggestions.

In southern Italy tuna is so highly prized that in Trapani, in May when the tuna season opens, there is a big celebration called the *mattanza*. The whole affair is presided over by an old learned fisherman who, for this festival, becomes *il rais* (Arabic meaning "the chief"), and he determines with absolute authority just where and how the first tuna will be caught. Fresh tuna is dense and quite firm but very tender. It has a pale, coral color but can have dark spots, especially near the backbone. It is considered an oily fish, but if it is absolutely fresh, its flesh stays moist during cooking. Here is an extremely simple way of cooking large pieces of tuna cut crosswise.

MENU SUGGESTIONS: Tomato Toasts (page 92) would be a good antipasto as would Bread and Cheese Skewers, Roman Style (page 93). As *contorni* you could have Mushrooms Roasted with Pine Nuts (page 239) and some Cauliflower in a Basket (page 229). Spumoni (page 296) would be refreshing and much appreciated after such a meal.

WINE: Trebbiano d'Abruzzo (page 298)

Trota ai Funghi

Trout in Casserole

SERVES 6

Trout are not necessarily associated with Campania, but the southern waters do have them. Of course, with modern methods of transportation, more ingredients go from place to place that previously did not. If you like trout, however, you may have noticed that the number of ways you can cook them is limited. This recipe will not only expand your repertory, but you may never cook trout any other way. This dish is not only delicious, it is beautiful. It is another of my friend Dottore Domenico Manzon's treasures.

MENU SUGGESTIONS: I would have no antipasto. Serve a *contorno* of Artichokes, Stuffed Agrigento Style (page 226), separately and before the trout. I would have another *contorno* of String Beans in Tomato Sauce (page 236) after the trout, and then I would have some Cream Puffs (page 256) for dessert.

WINE: Greco di Tufo (page 302) or Regaleali Bianco (page 310)

1 *pound cultivated mushrooms, cleaned and cut into thin slices*

6 *ounces (about 12 tablespoons) sweet butter, or q.b.*

Salt to taste

3 *or 4 grindings of fresh black pepper*

6 *trout, about 8 ounces each, cleaned (boned if you like), with heads and tails intact*

2 *large egg yolks*

1½ *cups heavy cream*

6 *large slices bread fried in some unsalted butter*

Fry the mushrooms quickly over high heat in about 2 ounces (4 tablespoons) of the butter, until the mushrooms reveal a tinge of gold on their edges. Salt and pepper to taste. Be careful not to burn the butter. Remove them from the pan, and put them into a bowl along with any butter left in the pan. Set them aside for later use.

Wipe out the frying pan, or use another one, and put 6 tablespoons of butter into it. When the butter is hot, but nowhere near burned, brown the trout on one side. Salt and pepper to taste. Turn them over, and brown them on the other side, and salt and pepper again. Do not let them overcook, because they require more cooking later. Remove the trout from the heat as soon as they have color on the sides, and reserve them in a warm place until later.

Preheat the oven to 375° F. Heavily butter an ovenproof casserole dish large enough to hold all of the ingredients, except the fried bread. Arrange the trout in the casserole so that they barely touch each other. In no case should you layer them. Scatter the fried mushrooms all over the trout. Beat the egg yolks and the cream together with a fork, making sure they are well integrated, and pour the mixture over the trout and mushrooms. Put the casserole into the oven, and bake it for 12 minutes, or until the cream is congealed a bit like custard and has nice buttery marks all over it. Do not overcook it.

While the trout are in the oven, fry the slices of bread in 2 tablespoons of unsalted butter until they are a light gold. Put a slice of the toasted bread in the center of heated plates. When the trout are done, put 1 on each slice of bread, and spoon on some of the juices from the casserole. Serve the trout very hot.

POLENTA FACILE (EASY METHOD)

1 *tablespoon salt*

2 *cups polenta*

Using only the top half of a double boiler, bring 2 quarts of water to a boil, and add salt. Meanwhile, put as much water in the bottom half of the double boiler as will be needed to actually cover the *bottom* of the *top part* of the double boiler when it is finally put in, and bring to a heavy simmer.

Put the polenta in a measuring cup from which you can pour it. With a slender but sturdy wooden spoon or a medium-strength whisk, create a vortex in the water in the top half of the double boiler by swirling it in one direction only. This is critical because, if you simply slosh the water around, you create lumps in the polenta that are almost impossible to remove.

While the water is swirling in a vortex, drizzle in the polenta *a pioggia* (like it is raining). You can do this very rapidly, but do not stop stirring. When all of the polenta is in, continue to stir but not so energetically. Keep stirring the whole time, being sure to scrape into the corners of the pot where the sides meet the bottom. Lower the heat so that the polenta intermittently bubbles on the surface and "spits" at you.

Continue to stir the polenta for about 5 minutes. When the polenta begins to thicken, place the lid on the pan, and fit it into the bottom half of the double boiler (with the simmering water below reaching up as high as possible underneath the top piece). Cook for about 1½ hours, stirring every 30 minutes or so. Taste for doneness. The polenta should be very yellow, smooth, shiny, and sweet tasting. If it is slightly bitter, cook it longer.

Polenta facile can be held in a slowly simmering double boiler in perfect condition for up to 4 hours. This makes it ideal for large parties or when you simply do not want too many last-minute dishes to worry about.

NOTE: One hardly associates polenta with the Abruzzese. The plain truth is that they used to eat polenta a great deal, especially field and stone workers. In these latter days polenta is not as popular, but the old-timers still appreciate it as an old and valuable friend and regale you with stories about it. Polenta, traditionally, is cooked in an unlined copper pot called a *paiòlo*. The unlined copper gives a brilliant color to the polenta, and the *intenditori* insist (and I am on their side) that the flavor is not only better, but characteristic. In any case, use only unlined copper for polenta, and barring that, you may use enamel, stainless steel, or glass; never aluminum or iron. If the *paiòlo* were large and in an old kitchen where the cooking was still done in the fireplace, it would have a curved bottom and a strong iron hoop handle that rests on a crane. The crane would be swung in over the fire and swung out whenever you wanted to inspect the ingredients in the pot or remove it from further cooking. The more modern *paiòlo* has a flat bottom and is smaller and obviously was designed to set on a modern stove.

Polenta Sulla Spianatoia

Polenta on a Board

SERVES 8

Of the hundreds of preparations of polenta, I think it would be hard to beat eating it this way. After the polenta is made, it is poured on a large, clean board. One's favorite sauce is generously splashed on, followed by mountains of snowy, freshly grated *pecorino*. The part that is so much fun is when all of the eaters who share the board as common dish proceed to eat with spoons and forks brandished as in a sword fight from an Errol Flynn movie. At more formal gatherings, I use clean, small cutting boards, and serve each eater individually.

There are two methods of cooking polenta. The old one requires constant vigilance and ends up spattering scalding polenta on your arms and wrists as it spits and bubbles its way to completion. The other method, which I call *polenta facile*, is just that; the easy way to do it; foolproof, spatterproof, and just about as good as the old method. This is one time when I approve of "progress."

MENU SUGGESTIONS: An antipasto of Mushrooms in Parchment (page 240) would be a good starter. On the polenta I would use some grilled or roasted Homemade Sicilian Sausage (page 188) and some Marinara Sauce (page 78), liberally sprinkled with grated *pecorino* cheese. Fresh fruit and a basket of Bitter Almond Cookies (page 278), along with some Aleatico di Puglia (page 298), would be fine closings to this meal.

WINE: Faro Rosso (page 309)

Lasagne di Carnevale alla Napolitana

Neapolitan Holiday Lasagna

SERVES 8 OR MORE

Lasagna has fallen on hard times. Its over-popularity in this country has caused it to lose some of its glamour. In Italy, however, *lasagne* are an occasion to celebrate either the eve or the end of Lent, when meat is allowed, or to rejoice in the fact that you happen to be lucky enough to have many ingredients in your pantry at the same time to add to the *lasagne*. When you see *lasagne* in this perspective, it is easier to contemplate, with excitement, putting ingredients together to signify an event that has its place in history.

See the Note at the end of this recipe for the local Southern Italian variations of this dish.

MENU SUGGESTIONS: *Lasagne* are a major dish. I would not have antipasto unless it consisted of some olives and celery or something very light. After the *lasagne*, I would have a Semifreddo (page 286) of choice and let it go at that. *Lasagne* are perfect for a buffet, and they could be among many dishes that could be served. For instance, you could have bowls of Almond Peppers (page 249), Sweet-and-Sour Baby Onions (page 234), Green Beans in Olive Oil and Lemon Juice (page 237), and some Deviled Broccoli (page 217).

WINE: Montepulciano d'Abruzzo (page 298) or Solopaca Rosso (page 304)

1 recipe of Neapolitan Tomato Sauce with Meat (page 75), made with 1½ pounds pork loin in one piece

1 cup fresh bread crumbs

2 large eggs

¾ cup grated Parmesan cheese

Salt to taste

Plenty of freshly ground black pepper

¼ cup finely chopped parsley

Olive oil for frying, q.b.

6 ounces Italian sausage, made with no fennel seeds, fried, skinned, and broken up (see Homemade Sicilian Sausage, page 188)

Lard or butter to grease casserole dish, q.b.

12 ounces freshly made pasta (page 123), 1/16 inch thick, cut into strips 2 inches wide and about 9 inches long, or commercial variety

1 pound Ricotta

2 cups Mozzarella, shredded or very thinly sliced

Make the *ragù* as directed, but substitute pork loin for the beef or veal. You need less meat for the *lasagne*, so the amount specified is 1½ pounds. You could certainly cook more and use it in other dishes. When the meat is well cooked, take it out of the sauce, and let it cool, unrefrigerated, on a plate. When it is cool enough to handle but still just a bit warm, chop the amount you need with a knife. The result should be very finely and evenly chopped meat. You could use a food processor, *but watch out that you do not make mush of it! (You could make the recipe up to this point 1 or 2 days ahead if you wish.)*

Mix the meat with the bread crumbs, eggs, ¼ cup of the grated Parmesan cheese, salt and pepper as needed, and the parsley. Make little meatballs the size of a large hazelnut, setting them aside as you make them. When you have finished, put some olive oil into a frying pan over high heat, and fry the meatballs quickly, until they have a light gold finish. They really do not need much cooking, because the meat is already cooked. Set them aside until later. *(You can make these the day before you assemble the lasagne, if you wish.)*

Fry the sausage very slowly over low heat in a small frying pan for about 12 minutes. When it is done, let it cool for a few minutes, and then remove the skin. Crumble up the meat, and set it aside for later use. *(You can do this 1 day ahead if you wish.)*

Grease a baking dish, 9 × 13, generously with lard or butter. Set it aside for later use. Boil 6 quarts of water in a large pot, and add 2 tablespoons of salt. Even though you will rinse the pasta later, the salt has an effect on the taste of the pasta that is essential later. Boil 2 or 3 pieces of *lasagne* at a time for about 1 minute. Immediately carefully take them out of the boiling water with a slotted spatula, and put them into a large bowl of cold water. Continue until you have cooked all the pasta. If you find that the water in the bowl gets too warm, throw in some ice cubes. Putting the boiled pasta into cold water stops the cooking, or else it will overcook and fall apart. Gently "wash" the pasta in the bowl to make it supple and manageable. Do not leave it in too long or it can soften too much. Lay the "washed" pasta on a damp kitchen towel. Continue this until you have finished all the pasta. (This operation takes lots of room. If you do not have enough counter space, line cookie sheets with damp towels, and put them on the floor or on chairs.)

Preheat the oven to 400° F, and move the rack to the upper third of the oven. Put one layer of *lasagne* down on the bottom of the greased baking dish, overlapping the pasta just a tiny bit to make a sheet. Spread about ⅓ of the Ricotta around on it and ⅓ of the Mozzarella. Then scatter on ⅓ of the sausage meat here and there and ⅓ of the meatballs. Put about 2 cups of *ragù* on next, but do not make it too wet; use your judgment. Start again with another layer of pasta, and continue thus to make layers. Be sure that you end up with a layer of pasta and that you have ⅓ of the Mozzarella and the rest of the grated Parmesan cheese left. Spread enough *ragù* on this final sheet of pasta to cover the top, sprinkle on the Parmesan, and then scatter the Mozzarella evenly over the grated cheese to cover as much of the top as you can.

Put the *lasagne* in the oven, and after about 10 minutes, cut the temperature down to 375° F. Let the *lasagne* bake for about 40 minutes, or until the dish is bubbling all over and the top has golden highlights all over. If it is cooking too fast, either reduce the temperature some more, or lower the rack 1 notch or so toward the center of the oven.

When the *lasagne* are done, take the dish out of the oven, and let it rest for at least 10 minutes. It is too difficult to handle otherwise. Serve the *lasagne* in cut squares or just scoop some of it out with a large serving spoon.

NOTE: In Catania, *lasagne* are made with eggplant, yellow peppers, tomato, capers, olives, and the inevitable anchovies. Ragusa has *lasagne* with layers of meat and cheese and meat sauce. Enna has *lasagne* with meat and meat sauce and cinnamon. Naples has *lasagne* for *carnevale,* after Lent, made with pork *ragù*, little meatballs, Mozzarella, and tomatoes. Calabria has *lasagne* with soft cheeses, mushrooms, and artichokes. In Puglia, there are *lasagne* with *sugo d'anguilla* ("eel sauce"), but in this case the *lasagne* are really like a wide noodle called *pappardelle,* and the dish is served like a regular dish of pasta with sauce. In Basilicata, the same situation exists, only this time with boiled fresh beans. In the Abruzzo, there is a wonderful lasagna that is really like a pie in that it has a bottom layer of dough that comes up the sides of the casserole, which is then filled with veal, beef, sauce, *prosciutto,* tomato, hard-boiled egg, and *pecorino* cheese. A second layer of pasta is put on top, and the whole thing is sent into the oven to be removed and enjoyed when it is bubbling hot.

Fregnacce

Stuffed Beef Bagatelles

SERVES 8

Here crepes or pasta squares are filled with meat, sausage, and tomatoes, all bound with eggs, covered with the same sauce without eggs, and cheese, and baked in the oven. If you use pasta dough, you cook it first, and then make little packages, sort of like blintzes. Either way, *fregnacce* is a dish a little like unlayered, individual *lasagne*. I've also eaten them in the shape of a triangle, which were delightful to look at on the plate. I had some another time stuffed with tuna, mushrooms, and red pepper flakes. *Fregnacce* means "nonsensical," "bagatelle," "trifle" in Italian. They are so good it must mean you can eat lots in a trifle.

Fregnacce are natural crowd pleasers and therefore a wise choice for large parties or buffets. Make them ahead and heat them at serving time.

MENU SUGGESTIONS: Antipasto of Sweet-and-Sour Baby Onions (page 234) and some Orange and Lemon Salad (page 242) would be good starters. In a bigger meal you could have Breaded Lamb Chops (page 186) after the *fregnacce*. Lemon Ice (page 291) with some Bitter Almond Cookies (page 278) would be a good light dessert.

WINE: Corvo Rosso (page 308)

2 tablespoons virgin olive oil

1 large onion, peeled and finely chopped

3 plain Italian sausages, or use Homemade Sicilian Sausage (page 188), finely chopped

6 ounces coarsely ground beef (or use ½ chicken, with the skin on, boned, and cut into ¾-inch cubes)

2½ pounds fresh tomatoes, peeled, cored, and well crushed, or 1 quart Marinara Sauce (page 78)

Plenty of salt

8 or 9 grindings of fresh black pepper

1 teaspoon red pepper flakes

3 large eggs

3 cups grated pecorino cheese

Butter for greasing casserole dish, q.b.

About 1 pound pasta dough, made with semolina, eggs, and water (see Strummed Macaroni, page 136)

Lightly brown the onions in the olive oil, add the chicken and sausages, and cook them until the sausage just loses color, stirring often. If you are using fresh tomatoes, add them to the meat mixture, and stir. If you are using Marinara Sauce, simply pour it into the mixture, and stir well. Add the salt, pepper, and the red pepper flakes, mix everything well, and let it cook at a gentle simmer for 20 to 25 minutes, stirring often.

Meanwhile, cut the pasta dough into 5-inch squares, about ⅟₃₂ inch thick. You should end up with 22 or 24 squares. If you are not ready to use the pasta squares immediately, cover them with plastic wrap. Butter 2 oven-proof casserole dishes, 8 × 14 inches, or use round or oval ones of similar capacity. Set them aside for later use.

When the sauce is done, pour it into a bowl, and cool it in the refrigerator. When it is cool, put half of it in another bowl, add the eggs, and mix it well. Add 1½ cups of grated *pecorino* cheese, and mix again. Reserve the other half of the sauce until you need it later.

Bring a large pot of salted water to a rolling boil, and throw the pasta squares in, 2 or 3 at a time. Cook them for about 1½ minutes, and remove them with a slotted spoon. Line them up as they are done on a wet kitchen towel. Continue until you have cooked them all.

Place the pasta squares on a table, and put about 3 tablespoons of the sauce and cheese mixture into the center of each one. Fold the top and bottom flaps onto the mixture so that they meet in the middle, and then fold the right and left edges up enough to contain the mixture and make a package. Turn the *fregnacce* over so that the seam side is down, and place them into the buttered casserole dish. Pour the reserved half of the sauce all over the *fregnacce*, and scatter on the rest of the cheese. Bake them in a preheated 350° F oven for 30 minutes, or until the sauce is bubbling all over. If the *fregnacce* begin to dry out a bit before they are hot, cover them with foil for 10 to 12 minutes. Remove the foil and check to see if they are moist and hot. Serve them really *al dente* and very hot.

NOTE: You can assemble the *fregnacce* up to the point of getting them ready for the oven up to 1 day in advance.

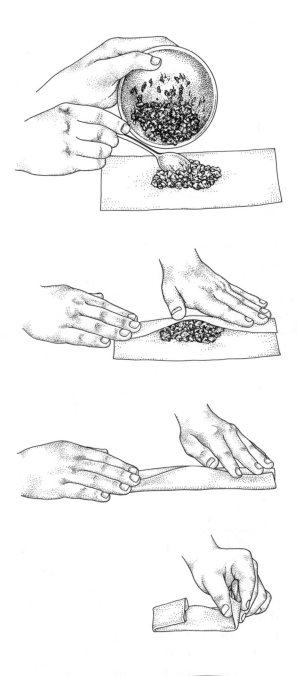

Cannelloni

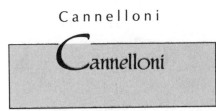

These tubes of fresh pasta are often filled with leftovers in various combinations, but they are just as often made for a special occasion. I provide three versions: one with cheeses, *prosciutto*, and tomato sauce; one filled with fish and spinach and bound together with *béchamel* sauce; and the last made with leftover meats.

Each recipe calls for about 1 pound of freshly made pasta rolled ¹⁄₁₆ inch thick. If you make it any thinner, you might as well be eating filling and no pasta at all. The pieces of pasta should be about 5 × 6 inches, and you should wind up with 20 pieces, more or less.

The pasta must be boiled for only about 40 seconds in plenty of salted water, rinsed, and then laid out on wet towels just prior to being filled. After they are filled and sauced, you can refrigerate them up to 1 day before baking them. Be sure to allow an extra 10 minutes or so of cooking time if you put them in the oven straight from the refrigerator.

Cannelloni are made by putting some of the filling down the center, lengthwise, of a flat piece of boiled pasta, and then rolling it up so that it looks like a fat cigar. The cannelloni are arranged in a buttered casserole dish touching each other, but never put more than 1 layer in a casserole. Sauce is spooned over the top, and they are baked in a hot oven until they are well heated all the way through. It is a very good sign if they have little golden spots on them here and there from the heat.

Cannelloni alla Sorrentina

SERVES 8 TO 10

WINE: Solopaca Rosso (page 304) or Five Roses (page 300)

1 *pound Ricotta*

4 *ounces* prosciutto, *thinly sliced and finely chopped*

6 *ounces shredded Mozzarella*

Salt to taste

Several grindings of fresh black pepper

2 *large eggs*

¼ *cup finely chopped parsley*

½ *cup grated Parmesan cheese*

1 *pound Pasta Dough (page 123), roughly 20 pieces, 5 × 6 inches wide, 1/16 inch thick*

About 3 cups of slightly loose Neapolitan Tomato Sauce with Meat (page 75)

Combine the first 7 ingredients, and mix them well. Add ¼ cup of the grated Parmesan cheese and reserve the rest for later. Mix everything well, and set it aside for later use.

Preheat the oven to 375° F. Butter a casserole dish, approximately 9 × 13, and set it aside for later.

Make the cannelloni as described on page 207, and set them into the buttered dish. When you have finished, spoon the *ragù* all over them, and sprinkle on the remaining Parmesan cheese. Bake the cannelloni for about 20 minutes, or until they are hot and bubbling. Serve them very hot.

Cannelloni alla Siciliana

SERVES 8 TO 10

Here is a recipe that does call for leftovers. In this case, it is leftover beef stew, which would be rare enough in Sicily. Sometimes veal, or a combination of both, is used.

WINE: Sangiovese di Aprilia (page 306), Torbato Secco di Alghero (page 308), or Frascati (page 305)

1 *pound stewed meat (beef or veal)*

1 *pound Pasta Dough (page 123), about 20 pieces, 5 × 6 inches, 1/16 inch thick*

About 3 cups of the stew juices

⅔ *cup grated* pecorino *cheese, or q.b.*

3 *ounces (about 6 tablespoons) sweet butter, or q.b.*

4 *large eggs, beaten*

Optional: ⅓ cup dry red wine and 1 whole clove

Chop the meat fine by hand, and mix it with about ¾ cup of its own juices. If you have not made the stew with wine and cloves you may add ⅓ cup dry red wine and 1 whole clove to the stewpot. Heat and reduce this mixture until it is dense enough to be suitable for the cannelloni filling. Be careful that you do not burn it; take your time. When the meat becomes dense, let it cool, and remove and discard the clove.

Butter a casserole dish, approximately 9 × 13, and set it aside. Preheat the oven to 375° F. Make the cannelloni as described on page 207, and set them into the buttered dish. Drizzle the remaining stew juices all over the cannelloni, and scatter the grated *pecorino* cheese all over them. Dot the cannelloni with butter at random.

Bake the cannelloni in the oven for about 25 minutes, or until they are hot and bubbly. Carefully take them out of the oven and pour the beaten eggs over the top. Shake the casserole back and forth with mitts or towels to protect your hands, and put the casserole back into the oven to bake for another 2 to 3 minutes, or until the eggs are set. Do not let them get too hard and overcooked. Remove the cannelloni from the oven, and serve them very hot.

1 pound any kind of rock cod, sea bass, or similar fish

6 peppercorns

1 bay leaf

Salt to taste

2 bunches fresh spinach, washed and trimmed, or use 1 package frozen spinach, thawed

1 pound Pasta Dough (page 123), roughly 20 pieces, 5 × 6 inches wide, 1/16 inch thick

1 cup Béchamel Sauce, (page 73)

5 or 6 big scrapings fresh nutmeg

2 cups fresh Marinara Sauce (page 78)

½ cup grated Parmesan cheese, or q.b.

Cannelloni
Ripieni di Pesce

SERVES 8 to 10

This is a recipe from Domenico Manzon. It is utterly delicious and would make a divine lunch or a starter course in a dinner.

WINE: Rapitalà (page 308) or Torre Quarto Bianco (page 301)

Put the fish, skinned, filleted, and laid flat, into a very small pan with a lid that will just hold it. Throw on the peppercorns, the bay leaf, add ½ cup of water and a pinch of salt, and put the lid on the pan. Put the pan over medium heat, and let the fish poach for about 5 minutes. Do not overcook it. Remove the fish with a slotted spoon to a dish to cool. Discard the bay leaf, the peppercorns, and the water. When the fish is cool, crumble it into small but not tiny pieces, and reserve it for later.

Put the spinach, with only the water in which it was washed clinging to the leaves, in a pan with a lid. Over medium heat, collapse the spinach, and let it cook for about 2 minutes. Drain the spinach in a colander, and when it is cool enough to handle, squeeze out as much water as you can. Put the spinach in a bowl, add the crumbled fish and the Béchamel, and scrape on the nutmeg. Mix everything well.

Butter a casserole dish, approximately 9 × 13, and set it aside. Preheat the oven to 375° F.

Make the cannelloni as described on page 207, and set them in the buttered dish. Drizzle the Marinara Sauce all over the cannelloni, then sprinkle on the grated Parmesan. Bake the cannelloni for about 20 minutes, or until they are hot and bubbly.

Spiedini di Maiale

Skewered Pork Rolls

SERVES 6

All Italians love food cooked over live coals, especially in the South. One preparation that responds marvelously to this kind of cooking is pork rolls.

This is a simple dish with tasty additions of *pancetta* and cheese. The *spiedini* cook quickly, and they are perfect for an evening meal when the weather is mild and you want to eat outdoors. You can make a respectable version of *spiedini di maiale* in your broiler.

MENU SUGGESTIONS: An antipasto of Chick-peas in Olive Oil (page 95), Potato Croquettes (page 231), and Roasted Peppers with Italian-Style Tuna and Clams (page 104) would be a very nice way to start the meal. After the *spiedini*, a *contorno* of Orange and Lemon Salad (page 242) would be perfect, followed by Cream Puffs (page 256).

WINE: Lacryma Christi del Vesuvio (page 305)

12 *slices of pork cut from the loin (about 2 pounds), about ¾ inch thick*

6 *slices very fresh soft* pecorino *cheese, or use Provolone or Caciocavallo, about ⅛ inch thick, about the same diameter of the meat, each cut in half*

12 *thin slices* pancetta, *about 4 ounces*

3 *large garlic cloves, peeled, each cut into 4 thin slices*

4 *tablespoons finely chopped parsley*
Salt to taste
Freshly ground black pepper to taste
Virgin olive oil for brushing, q.b.
Few pinches red pepper flakes, or to taste

Pound the pork slices with a meat bat or the flat side of a meat cleaver until they are quite thin, being careful not to break them. I find it easy to pound the meat between two pieces of plastic wrap. Several lighter blows are better than one or two heavy poundings. Arrange the meat in rows next to each other, and place a piece of cheese on each one. Gently uncurl a slice of *pancetta*, and spread it out on the cheese. Place a slice of garlic on each, and then sprinkle on about 1 teaspoon of chopped parsley over each. Dust each with salt and some freshly ground black pepper.

Place each slice of pork loin in front of you and fold the left and the right sides over the filling by about 1 inch. Starting from the bottom, roll the meat so that when you finish you have a neat little bundle, shaped roughly like a cigar. Secure the outer flap with a toothpick so that the filling does not fall out. Brush the *spiedini* with olive oil, and put them on a grill over a medium-hot live fire of oak, olive, or fruit wood, turning them often, until they are golden brown and look glossy and succulent. Put the *spiedini* on a warm platter, and serve them hot. Sprinkle on a little more salt and a touch of red pepper flakes. Serve plenty of crusty homemade Garlic Bread (page 91), which you can toast over the fire.

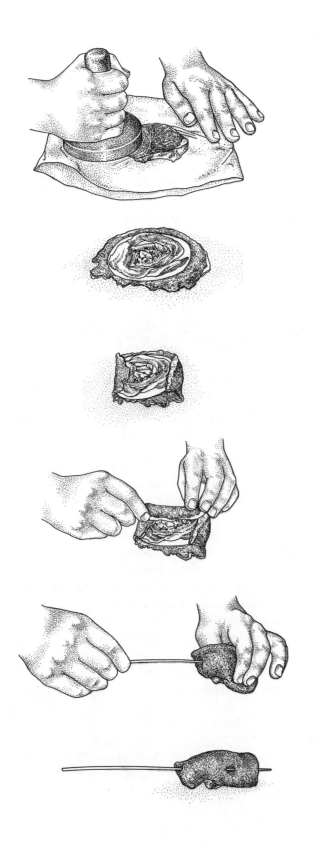

Pasta e Arrosto

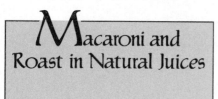

Macaroni and
Roast in Natural Juices

SERVES 6

The pasta in this irresistible dish shares equal importance with the meat. Usually the pasta, sauced with the pan juices and some of the chopped roasts added, is eaten as a separate course. The other meats are then served as a *secondo*. Sometimes they are served on top of, or just to the side of, the pasta, although this is less typical. The traditional meat here is pork, but it could be lamb, veal, or even leftover meats. There is often the addition of quail (in Italy they tend to be bigger). The most scrumptious way to flavor the pasta is to finish cooking it in the pan juices, provided you have enough.

MENU SUGGESTIONS: An antipasto of assorted sliced salami and some black and green olives and Marinated Zucchini (page 100) would be a good starter. Artichokes Stuffed with Ricotta and Salami (page 227) would be a substantial and delicious *contorno* eaten after the quail. A dish of Dessert Ravioli, Teramo Style (page 283), with some Monica di Cagliari (page 307), would be a nice finish to this meal.

WINE: Primitivo di Manduria (page 300)

1 or 2 tablespoons virgin olive oil

12 ounces pork or veal from the rib or top round area, in 2-inch cubes

3 or 4 fresh sage leaves

1 large sprig fresh rosemary or 1 teaspoon dried

6 quail, dressed for cooking

Salt to taste

Plenty of freshly ground black pepper

1½ cups dry red wine

1 pound macaroni of your choice, such as penne, rigatoni, etc.

1 cup grated pecorino cheese

Preheat the oven to 375° F. Put the olive oil into a small roasting pan, add the cubed meat, sage, and rosemary, and toss it well with the oil. Put the roasting pan into the oven, and roast the meat for about 20 minutes. Add the quail to the pan, and turn them every few minutes to be sure they get some color all over. Add some salt and freshly ground pepper. Every few minutes, pour on some of the wine until it is all added. If the pan seems to be dry, add hot water to make a small amount of sauce.

Meanwhile boil lots of well-salted water. Put in the pasta, and stir it well to be sure that it does not stick. As the pasta cooks, take the quail out of the roasting pan, and keep them warm on a plate by leaving the plate on the open oven door, and covering the birds with oiled or buttered parchment paper.

Remove the roasting pan from the oven, and remove the chunks of meat to a wooden chopping board. Chop the meat with a knife into little pieces about the size of a pea, and return the meat to the roasting pan with the juices.

When the pasta is a bit more than half cooked, which could take about 5 minutes, drain it, reserving about 2 cups of the cooking water until later, just in case it is needed. Add the pasta to the roasting pan, stirring it well to mix in the juices. Put the roasting pan back into the oven for about 12 minutes to finish cooking the pasta, stirring it frequently, and add half a cup of reserved pasta water from time to time if it seems to be too dry. The pasta should be juicy and succulent but not too wet or swimming in liquid. Perhaps the pan juices alone will be enough to moisten it properly.

When the pasta is done, divide it among heated plates, and sprinkle grated *pecorino* cheese on it. Serve the pasta at once. After the pasta is eaten, serve the quail as a *secondo*.

CONTORNI

Side Dishes

The side dishes presented here really do "contour" the second-course dishes, whether they are eaten before, with, or after them. Our good luck is that almost all of these side dishes easily change roles and can be *antipasti*. Conversely, many *antipasti* can be used as side dishes. How grateful we should be that these dishes give us endless variations on edible themes. The use of a side dish as a contour gives us the chance to play up or play down the importance of itself or of the second-course dish by having the *contorno* appear at different times for different emphasis. For instance, serving a *contorno* of Artichokes Stuffed with Ricotta and Salami before Braised Oxtails, Roman Style, emphatically gives equal stature to these two dishes; one is meant to "contour" the other, but unquestionably this is one dish separately served, so to speak. On the other hand, when Trout in Casserole, String Bean Bundles, and Italian Potato Pancake are all brought out together on separate plates, the prominence of the Trout is emphasized and the *contorni* seem to be relegated to a lesser role in that course.

These side dishes are so versatile that they can be used as *intermezzi* or even as quasi-*antipasti* to another course of food! For eaters who take little or no meat, side dishes provide an unforgettable, satisfying meal of major proportions, especially if you have a selection such as Sicilian Eggplant Relish with Garlic Bread, Signora Bonnano's Artichokes, Cauliflower in a Basket, Roasted Onions, Italian Potato Pancake, and some Almond Peppers; meat eaters may not even notice its absence when presented with an array as appetizing as the side dishes presented here.

Broccoli al
Diavolicchio

SERVES 6

1½ pounds (1 bunch) broccoli, broken
into flowerets, the trunk sliced the
long way into 3-inch lengths
All-purpose flour for dredging, q.b.

2 or 3 tablespoons olive oil, or q.b.

2 large garlic cloves, minced

About 12 Gaeta, Calamata, or
sun-dried black olives

½ teaspoon crushed red pepper flakes,
or to taste

Salt to taste

Clean the broccoli in cold water, and trim all of the woody parts from it. If it is very young and very fresh, you do not have to remove the membrane on each little stem. If it is older or has not been well cared for, remove the membrane to make the broccoli easier to enjoy. In either case, strip the membrane off the large trunk. Dry all of the pieces carefully.

Spread the flour in a low-sided dish, and dredge the broccoli in it. In a skillet, heat the oil over medium heat, and sauté the garlic for 2 minutes, or until it is light brown. Remove and discard. Fry the broccoli in the hot oil until it is slightly browned on all sides. Do not be concerned if quite a bit of the flour comes off, because it helps thicken the oil and juices. However, be sure that the heat is not so high that it burns the flour, as this affects the taste. Add the olives, sprinkle on the red pepper flakes, and add the salt, but be careful, as the olives generally are quite salty themselves. Cover the pan, and cook everything over low heat for 8 to 10 minutes, or until the broccoli is tender. Serve the *broccoli al diavolicchio* hot, and pour on any remaining oil and juices from the pan.

The clean, sparkly taste of these broccoli is due to the addition of red pepper flakes, a favorite condiment in the South. The whole idea is to produce little darts of fire in the mouth to wake up the taste buds. This dish is also known as *broccoli fra diavolo*, and it can be enjoyed without the olives, although you will lose the contrast between the natural sweetness of the broccoli and the tang of the olives. It is perfect both on an antipasto tray and as a *contorno*.

MENU SUGGESTIONS: These broccoli are delicious with Chicken Roasted with Rosemary (page 178) or as an accompaniment to Tuna and Fennel Seeds (page 201). Because of the piquancy of these dishes, a Semifreddo (page 286) of any flavor you like would be a good way to finish the meal.

WINE: Torbato di Alghero (page 308) with the chicken, Castel del Monte Bianco (page 299) with the tuna

Capunata o Capunatina

Sicilian
Eggplant Relish

MAKES 5 CUPS; SERVES
10 OR MORE

3 medium-sized fresh tomatoes peeled, cored, and diced small, or 1 15-ounce can, whole or chopped

⅓ cup Gaeta or Calamata olives

⅓ cup green Sicilian olives

2 heaping tablespoons black or white raisins

1½ tablespoons capers

⅓ to ½ cup virgin olive oil, or q.b.

1 large eggplant (about 1½ pounds), washed, dried, skin left on, and cut into ¾-inch dice

Salt to taste

Freshly ground black pepper to taste

1 cup diced celery (about 2 branches)

1 large Spanish or yellow onion, peeled and cut into ¾-inch dice

2 tablespoons wine vinegar (red preferred)

2 tablespoons toasted pine nuts

If ever a dish exemplified the "sweet and sour" influence of Saracen cooking in Sicily, it is this one. *Capunata* or, as it is more often called in Sicily, *Capunatina*, is the heart and soul of Palermo. Nowhere else can you get this age-old dish done as well. In and around Palermo, some cooks add lobster, shrimp, fresh tuna roe, or tuna packed in virgin olive oil. If you add any of these, put them in at the last moments of cooking lest they become tough and rubbery from overcooking. With lobster, boil it for about ten minutes, then let it rest and cool. Take it out of its shell, slice or chop the meat, and at the last moment of cooking, stir it in.

This dish is *simpatico* with so many foods that I keep a supply in my refrigerator. It is superb stuffed in medium-sized fresh tomatoes, cold or heated in the oven until the tomatoes just begin to soften. *Capunatina* is perfect hot, but traditionally it is eaten at room temperature with roast lamb, roast or fried chicken, roast pork, poached turkey, or as a relish with large slices of poached fish served cold or hot. You can use it very much like a fresh chutney for most anything. Sicilians prefer it with just some bread and a glass of red wine.

Capunatina keeps extremely well in a covered jar in the refrigerator for about five or six days. Don't bother to can it, as the

Put the tomatoes in a medium-sized bowl. Remove and discard the pits from the black and green olives, coarsely chop the olives, and put them in with the tomato.

Put the raisins in a separate small bowl to soak in warm water for about 20 minutes. Drain them, squeeze the excess water out of them, and add them to the tomatoes and olives. Add the capers as well.

In a frying pan large enough to hold all the ingredients, pour in about ⅓ cup of the olive oil, and heat it over moderately high heat until it is quite hot but not smoking. Carefully put in all of the diced eggplant, and after about 2 minutes, carefully move the mass of eggplant around with a wooden spoon or a spatula. The pieces must be well browned but not burned. This could take 15 minutes of frying and turning the diced eggplant frequently to color all sides of it. If you find that the oil has been soaked up into the eggplant, remove the pan from the heat, and set it aside. After about five minutes, you will notice the oil starting to drain out of the eggplant pieces. Return it to the heat, and continue cooking. Adjust the taste for salt and pepper. When the eggplant is browned on all sides, remove it to a large bowl. Add more oil to the pan if it is needed, add the celery, and over lower heat cook it for 10 to 12 minutes, or until it is slightly golden and soft. Adjust for salt and pepper. Add the celery to the eggplant. Add more oil to the pan if needed, add the onions, and over medium heat cook them until they are soft and golden. Adjust the taste for salt and pepper.

When the onions are done, return the cooked eggplant and celery to the pan, and add all the ingredients, stirring until everything is well mixed. Put the frying pan over low heat, and cook the whole mass for about twenty minutes. The flavors should be well blended, and yet every ingredient must be distinctly identifiable from every other ingredient. It should not be watery; it should be tight yet limpid and glossy.

When the *Capunatina* has finished cooking, put it into a ceramic or stainless steel dish to cool out of the refrigerator. Serve it with chunks of homemade bread.

NOTE: The three major ingredients, eggplant, celery, and onions, are cooked separately. Use the same pan, cooking one after the other. This is extremely important. Do not try to make this dish otherwise. The whole idea is to cook each of these ingredients to its fullest potential, and to salt and pepper them all a bit as you go along. If you were to mix them, first of all you would have too much volume to cook all at once, and second and more important, you would not be able to control the cooking of each ingredient. It would be rather a wet mass. The desired golden color from frying the components separately would be nearly impossible to achieve.

One of the prettiest and most delicious ways to use it is to serve it the way it is done in Gangi, in the central northern inland part of Sicily:

Boil some large artichokes. When they are done, let them cool. Spread the outer leaves out like a giant flower, and fold all the yellow inner leaves out also. Expose the choke, and carefully remove it with a spoon. Place a big spoonful of *capunatina* in the center of the artichoke, and there you have a most elegant and truly delicious first course or a lunch dish.

ingredients are available all year round. Freezing it should not even be considered.

MENU SUGGESTIONS: A starter of *capunatina* followed by Breaded Lamb Chops (page 186) or Fried Codfish, Roman Style (page 190), would be excellent. The *carciofi alla gangitana* make an excellent lunch with some Italian bread. Chocolate Bread (page 284) would be a tasty and not overwhelming dessert to have.

WINE: Etna Rosato (page 308)

Broccoli alla Siciliana

Broccoli and Cheese Casserole, Sicilian Style

SERVES 6

Broccoli alla Siciliana is a good example of the complexity of the cooking of the largest island in the Mediterranean. It is a show of talent that combines unlikely ingredients to produce a dish that is as much a part of history as it represents cooking of modern Sicily. Eaten with a piece of roast chicken or with a piece of fish, like cod, grilled over live coals, this is a dish that might be eaten by many a Sicilian family on a late Sunday afternoon.

MENU SUGGESTIONS: This would be good after an antipasto of "Phone-Wire" Rice Croquettes (page 96) and alongside Lamb Stew with Wild Mushrooms (page 164). A mild but tasty dessert would be Chocolate Bread (page 284) served with Nasco di Alghero (page 307).

1 *large bunch broccoli (about 1½ pounds)*

⅓ *cup virgin olive oil for frying, or q.b., plus a bit more for greasing casserole dish*

1 *large onion, sliced about ¼ inch thick*

   About ½ cup dry red wine, or q.b.

12 *black olives (oil-cured preferred, or use Gaeta or Calamata), pitted and coarsely chopped*

4 *anchovy filets, cut into pieces*

1⅓ *cups Provolone cheese, shredded or finely diced*

   Salt to taste

   Freshly ground black pepper to taste

Clean the broccoli in cold water, and then trim all of the woody parts from it. If it is very young and very fresh, you do not have to remove the membrane on each little stem. If it is older or has not been well cared for, remove the membrane to make the broccoli easier to enjoy. In either case, strip the membrane off the large trunk. Dry all of the pieces carefully and set them aside until you are ready to use them.

Gently fry the onions in olive oil over moderately low heat until they are soft, and reserve them. Cut the broccoli into thin slices or into flowerets. Gently sauté them in another pan in olive oil for 5 to 6 minutes, or until they are barely done. Add salt and pepper. Raise the heat, pour in the red wine, and cook the mixture until the wine is almost evaporated. Watch that you do not overcook the broccoli. If the broccoli appear to be done and there is a lot of liquid in the pan, remove them to a warm dish, and reduce the liquid over medium heat. Then recombine the two, and set them aside.

Grease a baking dish with a bit of olive oil, and place the onions all over the bottom. Lay the broccoli over this, and sprinkle the chopped olives, chopped anchovies, and shredded Provolone over the broccoli. Drizzle on some more olive oil, and bake the dish in a preheated 375° F oven until the cheese is melted and the whole dish is sizzling. But be sure the broccoli are tender. Stick a fork into the broccoli, and if they seem tender, remove from the oven. Do not overcook them, or let them dry out. Serve hot.

Artichokes

SOMEONE ONCE DESCRIBED THE ARTICHOKE as a vegetable that, when you finished eating it, you had more than when you began. You do pile up a lot of leaves when you devour a cooked artichoke, pulling away a leaf at a time until you get to the meaty heart.

Artichokes are delicious eaten that simply, but Italians find them to be supremely versatile. This spiny thistle is excellent boiled or steamed in water. Braising it in a combination of wine and olive oil is just as easy and even more flavorful. Baby artichokes, sometimes sold as "hearts," are very tender, and after the tough outer leaves are removed, they may be boiled, braised, or batter-fried. They also can be sliced paper-thin and eaten raw with a dip, or in a salad. Small, quartered artichokes also are delicious in a dish of braised chicken and mushrooms.

The best-known commercially grown artichoke is the Green Globe, available most of the year, at least in California, but most plentiful and cheapest in March, April, and May. The usual sizing is by the number in a case, 18 being jumbos and rare and very expensive; 48s are the mediums, and are the most commonly found on the market; babies are sold by the pound, and they can be as small as a large olive or as big as a duck egg. A single plant can yield artichokes in all these sizes, depending on when the artichokes are picked.

When artichokes are good, they are delicious, and when they are not good, it is the fault not only of the grower, but also of the grocery for accepting them for sale. Artichokes should be green, firm, and well shaped, with the leaves tightly hugging each other. If they are a little bit open, like a mature flower, you are getting one that is on its way to being a bit tough and dry. The leaves should pull off with a resounding snap if they are fresh and choice. If they have black spots here and there, don't worry. The spots are caused by frost or moisture from low-hanging fog, and will not affect the taste or texture. Be sure, though, when you encounter these spotted ones, that they are still firm and well shaped.

Before cooking artichokes, wash them well in a pan of cold water, holding them upside down and plunging them up and down so that any debris in between the leaves will float out.

When artichokes are cut or trimmed, they will turn black at the cut areas almost immediately. To prevent this, rub the exposed areas with a piece of cut lemon. An easier and cheaper method is to make acidulated water by adding either cider or white wine vinegar to a large pan of water. As you cut and trim the artichoke, keep dipping it in the water, and it remains pretty and fresh-looking. The taste is, if anything, enhanced.

Trim artichokes by peeling off about 2 rows of the tough outer leaves. Trim the little nubs that remain with a small, sharp knife to give it a neat appearance. Place the artichoke on its side and, with a large, sharp knife cut off the top 1 to 1½ inches of leaves, so that the top is flat and even. Keep dipping the artichoke in the acidulated water, or rub the cut surfaces with half a lemon.

From there, trim the rest of the leaves of any sharp tips, using scissors so there are neat rows of leaves all around. Unless I intend to serve the artichoke sitting on its bottom, I leave the stem attached, but I trim any long, inedible fibers. Use a sharp knife to peel the stem and pull off the fibers, as you would on a rib of celery. Cut the fibers off at the base of the stem.

Artichokes are handsome when served with the stems attached, particularly if the stem is long. And it gives you that much more to eat, because the flesh is the same as the artichoke's bottom, the choicest portion of the plant.

In any case, do not throw the stem away. If you must remove it, trim it, and cook it along with the artichokes, and enjoy it separately. After trimming the artichoke, you can either cook it or let it stand in acidulated water for up to 2 hours without hurting the texture or flavor.

COOKING ARTICHOKES

Most commonly, the artichoke is simply boiled in water with some lemon juice, peppercorns, olive oil, and a bay leaf until the bottom can be easily pierced with a dinner fork. It is eaten either hot or cold with the leaves dipped into melted butter, mayonnaise, or a vinaigrette.

Artichokes should be served either cold, or cool enough to handle, because you must pull the leaves off with your fingers. After you have eaten the meaty end of the leaves, you will reach the center, with much thinner, yellow leaves. Peel them off in little bunches and bite them in half, discarding the top spiny portion. Soon you will come to the fuzzy lining of the bottom. This is the "choke," and if the artichoke bud remained on the plant and was allowed to lengthen and blossom, these fuzzy fibers would be purplish petals of the rather spectacular-looking thistle. Using a table knife or a spoon, scrape away and discard this fuzz. What is left is the heavy, meaty, and utterly delicious artichoke bottom, which you should eat in large mouthfuls, really savoring and enjoying it.

ARTICHOKE BOTTOMS

Artichoke bottoms are like little bowls, perfect for filling. You can use almost anything you like for a filling. It is quite an elegant thing to serve and implies you have gone to some expense and effort. To prepare the bottoms, cook the whole artichoke as previously described, remove the leaves and the choke, and trim all around to give the bottom an appealing shape. Do not overcook them, especially if they are going to be reheated with a filling.

Be sure to save the leaves and serve them separately as *hors d'oeuvres*, or as a little scoop for dips.

Fortunately, baby artichokes, sometimes sold as "hearts," are available most of the time. They are a nuisance to trim raw, so I cook them, then trim, peeling away all the outer leaves until only the most tender heart is left. Then I shape them beautifully. You must be ruthless in this job, to end up with hearts that are perfect and perfectly tender and luscious. The fuzzy choke in these tiny artichokes is edible and quite good. It is a bit of a luxury to make them, but it is worth it. I serve them with a really fine vinaigrette of extra virgin olive oil, a hint of lemon juice, an even fainter hint of fresh garlic, some freshly ground black pepper, and a pinch of salt. Toss the hearts well, and enjoy them slightly warm. What a heavenly first course this is!

One of my favorite ways to eat baby artichokes is to clean and trim them well and then quarter them. If you do this quickly, there is no need to rub them with lemon juice. I will have already made a little egg batter: For 6 baby artichokes you will need 1 large egg beaten with a bit of salt and some pepper, some flour for dredging the artichoke quarters in a separate dish, and some olive oil for frying them, enough to come up the sides of the pan about ¼ inch. Dip the artichoke quarters into the flour, then into the beaten egg mixture. Heat the olive oil over medium heat, and when it is quite hot but not smoking, put the artichoke quarters in, and fry them until they are a deep golden color and just barely tender when pierced with a fork. Drain them on a cloth to remove any excess oil, and serve them as appetizers—neat; no sauce; nothing. If you insist on doing *something*, you can serve a little wedge of lemon to squeeze on them. But mainly just enjoy them.

One of the most delicious ways to serve artichokes is to stuff them. The Sicilians love them with bread crumbs and garlic. The recipe for Artichokes, Stuffed Agrigento Style, is the recipe that Mrs. Bonanno uses and the one that my family uses. Mrs. Bonanno also does a variation that I have never seen done in America, anywhere (see Signora Bonanno's Artichokes, page 225). Mr. Bonanno, however, likes to cook his artichokes in the fiercely glowing embers of a spent fire, heavily drizzled with extra virgin olive oil, some salt, pepper, and a good pinch of red pepper flakes (see Pietro Bonanno's Artichokes in Embers, page 224). We ate them one late fall evening near the wheat fields standing around the fire, waiting patiently for the *carciofi* to cook to perfection. We were solemnly handed thick pads of cloth to hold the broiling hot *carciofi* before Mr. Bonanno plucked them from the fire. We gingerly picked off the blackened, burned outer leaves and exposed the inner yellow flesh, which quivered from our hands shaking in the cold and also from our trying to juggle these red-hot gifts from the fire so that they would head straight for the eager open mouths gently blowing on them. To say that these *carciofi* were unctuous, delicious, succulent, and unforgettable would be damning them with faint praise. I will never forget that scene as long as I live.

ARTICHOKE "HEARTS"

Carciofi alle Brace

Artichokes in Embers

SERVES 6

This is a good recipe to make when you are barbecuing or have a fireplace going. It is a special dish to be enjoyed with close friends. This may well be the most delicious of all the artichoke dishes. The artichokes must have enough oil on them to keep them from drying out and plenty of salt and pepper. The red pepper flakes round out all the flavors and bring the whole dish together. (See Artichokes, page 221).

MENU SUGGESTIONS: Along with these artichokes I would have a big dish of Egg "Meatballs" (page 84), Fried Calzone (page 62), or any pizza you like; Codfish Salad (page 102) and some Snails with Oregano (page 171) for *antipasti*. A nice big plate of Grilled Swordfish (page 197) or some Rabbit, Ischian Style (page 182), would be ideal *secondi piatti*. Orange and Lemon Salad (page 242) as a *contorno* would be very good indeed. A plateful of Cream Puffs (page 256) is my choice for an end to this meal.

WINE: Cirò Rosso (page 302) or Etna Rosso (page 308)

6 medium artichokes, washed and trimmed as for Artichokes, Stuffed Agrigento Style (page 226)
About 6 ounces extra virgin olive oil

Plenty of salt
Plenty of freshly ground black pepper
1 tablespoon or more red pepper flakes

Be sure that the fire in the grill or in the fireplace is made with wood or mesquite. I do not recommend commercially made briquettes because they tend to be made with lots of chemicals, and they certainly make food cooked on them taste the same.

Bang the artichokes on a solid surface to open up the leaves so that you can get as much of the ingredients in among the leaves as you can. Drizzle on the olive oil, and then sprinkle on the salt, pepper, and red pepper flakes. Tap the artichokes down on a solid surface again to be sure that the ingredients are well distributed.

Be sure that the fire is spent, but that the coals are very hot and very bright. Make hollows roughly the size of the artichokes in the embers with a metal rod or long tongs. With long tongs place the artichokes into the hollows, and then very carefully heap the embers around the artichokes without putting them on top. You should be able to see the tops of the artichokes peeking out from the embers. Leave the artichokes in the embers for about 40 minutes, or until they are tender but not mushy. You can check for doneness by piercing them with long wooden skewers or a long trussing needle.

Remove the artichokes from the embers with the tongs, and place each one on a thick pad of paper napkins or on thick cotton kitchen towels. Hand an artichoke to each person, and have them gingerly pull off the burned outer leaves and discard them. Eat the rest of the artichoke with the fingers. When you get to the choke, it should be cool enough to remove with your thumbnail. Of course, you could serve the artichokes on a plate and offer a knife and fork, but I prefer eating them out-of-hand.

6 artichokes prepared as for
Artichokes, Stuffed Agrigento Style
(see page 226 and directions
below)

2 eggs, lightly beaten

6 tablespoons olive oil

1½ quarts Marinara Sauce (page 78)

½ cup or more grated pecorino
cheese

Carciofi alla Cura di la Signora Bonanno

Signora Bonanno's Artichokes

SERVES 6

Make a recipe of Artichokes, Stuffed Agrigento Style, but instead of trimming the artichokes with varying layers of leaves, make one blunt cut about one third of the way down from the top. Bang the cut surface down smartly on a solid surface to spread the leaves a bit, and proceed with the stuffing as described in the recipe. When you have stuffed all the artichokes, beat the eggs slightly, and brush them liberally all over the tops of the artichokes. Use more egg if you need it to get a good thick coating on the tops of the artichokes.

Meanwhile, heat the olive oil in a small frying pan over medium heat until it is hot but not smoking. Very carefully and very quickly turn the artichokes upside down (egg batter side down), into the hot oil, and fry them until the egg is golden and set enough to make a lid for the artichokes. Put as many artichokes into the pan as will fit; otherwise, do them one or two at a time.

Heat the Marinara Sauce in a deep pan that will hold all of the artichokes snugly. You should be able to submerge the artichokes, egg batter side up, in the sauce. Do not be concerned if you have too little sauce to cover the carciofi. Simply put a lid on the pan and baste the carciofi often to be sure that they get bathed in the Marinara Sauce. Cook them gently for about 45 minutes, or until they are tender.

Serve the carciofi with some of the Marinara Sauce, and sprinkle on plenty of additional pecorino cheese at the table.

There is an element of genius in this dish. The whole concept of stuffing an artichoke and then sealing it is the sort of thing Mrs. Bonanno, who wanted to create something special as a gift to friends at a great occasion, produced and then it was refined by many hands over many, many meals.

MENU SUGGESTIONS: An antipasto of Mussels with Saffron (page 103) and some Stuffed Pasta Dumplings (page 139) would be good starters followed by Lamb Stew with Wild Mushrooms (page 164) and a contorno of the carciofi. Roman Cheesecake (page 271) would be my choice for a dessert.

WINE: Salice Salentino (page 301) or Regaleali Bianco (page 310)

Carciofi "Ammudicata"

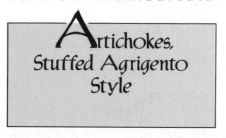

Artichokes, Stuffed Agrigento Style

SERVES 6

The artichoke is native to Sicily, and it was eaten and enjoyed there for a very long time before it made its way north into Tuscany, where it was considered an aphrodisiac. Catherine de' Medici reputedly ate many of them, possibly in preparation for her marriage to the future Henry II of France.

Carciofi "ammudicata" is everywhere in Calabria as well as Sicily. It is the kind of dish to which you can become addicted. In season, when artichokes are plentiful, plump, and cheap, you can make a whole meal of them. They are very refreshing to the stomach, very satisfying without filling you up, and ideal eaten at room temperature.

MENU SUGGESTIONS: As an accompaniment to lamb, these artichokes are perfect. For a cold lunch or a pre-theater party, they would be excellent with Chicken Infused with Bay Leaves (page 161).

WINE: Trebbiano d'Abruzzo (page 298)

FOR THE FILLING

1½ cups bread crumbs
1 cup grated pecorino cheese
½ cup chopped parsley
6 medium garlic cloves, minced
Salt and pepper to taste
6 firm, fresh medium-sized artichokes
½ cup olive oil, or q.b.

FOR THE COOKING WATER

10 whole peppercorns
2 large bay leaves
1 lemon, cut into 4 pieces

Combine the bread crumbs in a large bowl with the *pecorino* cheese, parsley, minced garlic, and plenty of salt and pepper. Set this aside for later use.

Trim the artichokes of excess lower leaves, and trim off the stem so that the artichoke will sit evenly without falling over, but save the stems for cooking along with the artichokes. Also trim off the little sharp points on the leaves. Rub the artichokes all over with a piece of cut lemon to keep the color nice.

Gently pound the top of the artichoke leaves on the corner of a table so that you spread them open to look sort of like a tight chrysanthemum. Set them aside. Mix the cheese and bread crumb mixture once more, and put it into the spread leaves, tapping the artichoke down gently. Fill the spaces full, but do not compact it too much. Place the artichokes in a heavy pan with a lid so that they just fit comfortably. Don't crowd them. Pour the oil all around the artichoke tops so that it gets on the stuffing evenly. Carefully pour some water into the pan to reach about 1½ inches up the sides of the artichokes, being careful not to get water into the stuffing. Throw the pieces of lemon, the peppercorns, and the bay leaves, torn in half, into the water. Put the lid on the pan, and cook the artichokes over low heat for 30 to 40 minutes, or until they are tender but still firm. Test them by sticking a long cooking fork in the top of the artichoke through the bottom. Do not overcook them or they will fall apart. Lift them out of the water with a slotted spoon, and let them sit for a few minutes to drain. Serve the artichokes hot or, as Italians often do, at room temperature. This is a good dish to make ahead of time, but do not store it in the refrigerator.

Juice of 1 lemon

3 young, tender, and prime medium-sized artichokes

10 whole black peppercorns

1 teaspoon salt

1 teaspoon virgin olive oil

FOR THE FILLING

½ pound Ricotta, or q.b.

1 egg, lightly beaten

½ cup grated pecorino cheese

6 thin slices salami, finely chopped

½ cup fresh bread crumbs, or q.b.

6 tablespoons cold, sweet butter, cut into thin slices

Butter for greasing the casserole, q.b.

Carciofi
Ripieni di Ricotta

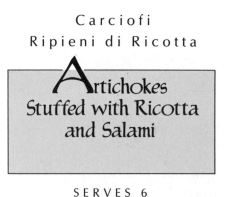

Artichokes
Stuffed with Ricotta
and Salami

SERVES 6

Cut the lemon in half, and keep it handy for rubbing on the artichokes. Carefully trim the artichokes of a few tough outer leaves. Rub the denuded areas with half of the lemon to keep them from turning brown. Cut off the little sharp points of the leaves with scissors, and rub the ends with the lemon half. Trim the stalk of any obvious fibers, but otherwise keep it intact. When the artichokes are trimmed, put them to soak in cold water to cover with the juice of half of the lemon for about 30 minutes.

Mix all filling ingredients together. Cover and set aside. Cut the artichokes in half the long way, including the stem. Scoop out the "choke" with a melon ball scoop or teaspoon. Pull out any purple leaves with sharp spines on the end, as they are inedible. Put the artichokes, cut side up, into a low-sided pan with a lid. Put in enough water to just cover the artichoke halves, and add the peppercorns, the juice of the remaining half of a lemon, the salt, and the olive oil. Bring the water to a boil, lower the flame, and gently simmer the artichokes until they are done, about 20 minutes. Check for doneness by sticking a dinner fork into the bottom of an artichoke. If it is soft (but not mushy), it is done. Carefully remove the artichokes from the water with a slotted spoon, and drain them upside down in a colander to get rid of excess water. When the artichoke halves are cool enough to handle, stuff each of them with one sixth of the Ricotta mixture, mounding it up to look like a mountain.

Butter an ovenproof casserole dish, and put the artichoke halves in it. Scatter the bread crumbs on top of the Ricotta mixture, gently pressing them on with the palms of your hands to be sure they stick. Lay the slices of butter on top of the bread crumbs, and bake the artichoke halves in a preheated 375° F oven until the butter melts and the tops are golden. Serve the *carciofi ripieni di ricotta* hot, and spoon on any butter that may be in the casserole. The *carciofi* are equally delicious at room temperature.

In Sardegna you can find the most succulent Ricotta imaginable, probably on a par with Roman or Sicilian Ricotta, which means the best. Artichokes stuffed with it are not served in the usual posture of sitting on their bottoms looking like dark, elegant flowers. Instead they are cut in half lengthwise, including the stems, boiled until they are tender, and then the inside choke is removed. The space that emerges is filled with Ricotta, other cheese, and salami. The finished dish is quite beautiful, and the taste is heaven. I don't know why such a dish has gone largely unnoticed in the literature.

MENU SUGGESTIONS: I would start with the Artichokes Stuffed with Ricotta and Salami as an antipasto. Then I would have a dish of Fiery Macaroni (page 138) or Macaroni with Arugula and Fresh Tomatoes, Andrian Style (page 135), followed by Braised Oxtails, Roman Style (page 187). A big bowl of fresh seasonal fruit would be my choice of dessert with a few cookies if you think you need something sweet.

WINE: Trebbiano d'Abruzzo (page 298) with the pasta; Cesanese del Piglio (page 304) with the oxtails

Carote al Prosciutto Cotto

Carrots in Cream Sauce

SERVES 4

This is a lovely dish for a buffet or a party because it is quite stunning, and can be made in fairly large quantities.

MENU SUGGESTIONS: An antipasto of Potato Croquettes (page 231) and some Roasted Peppers with Italian-Style Tuna and Clams (page 104) would be good. Lamb Chops, Calabrian Style (page 162), with a *contorno* of Carrots in Cream Sauce on the side would make a delicious meal. Sicilian Cannoli (page 261) would be my dessert in a festive meal like this one.

WINE: Montepulciano d'Abruzzo (page 298)

½ cup strong Homemade Chicken Broth (page 109)

1 pound carrots, scrubbed, trimmed, and cut into ¼-inch rounds

1 sprig fresh thyme

3 sprigs fresh parsley

1 bay leaf

3 ounces (about 6 tablespoons) sweet butter

1 small yellow onion, peeled and cut into tiny dice

4 ounces cooked ham, in one piece

1 teaspoon all-purpose flour

4 large egg yolks

¼ cup heavy cream
Confectioners sugar, q.b.

Heat the chicken stock in a small pan. Bring some water to boil in a saucepan, and add the carrots and the herbs. When the carrots just begin to soften, remove them, and discard the water and the herbs. Put the carrots in a large frying pan with the butter, and add the onions and the whole piece of ham. Sprinkle on the flour. Heat the carrot mixture until it is quite hot, then add the hot chicken stock, stirring. Cook the carrots over low heat until they are tender but not falling apart and the stock has been mostly absorbed.

Meanwhile, beat the yolks well with the cream. When the carrots are done, remove them from the heat, and let them set in the pan for about 1 minute. Remove the ham, cut it into small pieces, and reserve it. Pour the yolks and cream mixture over the carrots, which should have cooled just a bit, and mix everything well. The yolks should begin to firm up and thicken. If they do not, return the pan to low heat, and stir continuously until they thicken. Do not overcook them, or they will curdle and you will have scrambled eggs.

Put the carrots onto a heated serving dish, and sprinkle on just a very light veil of powdered sugar; not much. Scatter the pieces of ham over the surface. Serve the carrots immediately.

1 *large cauliflower with good-looking green leaves and stems*	*All-purpose flour for dredging cauliflower, q.b.*
Salt and pepper to taste	½ *cup olive oil for frying*

Cavolfiore Fritto

Cauliflower in a Basket

SERVES 6

Cut the green stems and leaves off the cauliflower in one piece and reserve them for a serving "basket." This is not difficult, but it is a bit painstaking. Be careful that you do not break the "basket." The best way to remove the stems and leaves in one piece is to insert a small, sharp knife in between the stems and into the core to cut it enough to weaken it. Do this all around until you have loosened them completely. If the leaves and stem look a little dry, soak them in ice-cold water for about 15 minutes, then wrap them, still wet, in a kitchen towel, and put them into the refrigerator for 2 to 3 hours.

Wash the cauliflower in cold water. Place the whole cauliflower in a pan just big enough to hold it with cold water to cover, salted to the ratio of 1 teaspoon of salt to 1 quart of water. Bring the water to a boil, and then reduce the heat. Simmer the cauliflower for 10 minutes more, or until it is barely tender. Do not overcook it. It is better to slightly undercook it if there is any doubt.

When the cauliflower is done, drain it well, and set it aside to cool. Spread some flour in a low-sided dish. When the cauliflower is cool enough to handle, cut it into golf-ball-sized pieces, and dredge them in the flour. Heat the oil in an 8-inch frying pan until it is hot but not smoking and fry the pieces of cauliflower until they are a deep golden color. Drain them on kitchen or absorbent towels as they are finished. While they are hot, sprinkle on plenty of salt and freshly ground pepper. You can keep them warm as you finish cooking the other pieces by putting them into a warm oven with the door slightly ajar, as this keeps them from getting soggy.

When you have finished, place the stem-and-leaf basket on a serving platter or in a deep serving dish, which gives it more stability, and arrange the fried cauliflower pieces in it to look as natural as possible. Serve the cauliflower hot. Or you can dispense with the basket and simply heap the pieces on a serving dish. People who don't like cauliflower will eat several of these pieces and enjoy them.

The idea of shaping cauliflower into a basket is not strictly Sicilian, but it is a nice idea anyway. This serving method is described in the recipe that follows. Often it can be part of an antipasto as well as a *contorno*, and it is particularly good if you make a *fritto misto*, a mixed assortment of fried foods that could include fish and other vegetables.

MENU SUGGESTIONS: The cauliflower would be good as a separate *contorno* or even as a part of an antipasto followed by Homemade Sicilian Sausage (page 188). It is particularly good in a mixed platter of Fried Squid (page 174). "Drowned" Ice Cream (page 293) of any flavor would be refreshing after this rather substantial meal.

WINE: Rosato del Salento (page 300)

Cavolfiore Gratinato

Cauliflower au Gratin

SERVES 6

½ cup melted butter

1 large cauliflower

6 quarts water for boiling

1 tablespoon salt for boiling water

1 large garlic clove, finely chopped

3 tablespoons chopped parsley

½ cup grated Caciocavallo cheese

¼ cup bread crumbs made from fresh bread

Salt to taste

Freshly ground pepper to taste (use plenty)

You will like cauliflower prepared this way because the combination of flavors really complements the underlying taste of the vegetable, which is rather bland when cooked and eaten plain.

Considering the complexity of Sicilian cooking, I am surprised that there are no anchovies or black olives in this dish. Actually I added Gaeta or Calamata olives, and it is even better.

The use of butter is unusual also. This means this dish is a little newer or it must have been used in a house that had some foreign influence. In this case "foreign" might well mean the mainland of Italy.

MENU SUGGESTIONS: At room temperature this dish could be included in any array of antipasti. It would be perfect to accompany Fried Codfish, Roman Style (page 190), or served as a separate contorno, followed by Chicken, Potenza Style (page 179).

WINE: Bianco Alcamo (page 308) with the fish; Aglianico del Vulture (page 301) with the chicken

Use a small amount of the melted butter to grease an ovenproof dish that will hold all the flowerets of cauliflower. The dish should have low sides to encourage the coloring of the cavolfiore. High-sided dishes tend to make the cavolfiore bake more than roast, making the color not so good; plus the dish could become too liquid. Set the dish aside for later.

Wash the cauliflower in lots of cold water. Strip off the outer leaves, and discard them. Bring the water to a boil, and add the salt. Boil the cauliflower, whole, for 12 minutes, or until it is almost done. (If you prefer, you can cut off the flowerets first and cook them briefly, around 4 to 5 minutes, in the boiling water. Drain the flowerets well. Proceed with the recipe.) Drain the cauliflower, and set it aside to cool.

When the cauliflower is cool enough to handle, break it into large pieces, perhaps the size of a small lemon, and put them into the buttered baking dish. Scatter on the garlic, parsley, grated Caciocavallo cheese, and bread crumbs. Sprinkle on some salt, grind on plenty of fresh black pepper, then drizzle the melted butter over the top. Bake the cavolfiore in the top third of a preheated 375° F oven for 20 minutes, or until the cauliflower looks golden. Serve it hot.

2½ pounds russet, or other farinaceous "old" potatoes

4 to 5 tablespoons sweet butter

1⅔ cups grated pecorino or Parmesan cheese

1 large garlic clove, finely chopped or puréed

3 tablespoons coarsely chopped parsley

Plenty of salt

Plenty of freshly ground pepper

1 whole large egg and 2 large yolks

All-purpose flour for dredging or dusting, q.b.

Bread crumbs, q.b.

Whites of 2 large eggs, very gently beaten until just frothy

1 cup olive oil for frying, or q.b.

Cazzilli o
Crocchetti di Patate

Potato Croquettes

MAKES ABOUT 20 CAZZILLI

Peel and quarter the potatoes, and cook them in salted water over medium heat for about 20 minutes, or until they are barely tender. Do not overcook. Drain them well, and put them back on the heat for a couple of minutes to dry them well. Keep shaking the pan or stir them around while they are drying.

While the potatoes are still warm, mash them or put them through a potato ricer. Add the butter, cheese, garlic, and parsley, and correct for salt and pepper, if needed. Set the potato mixture aside to cool completely. If the potato mixture is too soft, add a *little* flour, 1 tablespoon at a time, and mix well. The potato mixture should be stiff and firm. Add the whole egg and the 2 egg yolks.

The usual way to make *cazzilli* is to gently roll about half the mixture into a thick baton about 1½ inches across, gently flatten it so that it is oval, then cut the baton into 2-inch-long pieces. Repeat the procedure with the remaining potato mixture. Otherwise, you could take 2 to 3 tablespoons of the potato mixture at a time and shape it any way you like. Some people like to shape them into oblong balls, sort of like miniature footballs. But you could make them round if you wish, or you could just let the mixture be free-form as it drops from the spoon.

After you have shaped the *cazzilli*, lightly dust them all over with flour, or roll them gently in a bowl or dish of flour, and set them aside. Be sure to work quickly and diligently because if the *cazzilli* sit too long, they become soggy and have to be refloured.

Spread the bread crumbs in a low-sided dish. Put the floured *cazzilli* into the lightly beaten egg whites, coat them well, then roll them in the bread crumbs. Meanwhile, heat the olive oil in a heavy frying pan over medium heat. Do not have the oil too hot or it will burn the potatoes before heating them through. The ideal temperature is around 360° F. Place the *cazzilli*, a few at a time, in the hot oil, and fry them gently until they become a dark golden color. Serve them hot.

Cazzilli can be made ahead of time, perhaps several hours, and reheated in a 400° F oven for a few minutes with the door ajar, but they are best if served right after frying them.

Potatoes are not frequently seen at the Sicilian table. Of course, the Sicilians have a particularly inventive hand when it comes to vegetables. This is another of those dishes that are heartwarming and earthy, but can also be served at the most formal meal. In any setting I have yet to see them go un-eaten. *Cazzilli* should be very moist and tender and yet be able to hold their shape. The use of bread crumbs as a casing for them helps keep them moist and tender, but they are equally good, if not better, without. You could use leftover mashed potatoes here, but in our family there were seldom any leftovers.

MENU SUGGESTIONS: Mushrooms in Parchment (page 240) would be a good starter, followed by a plate of Potato Croquettes piping hot and just plain, and then followed by Trout Vernaccia (page 177) and some Spinach, Roman Style (page 245), as a *contorno*. Pears in Chocolate (page 285) would be a fine ending.

WINE: Bianco Alcamo (page 308)

Ciamotta

Mixed Vegetable Stew

SERVES 6

1 *large eggplant, about 1 pound, washed*

1 *pound large, firm potatoes, washed*

4 *bell peppers, red and green mixed if possible, washed*

1 *pound ripe, firm tomatoes (use same amount canned if necessary)*

Virgin olive oil for frying, q.b.

2 *large garlic cloves, peeled and crushed almost to a purée*

Salt to taste

7 *to 8 grindings fresh black pepper*

Sometimes called *ciambotta*, this dish is similar in preparation to *capunatina* (page 218) in that the ingredients are cooked separately and then recombined later on. This is a hearty dish and would be perfect for large parties because it looks beautiful in a big rustic casserole dish or bowl. Unlike so many vegetable dishes from the South, this one is eaten not at room temperature but hot. The nice thing about it, besides being delicious, is that you can prepare some of the ingredients ahead of time. Then, shortly before serving, you can finish cooking it in a casserole dish that can go to the table or buffet.

Two women, separately, recited the ingredients to me just as they are shown. However, one said that you did not have to salt and weight the eggplant. The other insisted it must be done. Let the condition of the eggplant determine whether to salt and weight it or not.

MENU SUGGESTIONS: This *contorno* is good with any roasted fowl or meat, be it beef or pork or veal, etc. It is awfully good as a *contorno* with Fried Codfish, Roman Style (page 190), or Fried Squid (page 174).

WINE: Regaleali Rosso (page 310) with the meats; Est! Est!! Est!!! (page 304) with the fish

Trim off the stem and leaves from the eggplant, and cut it crosswise into ¼-inch-thick slices. (If you are going to salt it, see note at the end of this recipe.) Peel the potatoes, and cut them crosswise into ⅛-inch-thick slices. Core the peppers, discard the seeds, cut them in half and then into ¼-inch-thick slices lengthwise. Peel and core the tomatoes, and crush them very well with your hands.

Put enough olive oil in a large frying pan to come up the sides about ⅛ inch. When the oil is very hot, fry the eggplant slices until they are nicely browned on both sides, then remove them with a slotted spoon to a casserole dish large enough to hold everything. Add more oil to the pan if necessary, fry the sliced potatoes until they are golden, and add them to the eggplant. Fry the peppers until they are just barely soft, adding a bit of olive oil if you think they need it. When the peppers are done, put them into the casserole with the other cooked ingredients. Preheat the oven to 375° F. (You could make the fried ingredients a few hours ahead of time and put them into the casserole dish. When you are ready to continue the recipe, put in the other ingredients and proceed as directed.)

Scatter the crushed tomatoes on the ingredients in the casserole, add the crushed garlic, and gently mix all the ingredients. Add some salt and freshly ground pepper, and stir again. Bake the casserole in the oven for 30 minutes, or until it is bubbling. This dish is well cooked, and it is meant to be that way. Serve it hot from the casserole dish.

NOTE: To remove excess water from eggplant, sprinkle salt on both sides of each slice and put them in a colander overlapping one another. Place a bowl inside the colander and weight it down with a heavy object. Let stand for 1 hour. Rinse the slices quickly under cold running water and pat dry.

Cipolle Arrostiti

Roasted Onions

SERVES 6

6 Spanish (yellow) onions, all
uniformly about 3 inches in
diameter (if possible)

Virgin olive oil, q.b.

Plenty of salt and pepper

⅓ cup red wine vinegar

Leave the outer brown skins on the onions, rub them gently with plenty of virgin olive oil all around, and sprinkle on the salt and pepper.

Place the onions on a baking sheet with borders, and bake them in a 375° F oven for 1 to 1½ hours, or until the onions are soft but not mushy. When they are done, remove them to a serving platter, and cut them in half vertically, leaving the outer brown skin in place.

The roasting pan will now have quite a bit of caramelized natural sugar from the juice of the onions exuded during the baking. This is the basis for the sauce that goes on the onions. To deglaze the roasting pan, place it over a burner on top of the stove, and pour in the red wine vinegar. Scrape the pan well with a wooden spoon to dislodge all of the "caramel," and let the vinegar alcohol burn off for about 4 minutes over low heat. This will help reduce the juices and vinegar and make the sauce thicker. Push aside any large pieces of outer onion skin that may be left in the pan. Use a pastry brush to brush the sauce over the open faces of the onion on the serving platter. If there is any sauce left over, save it for brushing on barbecued chicken or grilled fish.

These onions were probably originally thrown into a fire, allowing their skins to become a case to protect the flesh from the flames. Over the years they were roasted in spent baker's ovens. No matter what their beginnings, these humble bulbs are a big hit whenever and wherever they are served.

SERVING SUGGESTIONS: Make more onions than you need, and save them for later use. They keep in the refrigerator in good condition for about 4 days. Take the skins off, and use just the succulent insides in a salad. Cut the insides of the onions into thick strips, and combine them with coarsely chopped tomatoes. Sprinkle on plenty of virgin olive oil, salt, pepper, and oregano (fresh if you can get it). Additionally, you could add quartered or chopped hard-boiled eggs and a few anchovy filets, either chopped or whole, as you like.

The original way to make this salad is to use green tomatoes. If you have your own garden or can get to some tomatoes growing on a vine, pick them just before they begin to get their red color. This is a very special salad and is awfully good, especially if you can find underripe tomatoes.

MENU SUGGESTIONS: Use these onions as an antipasto. They make excellent relishes for chicken, pork, beef, and larger grilled fish of all types.

WINE: Favonio Pinot Nero (page 299) for the meat and chicken; Etna Bianco (page 308) for the fish

Cipolline in Agrodolce

Sweet-and-Sour Baby Onions

SERVES 6 TO 8

Cipolline in agrodolce is a favorite vegetable for all Italians. The baby onions should be soft but not mushy; beautifully dark but not scorched; and perfectly caramelized without being burned and bitter.

To facilitate peeling, soak these little onions in cold water for about 20 minutes. This softens the skin, but it also strengthens it so that when you pull, it tends to peel off rather than just break. As you peel each one, place it in a bowl of fresh cold water. Continue until you have finished.

MENU SUGGESTIONS: Serve the onions hot as a relish for roast pork, chicken, lamb, or even fish such as Fried Codfish, Roman Style (page 190). At room temperature they are superb as an ingredient in an antipasto.

WINE: Trebbiano di Aprilia (page 306)

2 ounces (about 4 tablespoons) sweet butter, or q.b.

2 pounds small white boiling onions, peeled

⅓ cup granulated sugar

1 cup white wine vinegar

1 cup water

Freshly ground black pepper to taste

Put all of the ingredients in a heavy saucepan, cover it with the lid, and bring it to a boil. Reduce the heat, and simmer the onions for about 40 minutes, shaking the pan often and occasionally stirring the onions around with a wooden spoon. Be careful that you do not break them up. When the onions appear to be glossy and begin to turn a little bit brown, test them for doneness using a trussing needle or a long bamboo skewer, which should easily push into the onion. Be sure that they are not mushy. When they are almost done, you will be ready to do the final cooking of the onions to give them their characteristic look and flavor.

Uncover the pan, and continue cooking the onions. Let the sugar caramelize, and shake the pan often. If there seems to be a lot of liquid, use a higher heat to speed up the evaporation. *Do not let the onions burn!* Just before the onions are as dark and beautifully fragrant as they should be, remove them from the heat so that they can continue to cook, but not overcook, and the sugar does not caramelize more than it should.

If the onions are glazed and cooked and the liquid has not reduced enough, remove the onions with a slotted spoon, and put them aside. Finish reducing the juices and sugar over medium heat until they are thick and dark, then remove the pan from the heat, and let the juices cool for a few minutes. Recombine the onions and the juices.

¾ *pound green string beans (about 60)*

12 *scallion tops or chive blades*

2 *large eggs*

Salt and pepper to taste

All-purpose flour for dredging

1 *cup olive oil for frying*

Fagiolini Legati

String Bean Bundles

SERVES 6

Trim the beans, making sure that any strings are removed and that the beans are clear and smooth. Make them the same length, leaving them about 5 inches long.

Boil about 6 quarts of salted water in a large pot. Throw the beans in, and let the water return to the boil. Cook the beans at a medium boil for about 3 minutes. *Be careful!* Do not overcook them! Test them after 3 minutes; they should be *very* crunchy. Drain them in a large colander immediately, scatter them on a kitchen towel on a cookie sheet, and let them cool.

When the beans are cool, assemble them into small bundles of 5 each, and tie them in the center with a blade of chives, or use the green top of a scallion. If the green top is too fat, cut it lengthwise once or twice. Chives work the best. Make a very pretty knot, and if the ends are too long, cut them at a diagonal to make them tidy. Set them aside. (This part of the job can be done as much as a day ahead, but be sure to refrigerate the beans.)

Beat the eggs in a low-sided dish, and season them with salt and pepper. Spread the flour in a low-sided dish. Dip the bean bundles in the beaten egg, shake them well to remove excess egg, then roll them in the flour. Heat the oil in a frying pan over medium heat to about 360° F, place the bundles in the hot oil, and fry them until the beans are a golden color all over, turning them several times, if necessary, to get an even color. Do not overcook them. The beans are partially cooked already, and this last step simply heats them through, because they are sealed with the egg and flour mixture. Add more oil if you need to.

Remove the beans from the oil with a slotted spoon to drain on absorbent towels. If you have a lot of bundles to fry, keep the finished bundles on a platter in a warm oven with the door ajar until you have finished the job.

Serve the bean bundles at once. These do not "hold back" very well.

When these beans are made correctly, they are as good as the *tempura* in Japanese cooking. Sometimes they are called "Golden Beans." Originally they were tied with a string, and then at serving time you were faced with the tedious job of cutting off all the strings and carefully unwrapping the bundle before you could put the beans on a plate. Tying the bundles with chives or scallion tops saves time and makes them look attractive on the plate. *Fagiolini legati* are special. I think they are worthy of being served as a separate course.

MENU SUGGESTIONS: These would be very good as a separate *contorno* served before Mussels with Saffron (page 103). They would also be wonderful as part of a mixed fry including Fried Codfish, Roman Style (page 190). They would also be fine as a *contorno* for Skewered Pork Rolls (page 210).

WINE: San Severo Bianco (page 301)

Fagiolini al Pomodoro

String Beans in Tomato Sauce

SERVES 4 TO 6

Fagiolini al pomodoro is a popular dish, but it may be only in second place after Swiss chard done exactly the same way, and perhaps it is neck and neck with spinach, which is also done the same way. They are all marvelous dishes, and you will be amazed at how different each green ingredient interacts with the other ingredients. Just as the beans can be eaten cold, so can the Swiss chard and the spinach. Also this dish, cold, is good even without the addition of vinegar and oil as suggested in the recipe.

Fagiolini al pomodoro is also known in Sicily as a Calabrian dish. This is normal, because there are vast similarities in many southern Italian dishes. Names of dishes are often interchangeable. One region may have a traditional dish that is eaten and cooked by everyone living there and called by a name that implies it is from elsewhere. When it shows up as *Calabrese*, these beans are accompanied by small raw, red onions that have been thinly sliced and soaked in cold water for about an hour and then towel-dried before they are eaten. *Fagiolini al pomodoro* and raw red onions, accompanied by a basket of Garlic Bread (page 91); now there is a real meal.

MENU SUGGESTIONS: This dish is perfect as a *contorno* for the Tuna and Fennel Seeds (page 201). In a cold meal Chicken Infused with Bay Leaves (page 161) would be a natural choice. String Beans in Tomato Sauce would be a good choice to accompany Braised Beef, Roman Style (page 184).

WINE: Fiorano Bianco (page 305) with the tuna; Ravello Rosso (page 303) with the chicken or beef

1 *pound fresh string beans*

2 *tablespoons virgin olive oil, or q.b.*

2 *large garlic cloves, well mashed*

  Salt and pepper to taste

2 *large ripe tomatoes, peeled, seeded, and chopped, or 1 15-ounce can chopped tomatoes*

Wash and trim the beans of any blemishes or strings, and break or cut them into 3-inch lengths. Boil them in rapidly boiling salted water for about 2 minutes. Drain them well, and scatter them on a plate or a towel to dry and cool slowly. Set them aside.

In a large heavy pan heat the olive oil, lightly brown the garlic, and then add salt and pepper. Add the chopped tomatoes, and cook them for 15 minutes over high heat.

Next, lower the heat, add the beans, stirring them well, and cook them, covered with a lid, for 5 to 6 minutes, or until they are just tender. Watch that you do not overcook the beans. They should be *al dente*.

Serve the beans hot, but any that are left over are also good cold with a tiny splash of red or white wine vinegar and a drop of virgin olive oil.

1 *pound string beans*   *Juice of ½ large lemon*

   Salt to taste   *Freshly ground pepper to taste*

2 *tablespoons olive oil, or q.b.*

The beans should be small and crisply fresh. Trim them of any strings, take off the tops and tails, and then break them into 4-inch pieces. Wash the beans in cold water, and set them aside.

Bring 6 quarts of salted water to a rolling boil over high heat. Throw all the beans in the water at once, bring the water back to a boil, and from that time cook them for exactly 6 minutes. Remove them from the heat, drain them immediately, and put them into a bowl. Add the olive oil, lemon juice, plenty of freshly ground pepper, and taste for salt.

Serve the beans hot. If you are not going to serve the beans immediately, keep them in a colander or on a towel after you have drained them. Later, when you want to serve them, put the beans in a pan of any kind with the oil, and heat them over medium heat, shaking the pan often. When the beans are hot, squeeze on the lemon juice, add the ground pepper, and taste for salt. Do not put the lemon juice on them until they are just ready to be served, because the beans turn yellow if they sit in it for more than 5 minutes. Leftovers are good cold in a salad or served as a cold vegetable.

Fagiolini Verde

Green Beans in Olive Oil and Lemon Juice

SERVES 4 to 6

One of the best recipes I know to bring out the clean, sweet taste of fresh beans.

MENU SUGGESTIONS: *Fagiolini* are excellent to use as a hot or cold antipasto. They are also good as a *contorno* for Chicken Roasted with Rosemary (page 178) or Mussels and Sausage (page 194).

WINE: Favonio Pinot Nero (page 299)

Fave e Cicoria

Fava Beans and Chicory

SERVES 8 OR MORE

This may well be *the* regional dish of Puglia. It is certainly one of the most revered of all the old dishes. Other regions have their versions, but in Puglia, *fave e cicoria* is king. You really need *cicoriella*, a wild green much like dandelion, but that is not available to us, so the next best thing is chicory or curly endive. This recipe is dedicated to the English soprano Margaret Hayward, Siren of Lecce.

MENU SUGGESTIONS: An antipasto of a Pizza Margherita (page 49), Sweet-and-Sour Baby Onions (page 234), and some Mussels with Saffron (page 103) followed by a *primo* of Fiery Macaroni (page 138) would be a good start. You could then have some Fried Codfish, Roman Style (page 190), with a *contorno* of Fava Beans and Chicory. Rose Wheels (page 264) would be my choice for dessert.

WINE: Per'e Palummo (page 303)

1 *pound dried fava beans*
2 *large heads chickory or young, tender curly endive*
   Salt to taste
Freshly ground black pepper to taste
Plenty of extra virgin olive oil
Optional (but often served):
1 red (Bermuda) onion

Soak the beans overnight in lots of cold water. Drain them, and when you are ready to cook them, put the beans into a large pan with fresh water to cover 3 inches above their surface. Bring the water to a boil, and then reduce the heat so that the *fave* simmer. Cook them for about 1 hour. Turn the heat off, and let the *fave* cool enough so that you can handle them. Peel the outer covering off them, and discard it. This is easily done if you peel the butt end off, and then you can easily squeeze the bean out. Put the peeled beans into a bowl, and mash them well with a fork. They must not be too smooth. Set them aside until later.

If you are going to serve red onion with this dish, peel it, and slice it very thin. Put the slices into very cold water for about 1 hour before serving them, and dry them on a towel.

Wash and carefully trim the endive, and break it into branches. Put them into a heavy pan, and barely cover them with water. Cook them for 12 minutes, or just until they are tender and sweet. Meanwhile, gently and carefully heat the *fave* purée in a small, heavy saucepan. Drain the endive well, and gently squeeze out any excess water. Be careful, as they will be very hot.

On a heated plate put a mound of hot, cooked endive and a few spoonfuls of *fave* purée next to it. Sprinkle on some salt, grind on some fresh black pepper, and drizzle on quite a bit of extra virgin olive oil. Offer more oil at the table. If you are using the sliced onions, put a few on the plate. The persons eating this dish either eat each component separately, or they may take small bits of everything and put them together to make a mouthful. Either way is correct.

This is a wonderful *contorno*, but it is great as a snack. *Fave e cicoria* is delicious at room temperature, so it is a good make-ahead dish, but do not refrigerate it. And do not put the oil on it until you serve it.

NOTE: In some instances the outer skins of the *fave* are removed after the beans have soaked and before they are boiled. This results in a much whiter version than what I have described. Either way is correct, but it is nice to have that agreeable white purée.

1¼ pounds very large mushrooms
  (fresh porcini caps are ideal)

1 lemon, cut in half

⅓ cup virgin olive oil, or q.b.

2 large garlic cloves, minced

⅓ cup or more shelled pine nuts

Salt to taste

Freshly ground pepper to taste

2 teaspoons red pepper flakes, or to
  taste

Funghi
Arrosto con Pignoli

Mushrooms
Roasted with Pine
Nuts

SERVES 6

Brush the mushrooms to clean them, and rub them all over with the lemon to keep them from turning too dark. Gently pull the stems out of the caps, and put them into a separate bowl. If the mushrooms are very fresh, as they should be, the stems should snap right out but they may not break off completely. Do not be concerned, as this is normal. If the ones that have done this look odd, trim them with a paring knife. Cut the stems crosswise into thin slices that resemble a nickel. Reserve them for later use.

Preheat the oven to 400° F. Place the mushroom caps (inside facing up) in a well-oiled ovenproof dish from which you can serve. Use a dish that has low sides; if you use a deep one, the mushrooms will not take on color as well. They will be more baked than roasted and will exude liquid, which substantially changes the dish. It will still be good but not as characteristic as it should be. Use about ⅓ of the oil that is called for to oil the dish. The mushrooms must not be swimming in oil, but they must have enough or they will be dry and uninteresting. None of the other flavors will come together well if you do not have enough oil. The mushrooms should fit snugly in the dish, but do not force them together. Scatter the pieces of mushroom stems, garlic, pine nuts, salt, plenty of pepper, and the red pepper flakes evenly on top of the caps. Drizzle on the rest of the olive oil, plus more if you like.

Bake the mushrooms in the top third of a hot oven for *about* 15 or 20 minutes, or until the pine nuts begin to color. Serve them hot.

This is another example of how inventive Sicilians are with vegetables.

MENU SUGGESTIONS: These mushrooms would be good as an antipasto, hot or at room temperature. They would be delicious as a *contorno* to Skewered Pork Rolls (page 210) and Breaded Lamb Chops (page 186) and they would also be wonderful to have with Polenta on a Board (page 203).

WINE: Corvo Rosso (page 308) or Faro Rosso (page 309)

Funghi 'Ncartati

Mushrooms in Parchment

SERVES 4

Mushrooms, anchovies, and lemon juice seem simple enough at first. But when you see just how they come together, you get an idea of the effortless complexity of Sicilian cooking. This is truly a great dish.

MENU SUGGESTIONS: Mushrooms in Parchment is a terrific hot antipasto. A larger portion makes a lunch dish with some bread, followed by a bowl of fruit or a plate of Bitter Almond Cookies (page 278) served with some Marsala Fine (page 309).

1 *pound fresh, plump mushrooms of your choice*

6 *anchovy filets, finely chopped*

4 *heaping tablespoons finely chopped parsley (Italian preferred)*

Plenty of freshly ground black pepper

2 *large garlic cloves, finely chopped*

4 *tablespoons bread crumbs*

About 4 tablespoons virgin olive oil, plus extra for brushing

Juice of 1 lemon

6 *squares parchment paper, about 12 × 12 inches each*

6 *thin lemon slices for garnish*

Brush the mushrooms well. Do not wash them unless it is really necessary to clean them. They get soggy easily. Cut them into thin slices, and place them in a medium-sized bowl. Add all the other ingredients, except the lemon slices and the parchment paper. Mix everything very well with your hands or with cooking spoons.

Preheat the oven to 375° F. Lightly brush some olive oil on each sheet of paper. Place one sixth of the mushroom mixture on the paper a little off-center. Place one of the lemon slices on top of the mixture, and plait (crimp fold) the parchment to form a neat, secure little package. Place the parchment packages on a cookie sheet. (You can prepare the *funghi 'ncartati* to this point up to 8 hours ahead.) Bake the mushrooms for 7 to 8 minutes, but no more.

Serve the package on a heated plate. Have each person open his own package by tearing open the top and folding it back on itself, perhaps with three folds.

Any leftover mushrooms are delicious cold as an antipasto, and they are a good relish for hot or cold roast beef, lamb, or chicken.

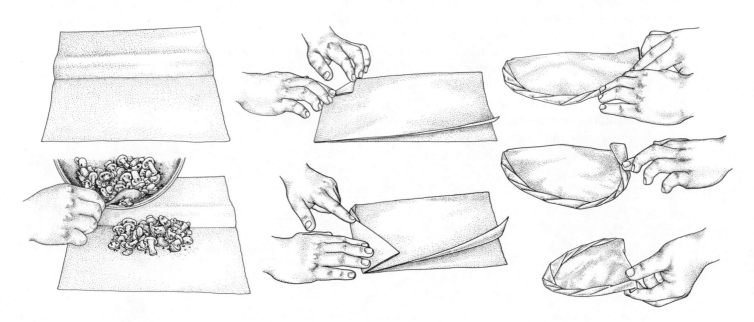

8 *very large leafy branches fresh oregano, or 1 teaspoon dried*

½ *cup extra virgin olive oil, plus more for basting, or q.b.*

2 *garlic cloves, peeled and finely chopped*

Big pinch of salt

¼ *cup white wine vinegar, or q.b.*

1 *large eggplant, washed, skin on, and sliced about ¼ inch thick*

6 *leaves fresh mint, finely chopped*

Tie the oregano branches together with a string to form a sort of brush. Gently mash the brush of oregano with the lower palm of your hand to crush it slightly. It should give out a heady perfume.

Mix the olive oil, garlic, salt, and vinegar in a low, very wide platter using the oregano brush as a whisk. Shake off any excess dressing, and reserve it and the oregano brush for later. (Or use a pastry brush if fresh oregano isn't available.)

When the fire is quite lively but not roaring, baste the slices of eggplant with some olive oil, using the oregano brush (or the pastry brush), and put them on the grill. Grill the slices, basting them with olive oil often, until they are soft and have burned spots all over them like little flecks. This is essential to the appearance of the dish, and it has everything to do with the taste. The eggplant slices should look utterly appetizing while they are cooking. Cook them on one side until they are flecked with burned spots, and then turn them over to cook on the other side.

As the eggplant slices are done, put them onto the platter with the olive oil mixture, and turn them over again and again in the mixture. Do this every time you add new slices to the platter. When you have finished grilling the eggplant slices, be sure that they have all been well anointed with the mixture on the platter. If they look too dry, drizzle on some more oil and a tiny splash of vinegar. Scrape the leaves off the oregano brush, and throw them onto the platter. Or scatter 1 teaspoon of dried oregano onto the eggplant slices in the platter. Add the chopped mint, and toss the eggplant slices well to be sure they absorb all the flavors.

You can eat the eggplant hot or cold. I think it is one of the best dishes I have ever had. I would serve it hot with large chunks of homemade bread and a big red wine as a separate and very important course in the meal.

Melanzane, "Non So Come Si Chiamano"

MAKES 4 SERVINGS

My cousin Mary's eggplant dish is so old it is ancient, and according to her, no one has ever known the name. With the mesquite vogue still raging, this is a perfect dish to make while you are grilling other things. In Italy, of course, the usual wood for live fires is oak or olive. Don't be a slave to the recipe. When you read it, you will get a feel for it.

MENU SUGGESTIONS: A dish of Potato Croquettes (page 231) as an antipasto would be good along with the eggplant followed by Pepper-Sprinkled Mussels (page 169). A *primo* of Fettuccine, Roman Style (page 132), would be a delicious other flavor to introduce. If you are still hungry, you could have Chicken Roasted with Rosemary (page 178). A Semifreddo (page 286) would be my choice for dessert.

WINE: Brindisi Rosso (page 298)

Insalata di Arancia e Limone

Orange and Lemon Salad

SERVES 4 OR 6

Here you have the sweetness of orange, the tartness of lemon, and the sharp tingle of mint (or basil) and onion. When you have gone this far, you must add black pepper and olive oil.

Sicilians often eat this salad with bread as a meal. White wine is good with it, and it does not seem to disturb the palate at all. Without trying dishes like this one you can never hope to understand the taste values of the South. If you can find blood oranges, use them. The color is astounding, and the flavor, if they are ripe, is magnificent.

MENU SUGGESTIONS: On a warm day this would be an ideal antipasto. It is also good for a light lunch. It is particularly refreshing after a meal of roast meat or fowl, or Trout Vernaccia (page 177).

WINE: Torre Quarto Bianco (page 301)

4 medium navel oranges (blood oranges are preferred but very difficult to find)

2 medium very ripe lemons

1 small red (Bermuda) onion, peeled and sliced thin or finely chopped

6 leaves fresh mint, finely chopped
Freshly ground black pepper to taste

2 tablespoons virgin olive oil, or q.b.

Optional: Use sweet basil instead of mint, or use it as well as the mint (dried will not do here)

Peel the oranges and lemons, totally removing the pith (white spongy part). This is best done by slicing off the peels, including the pith, using a sharp paring knife. Peel them over a plate so that you can catch and reserve for use any juices that collect.

Slice the oranges about ¼ inch thick. Slice the lemons about ⅛ inch thick, cutting right through the seeds with a very sharp knife. Seeds are normal, and Italians are used to eating fruit with seeds in it. The seeds can be removed by the eater later. Spread the sliced oranges out on a platter with low sides, and then arrange the sliced lemons on them in a neat pattern. Pour on any reserved juices from the peeling and slicing. Put the sliced or chopped onion all over the sliced oranges and lemons, and then scatter on the chopped mint and/or basil. Grind on the fresh black pepper to taste, and then drizzle the entire surface with the olive oil, using a bit more if you like. Let the platter stand for about 2 hours at room temperature. The salad should be served at room temperature.

2 *pounds firm, young "white" waxy*
potatoes

⅓ *cup virgin olive oil, or q.b.*

3 *to 5 teaspoons red pepper flakes, or*
to taste

Big pinch of salt, or to taste

Wash the potatoes and then place them, unpeeled, in a large pan of cold water to cover. Bring the water to a boil over high heat. When it just begins to boil, lower the heat and maintain a gentle boil for 25 minutes, or until the potatoes are done. They are done when a fork can penetrate easily, but the potatoes must not be too soft or they will fall apart. Remove them from the hot water with a slotted spoon and cool them until you can handle them. Peel them, and cut them into ¼-inch slices. Arrange half of the sliced potatoes in a serving dish that eventually will hold them all and sprinkle with salt. Reserve the other half until later.

Heat the olive oil in a frying pan over high heat. When the oil is hot, add the red pepper flakes. Stir the flakes well and do not let them burn. The oil should be tinged with red. Spoon half of the oil and red pepper mixture over the potatoes in the serving dish. Quickly put the other layer of potatoes over the first layer, add more salt, and then pour the rest of the olive oil and red pepper mixture over them, using a rubber spatula to get it all out of the frying pan. Serve the potatoes immediately or leave them for eating later. Do not refrigerate them.

Patate al
Diavolicchio

SERVES 6 OR MORE

In and around the ancient city of Matera, this dish is highly regarded, as well it should be.

MENU SUGGESTIONS: A large serving of Mussels and Sausage (page 194) would be a good meal with *contorni* of Hot Devil Potatoes and Artichokes, Stuffed Agrigento Style (page 243). Some Bitter Almond Cookies (page 278) with Moscato di Pantelleria (page 309) would be a very mild and pleasant finish to the meal.

WINE: Locorontondo (page 300) or Corvo Rosso (page 308)

Pomodori alla Siciliana

Sicilian Tomatoes

SERVES 6

The Sicilians and other Southerners like to eat their tomatoes in a slightly underripe state in dishes such as the one that follows. They save the really ripe and sweet tomatoes for sauces or eat them plain with bread.

MENU SUGGESTIONS: An antipasto of Mussels with Saffron (page 103) with some Garlic Bread (page 91) would be a good starter course. Linguine with Clams (page 134) would be an excellent *primo piatto*, followed by Lamb Chops, Calabrian Style (page 162), with a *contorno* of the Sicilian Tomatoes (page 244). A big piece of Golden Christmas Bread (page 280) with a little glass of Moscato di Trani (page 300) also would be delicious.

WINE: Merlot di Aprilia (page 306)

6 *medium tomatoes, a little underripe*

2 *or 3 tablespoons olive oil, plus more for brushing and oiling on later, or q.b.*

1 *large onion, peeled and finely chopped*

1 *small tin anchovy filets, finely chopped, plus the oil in the can*

3 *tablespoons chopped parsley*

2 *tablespoons coarsely chopped capers*

½ *cup black olives, Gaeta or Calamata, pitted and chopped into pea-sized pieces*

½ *cup bread crumbs*

Salt and pepper to taste

Cut off the top ¼ of the tomatoes and save them for later. Squeeze out the seeds and juice and scoop out as much of the remaining pulp as you can without breaking through the sides, reserving everything. With a knife, chop the tomato pulp into pieces about the size of a pea, and set it aside.

Heat the olive oil in a medium-sized frying pan, add the chopped onions, and fry them until they are golden and soft. Add all the other ingredients, except the scooped-out tomato skins, salt and pepper to taste, and cook everything together for a minute or two.

Lightly oil a baking dish with some of the olive oil. Stuff the scooped-out tomato skins with the pulp and onion mixture, put the top back on, and place the tomatoes in the oiled baking dish. Lightly brush the stuffed tomatoes with a little more olive oil, and then bake them in a preheated 350° F oven for 20 minutes, or until they are soft and slightly wrinkled but not mushy. Serve the tomatoes hot.

Any leftover stuffed tomatoes are very good at room temperature with bread and wine.

3 *tablespoons of the smallest available raisins, black or white*

4 *medium-sized bunches spinach (about 2½ pounds), washed at least twice in cold water and trimmed of roots*

⅓ *cup virgin olive oil, or q.b.*

5 *medium garlic cloves, peeled and well crushed*

4 *tablespoons pine nuts*
Big pinch of salt

6 *or 7 grindings of fresh black pepper*

Spinaci alla Romana

Spinach, Roman Style

SERVES 4

Spinaci is practically a requirement with roasted baby lamb. It is also good with roast veal, pork, or chicken. It is often enjoyed by itself as a *contorno*.

MENU SUGGESTIONS: Savory Bread Salad (page 94) as an antipasto would be perfect followed by Trout Vernaccia (page 177) or Braised Beef, Roman Style (page 184), or Chicken Roasted with Rosemary (page 178), with a *contorno* of Spinach, Roman Style. Spumoni (page 296) would be a very tasty finale.

WINE: Locorotondo (page 300) with the trout; Sangiovese (page 306) with the beef or chicken

American raisins tend to be very sweet and do not have much depth of flavor. The sweetness is all pervading. To help expel some of the natural sugars, put the raisins in a small bowl covered with enough warm water to soak them for about 15 minutes. Set aside.

Put the spinach in a frying pan large enough to hold it all and cook over high flame until it collapses and turns dark green, stirring it well and shaking the pan the entire time. After this stage, cook it about 4 minutes longer. Try to drive out any moisture left in it. Remove the cooked spinach to a bowl and set it aside. If the frying pan is wet, wipe and dry it out.

Heat the olive oil in the frying pan, add the garlic, and brown it, but do not burn it. Meantime, take the raisins out of the water and squeeze them as dry as you can. Remove and discard the garlic from the oil, add the pine nuts and the raisins, and cook them carefully until the pine nuts take on a deep golden color. Watch out because the pine nuts can burn in a second. Never leave the pan, even for a moment. Return the spinach to the pan, stir it all around with a fork, and add some salt and pepper. Mix all the ingredients so that the flavors come together and cook them for about 3 or 4 minutes. You may add additional olive oil if you think the *spinaci* look a little dry. You can also serve additional oil at the table to be drizzled on the portions. Serve the *spinaci alla Romana* hot.

Tortino di Patate

Italian
Potato Pancake

SERVES 4 AS A MAIN
COURSE OR 6 AS A
SIDE DISH

This little *tortino* (the name cannot really be translated, although the root word is *torta*, for "cake," and sometimes it is called a *frittata*) is a dish important enough to serve as a separate course.

MENU SUGGESTIONS: I would use this as a *primo piatto* after an antipasto of Roasted Peppers with Italian-Style Tuna and Clams (page 104) and then have some Homemade Sicilian Sausage (page 188) with a *contorno* of Mixed Vegetable Stew (page 232). Almond Tart (page 270) is a good closer to this meal.

WINE: Cacc'e Mmitte di Lucera (page 299)

2 *pounds russet or any "old" potatoes*
½ *pound* pancetta, *cut into ¼-inch squares*

Plenty of salt and freshly ground black pepper

Wash the potatoes, put them, whole into a pan large enough to hold them comfortably, and cover them with cold water. Bring the water to a boil and cook them until they are soft and done. If the potatoes weigh 7 to 8 ounces each, they may take about 30 minutes to cook. When they are done, drain them, and let them cool until you can handle them.

Meantime fry the *pancetta* in a 9-inch heavy frying pan. When the *pancetta* is deep gold in color, remove it from the pan. Reserve 2 tablespoons or a bit more of the remaining fat for use later. If there is less than 2 tablespoons, add about 1 tablespoon lard or butter.

Mash the potatoes in a ricer, or by whatever method you like, and add plenty of salt and pepper. Mix it well, add the *pancetta*, and mix again. Reheat the 2 tablespoons of the reserved fat in the pan, and when it is fairly hot, put the mashed potato mixture into it carefully so that you do not splash the hot fat. Mold the potato mixture into a thick pancake, lower the heat, and watch that you do not burn it. If it seems to be browning quickly, remove the pan from the heat for a moment or two, then replace it over lower heat. When the *tortino* is a deep gold on the bottom, loosen the sides, and slide it around a bit in the pan so that it does not stick. If it is stuck, gently put a flexible spatula under the bottom of it and try to unstick it. (This is one case where a nonstick pan could be very useful, but remember that this is not a license to reduce or eliminate the fat. Without it you might as well eat a plain boiled potato.)

Place a dinner plate over the top of the frying pan, very carefully invert the *tortino* onto the plate, then slide the *tortino* back into the pan and brown it on the other side. Serve it very hot, immediately. Cut it into wedge-shaped pieces as you would a cake.

1 large eggplant, about 1 pound

3 cups water for boiling

½ cup fine fresh bread crumbs

½ teaspoon salt

½ cup grated pecorino cheese

All-purpose flour for dredging, q.b.

Olive oil, q.b.

Lard, q.b.

Wash the eggplant, trim off the stem and leaves, and cut it in half lengthwise. Put the water into a shallow wide pan with a lid and bring it to a boil. Lay the eggplant, skin side down, into the boiling water and put on the lid. Lower the heat and simmer the eggplant for 30 minutes, or until it is quite soft. If the water should all boil away, add a bit more, but just enough to keep the eggplant from burning. Remove the eggplant from the pan with a slotted spoon and drain it very well by putting it into a colander and letting it set for about an hour.

Knife chop the eggplant into very small pieces. Put the chopped eggplant into a bowl, and add the bread crumbs, salt, and the cheese. Mix it all well with your hands. If it seems very loose and hard to shape, add a few more bread crumbs. Form the eggplant mixture into balls about 2 inches around and set them on a flat plate as you make them. (You can make the eggplant balls to this point up to 1 day ahead and refrigerate them.) Spread some flour for dredging on another flat plate. Put equal amounts of olive oil and lard to come up the sides of a frying pan about ¼ inch. When the oil is quite hot, roll the eggplant balls around in the flour and put them into the hot oil. When they have become brown and crusty on one side, carefully turn them over with a fork or tongs and fry the other side until it, too, is brown. Remove the balls to an absorbent towel to drain any excess oil from them. Serve them piping hot.

NOTE: You can complete the recipe and set the balls aside to be reheated in the oven later on. This is not ideal, and I would do it only if you have no alternative. It would be better to make them ahead as described and finish frying them at the last moment. They take almost no time to brown.

Polpette di Melanzane

Eggplant Dumplings

MAKES 12 DUMPLINGS, APPROXIMATELY 2 INCHES AROUND

The inside of these dumplings is luscious and soft, and the outer part, which produces a crunchy sensation in the mouth, enhances the flavor of the eggplant. The taste might easily be mistaken for artichoke. The classic method of cooking this dish is to boil or steam the eggplant. But, if you are so inclined, you can roast it instead and get an even more pronounced flavor.

MENU SUGGESTIONS: Golden Fried Pumpkin (page 101) and some Chick-peas in Olive Oil (page 95) would be good *antipasti*, followed by Rabbit, Ischian Style (page 182), with a *contorno* of Eggplant Dumplings (page 247). Flaming Chestnuts (page 281) would be an appropriate and festive finish to this meal.

WINE: Torre Quarto Rosso (page 301)

Sedano Fritto

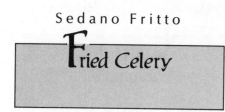

Fried Celery

Celery is essential to stocks, soups, roasts, and stuffings, but it is not high on anyone's list as a favorite vegetable. *Sedano fritto* is simple to make, and for those who are not enamored of cooked celery, I urge you to try this. It is a perfect accompaniment to spicy roast chicken dishes, and it is equally good with fried fish or as part of a *fritto misto* ("a mixed fry").

All of the ingredients in the recipe are q.b., depending on the number of servings you desire.

MENU SUGGESTIONS: Fried Celery is good as a snack or even for a cocktail party where you are serving semidry or fruity sparkling wines. It is also good as an antipasto along with some Chick-peas in Olive Oil (page 95) and thin-sliced salami. It would make a good *contorno* with or just after some Trout in Casserole (page 202). Finish with Rose Wheels (page 264) and a nice glass of Moscato di Trani (page 300).

WINE: Solopaca Bianco (page 304) or Brindisi Rosato (page 298)

Celery, cleaned and cut into 3- or 4-inch lengths
All-purpose flour for dredging

Large eggs, lightly beaten
Olive oil for frying
Salt to taste

Boil the celery in salted water for 6 to 7 minutes, or until it just begins to lose its crunch. Drain well and lay out on a large towel to cool and dry completely.

Put enough olive oil to come about ½ inch up the sides of a low-sided frying pan and heat the oil to about 360° F—hot but nowhere near smoking. Spread the flour in a shallow dish, and lightly beat the egg in another low-sided dish. Toss the cooled celery around in the flour, then roll it around in the beaten egg, and then fry it in the hot oil until it is a deep gold. Remove it from the oil with a slotted spoon, and put it onto a draining cloth or absorbent towels to absorb any excess oil. Sprinkle it with salt the moment it comes out of the hot oil. Serve it very hot.

Mandorlata di Peperoni

Almond Peppers

SERVES 8 OR MORE

¾ cup almonds, well toasted, slivered, or coarsely chopped

5 medium bell peppers, 3 red and 2 green (preferably)

4 tablespoons virgin olive oil, or q.b.

½ cup raisins, black or white or mixed

1½ teaspoons granulated sugar

¼ cup red wine vinegar

Salt to taste

If the almonds are not toasted, place them on a cookie sheet with sides, and put them into a preheated 350° F oven for 15 to 20 minutes, stirring them often and watching them carefully, as they burn easily. Take the almonds off the cookie sheet and cool them before using them.

Wash and core the peppers, removing the seeds and any white pith found inside. Cut the peppers lengthwise into ¼-inch slices and fry them in the olive oil over medium heat until they are soft but not really limp. The peppers should have nice dark gold burn spots all over them, but they should retain their color and have some body. They must not be undercooked. They must be cooked enough to develop their own sugar, which happens only under heat for a period of time. Throw in the raisins and stir everything around for about 2 minutes. Sprinkle on the sugar and stir again. Scatter on the almonds and stir again. Pour in the vinegar, salt to taste, and let the mixture cook for about 5 minutes.

Serve the Almond Peppers hot or let them cool to room temperature. They will keep, well covered, in the refrigerator for about 3 or 4 days. Allow Almond Peppers to come to room temperature before serving.

The sweetness of well-cooked peppers and the toasty crunch of almonds is a classic combination in Basilicata, where both grow in abundance. This dish, like so many Italian dishes, is good either hot or cold. Mandorlata di peperoni is as wonderful as a relish as it is a vegetable. With roasted meats and fowl, it is a natural.

MENU SUGGESTIONS: Almond Peppers are good cold as an antipasto. They are also very good as a contorno for roasted meats and fowl, such as Breaded Lamb Chops (page 186), or as a side dish to Pizza, Lanciano Style (page 52). With this particular meal, I think Lemon Ice (page 291) would be a refreshing way to end.

WINE: Monica di Sardegna (page 307)

Desserts and Sweets

Desserts imply the end of a meal, a mighty fine time to eat them. But the desserts here are equally good and possibly more appropriately eaten, as the Italians often do, as midmorning or midafternoon treats, and to honor guests at times when a meal may not be wanted or possible. Many desserts eaten by Italians come from bakeshops that have managed to retain homemade quality. The ones given here are all within the ability of home cooks to make. Desserts always imply good times and festivities, special days, rewards for deeds well done, banishing the blues, or just plain sharing. Who could refuse a proffered plate of Rose Wheels and White Meringues with coffee or wine when friends, or strangers about to be friends, gather, or Miniature Sweet Buns and Saint Agatha's Nipples with morning coffee, or Hazelnut Semifreddo or Lemon Ice on a hot afternoon, and what about Flaming Chestnuts and Dessert Ravioli, Teramo Style, after a cold evening of playing or shopping or working? Who can say no?

Pasta Soffiata

MAKES ABOUT 25
TINY CREAM PUFFS
OR ABOUT 8 TO 12
SMALL (3-INCH)
CREAM PUFFS

1 cup water

½ cup (8 tablespoons) butter (if using sweet butter add ¼ teaspoon salt)

1 tablespoon granulated sugar

1 cup all-purpose flour

4 large eggs at room temperature

Put 1 cup of water and the butter and sugar in a heavy saucepan and bring to a boil over high heat. Add the flour all at once, lower the heat, and stir vigorously with a wooden spoon until the batter makes a soft cohesive mass that does not stick to the sides of the saucepan. It will make a sizzling sound. Keep stirring the batter over the heat. All this should take about 2 minutes. When the dough is quite cohesive and maintains a ball shape as you spin it around the pan, remove the pan from the heat. Transfer the mass of dough to a bowl to cool for about 10 minutes. When it is tepid, add one egg at a time, beating it in thoroughly. Keep this up until 3 of the eggs are used. Before putting in the last egg, test the batter. It should be firm enough to stand up in peaks. The more eggs you can incorporate, the fluffier the baked or fried result will be. But you must be careful that you do not make the dough too soft. It must hold its shape readily when you push it around with a spoon.

This dough is best used just after making it. However, you can store it, well covered, in the refrigerator for up to 2 days. Be sure to let it come slowly to room temperature before you use it, and also be sure to re-beat it. Use it wherever it is needed in desserts or other dishes, such as baked cases for savory fillings, etc.

This dough is the basis for making that age-old celebrated dish served on Saint Joseph's Day, without which no southern Italian could live: *sfinci di San Giuseppe*. *Sfinci* show up everywhere and are simple to make. The same dough is also used to make Tiny Cream Puffs (page 257) filled with whipped cream and smothered in melted chocolate. Some of the best I have eaten were made in San Giuseppe Jato by the Albanian population that resides in the Piana degli Albanese in Sicily. Cream Puff Pastry has been used extensively in Italy since the early sixteenth century and probably found its way South even earlier.

1 *recipe Cream Puff Pastry (page 255)*

1 *large egg, beaten, or q.b.*

1 *recipe Pastry Cream (page 260) for the filling*

Pasticcini Ripieni

Cream Puffs

MAKES 12 CREAM PUFFS

All over Southern Italy there are dessert tables in restaurants resplendent with dishes of *pasticcini* or *profiteroles* ("tiny cream puffs") sitting in chocolate sauce. Here's an easy recipe for both of them.

Preheat the oven to 400° F. Line a baking sheet with parchment paper, or lightly grease the sheet and dust it with flour. Tap the sheet to shake off any excess flour. Either pipe or spoon on the Cream Puff Pastry, leaving a good amount of space between each one. The puffs should triple their volume, so let that be your guide. For cream puffs, put down a round patch of batter and surmount that with a smaller patch to give it good shape. Brush the tops and sides with the beaten egg. Place the baking sheet in the lower third of the hot oven. Check the puffs after 15 minutes. Open the door a tiny bit and leave it like that so that there is no huge loss of heat, then slowly open it more—as much as you need to see in. If the puffs are baking too fast and developing too much color, lower the heat to 325° F or so. When the puffs are set and firm, but not yet done, remove them and make a couple of small horizontal slits in their sides with a sharp knife to let out any steam. Continue to bake them until they are an even deep gold all over. Total cooking time from 25 to 35 minutes.

Cool the cream puffs on a rack for at least 1 hour before serving them. Do not cover them with anything while they are even slightly warm or they will become soggy. For optimum taste and texture, fill them just before serving, although you could fill them several hours before using them. Store them in a cool place but out of the refrigerator, if possible. When refrigerated, they tend to get condensation on them and become soggy.

The baked, empty shells freeze very well. They will keep at room temperature, well covered, for 2 or 3 days, but they mold easily, so watch out.

Fill cream puffs with Pastry Cream, zabaglione cream, or whipped cream flavored with chocolate or vanilla, etc. The ideal way to do this is to use a pastry bag fitted with a Bismark tip. This is a small metal tube shaped like a baby funnel but with the tip end cut at a diagonal. This makes it sharp enough to pierce the cream puff and fill it without damaging it. Most good kitchen supply stores will have pastry bags and Bismark tips. Dust the cream puffs well with confectioners sugar and serve.

1 recipe Cream Puff Pastry (page
    255)

2½ cups whipped cream (produced
     from 1¼ cups whipping or heavy
     cream)

¼ cup confectioners sugar

1 cup semisweet chocolate

1 cup hot water

1 tablespoon sweet butter

2 tablespoons heavy cream

Proceed as in Cream Puffs (page 256) and fill Tiny Cream Puffs with whipped cream sweetened with confectioners sugar. When you have finished filling them, melt the semisweet chocolate and add hot water slowly, stir the mixture all around until it is smooth and shiny. Let it "cook" over very low heat or, better yet, in a bain-marie, for about a half hour. Take the chocolate sauce off the heat, stir in butter and heavy cream, and continue stirring well. Let the sauce cool, then drizzle it all over the *profiteroles*. If there is any sauce left, you can serve it separately. Done this way, you can make the *profiteroles* several hours ahead.

Profiteroles

MAKES ABOUT 25 TINY
CREAM PUFFS

To make *profiteroles* as they do in San Giuseppe Jato, Piana degli Albanese, the Albanian Plains in Sicily, make the cream puffs much smaller.

Pasta Frolla

Tender Pastry

MAKES ENOUGH
DOUGH FOR
2 9-INCH TARTS

2½ cups all-purpose flour

½ cup granulated sugar

½ teaspoon salt

½ cup sweet butter at room temperature

Optional: *rind of 1 lemon*

4 *to 5 tablespoons ice water (or use wine or whiskey, but be sure it is cold)*

Of all the tarts and pies that Italians make, surprisingly few of them call for prebaking the crust. This seems to be more a commercial technique.

Most people overwork the dough. This is fine in bread dough because it activates and encourages the formation of gluten. You want the reverse when making pie and tart doughs, known as "short doughs." This refers to the fact that they are made with shortening, otherwise known as fat. The fat can be vegetable shortening, lard, butter, or oil. The addition of fat helps to reduce the formation of gluten. Therefore, tart crust is not chewy and pully like bread, instead it is crumbly and flaky and very tender.

The idea of rubbing fat and flour together is to coat the flour molecules so that the "gluten networking" will be hindered. Moisture must be added to the flour and fat mixture or the mixture will not hold together, but it cannot be excessive. It must merely help to bind the flour and the fat. The moisture can be milk, water, eggs, wines, or whiskey. Each one or a combination of them gives different results. Short doughs must not have heat either from external sources such as a hot room or from the hands because that, too, produces gluten. That is why you are always instructed to "work fast."

Short doughs should always look like they require more mixing. Most people mistakenly mix until they look nice and

If you are using a marble slab to make the dough by hand, place the flour, sugar, salt, and lemon rind (if desired) in a mound. Then use your fingers in a circular motion to create a "well" in the mound of flour. Break the butter into little pieces about the size of grapes and throw them into the well. Then pull some of the flour onto the butter and combine them. Do this very quickly and do not overmix. Add the water and very quickly mix the dough so that it just holds together. This should take about 1 minute. (You can do all of this in an electric mixer using the paddle or flat beater attachment. I find that a food processor makes the dough too wet, and I don't like the results. Use one if you wish and if you know what you are doing.) When the dough just holds together and is not crumbly, wrap it in plastic or foil and let it rest out of the refrigerator, but in a cool place, for about half an hour.

Roll out the dough with a heavy rolling pin, but do not put too much pressure on it. It will be quite fragile. Lightly dust with flour as needed to keep the dough from sticking to the marble or to the rolling pin. If the dough breaks, do not be concerned because it is easily repaired. Simply push it together again, or break a piece off the edge and use it like you would modeling clay to repair any tears or breaks. Gently but firmly, grasp the top edge of the dough and lay it over the rolling pin. Then roll the dough and the pin toward you and keep rolling the dough onto the pin. Put the dough into a tart pan. Lay the loose end of the dough on the edge of the pan and then unroll the dough slowly and gently, in the reverse direction, and let the dough fall into the pan. Adjust it after it is in the pan, if necessary. If the dough breaks while you are putting it in the pan or even afterward, simply repair it as described earlier. Prick the dough, at random, all over the bottom with an eating fork. Cool the dough in the refrigerator for at least 3 hours.

When you are ready to bake the crust, put wax paper or lightweight foil on top of the dough. Fill the tart with dry beans or rice as a weight to keep the dough from ballooning while baking. Medium-sized gravel also would be good to use. It never breaks or becomes rancid because you can soak it in detergent occasionally, rinse it well, and reuse it indefinitely. Gravel is cheap and readily available at pet or hardware stores.

smooth and perfect. That appearance usually means you have gone too far already. The results may be tolerable but not optimal. Dough, when it is properly mixed, will look like it has little clumps of unincorporated flour and/or fat. That is just the way it should look. For a really flaky, tender crust you should see rather large globs of fat, perhaps the size of a dime or a nickel in your dough. Those doughs are the best.

If the dough requires more mixing, it will get it when you go to roll it out for use. You are better off trying to correct undermixed dough than overmixed dough.

Short doughs need to rest a lot between handlings. The more you let dough rest, in a cool or cold place, after mixing it and before rolling it, the better. After you have rolled it and put it into a pan, let it rest in a cool spot again. The ideal way to approach making short dough is to think ahead. Make the dough the day before you need it. This also saves chaos and last-minute rushing in the preparation of the meal. On the morning of the evening you want to serve the tart, roll the dough and line the pan. Let it rest in the refrigerator for several hours. Prepare the filling. When the time comes to actually bake the tart, put in the filling. While you do that, preheat the oven, always a good practice for any baking or roasting. Then with virtually no struggle you can produce a very tasty tart without lots of trauma.

If you cannot make the dough in a leisurely way, ahead of time, you can speed up the waiting process by putting the dough into the freezer after every step. Be sure you don't freeze it, though; just chill it for about 10 or 15 minutes between each step.

You can also make up a batch of dough and freeze it well wrapped for up to 2 weeks. Defrost the dough overnight in the refrigerator and then use it as described above.

Crema Pasticciera

Pastry Cream

MAKES ABOUT
2 ½ CUPS

Pastry Cream is delicious as it is, but you can add the zest of a lemon to make it even tastier. It is the perfect filling for Saint Joseph's Day Fritters (page 289).

2 cups milk

6 large egg yolks

¾ cups granulated sugar

1 teaspoon vanilla extract

½ cup all-purpose flour

1 tablespoon sweet butter

In a small saucepan heat the milk to scalding. Set it aside. Combine the egg yolks, sugar, and vanilla together in a heavy nonaluminum saucepan, and whisk very well until the mixture is light yellow and in the "ribbon" stage (that is, you can drizzle a design on top that takes 3 seconds to disappear). Add the flour and continue to whisk well. Pour on the hot milk and stir well with the whisk. Place the pan over medium heat and continue whisking until all is smooth and well mixed. Let the cream cook gently until a few small bubbles appear, indicating that the mixture is about to boil. Turn down the heat and, whisking all the time, cook for about 2 more minutes. Be sure you don't burn the bottom of the pan! Remove the cream from the heat, and whisk in the butter. Cover the surface with buttered parchment paper or some buttered plastic wrap, pushing either one right down on the surface to keep it from "skinning over." Let the mixture cool.

Use the cream for filling cream puffs, lining tarts, and putting in between layers of cake. You can also spoon some over poached fruit, on cake or cookies. This cream can also be frozen. When you want to use it, let it come to room temperature and whisk it very well. Use as directed in recipes calling for Pastry Cream.

NOTE: You can use an electric mixer to beat the yolks, sugar, and vanilla on high speed. When the mixture is very thick and yellow, slow down the speed to very low, swirl in the flour, and then pour in the hot milk. The minute the mixture is well blended, put it all into a saucepan and continue as described in the recipe.

2 cups all-purpose flour

½ teaspoon salt

1 tablespoon lard or shortening

1 tablespoon granulated sugar

½ cup sweet or dry Marsala, or q.b.

1 large egg, lightly beaten

1 quart olive oil for frying

FOR THE FILLING

2 pounds Ricotta

¾ cup confectioners sugar, or q.b.

3 or 4 tablespoons finely chopped candied orange and/or lemon peel (page 24)

4 tablespoons finely chopped semisweet chocolate

3 or 4 tablespoons orange flower water and/or Curacao or Cointreau

Heavy cream (if needed), q.b.

FOR DECORATION

6 tablespoons chopped pistachio nuts (or use toasted almonds, chopped)

6 tablespoons finely chopped chocolate (or use maraschino cherry halves)

Cupcake papers

Confectioners sugar for dusting

Cannoli alla Siciliana

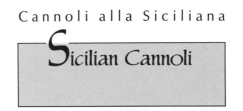

Sicilian Cannoli

MAKES ABOUT
24 CANNOLI

Cannoli are justifiably world famous. It is worthwhile noting that three of the best known and loved Italian desserts are from Southern Italy: spumoni, cannoli, and zabaglione. And while spumoni and zabaglione are soft and creamy, in cannoli you get a very tender, crunchy pastry shell *plus* a soft creamy filling. It is hardly possible in the deep South of Italy to conduct a major celebration without cannoli.

TO PREPARE THE CANNOLI

Place the flour, salt, lard, and sugar on a board or on a piece of marble and mix it all thoroughly with your fingers. Make a well about 9 or 10 inches around and add some of the Marsala, a little at a time; keep mixing as you would for pastry dough until you have a soft ball that is not crumbly. Then knead the dough for 7 to 8 minutes, or until it is supple and slightly glossy and a little pockmarked like orange peel. You can use an electric mixer with a flat beater or a food processor to mix the dough. But beware that in the food processor the dough does not get too moist because of the way the blade mixes. You may have to add a spoonful or two of extra flour. In the electric mixer you will end up with some rather large balls of dough. Just take them out and finish kneading them by hand for about 1 to 2 minutes to incorporate them into one ball of dough. Then proceed with the recipe as directed.

Cover the dough by placing an inverted bowl over it to keep it from drying out, and set it aside for about a half hour. Do not put it into the refrigerator unless you intend to use it the next day. If so, wrap the dough in plastic wrap. Let the dough come to room temperature before attempting to use it. It would be too firm to work otherwise.

Cut the dough into two pieces and roll each out as thin as possible with a rolling pin. If you have a pasta machine, you could use that. The dough can be rolled out by hand into a circle or, if you are using a pasta machine, into a long, wide strip. It should be about ⅓₂ inch thick. To prepare small pieces of rolled-out dough for the cannoli, use a 4-inch round cookie cutter, or use a sharp knife or straight razor to cut 4-inch squares. Reserve the scraps in a bowl, gently knead them together again, and roll and cut it once more. (Save any odd-shaped pieces to be fried later, and sprinkle them with con-

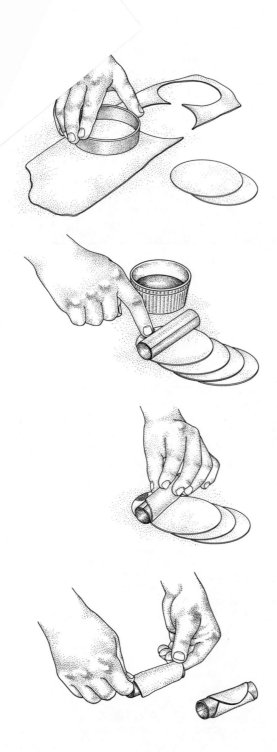

fectioners sugar. Eat them with fresh fruit and coffee or Moscato wine. These fried scraps are very much like a dish called *cenci* ["rags"].)

To prepare for the frying of the cannoli, line up all of the cut pieces, round or square, overlapping each other a bit, in a vertical row on a table. If you are using squares, place them so that they look triangular to you. Break the egg into a small bowl and beat gently with a fork for a minute or so. Place the bowl with the egg near the dough pieces. Line up all of the cannoli forms that you have just to the left of the dough pieces. Put the dough onto the cannoli forms in this way: Lay a *cannolo* form horizontally across the center of the first piece of dough, dip your finger into the beaten egg, and put just a little spot of egg on the bottom portion of the dough. (This egg spot will act as a kind of glue to hold the tube together at that part.) Pick up the top part of the dough and lay it over the *cannolo* form and gently roll the form, with the dough partially wrapped around it, toward you so that the top part of the dough rolls onto the egg-washed spot. At this point apply gentle pressure on the form to make a good, firm seal. Be very careful that you do not get any egg on the form itself because if you do, when the cannoli are fried, you will have created a bond of dough and egg onto the form that acts like glue, and you will have to break the fried *cannolo* to get it off. Put the finished *cannolo* just to the right of the row of dough pieces and continue thus until you have used up either all of the dough or all of the cannoli forms. (This method is very good to help you get organized, the most neglected aspect of cooking.)

If you do not have enough cannoli forms to complete the wrapping, stop and fry the ones you have done. By the time you have finished frying all of the prepared ones, the forms will be cool enough to handle, and you can simply use them again immediately. The forms will be oily, but that does not matter. Do not wash them.

After you have wrapped all of the cannoli forms with the dough, heat the oil to no hotter than 375° F, in a small but heavy pot just wide enough to fit the length of the cannoli forms. Have on hand the following: tongs with which to remove the fried cannoli from the oil; 2 thick kitchen towels, folded, to make a protective, absorbent pad in which to hold the cannoli after they come out of the hot oil; a pair of pliers with which to grasp the exposed metal part of the cannoli forms and pull them out of the fried pastry tube; a shallow dish lined with paper towels or kitchen towels to serve as a draining pad for the finished cannoli; and a fat thermometer is handy when you are not using an electrically controlled deep fryer.

Carefully place 2 dough-wrapped cannoli forms into the hot oil. Do not throw them in, or the oil will splash and burn you. You cannot successfully fry more than 2 at a time unless you are highly experienced.

The cannoli fry so very quickly, in about 1 minute, that you don't dare neglect them. Fry them until they are a golden brown, and remove them from the oil with a slotted spoon or the long tongs, and set them on the dish lined with absorbent towels to drain. Wait about 10 seconds, then pick up the metal part of the tube that should be showing (it is red-hot, so look out) with the pliers, and with the thick folded kitchen towels, carefully grasp the cannoli and pull the tube out. Stack the cannoli in a dish lined with absorbent towels. When the tubes are cool enough to handle, repeat the procedure until you finish. The oil may be cooled and stored in a sealed bottle for future use.

Cannoli shells freeze beautifully, so make a lot and freeze them (unfilled!), carefully wrapped. You can also easily store them in an airtight container for about 10 to 14 days. If they become slightly stale, place them in a preheated 325° F oven for about 3 minutes. Cool them, and then use as described.

TO PREPARE THE FILLING

Mix the first 5 filling ingredients together in a large bowl. If the mass seems too dense and not luscious enough, you can add a few tablespoons of heavy cream to soften it. If the liqueur is not too pronounced, you could also add a bit more of it, but it must not taste too much of the alcohol, just a hint.

Pipe the filling into the shells. The filling should come just barely over the outside edge of each end. You can use a spoon or a knife, but this takes forever. If you learn to use a pastry or piping bag, you can fill all 24 shells in about 5 minutes. This is important because you cannot fill the cannoli very far in advance, preferably not more than an hour or two before serving, or they become soggy. Decorate the ends with chopped pistachio nuts or half a maraschino cherry and finely chopped chocolate or chopped toasted almonds. Place them in cupcake papers to resemble a flat flower basket so that they will not roll around on the serving plate. Sprinkle the cannoli liberally with confectioners sugar, and serve immediately. (Sprinkle them with confectioners sugar after they are in the papers for two reasons: One, if you handle them after they have been sprinkled you see fingerprints all over them. Two, the sugar partly obscures the end decorations so that there is not a sharp and severe color demarcation but a soft and natural one very typical of the times when these are served, namely, Christmas, Easter, and at weddings.

Eat cannoli with your hands. If you try to eat them with a fork, you are likely to send them sailing across the table.

Cartellate o "Rose"

Rose Wheels

MAKES ABOUT
30 PIECES

This is a traditional Christmas dish in Apulia. You can, however, find them out of season in many *trattorie*. In many small eating establishments the *rose* are placed in a huge basket near the door, and when you leave, having eaten very well, you are encouraged to eat a little bit more, free of charge. Who can say no?

These little pastries are crunchy and absolutely irresistible with fresh-brewed coffee. They can be equally good with a glass of red or rosé wine or even a slightly dry dessert wine.

MENU SUGGESTIONS: These are wonderful after a festive meal, especially if you can bring out a big plate of them. They would be wonderful to eat after a meal with Breaded Lamb Chops (page 186) and some Spinach, Roman Style (page 245).

WINE: Nasco di Alghero (page 307) or Malvasia delle Lipari (page 309) for the rose

1 pound (about 3⅓ cups) fancy durum flour

1 large egg

⅓ cup very warm olive oil, plus q.b. for frying

½ cup warm white wine

FOR THE FILLING

2 pounds (3½ cups) grape jelly or red currant jelly

⅔ cup honey

About 2 cups wine (dry red wine or sweet dessert wine can be used; water can be used in a pinch)

1 cup olive oil for frying

FOR DECORATION

Ground cinnamon, q.b.

Ground cloves, q.b.

Superfine sugar or "thousands and millions" (multicolored candy sprinkles), q.b.

TO PREPARE THE ROSE WHEELS

Place the flour in a mixing bowl (of electric mixer, if you like), add the egg, and mix well. Add the warm olive oil all at once and mix well. Add the warm wine, and mix well again. The dough should resemble regular pasta dough. If it does not, add a bit more wine as needed. After the dough is well mixed, whether by the electric mixer or by hand, knead it well for another 4 minutes. Wrap the dough in clear plastic, leave it for about 15 minutes, and then roll out the dough just as you would for pasta, by hand or with a machine. The dough should be slightly under ⅛ inch thick.

With a pastry wheel cut the dough into strips about 1½ inches wide and about 12 inches long. Using a pastry brush, moisten the top edge lengthwise with a bit of wine. Place the tip of your index finger vertically 1 inch from either edge. Lift and pinch the top and bottom edges around your finger to form a cup (hole). Continue the process the length of the dough. You should have about 8 or 9 openings of about ⅜ inch with pinched or pressed dough between each one. The result will look like a kind of necklace with a bead (hole) and string (pinched dough). Curl the length of dough onto itself by holding one end and carefully spinning the remaining length until the whole thing looks like a wide flat rose. (See illustration.) Carefully place the rose on a cookie sheet and proceed with the next one. Continue until you have used all the dough. Let the roses set *uncovered* overnight. They will become dry and hard. The next day make the filling.

TO PREPARE THE FILLING

Place all the filling ingredients, except the olive oil, in a saucepan or a bain-marie over medium heat for an hour, or until all is smooth and liquid. Take

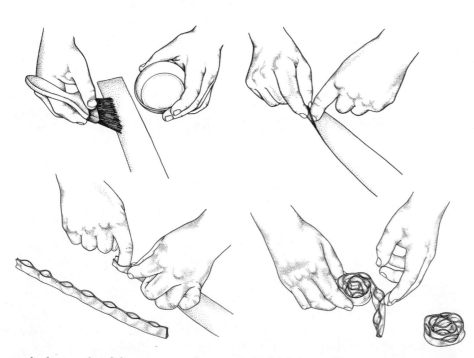

a little sample of the mixture, place it on a cold dish, and let it cool thoroughly. If it is the consistency you like and will hold its shape (it must be firm enough to set up, like thick honey, but not become firm enough to become lumpy), proceed with the recipe. If not, let it cook down a bit, and test it again. If by chance the mixture gets too thick, add some more wine, and thin it again. If you do this be sure to add the wine a little at a time because it takes a while for it to absorb into the mixture properly. When the mixture is just right, keep it hot in the bain-marie or over very low heat watching it constantly.

TO FRY THE ROSE

Heat the olive oil to 375° F. in a deep 8-inch pan, place 2 or 3 of the dough flowers in at a time, and fry them until they are an even very light gold color. Drain them upside down on a rack with a pan or kitchen towels underneath. When they are drained and still very hot submerge each flower into the filling mixture for a minute or two. Carefully lift them out with tongs or a slotted spoon or a cooking fork, and set them right side up with all the little openings filled with jam on a draining rack. Proceed with the others and arrange them on a plate. Before serving they should be sprinkled with a bit of ground cinnamon and, if you like, a bit of ground cloves. Additionally, you can either sprinkle on some superfine sugar or throw on some "thousands and millions" (little multicolored candy sprinkles).

Cassata Siciliana

Sicilian Cassata

MAKES 1 9 × 4½ × 2½-
INCH LOAF SHAPED
CAKE

Cassata is easily as old as the Arab occupation. In Arabic the term *quasat* means a round pan or bowl thus giving cassata its descriptive name. Nowadays cassata is made in shapes as diverse as the cooks who produce them, like a normal round layer cake, or in a loaf pan as for baking bread, or in a bombe (*bomba*) much like the shape of the famous Tuscan dessert *zuccotto* (supposedly shaped like a pumpkin). Cassata was the ultimate Easter dessert for the Sicilians and Campanians. It was all the rage. It is made at other times of the year now for festive occasions, but it is still most eaten at Easter.

As in so many other cases, probably the best makers of cassata were the nuns in the convents. They were enormously skilled bakers and had enough good ingredients at hand to make rather substantial confections. These baked goods were sold to raise money for the convent. To this day this practice can still be found in some of the really old convents that have never lost the old ways. So popular was this cake that in 1575 the diocese at Mazara del Vallo temporarily prohibited the nuns from making it because in their zeal to do a good job and to make many *cassati*, they neglected their religious duties.

Cassata is easy enough to make. It has a basic yellow cake as the base and essentially the same filling as cannoli. The usual cake is *pan di Spagna* which is made mostly with potato starch (see Note #1). For those of you who cannot get potato starch I provide instead *pasta Genovese*, a cake so delicious it is worth eating plain.

Decorating the *cassata* is fun and a good way to express yourself. A thick chocolate covering festooned with piped chocolate details, highlighted by green pistachio nuts and beautiful little sections of candied citrus peel puts this cake in a special class.

6 large eggs

¾ cup granulated sugar

1 teaspoon vanilla extract

1¼ cups sifted all-purpose flour

½ cup sweet butter, melted and cooled

FOR THE FILLING

1 pound Ricotta

¼ cup or more semisweet chocolate, finely chopped

⅓ cup confectioners sugar

1 teaspoon vanilla extract

2 tablespoons mixed glacéed fruit, or just citron or orange, finely chopped

4 tablespoons chopped pistachio nuts and/or toasted almonds

¼ cup heavy cream

FOR MOISTENING THE CAKE

¼ cup orange-flavored liqueur such as Curaçao or Cointreau

FOR FROSTING # 1

1 cup heavy cream

3 tablespoons confectioners sugar

FOR FROSTING #2

3 cups semisweet chocolate, cut into small pieces

¾ cup cold espresso coffee

½ pound sweet butter, chilled and cut into small pieces

1 tablespoon dark rum

FOR DECORATION

Candied citrus peel (page 24), finely chopped or in chunks

OPTIONAL DECORATION

Coarse ground toasted nuts of your choice, q.b.

Semisweet chocolate, finely chopped or in small chunks

Pasta Genovese

Genoise

MAKES 1 17 × 12 - INCH
CAKE

TO PREPARE THE CAKE

Preheat the oven to 350° F. Lightly butter and flour the cake pan or use parchment paper and set aside until later. Place the eggs, sugar, and vanilla in the bowl of an electric mixer and place it in another bowl of very hot water from the faucet. Stir the mixture several times. It must be very warm but watch that the eggs do not curdle. Put the mixing bowl on the mixer and beat at high speed until the eggs are light yellow and about 3 times original volume, about 6 or 7 minutes. Stop the machine, remove the bowl, and fold the flour in using a rubber spatula. Sift the flour on the surface of the batter in 3 batches, folding after each addition. Work quickly. Drizzle in the butter in 2 batches and fold after each addition. Quickly pour the batter into the prepared pan and bake for about 25 minutes or until the cake is a light golden color and firm to the touch. Let it cool about 5 minutes and then turn it out of the pan onto a cooling rack. The cake can be made up to 2 days ahead and stored out of the refrigerator wrapped in clear plastic wrap. The *pasta Genovese* so wrapped can be frozen until it is needed. Simply unwrap and defrost before you want to use it.

TO PREPARE THE FILLING

Combine all of the ingredients for the filling in a bowl, except the heavy cream, and mix well. Whip the cream until it is thick and fold it into the other ingredients in the bowl. The filling can be made up to a day ahead and stored in the refrigerator.

TO PREPARE THE CASSATA

Line the loaf pan with parchment paper. Cut the cake to fit on the sides and bottom of the pan in a single layer. Sprinkle the cake slices with half the orange-flavored liqueur. Put half the Ricotta mixture on the bottom layer of cake. Put another slice of cake on the filling and sprinkle on the remaining liqueur. Top the final layer of filling with another slice of cake. Cover the *cassata* with clear wrap and put it into the refrigerator overnight or at least several hours to set. When you are ready to frost the *cassata* carefully unmold it on a serving dish after it has set and remove any paper that may have clung to it.

TO PREPARE THE FROSTING AND
DECORATE THE CASSATA

For frosting #1, place the cream in a bowl, and whip it until it forms stiff peaks but is very smooth and shiny. You can do this in an electric mixer if you wish, then slow the beating down considerably, and gently fold in the sugar a tablespoon at a time. With a palette knife smooth the whipped cream onto the cake to cover the sides and the top. You can make it very thick and then sprinkle on the ground nuts and chocolate or candied fruit. Let the *cassata* rest in the refrigerator for a couple of hours before cutting it. Or put on a thinner covering of the whipped cream, put the leftover cream into a piping bag, and make any kind of design you like all over the cake. They could be rosettes or ropes or whatever strikes your fancy. Highlight the decorations with the nuts and/or chocolate and candied citrus peel. For frosting #2 slowly and carefully melt the chocolate in the coffee over hot water in a double boiler until it is shiny and there are no lumps in it. Take the mixture off the heat, and add the butter, a piece at a time, stirring continuously. Add the rum and stir it in. When all the butter is in, cool the mixture to a spreading consistency. You can easily check this by simply smoothing some onto the side of the *cassata* and ascertaining whether you can work with it. It may need to go into the refrigerator for a while if you are in a bit of hurry but be careful that it does not get too cold to be spreadable. Spread the frosting on the cake, and decorate with abandon. Use designs you have always wanted to use but never had the chance. This is a cake for celebration and release. You can use contrasting colors, like bright green pistachio nuts, whole or chopped, or candied orange peel scattered here and there. Make it opulent.

Refrigerate the decorated *cassata* long enough to set the decorations before serving it. The *cassata* should be served cool but not ice cold. Slice 1-inch pieces. It is very rich, and you may not be able to eat a lot of it.

NOTE #1: PAN DI SPAGNA

Makes 1 17 × 12-inch sheet cake

6 *egg yolks*

¾ *cup granulated sugar*

  Zest of 1 lemon

1 *teaspoon vanilla*

1 *cup* fecula *(potato flour)*

6 *egg whites*

  Butter and flour for pan, q.b.

Preheat the oven to 350° F. Lightly butter and flour the cake pan or use parchment paper and set aside until later. Separate the yolks. Put the whites aside in a bowl. Beat the yolks and sugar until they are pale yellow and triple their volume, by hand or in an electric mixer. Add the lemon rind and vanilla. Stop the machine and remove the whisk. Scatter the fecula onto the surface of the egg yolk mixture using a sieve and fold it in well. Immediately, beat the whites very stiff. Fold them into the egg yolk mixture. Pour the mixture into the cake pan. Bake in the oven for 25-30 minutes. When the cake is done take it out of the oven and let it cool for about 5 minutes. Turn the pan over onto a cooling rack and gently rap the bottom of it to dislodge the cake. It should fall right out. Peel the parchment paper off the bottom and discard it. Let the cake cool thoroughly before using it.

NOTE #2: If you cannot get *fecula* (potato flour), you can use pastry flour instead. The cake will be a little firmer but quite good.

Crostata di Mandorle

Almond Tart

MAKES 1 9-INCH
TART

The dough here is Tender Pastry (page 258). You should always have on hand some jam and almonds. Eggs and flour are certainly to be found in anybody's kitchen. There, you have the makings of this tasty and satisfying tart!

MENU SUGGESTIONS: A dish of Potato Croquettes (page 231) would make a good antipasto followed by Chicken Roasted with Rosemary (page 178) with a *contorno* of Almond Peppers (page 249). Almond Tart would be not only a good finish to this meal, but it would show how different almonds can be in diverse dishes, such·as the two included in this menu.

WINE: Greco di Tufo (page 302) with the chicken; Marsala Superiore (page 309) with the tart

1 *recipe of Tender Pastry (page 258) (you will have a little left over)*

3 *large egg whites*

½ *cup apricot jam (chunky pieces)*

1 *pound almonds, skinned or not*

½ *cup semisweet chocolate, finely chopped*

1 *large egg, beaten, for egg wash*

If the almonds are raw, toast them, dry, until they are golden, being careful not to burn them. Cool and grind them very fine in a food processor or in a nut mill. Set them aside for later use.

Roll out the pastry dough to a generous ⅛ inch thick. Line a false-bottom tart pan (one with a removable bottom) with the dough, letting some of it hang over the edges by about 1 inch. Trim the edges even with the top of the pan and set it aside in the refrigerator, for about half an hour. Gather the remaining dough into a ball and roll it out again to the same thickness as the tart dough. Using a pastry crimp cutter, cut about 9 strips of dough about ¼ inch wide. Lay them on parchment or wax paper and reserve them in a cool place for later use.

Preheat the oven to 375° F. Line the tart dough in the pan with wax paper or foil and load the inside of the pan with beans or rice or anything that will keep the bottom of the tart from ballooning during baking. Bake the tart on a cookie sheet on a rack in the lowest part of the oven for about 20 minutes, or until the crust begins to firm up. When you see that it is firming, yet the dough is still very pale, take it out of the oven and remove the weights. (You can make the tart up to this point a day or two ahead. Simply cover the tart with plastic wrap and store it in a cool place, unrefrigerated, until you are ready to use it.)

Beat the egg whites until they are thick, glossy, and hold their peaks well. Set this meringue aside for a moment. Spread the apricot jam on the bottom of the baked dough. Work quickly so that you do not make the dough soggy. Fold the almonds and the chocolate into the meringue and spread the meringue all over the jam. Lay the reserved strips of raw dough over the top of the tart in a crisscross fashion, trimming them to fit, if necessary, but trim each strip about ⅛ inch longer than you need at each end. Push the ends into the apricot mixture in the tart with a small knife. This makes a neat appearance. Brush the strips with a bit of the egg wash and put the tart into the oven to bake in a preheated 375° F oven for another 30 minutes or so. The almond meringue should be slightly puffy and the pastry strips should be golden and cooked. The strips might be partially submerged in the meringue and not have a distinctive pattern. This is normal. Serve the tart while it is warm, or it can be eaten cold but not refrigerated.

NOTE: You could use grape jelly in the filling, with plenty of chopped, toasted almonds and toasted walnuts, pieces of candied orange peel, and the zest of 1 or 2 lemons. Cover this mixture with strips of dough. Do not use meringue. Proceed as described.

1 *recipe Tender Pastry (page 258)*
  (there will be leftover)

FOR THE FILLING

½ *cup dark or light raisins*

3 *or 4 tablespoons dark rum*

1½ *pounds Ricotta*

½ *cup almonds, slivered, sliced, or*
  chopped (blanched almonds
  preferred)

2 *large eggs, lightly beaten (save a*
  little for brushing pastry later)

  Zest of 1 lemon

  Zest of ½ orange

½ *cup sugar*

1 *teaspoon vanilla extract*

3 *tablespoons all-purpose flour*

⅓ *cup finely chopped candied orange*
  peel (page 24)

Crostata di Ricotta

Roman Cheesecake

MAKES 1 9-INCH,
DEEP TART, PLUS
PASTRY STRIPS
FOR TOP

Crostata di ricotta is famous not only in Lazio, especially around Rome, but it is eaten with gusto in Calabria and Sicily and Sardinia. Of course, the Romans are justifiably proud of their Ricotta. This *crostata* is appreciated mostly at Easter, but any holiday would justify its being made.

TO PREPARE THE FILLING

Soak the raisins in the rum for 20 minutes. In a medium-sized bowl or in an electric mixer bowl, combine all of the other filling ingredients. Add the raisins and the rum. Preheat the oven to 375° F.

TO ASSEMBLE

Pat the dough into a round, thick lozenge. Flour it a little bit to keep it from sticking to the work surface. Roll the dough out into a sheet about ³⁄₁₆ inch thick. (If possible, use a 9-inch round flan ring on a baking sheet, both made of dark metal. The ring should be 2 inches high. The dark black metal baking units give a better-colored and better-cooked crust. Otherwise the next best thing to use is a 9-inch springform cake pan. If you can get a darker metal one, so much the better.) Line the flan ring with *pasta frolla*, leaving 1½ inches of the dough hanging over the edge of the ring. With the leftover pastry dough, make 8 or 9 strips with a crimp cutter for crisscrossing the top of the *crostata* later. The strips should be about ¼ inch thick, ½ inch wide, and long enough to reach a little more than across the top of the *crostata*.

Preheat the oven to 375° F.

Pour the Ricotta filling into the crust base that lines the flan ring. Lay the dough strips on top of the filling in a crisscross fashion. Tuck about ½ inch of the ends of the dough strips down around the edges into the filling itself to make a neat appearance. Take the flap of dough left around the edge of the ring and roll it up on itself to make a scroll inside the metal ring, hiding the tucked-in ends of the crisscrossed dough strips. You can leave it as it is or make crimp designs on it for a more decorative look.

Brush the surface of the *crostata* all over with the beaten egg and sprinkle on about 1 tablespoon or more of granulated sugar. Place the *crostata* in the lower third of the oven and bake it for 45 minutes to an hour, or until the crust is golden brown on the bottom, sides, and top. It will move ever so slightly if shaken and be a little puffed up. Remove it from the oven and cool for about 1 hour. (It will shrink a little in the process.) Remove the flan ring or the springform ring and place the *crostata* on a serving plate. Serve it warm or cold but not refrigerated.

Maritozzi

Miniature Sweet Buns

MAKES
12 OR 14 BUNS

Traditionally eaten during Lent, these little buns are good at any time. All the various methods that I found to make *maritozzi* have one thing in common: You must start out with very soft and moist bread dough, and you must put some olive oil in it. These little buns would be perfect to make if you are making bread. Save part of the dough for *maritozzi*.

The tops of the buns are very deep brown but not burned. The surface is painted with a sugar solution that produces a crusty sweet glaze.

MENU SUGGESTIONS: These buns are perfect for midmorning coffee or tea breaks. They are wonderful to have on hand for afternoon visitors when you offer Marsala (page 309) or Aleatico di Puglia (page 298) or sweet vermouth. While brunch is definitely an American peculiarity, I think some Roman *maritozzi* would be a perfect bun to take the place of the overworked croissant.

⅓ cup black raisins

1 recipe very soft, proofed Basic Bread Dough (page 47)

All-purpose flour for dusting table and kneading, q.b.

2 large eggs

3 tablespoons virgin olive oil

2 tablespoons pine nuts

⅓ cup granulated sugar

⅓ cup candied orange peel, cut into tiny dice

Unsalted butter, q.b., for greasing

FOR THE ICING

½ cup granulated sugar

¼ teaspoon vanilla extract

⅛ teaspoon cinnamon

Put the raisins in a bowl of warm water for about half an hour to soften and hydrate them. Drain them well and set them aside for later use.

TO PREPARE THE DOUGH

Put the bread dough on a table and work in the 2 eggs. Use small amounts of flour to keep the dough from sticking to the table as you work. It will be messy, so you could use an electric mixer with a dough hook, if you like. The dough should end up being smooth and shiny. If it is impossibly wet, add a bit more flour, though the dough must be very soft.

Work in the olive oil, raisins, pine nuts, sugar, and the candied orange peel. Knead a long time to be sure that everything is well amalgamated. Lightly butter a clay or metal bowl, put the *maritozzi* dough in to rise, and cover the bowl with a clean kitchen towel and then a bath towel folded at least once. The rising place should be only moderately warm, no more than 70° F, because you want the *maritozzi* dough to rise slowly, taking about 6 hours or more. (I make my dough mixture late at night and let it rise until morning. You could make the dough in the morning and put it into the refrigerator for at least 1 full day. Bring it to room temperature and then proceed with the rising.)

When the dough has risen, punch it down and shape it into 12 to 14 oval buns. Butter a baking sheet and place the buns on it. Cover them lightly with a clean kitchen towel and let the buns rise about 3 hours in a slightly warmer place, about 75° F. When the buns are very plump and have doubled in size, preheat the oven to 375° F.

TO PREPARE THE ICING

Put the granulated sugar, vanilla, and cinnamon in a small bowl and drizzle on enough water to make a rather thick but easily spreadable paste. (Sometimes I use lemon juice, but water is normally used.) Set the icing aside for later use.

TO COMPLETE THE BUNS

Put the buns in the middle of the oven. After about 7 minutes, carefully open the door and check them for color. When they are a very deep gold, quickly remove the pan from the oven, and using a pastry brush, wash the tops of the *maritozzi* with the sugar icing. Put them back in the oven for another 4 to 5 minutes, or until the icing on top has set and looks white and crunchy. If not, leave them in for a minute or so longer. Remove the *maritozzi* to a cooling rack and let them rest for about half an hour. Serve them any time after that.

FOR 1½ CUPS CREAM FILLING

1 *cup milk*

4 *large egg yolks*

½ *cup granulated sugar*

¾ *teaspoon vanilla extract*

6 *tablespoons flour*

2 *teaspoons sweet butter*

⅓ *cup semisweet chocolate, cut into tiny pieces*

1 *tablespoon finely minced candied orange peel (page 24)*

FOR THE DOUGH

1 *recipe of Tender Pastry (page 258)*
Egg yolks, beaten, for sealing the dough, q.b.

FOR FINISHING THE COOKIES

2 *large egg whites*
Pinch of salt
Confectioners sugar for dusting, q.b.
Optional: ½ maraschino cherry on each cookie before baking

Follow the directions for Pastry Cream (page 260), using the ingredient amounts given above. Mix together the cream, chocolate pieces, and candied orange peel. Set aside in the refrigerator for later use.

Preheat the oven to 350° F, and place the rack in the middle of the oven.

Roll out the Tender Pastry into 2 sheets 22 inches long, 6 inches wide, and ⅛ inch thick. Paint one of the sheets all over with the beaten egg yolk, then distribute the cream mixture in little mounds of about 1½ tablespoons each, leaving 1¼ inches of space all around each one. Carefully lay the other sheet of dough on top. With a round, individual ravioli cutter about 2½ inches across, press down and make the cookies. The cutter should seal and cut at the same time. You can do this same procedure without the ravioli cutter. Simply press the dough all around each mound of cream to make a good seal, and then, with a fluted cookie cutter or a pastry crimping wheel, cut out the individual cookies. Be sure the edges are well sealed.

Put the *minni* on a cookie sheet, leaving about 1 inch between each one. In a small bowl, add a pinch of salt to the egg whites and beat them until they form soft peaks. Carefully smear the beaten egg white, ¼ inch thick, all over the cookies with a small metal spatula. Put ½ of a maraschino cherry in the center of each *minni*, if you are using them. Bake cookies in the middle of the oven for 20 minutes, or until they are golden on the top and bottom. You can serve them barely warm or cold but not refrigerated. Before serving the *minni di Sant'Agata*, dust them liberally with confectioners sugar.

SICILIA

Minni
di Sant'Agata

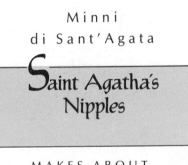

MAKES ABOUT
24 COOKIES

In Sicily the profound devotion to church and religion is equaled only by seeming irreverence. In fact, this unbelievable name for a sweet is a matter of devoutness for the saint who repelled amorous advances by a prefect of Catania and was, because of her virtue, tortured by having her breasts cut off. Saint Agatha is the patron saint of both Catania and Palermo, but the Palermitani have still another exalted patron saint in their corner, Saint Rosalia.

On their own gustatory merits, the Saint Agatha's Nipples are truly delicious and well worth making. The approach to making them is much like making ravioli, so they should present no problem.

WINE: Moscato di Pantelleria (page 309)

Pastiera Napolitana

Neapolitan Easter Pie

MAKES 4 8-INCH
TARTS

Whether you make it at Easter or not, *pastiera* in Italy celebrates spring and rebirth. Whole wheat berries are soaked and then combined with Ricotta, candied orange peel, lemon zest, and vanilla, and the whole thing goes into a crust just waiting to be eaten. Some Neapolitans add a bit of Pastry Cream (page 260).

You should try to get soft spring wheat for this tart. If you do not, you will find that a day or so after making the tart, the berries will harden. You can also get good results by using cracked wheat, in which case you simply soak the berries for a couple of hours as opposed to the normal 3 days. You could also cook the berries as directed on the package, drain well, and use them in the recipe.

It is perfectly authentic to use barley, if that is all you can get. It soaks faster and stays softer longer. The real oldtimers I have spoken to tell me that they used to soak the wheat for 15 days, changing the water every day. Their story has been corroborated in old cookbooks. I have done it that way, and the result is good, but you must be very patient indeed.

1¼ cups soft spring whole wheat berries, or use barley	⅓ cup candied orange peel (page 24), finely chopped
1 teaspoon lard	5 large egg yolks
2½ cups milk, or q.b.	2 recipes Tender Pastry (page 258)
1¼ cups granulated sugar	3 large egg whites
12 ounces Ricotta	2 additional large eggs for brushing dough
Zest of 2 lemons	
1 tablespoon orange flower water	Granulated sugar for sprinkling, q.b.

Soak the wheat in plenty of cold water for at least 3 days, changing the water daily. You can soak it for several more days, if you wish, and soften it even more.

Drain the wheat and cover it with plenty of fresh cold water in a deep pot. Bring the water to a simmer and cook the wheat for 1 hour or a bit more. Drain the wheat well. Put the drained wheat, lard, and milk in the top of a double boiler and cook the mixture for about 3 hours over moderately high heat. If the wheat seems very dry and unmanageable, add about ⅓ cup more hot milk and stir well. You may have to do this more than once, depending on the wheat and how it cooks. In any event, the wheat should be soft and in separate grains, like rice, and not too gluey or too dense and hard. When the wheat is almost done, add the sugar and cook another half hour or so. Cool the wheat mixture and set it aside for later use. It should look moist and plump but not wet. If it seems too dry, add just a little bit of warm milk to moisten it. The milk will absorb as the wheat cools.

In a large bowl combine the Ricotta with the lemon zest, orange flower water, vanilla, candied orange peel, and egg yolks. Add the cooked and cooled wheat, and mix everything well. Set it aside for later use.

Roll out the pastry to about ⅛ inch thick, and line the tart shells with it, trimming the dough even with the top of the tart pan. Gather the scraps of dough and gently re-roll them to make a large sheet about ⅛ inch thick. With a crimp cutter, cut strips of dough about ⅜ inch wide and about ⅛ inch longer at each end than the diameter of the tart shells. These will be the lattice work on the tarts when they are finished.

Preheat the oven to 375° F and move the rack to the middle of the oven. Beat the egg whites until they are fairly stiff. Put ¼ of the egg whites into the Ricotta and wheat mixture to soften it, then fold in the rest of the beaten egg whites. Fill the tarts with the mixture, dividing it equally among the 4 shells. Make a lattice design on top of the *pastiere* with the strips of dough. With the point of a small knife, push the end of the dough strip against the dough that lines the tart pan and the filling itself. This will hold the lattice in place and make the *pastiere* neat. Beat the 2 additional eggs, and brush the tops of the *pastiere* with the wash. Sprinkle on some granulated sugar, and bake the *pastiere* for 45 minutes, or until the crust is just golden.

The *pastiere* are best when cooled and barely warm. They are very good cold, too. The *pastiere* will keep, covered in plastic wrap, for 3 days in the refrigerator.

MENU SUGGESTIONS: Bread and Cheese Soup (page 118) could start your meal. Then you could have Braised Oxtails, Roman Style (page 187), with a *contorno* of Spinach, Roman Style (page 245), on the side. The *pastiera* could be the end of this homey, earthy meal that is good enough to serve your most treasured guests.

WINE: Cirò Rosso (page 302)

Torta di Noci #1

Walnut Cake #1

MAKES 1 9-INCH
"CAKE"

Why this is called a "cake" I do not know, except that perhaps it looks like a cake; it has a top. But then again similar sweets have tops and are called, quite correctly, *crostata*, or tarts.

This "cake" is very nutty and dense, and it keeps several days, covered with plastic, out of the refrigerator. It is quite tasty and has the characteristic taste of a Fig Newton, only better. It is ideal as a snack, or it can be really delicious eaten as a dessert after a simple meal.

The key elements are the walnuts and the *mosto cotto* ("cooked wine must"). For those of you lucky enough to be able to get wine must (juice freshly squeezed from grapes), you can make your own *mosto cotto*. Simply boil the must until it has a thick, jellylike consistency, cool it, and use it as you would jelly, or cook with it. A good substitution for *mosto cotto* in this recipe is red currant jelly or grape jelly. I prefer the red currant because the taste is a little lemony and tart.

FOR THE DOUGH

2 cups all-purpose flour

4 tablespoons lard

2 ounces (4 tablespoons) sweet butter

⅓ cup granulated sugar

Zest of 1 lemon

1 large egg

3 large egg yolks

1 large egg, lightly beaten, for brushing dough

Or use ⅔ recipe Tender Pastry (page 258) approximately 1 pound

FOR THE FILLING

2 cups shelled walnuts, well crushed

½ cup raisins

¼ cup candied orange peel (page 24), finely chopped

1⅓ cups mosto cotto or currant jelly (see notes accompanying recipe)

Put the flour, lard, butter, sugar, and lemon zest into the bowl of an electric mixer. Use the flat beater and mix the ingredients well, until they look like small pebbles. Add the whole egg and the egg yolks, and continue to mix until the dough just barely comes together. If it looks too wet, add a teaspoon of flour at a time to correct it. If it looks too dry or won't hold together, add 1 more egg yolk. Dump the ingredients out onto a work surface and push and knead for about 1 minute into a soft dough. Wrap the dough in plastic wrap and refrigerate it for about 1 hour.

Meanwhile, combine all the ingredients for the filling in a bowl, mixing well, and set it aside for later use.

Roll the dough out about ⅛ inch thick, and line a false bottom 9-inch tart pan (one with a removable bottom), leaving about a 1½-inch overhang of dough. Gather the remaining dough and roll it out large enough for a top. Spread the filling into the pastry shell, and smooth it out with a spatula so that it is relatively flat. Lay the other sheet of pastry on top, leaving about a 1½-inch overhang. Preheat the oven to 375° F.

Press the two overhanging pieces of dough together to secure them. Then carefully roll them up and onto the edge of the flutes on the pan and resting on the main body of dough. Use a fork or your fingers to make a little decoration on the roll of dough going around the edge. If you have any dough scraps left over, you could roll them out pencil thin and twist them like a rope or braid. Brush the entire top of the *torta di noce* with the beaten eggs, and lay on the braid in a circle somewhere in the middle. (The braid is not necessary, and if you have no extra dough, you could simply eliminate it. The egg wash should be applied in any event.) Make a little steam chimney in the middle of the *torta*. Use a pastry tip. Just gently stick it into the dough, with the small end down and it will break through. This allows steam to escape and helps keep the *torta* from bursting. You could use a small piece of foil or parchment paper to make the chimney, if you wish. Additionally, make little knife slashes here and there all over the surface of the dough to help steam escape.

Bake the *torta* in the middle of the oven for an hour, or until the dough is brown on the bottom and the top. To facilitate removing the *torta* from the false-bottom pan, place it, while it is still very hot, on a heatproof bowl that is smaller than the ring around the edge, or on a #10 can of fruit or tomatoes, etc. The ring will slip down, and the *torta* will be supported by the metal bottom, which can be removed later when it cools. If the ring does not want to slide down of its own accord, gently put pressure on the edge, and that should loosen it.

The *torta di noci* can be eaten warm or at room temperature. It should keep well for at least 5 days covered with plastic wrap in the refrigerator.

4   *ounces (8 tablespoons or ½ cup)*
    sweet butter at room temperature,
    and q.b. for buttering cake pan

⅔   *cup granulated sugar*

1   *large egg*

2   *tablespoons Jamaican dark rum*
    Zest of 1 lemon

1   *teaspoon vanilla extract*

1½ *teaspoons baking powder*

2¼ *cups finely ground shelled walnuts,*
    resembling meal

1   *cup all-purpose flour, and q.b. for*
    dusting cake pan
    Confectioners sugar, q.b.

Torta di Noci #2

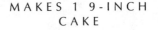

MAKES 1 9-INCH
CAKE

Preheat the oven to 350° F. Grease a 9-inch cake pan with butter and sprinkle flour all over it, shaking the pan well to get a thin, even coating. Bang the pan once to dislodge excess flour, and discard flour.

Cream the butter with the sugar in an electric mixer with the whisk attachment. When the butter and sugar are well creamed and very soft and smooth, add the egg, rum, lemon zest, vanilla, and the baking powder, and mix well. Add the walnuts, a little at a time, and keep mixing. When all the walnuts are in, add the flour, a bit at a time, from a sifter or sieve. This will keep it from lumping. The batter should be rather dense.

Pour the batter into the prepared cake pan, spreading it evenly with a spatula to make the top level, and place the cake in the top part of the oven to bake for about 1 hour, or until it is firm to the touch. Take it out of the oven and carefully turn it out of the pan to cool on a cooling rack. The *torta di noci* is actually better the next day. When it is cool, wrap it in plastic wrap, but do not refrigerate it. Wrapped thus, it will keep for about 4 days. Just before serving it, sprinkle confectioners sugar all over the top.

This is a completely different cake from the first. It resembles a real cake, and it is very smooth and subtle. Although it is meant to be eaten very simply and with only confectioners sugar sprinkled on top, you can cut it in half crosswise and fill it with jam or buttercream. You could even put frosting on it. I prefer it in its pristine state. Like all Italian cakes, this one is shallow.

Amaretti

Bitter Almond Cookies

MAKES ABOUT
28 COOKIES

These cookies show up in many parts of Italy mostly known as *amaretti*, but it is not out of the question that they might have been developed in Oristano or at least refined there. The hardest part of making these cookies, besides finding the bitter almonds, is to keep from eating them as they come out of the oven. Bitter Almond Cookies must be soft and moist in the center even after they have been stored for a long time. If you make them as I describe, you will have no trouble in attaining the standard. *Amaretti* have no relationship with the commercial *amaretti* so charmingly wrapped up in filmy paper. Those are made with egg whites and almond paste and are very dry and brittle, yet tasty.

If you cannot find bitter almonds in health food stores, try asking for apricot kernels. If all else fails, get everyone you know to save pits from peaches, apricots, nectarines, and large plums. Crack the pits open with a nutcracker and take the kernels out. If you do not use them immediately, dry them in the sun or in a low-temperature oven and store them in a jar for later use. If you do not dry them well, they mildew. Read the Italian Pantry section (page 20) for more information. *Amaretti* can be stored in a covered jar for about a month in perfect condition. You can keep them on hand to have with afternoon sweet wine or coffee or as an accompaniment to ice cream or fruit.

¾ cup almonds

¼ cup bitter almonds or apricot kernels, with or without skins, ground as finely as possible

⅓ cup granulated sugar, plus q.b. for sprinkling

3 large egg whites

Butter for greasing the pan, q.b., if needed

All-purpose flour for dusting the pan, q.b., if needed

If the almonds have skins on them, remove them by throwing the almonds into boiling water and leaving them there for about 45 seconds. Drain them and slip off the skins. Dry the almonds in a very low oven for about 20 minutes, then grind them to a fine powder using a nut mill or a food processor. Do only 2 or 3 ounces at a time or you risk overgrinding, thereby heating some of the nuts and turning them into nut butter.

Combine all the ground nuts with the sugar, and mix well with your hands to get an idea of the texture of the mixture. Add the egg whites and, still using your hands, mix the ingredients until you get a soft, pliable mass. If the mixture is too thick, you will have trouble piping or spooning it onto a cookie sheet, so add a bit more egg white. If the mixture is too loose, the *amaretti* will lose their shape immediately, so add a bit more ground almonds.

Preheat the oven to 350° F. Line a baking sheet with parchment paper, or, if you do not want to use that method, lightly butter a cookie sheet, sprinkle flour on it, shaking the pan back and forth to evenly distribute the flour, and then bang the pan on the counter to dislodge any excess flour. Discard the excess flour. To be sure that the bottoms of the cookies do not overcook, put the prepared cookie pan into another one, giving you a double thickness on the bottom.

Spoon or pipe the nut mixture onto the pan in even rows, leaving about 1 inch between each one. The cookies should be about 1¼ inches across and about the same height. The mixture should be firm yet supple. If the shape is a little off, you can moisten the ends of your fingers with water and push the little balls into shape. They should resemble large marbles with flat bottoms.

When you have finished placing the cookies on the pan, sprinkle them lightly with more granulated sugar. It is easy to do if you use a sugar dredger or put some sugar into a small strainer and gently shake it over the tops of the cookies. Do not use much. Let the cookies rest for about 15 minutes and then bake them in the middle of the oven. Check them for color after 10 minutes. If they have little dark spots on top, that is all right. After another

5 minutes, check them again and continue to do so until they are a light gold color all over and the inside is moist and supple. They should be done within 15 to 20 minutes, depending on your oven. Remove them from the oven and cool them on a platter. Do not stack them.

When the *amaretti* are completely cool, you may store them in a sealed tin or jar for up to a month. The insides should remain soft.

MENU SUGGESTIONS: Use *amaretti* with Ice Creams (page 292) or a Semifreddo (page 286) or as afternoon snacks. They make perfect gifts because they are not fragile, and they have a long shelf life.

WINE: Malvasia delle Lipari (page 309) or Moscato di Pantelleria (page 309)

SARDEGNA

3 *large egg whites*
  Pinch of salt
¾ *cup granulated sugar*
⅓ *cup almonds, blanched, toasted, and coarsely chopped*

Butter for greasing, q.b., if needed
All-purpose flour for dusting, q.b., if needed

Bianchini

White Meringues

MAKES ABOUT 2 DOZEN SMALL COOKIES

These little clouds of nutty sweetness are also called *bianchittus*. They are meringues with sugar and nuts folded in and are perfect to have with midmorning coffee or with semisweet wines or coffee in the afternoon. In Sardinia the *bianchini* are so sweet they make your teeth rattle. I have cut the sugar down a bit because I think it is not necessary to have so much. This is one of the very few classic recipes I have tampered with.

Preheat the oven to 250° F. Line a baking sheet with parchment paper, or, if you do not want to use that method, lightly butter the cookie sheet, sprinkle flour on it, shaking the pan back and forth to evenly distribute the flour, and then bang the pan on the counter to dislodge any excess flour. Discard the excess flour. To be sure that the bottoms of the *bianchini* do not overcook, put the prepared cookie pan into another one, giving you a double thickness on the bottom.

Put the egg whites into the bowl of an electric mixer, and add a pinch of salt. Start the mixer on a low speed and mix for 2 minutes, or until the egg whites look foamy. Turn the mixer to high speed and beat the egg whites until they begin to stiffen. Add 1 tablespoon of the sugar and beat until the egg whites look glossy and smooth and hold their shape really well. Stop the mixer, and remove the bowl. Scatter half of the chopped almonds on the surface of the egg whites and about half of the remaining sugar, and fold them in well. Repeat this with the remaining almonds and sugar. With a tablespoon, drop little mounds of batter about 1 inch apart onto the prepared cookie pan. You can make the cookies bigger or smaller as you like.

Bake the cookies in the middle of the oven for about 1 hour. The *bianchini* should be firm and dry on the outside, and they should remain as white as possible. They may be a little moist on the inside, which is good, but not too moist, or they will not keep well. If you plan to store them any length of time, lower the heat in the oven and continue to bake them until they are completely dry.

Pangiallo

MAKES 4 SMALL LOAVES

Like so many Italian sweets, *pangiallo* is unpretentious. It is not decorated and resembles a little round loaf of ordinary bread. But its appearance is deceptive. Inside is a dense ball of dried figs, nuts, and jam. *Pangiallo* is especially savored as a midmorning or midafternoon *merenda*, or "snack," with coffee. A glass of sweet wine is equally welcome.

MENU SUGGESTIONS: *Pangiallo* is an earthy, obviously homemade dessert bread. Accompanied by fresh seasonal fruit and a suitable wine, it is a perfect light meal. It is particularly good after meals barbecued outdoors, perhaps Homemade Sicilian Sausage (page 188) or Breaded Lamb Chops (page 186).

WINE: Per'e Palummo (page 303) with the meat; Anghelu Ruju (page 306) with the *pangiallo*

1 recipe Basic Bread Dough (page 47) made with olive oil, once risen

All-purpose flour for rolling dough, q.b.

Virgin olive oil for brushing finished loaves, q.b.

FOR THE FILLING

1 pound dry black figs, ground medium fine

½ cup whole pine nuts, toasted

¾ cup whole hazelnuts, toasted

¾ cup almonds, toasted and coarsely chopped

2 tablespoons candied orange peel (page 24), finely chopped

⅓ cup apricot preserves

Have handy a sheet of wax paper about 9 × 9 inches. Put the filling ingredients into a large bowl, and mix everything very well using your hands, which is the most efficient way. (Rubbing your hands with a bit of the olive oil will help keep the filling from sticking to you.) While your hands are a bit of a mess, divide the filling into 4 equal parts and gently form each one into a sort of ball. Lay the finished balls on the wax paper for later use.

Divide the bread dough into 4 equal parts and gently roll them around with your hands to form a ball. Roll each ball into a circle ¹⁄₁₆ inch thick.

Put one fig ball in the center of each of the rolled dough pieces. Pick up the edges of the bread dough and bring them all together just above the center of the fig ball. Gently grasp them and twist them so that the resulting

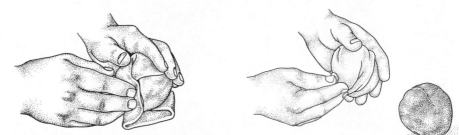

design looks like a swirl. This seals the bread and keeps the stuffing inside. Try not to make this part of the dough too thick. It should be as uniform as possible all around. Brush the loaves all over with virgin olive oil, not too much, just so they glisten. Preheat the oven to 375° F, place the *pangialli* on a baking sheet, and let them rest in a warm place for as long as it takes your oven to attain the desired temperature.

Put the *pangialli* in the middle of the oven and bake them for 30 minutes, or until the dough is a deep gold all over, including the bottom. Take them out of the oven to cool on a rack. They are best eaten several hours later. If you wrap them in plastic, you can keep them, unrefrigerated, for about 3 days. If you must keep them longer, you can wrap them in plastic and store them in the refrigerator. Three hours before you want to use them, gently warm them in a preheated 375° F oven for about 5 to 6 minutes.

1 *pound large, plump chestnuts*	¼ *cup water*
1 *cup granulated sugar*	⅓ *cup rum*

Preheat oven to 425° F.

Make a long horizontal cut across the curved side of the chestnut between the tip and the end of the chestnut. Cut just deep enough to get through the tough outer skin and barely scrape the inner skin. Use a short, strong paring knife if you don't have the Italian knife called a *castrino,* "castrating knife." Place the chestnuts on a cookie sheet or in a large pie pan, and put them into the oven to roast for about 30 minutes. When they are done, you will notice that the meat has pushed through the cut outer skin and is well exposed. This will greatly facilitate peeling them completely. (This very old method makes peeling chestnuts a breeze, and I do not know why everyone does not know about it.)

Put the chestnuts into a deep bowl lined with a kitchen towel and cover them with another kitchen towel. Leave them to rest for a few minutes, and when they are still very hot but handleable, peel them, putting the peeled ones in another bowl covered with a kitchen towel to keep them warm until you make the syrup.

Place the sugar and water in a heavy pan large enough to hold the chestnuts later, and heat it over medium heat, stirring for 5 minutes, or until the syrup is well melted and clear. Do not caramelize the sugar, although if it turns a very light gold, it would not hurt, except that when it cools, it may turn into crackle. This is not desirable. Add the chestnuts and stir them around to coat them well. Take your time. When the chestnuts are nicely coated with the syrup, place them in a flameproof dish or chafing dish and pour on the rum. *Carefully* put a match to the dish and flame it, turning the chestnuts all around with a long metal spoon. Do this with a bit of showmanship. Keep it up until the alcohol has all burned off. You may see little scorch marks on the chestnuts as you do this, but don't worry; it makes the chestnuts look and taste nicer. (*Do* be very careful not to flame the chestnuts near anything flammable.)

Serve 4 or 5 chestnuts and some of the syrup to each person. Warn your guests that the chestnuts are very hot and to use caution when eating them. Sugar burns can be disastrous, especially in the mouth. Fortunately, the chestnuts cool rapidly. In a moment or two, you and your guests will be enjoying this very special treat. (See the Italian Pantry notes on chestnuts, page 22, for further information.)

Castagne alla Fiamma

MAKES 1 POUND
FLAMING CHESTNUTS

Flaming Chestnuts are eaten in all parts of Italy. It is a dish that is particularly enjoyed in the North, but so many of the chestnuts in use the world over are from Southern Italy; hence my inclusion of this dish here. In Abruzzo Flaming Chestnuts are especially prized. Though they were pointed out to me as a dish of substantial use there, I actually learned this version from Contessa Giovanna Calini of Bologna. The Calini version could be accepted as the standard recipe for *castagne alla fiamma.* When I ate them in the contessa's living room, they were served on heavy little silver plates decorated with dainty napkins in the shape of doilies.

Frittelle alla Lucana

Lucanian Fritters

MAKES ABOUT
40 PIECES

Lucania, as Basilicata used to be called, is famous for its dried sausages and its chestnuts. It is an isolated region and it has not been a tourist attraction. I have found that the less tourism a city, or province, or region has, the less complicated and sophisticated the food. Without all the influence of strangers, and the inevitable need or desire to accommodate them, insular places remain untouched and are slower to modernize or be worldly. This is either a fault or a virtue, depending on your point of view. The little *frittelle* are ancient and are an example of the originality of a dish and the lack of need to change it. You taste the subtlety of the bay leaf and just the essence of wheat flour. *Frittelle* are a treat after dinner or for a hot snack when you have afternoon visitors. I like them with coffee or with a dark sweet wine like Marsala (page 309).

MENU SUGGESTIONS: Pizza, Lanciano Style (page 52), served warm as an antipasto would be a good starter, along with Roasted Onions (page 233). A dish of Snails in Tomato Sauce (page 172) would be good with a *contorno* of Green Beans in Olive Oil and Lemon Juice (page 237). Lucanian Fritters would finish this meal nicely.

WINE: Merlot di Aprilia (page 306)

Olive oil for frying and greasing
  the wrap, q.b.
1⅓ cups all-purpose flour
⅔ cup semolina
1 large bay leaf
1 teaspoon salt
4 teaspoons virgin olive oil
Plenty of confectioners sugar for
  dusting

Very lightly oil a piece of plastic wrap or aluminum foil about 12 × 15 inches and set it aside.

Sift the flour to be sure that there are no lumps whatsoever. Lumps solidify when they come in contact with the hot water and remain as lumps, and you don't want lumps. Combine the flour and the semolina in a bowl and set it aside for later use.

Put 3 cups water, the bay leaf, salt, and virgin olive oil in a small pan over medium heat. When the water starts to boil violently, remove the pan from the heat and set it aside. Add the flour and semolina mixture into the hot water all at once and stir energetically with a wooden spoon until the mixture begins to become an integrated mass. Put the pan back on the heat and continue to briskly stir for about 3 minutes more. The dough should be very stiff and hard to manage.

Using a rubber spatula, scrape all of the dough out of the pan onto the oiled plastic wrap or foil. Remove the bay leaf and discard it. Moisten your hands with water and pat the mass into a square or rectangle ½ inch thick. Keep wetting your hands as necessary. Let the dough cool for 30 minutes or more. (You can make the recipe to this point up to 1 day ahead of time. Cover the dough in plastic and refrigerate it if you do not use it immediately.)

When you are ready to serve the *frittelle*, cut the dough into 2-inch squares and put them on a flat dish. Heat enough olive oil in a small frying pan to come up the sides ⅛ inch. (You can use more oil if you wish, but I find it unnecessary.) Carefully put in a few squares of dough, fry them until they are a very deep gold on one side, then turn them over with a fork or a small spatula to fry on the other side. Their color must be very dark gold but not burned, or they will have an "off" taste. As the *frittelle* are fried, put them on absorbent towels to absorb any excess oil.

Arrange the fried *frittelle* on a serving dish, sprinkle them liberally with confectioners sugar, and turn them over to sprinkle them again with the confectioners sugar. Serve the *frittelle* very hot, but warn the eaters. The *frittelle* will remain hot enough to eat for about 7 minutes after you make them, but they are optimum served immediately.

1 cup all-purpose flour
Pinch of salt

2½ tablespoons granulated sugar
Zest of 1 lemon

4 tablespoons olive oil

2 to 3 tablespoons dry white wine

½ cup or so block chocolate (prefer bitter but semisweet will do), chopped medium fine

⅓ cup or so almonds, toasted and chopped coarsely

4 tablespoons jam, or q.b. (any kind you like)

2 cups olive oil for frying
Milk or lightly beaten egg for sealing dough, q.b.

Honey, q.b.

Cuscinetti di Teramo

Dessert Ravioli, Teramo Style

MAKES ABOUT 30 "RAVIOLI"

Place the flour on a pastry board and add the salt, sugar, lemon zest, oil, and enough wine to make a firm but tender dough. Knead it well, but it is not necessary to knead it a long time; 5 minutes should do. Let the dough rest, covered with clear wrap, for about a half hour at room temperature.

In the meantime, make the filling by mixing the chocolate, nuts, and jam together. Set this aside for use later.

Roll out the dough to a thin sheet about ⅓₂ inch thick and, using a cookie cutter or a glass with a 3-inch circumference, make rounds about 3 inches around. Place a little of the chocolate filling on each circle of dough, moisten the edges of the dough circles with milk or the beaten egg, fold the dough over like a turnover, and press it shut with a fork or your fingers. Line raviolis up on a lightly floured kitchen towel or a lightly floured cookie sheet until you are ready to fry them.

Heat the oil in a deep pan to 350° F, and fry the ravioli until they are a deep golden color. Remove them with a slotted spoon to drain on paper or kitchen towels. Brush the little ravioli with honey while they are hot. Serve them hot or cold.

Dessert ravioli are awfully good to eat as a snack in the afternoon with sweet wine or coffee. They are ideal as house gifts when you visit friends, and they keep for several days stored in a jar. If you have a pasta machine, you can save yourself some work, which should encourage you to make *cuscinetti* more often.

MENU SUGGESTIONS: *Cuscinetti* would be ideal for picnics and for eating *al fresco*. On a balmy evening you could grill some Homemade Sicilian Sausage (page 188) outdoors and have a big platter of Mixed Vegetable Stew (page 232) or some Almond Peppers (page 249) with it. Afterward you could have a bottle of Moscato di Trani (page 300) and some Dessert Ravioli, Teramo Style.

Parrozzo

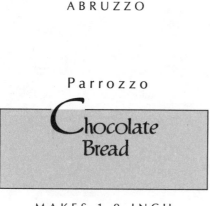

Chocolate Bread

MAKES 1 9-INCH
CAKE

Parrozzo is a soft nutty bread covered with pure chocolate. In the old days the *contadini* ("peasants") made bread with corn flour and baked it in the oven, if they had one, or on the hearth under a special iron cover, which was so constructed as to hold hot coals on top of it, called a *coppo*. Often the bread was eaten hot. This bread was called *pane rozzo*, which means "rough bread." Eventually the name was left to romanticize a bygone era and the delicious *parrozzo*. As far as I can find, the earliest versions of the modern *parrozzo* were not covered with chocolate; that came later. The bread is delicious with or without it.

MENU SUGGESTIONS: An antipasto of Mussels with Saffron (page 103) and Roasted Peppers with Italian-Style Tuna and Clams (page 104) followed by Chicken Roasted with Rosemary (page 178) would be appropriate dishes to precede a big slice of Chocolate Bread, served with Malvasia delle Lipari (page 309).

1 cup blanched almonds

5 or 6 bitter almonds (see almonds in Italian Pantry, page 20)

5 tablespoons sweet butter

½ cup all-purpose flour

6 tablespoons fecula (potato flour) or cornstarch

⅛ teaspoon cinnamon

5 large eggs

¾ cup granulated sugar

FOR THE TOPPING

5 ounces semisweet chocolate, chopped in tiny pieces

Grind all the almonds into fine powder using a food processor or a nut mill. It helps to add just a bit of the sugar if you are using the food processor. It seems to help hold the little nut particles apart, which makes a better grind. Set aside. Use some of the butter to grease a 9-inch cake pan, and use a little of the flour to dust the pan. Set the pan aside. Melt the remaining butter in a small pan over low heat, but do not cook it. Remove it from the heat, and let it cool. Sift the flour, *fecula,* and cinnamon together in a large bowl.

Preheat the oven to 375° F.

Separate the egg yolks from the whites, and put them into separate bowls. Beat the egg yolks, adding one at a time, in a medium-sized bowl, and gradually add the almonds and sugar until the mixture is white and fluffy. Add the flour mixture and the cooled butter, beating vigorously between each addition. Beat the egg whites until they are stiff and glossy, and fold them into the batter. Pour the resulting mixture into the prepared cake pan and bake it for 40 minutes or until the top is golden and the cake is firm. You can test it for doneness by sticking a toothpick into the center of the cake and pulling it out. If it is done, the toothpick will be clean. Let the cake cool in the pan for 15 minutes or more before turning it out onto a cooling rack. Let it thoroughly cool before attempting to glaze it with the chocolate.

Melt the chocolate in a double boiler over very low heat. Actually, if you put very warm tap water into the bottom of the double boiler, it should be hot enough. When the chocolate begins to melt, add 2 tablespoons of warm water and stir constantly until the chocolate is glossy and smooth. The water will keep the chocolate from getting brittle when it dries. If, for some reason, the chocolate binds and becomes a thick mass, add a few more drops of warm water and whisk vigorously for a few minutes with a fine wire whisk.

Put the cooling rack with the cake on it on a cookie sheet to catch any drippings from the glaze. Pour the melted chocolate on top of the cake, and spread it quickly with a palette knife or spatula. (Some people like to cover the whole cake, including the sides. Some like to just have a heavy layer of chocolate on the top, with little drizzles coming down the sides. I usually cover the whole cake if I am using the chocolate.) Let the chocolate cool completely and serve the cake at room temperature. Store any leftover cake under a glass dome out of the refrigerator.

Butter for greasing casserole dish, q.b.

6 pears, Bosc or other firm type

4 tablespoons mild honey

4 ounces semisweet chocolate

2 large eggs

1 tablespoon confectioners sugar

Pere al Cioccolato

Pears in Chocolate

SERVES 6

The addition of honey on these pears provides the chocolate with a hint of the tastes of nutmeg and allspice.

MENU SUGGESTIONS: An antipasto of Tomato Toasts (page 92) and Golden Fried Pumpkin (page 101) followed by a Pizza Margherita (page 49) and a tossed green salad would be a nice easy meal to have before.

WINE: Ravello Rosso (page 303)

Preheat the oven to 375° F.

Butter an ovenproof casserole dish from which you can serve later. Peel the pears, leaving the stem on, and stand them up in the casserole. If they are unstable, cut off a little slice of the bottom to make it flat. Pour ½ cup water into the casserole and put the pears in the oven for about 40 minutes, or until they just begin to soften. This depends on how ripe they are, but remember that Bosc pears are, by nature, firm and crunchy. Baste them with the water every 10 minutes or so. Do not overcook them. If the water evaporates, add a little more boiling water. (Cooler water will stop the cooking and it might break the casserole dish if it is made of clay.)

When the pears seem done, check if there is any water left in the casserole. If there is, tilt the casserole and spoon the water into a bowl, and mix it with the honey. If there is no hot water in the casserole, use about 2 ounces from the tap or boil that amount. Spoon the honey mixture all over the pears several times. Leave them in the oven for another 5 minutes or so, and let the honey lightly coat the pears. Take them out to cool completely. Every so often, spoon any honey mixture that has dripped off them back onto the pears.

When you are ready to serve the pears, melt the chocolate in a warm water bath or double boiler. Do not get it too hot. Separate the 2 egg yolks from the whites. Cool the chocolate, and when it is quite cool but still very liquid and glossy, beat in the egg yolks with a whisk. Make sure they are well amalgamated with the chocolate. Set the chocolate sauce aside and whisk the egg whites until they are very frothy and begin to hold peaks. Sprinkle on the confectioners sugar and continue to whisk until the whites are at the glossy, very, very soft peak stage. You should be able to actually pour the whites, but they should be slightly firm. Fold the egg whites into the chocolate sauce, but do not overmix. Make a very nice fluffy but loose texture that can be spooned over the pears. If bits of white show, do not be concerned. Spoon the sauce over the pears and take them to the table on dessert plates. Set a spoon and fork with which to eat them.

Coviglia

Semifreddo

MAKES ABOUT 6
5-OUNCE CUPS

Probably everyone knows the famous Neapolitan semifreddo dessert biscuit tortoni. A Neapolitan by the name Tortoni made it famous in Paris in the early nineteenth century. The word *semifreddo* is used with abandon, which is only fair because it is so hard to define just what it is. This luscious cream-and-egg-based dessert is called *coviglia* in Naples, and only there. It has many faces, all legitimate. Semifreddo flavors can change from season to season, such as strawberries and raspberries in summer, and coffee and lemon anytime at all; or crushed, toasted nuts in winter. Bananas or cooked pineapple are delicious, as are large cookie crumbs gleaned from the bottom of the jar and some cake crumbs from other pastry projects. In short, anything that makes culinary sense can be used to make *coviglie*. Use combinations of the aforementioned to get really exotic results.

The following recipe gives the base for making semifreddo. After carefully reading and understanding how it works, you can then set out to make your very own renditions. I include *coviglia* recipes using almonds or hazelnuts, chocolate, coffee, and strawberries as examples. From there you can have a free hand in making your own.

4 *large egg yolks*
½ *cup granulated sugar*
   Flavor of your choice: Use ½ cup toasted and crushed nuts; or ⅓ cup shredded chocolate; or ½ basket whole strawberries, or make purée; or 2 ounces very strong espresso, cold

3 *large egg whites, stiffly beaten*
1 *cup heavy whipping cream*
   Optional: *add ½ cup stiff Pastry Cream (page 260) at the same time you add the flavor. This results in an even creamier dessert and yields about 2 more 5-ounce portions.*

Put the egg yolks and sugar into the bowl of an electric mixer. Using the whisk, beat them on low speed until the yolks and sugar are well mixed and begin to turn pale yellow. Turn the speed to high and beat the yolks until they have tripled in volume and you have reached the ribbon stage.

At this point add the flavor you want. You can also add the optional Pastry Cream now, but it must be folded in so as not to collapse the volume of the yolks. Whatever you add, generally it must be as thick as the yolk mixture, or the resulting semifreddo will be too soft. If this ever happens, you can usually save it by freezing it, unless it is very liquid indeed, in which case you should start the recipe again and make milk shakes with the "disaster." If the semifreddo is meant to be eaten as a cold pudding or soufflé, the yolks, cream, and egg whites must be thoroughly and well stiffened. If the semifreddo is to be eaten frozen by intention, then the stiffness of the aforementioned ingredients is not so critical. When you add flavors such as the espresso, you must be sure the cream and the egg whites are beaten really stiff to compensate for the liquid.

The ideal added flavor ingredients are bits of chocolate, cookie crumbs, and cake crumbs; or toasted, cooled, and chopped nuts because they are dry and add body to the semifreddo. If you use fresh fruit such as strawberries or peaches, be sure they are ripe but very firm, as they will exude too much juice and liquefy your dessert. Cut them into rather small pieces or they will be too bulky. But remember, if you have added flavor ingredients that might cause that problem, plan on serving the semifreddo frozen. That should take care of most any situation.

Meanwhile, beat the cream with another mixer or by hand until it is quite stiff and looks as though it is grainy and about to become butter. Pour about 20 percent of the yolk mixture into the whipped cream and mix it well to loosen the mass of cream. Pour the egg yolk mixture onto the surface of the lightened whipped cream and fold in the rest of the yolk mixture.

Folding is accomplished by plunging a rubber spatula into the center of the mixture, clear to the bottom, while you are firmly holding the bowl with the other hand. Angle the spatula to the right and slice across the bottom of the bowl coming left and continue up the left side of the bowl, bringing some of the mixture from the bottom up and over so that it lands on the top. Quickly rotate the bowl a quarter turn in any direction, plunge the spatula into the mixture again, and repeat the fold. Keep doing this as rapidly as you can, being sure to bring mixture from the bottom to the top by the folding action. Theoretically, you should finish the entire mixing within 12 folding operations.

Set the mixture aside in the refrigerator and beat the egg whites until they are quite stiff and shiny. They must be quite stiff, or they will liquefy the yolk and cream mixture and make it collapse. Add a pinch of salt to the mixing bowl if it is not made of clean unlined copper, well cleaned. If it is, no salt is necessary. When the whites are quite stiffly beaten, put them on top of the yolk and cream mixture, and fold them together.

Immediately scoop the mixture into glasses, cups, or paper molds. Put them into the refrigerator if you want a very soft, creamy, and unctuous dessert. Otherwise freeze them and the *coviglie* will become like semisoft ice cream. Frozen and well covered, the *coviglie* can be stored for a month or two. You can make the *coviglia* in one large bowl if you like.

When you serve the *coviglie*, be sure they soften for a few minutes out of the freezer. They should hold their shape but be very soft, silky, and luscious.

NOTE: By simply adding chocolate or vanilla extract or lemon juice you can make very respectable ice cream with the base for semifreddo. As a matter of fact, I make almost all my ice cream with this method. I have no need for a crank, although I own one. The resulting ice cream with this method is more like ice cream should be: softer, more supple, and very tasty because it is not in a cold, hard block as commercial ice creams are. Many of my students who have learned this method of making *coviglie* use the base for ice cream of almost any flavor they like with consistently excellent results.

Coviglia di Caffè

SERVES 6

1 *recipe Semifreddo base (page 286)*
¼ *cup very strong espresso, cold*
6 *espresso coffee beans*

Make the recipe for Semifreddo base as directed. Add the coffee beans as a decoration. They are crunchy and delicious.

The coffee flavor in this *coviglia* really must be espresso, made with those shiny black Italian roast beans, easily found in good coffee stores everywhere.

Coviglia di Cioccolata

SERVES 6

Almost everyone loves chocolate. You should use the best-quality chocolate you can get, and it should be semisweet. Do not pulverize the chocolate, or it will make your semifreddo a muddy, off-color. It should be cold and then chipped off in little pieces with an ice pick or a small knife.

1 *recipe Semifreddo base (page 286)*
⅓ *cup semisweet chocolate, chopped tiny or to taste*

Make the recipe for Semifreddo base as directed. Add chocolate pieces on top.

CAMPANIA

Coviglia di Fragole

SERVES 6

If you ever come across *fragole del bosco* ("wild strawberries"), those little rubies of flavor and elegance, by all means get some and make this semifreddo. If you have to make do with ordinary strawberries, make sure they are very red, very ripe but firm and as sweet as if they had been soaked in sugar. Cut the strawberries into 4 or 6 pieces and drain in a sieve for a while before you fold them into the semifreddo. Add more as a decoration just before serving to dress up the *coviglia di fragole*.

1 *recipe Semifreddo base (page 286)*
½ *basket strawberries, washed, dried, and cut into pieces, plus additional strawberries as decoration*

Make the recipe for Semifreddo base as directed using the strawberries. When ready to serve, add 1 or 2 strawberries on top of each for decoration.

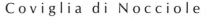

Hazelnut Semifreddo

SERVES 8

1   *recipe Semifreddo base (page 286)*

½   *cup Pastry Cream (page 260)*

⅓   *cup toasted, peeled, and crushed hazelnuts (or use toasted almonds)*

Zest of 1 orange and/or 1 teaspoon finely chopped candied orange peel (page 24)

Make the recipe for Semifreddo base as directed using the Pastry Cream, nuts, and orange.

This is my favorite *coviglia*, possibly because it has *crema pasticciera* in it. I like it either cold as it comes from the refrigerator or frozen. If I want a more sensual dessert, I simply put it into the refrigerator. The texture then is so smooth and luscious that I literally lick it off the spoon, slowly. Otherwise the freezer treatment is perfect.

SICILIA

Sfinci di San Giuseppe

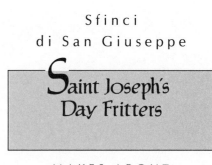

Saint Joseph's Day Fritters

MAKES ABOUT 25 FRITTERS

1   *quart olive oil*

1   *recipe Cream Puff Pastry (page 255)*

Confectioners sugar, q.b.

Heat 1 quart of olive oil or other good cooking oil to 350° F. Take a tablespoonful of pastry batter and carefully drop it into the oil, using your finger or another spoon to dislodge the dough. Do not put in too many, or you will cool off the oil too much and make the fritters soggy. The fritters will turn themselves over (as the bottom cooks it expands and becomes lighter than the top, and this makes the *sfinci* keep turning). If they don't, give them a little nudge with a spoon or a stick. You must be there to supervise the gyrations. The first puffing takes place and then there may be 3 or 4 more puffings. They should triple in volume. When the fritters are golden brown, remove them with a slotted spoon to a dish with an absorbent towel in the bottom to drain excess oil.

Dust the *sfinci* generously with confectioners sugar, or tear them open and fill with Ricotta mixture (see Sicilian Cassata, page 266, or Cannoli filling, page 261) or Pastry Cream (page 260), and then dust them with confectioners sugar. Either way, serve them as soon as possible. They are at their best when they are hot, do not keep well, and cannot be reheated successfully. Heap them up on a plate and serve. Eat them with your fingers.

These soft, puffy morsels are good plain with a dusting of confectioners sugar. They are even better filled with pastry or cannoli cream.

Cremolate
Soft Ices

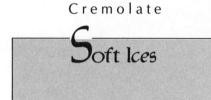

Soft Ices are made with fruit, fruit juices, sugar, and water. Occasionally the flavors will vary to include chocolate, in which case there is the rare change of ingredient, milk.

Cremolate are always soft and just barely on their way to becoming slightly granular, but this is more a perception than a fact. The simplest ones are peach, apricot, mandarin orange, and lemon. They are also the best. Keep in mind that Italian desserts may be considered very sweet by contemporary standards, but they also have an enormous depth of flavor. In commercial American and French pastries and ice creams, you get loads of fat in the form of butter or lard, and in Italian ices you get sugar.

The ices given here should be made with fresh fruit. If you reduce the amount of sugar, you will end up with a very grainy texture. Sugar in heavy doses will not freeze. The same is true of alcohol. Sugar, more than ice and salt ratios, determines the texture of ice creams and sherbets. Above the scale of 22 on the Baumè sugar meter (specific gravity), ice creams will not harden. They are like a slush, and they remain that way. If you add too much alcohol to ice creams, the same thing happens. You get slush. Antifreeze in your car radiator has a high alcohol content, which prevents freezing of the liquid in the motor. If you had only water in the radiator and were in freezing weather, the expansion of the frozen water would split the engine block.

If you get below 13 or 14 on the Baumè meter, you get the coarse textures and ice shards that are absolutely necessary in *granite*. *Granita* would not be *granita* without the shards. The ideal Baumè reading for *granite* is about 10 or 11, but it is good at up to 13.

If you use a little less salt than called for in the freezing process, it will take longer for the ice cream to set up, and the texture will be finer and smoother. If you add more salt than is recommended, the freezing time will be shortened and the ice cream will surely be more granular.

If you follow the ratios of the recipe for Lemon Ice that follows, you will be able to make other ices, as mentioned above. I include a recipe for Chocolate Ice also. For those who like a smoother result, add to the recipes that follow 3 large egg yolks whisked with some of the sugar to the ribbon stage. Then, when the other part of the mixture is still hot, pour it into the egg yolk and whisk it well and vigorously. Continue as the recipe describes.

2 cups sugar
Zest from 2 lemons

1½ cups lemon juice
1 teaspoon vanilla extract

Put 3 cups water and sugar into a nonaluminum pan and bring the water to a boil. When it looks clear, that means the sugar has melted. Add the zest, lemon juice, and vanilla. Remove the pan from the heat and let it cool. When it is cool, test it for the amount of lemon taste you want. Remember, though, the flavor tempers considerably after freezing and curing. So if it seems a little too lemony while it is warm, it may be perfect after it freezes. Add more lemon juice if you like and stir well. If, on the other hand, it is too lemony for you, add more water and sugar in the same ratio as before, and heat the mixture to be sure the sugar melts. Cover the mixture and put in the refrigerator for at least 6 hours, but overnight is better.

Put the cold mixture into the freezer can and put the dasher in. Churn the ice until it is quite firm. Quickly put the resulting *cremolata* into a glass or plastic container, cover it, and let it "cure" in the freezer, preferably for 1 day.

Cremolata di Limone

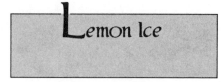

MAKES ABOUT
1½ QUARTS

This lemony ice is better if you let it "cure" in the freezer overnight. Covered, it will last in the freezer, in good condition, for about 2 weeks. Serve some cookies or a piece of plain cake with the ice and you have a wonderful dessert. Lemon Ice on a warm afternoon is a good way to beat the heat.

Cremolata di Cioccolata

MAKES ABOUT 5 CUPS

6 tablespoons cocoa

4 cups milk

1 cup superfine granulated sugar

Put 1 cup water into a pan with the cocoa, bring to a boil, and then turn the heat down. Let the mixture simmer for 5 minutes, remove it from the heat, and let it cool. When the mixture cools, add the milk and the sugar, and stir it for perhaps 10 minutes, or until the sugar is completely melted. Put the covered mixture into the refrigerator for at least 6 hours, but overnight is better.

Put the cold mixture into the freezer can and put the dasher in. Churn the ice until it is quite firm. Quickly put the resulting *cremolata* into a glass or plastic container, covered, and let it "cure" in the freezer, preferably for 1 day.

Chocolate is highly regarded in Italy, but it is not eaten with such passion as on our shores. This recipe for Chocolate Ice is made with bitter chocolate cocoa. It makes for a bit of graininess, but the flavor is good and chocolaty.

Gelati

Ice Creams

Sicilian and Neapolitan ice creams are, without doubt, the best in the world. They are best eaten on the spot. Italians do not ordinarily make their own ice cream. It is not only easier but more fun to make a *passeggiatta* ("promenade") to the local *gelateria* ("ice-cream parlor") and gorge.

The following recipes give two ice creams that are favorites of mine: hazelnut and vanilla. You will see that they are not made with cream but with milk. These ice creams have less fat, but they are closer to the taste you would get in Italy. Once you acclimate your mouth to these ice creams and then taste typical American ice cream, you will see the difference.

Remember, though, no matter what brand of ice-cream freezer you use, the ice must be crushed to get the best results, and you must have enough salt. Most people fail to crush the ice fine enough and are stingy with the salt.

Prepare the ice-cream freezer according to the manufacturer's directions. In any event, wash the can, the dasher, and the cover in hot soapy water, even if you did that before putting it away after the last use. Rinse well, and then dry thoroughly. You must have a scrupulously clean can to jell the ice cream.

In the case of the Waring Ice Cream Parlour, which uses ice cubes, I find that using miniature ice cubes works better than the usual ones. You can buy ice trays that make those baby cubes. It saves having to crush ice, and they are usable for other purposes in the same way as the big ones.

Please read the sections on Ices (page 290) and Spumoni (page 296) for more information.

Gelato Affogato

"Drowned" Ice Cream

This hardly constitutes a recipe, but the combinations are infinite and after a while, after you have grown used to the idea, you will spend the rest of your days experimenting.

The portions must be big or this is not a dessert to bother with. Serve 1 cup of ice cream per person. For this amount of ice cream you should use a pony of whiskey. If you are using aqua vitae use about an ounce.

Chocolate goes very well with Scotch; or vanilla and almonds or chocolate and almonds. There is also peach ice cream with peach brandy on it or raspberry ice cream with Grappa. Dark chocolate and Grappa were made for each other. You could use some of the sweet liqueurs but I think the sharp alcohol of something dry like whiskey or straight brandy is the best for my taste. This is one time you can get carried away with your imagination.

MENU SUGGESTIONS: After a festive meal or for a totally fuss-free dessert, "Drowned" Ice Cream is a natural. It is particularly good after something like Fried Codfish, Roman Style (page 190), Breaded Lamb Chops (page 186), or Trout in Casserole (page 202).

Gelato di Vaniglia #1

MAKES
APPROXIMATELY
6 CUPS

Vanilla ice cream is a good friend to so many other flavors. It is tasty and yet has a nonassertive character that allows you to use it in many interesting ways. Sometimes just sprinkling cookie or cake crumbs on it makes it epicurean, depending on who made the cake. I find vanilla ice cream perfect to use in "Drowned" Ice Cream (page 293). Almost any whiskey or liqueur you can name seems to be just right with it.

| 10 | *large egg yolks* | 4 | *cups milk (or half and half)* |
| 1½ | *cups granulated sugar* | 2 | *teaspoons vanilla extract* |

Scald the milk by putting it into a pan over low heat and bringing the temperature up to 180° F. Take the milk off the heat and stir in the vanilla. Let it rest for about 15 minutes.

Meanwhile beat the egg yolks and the sugar with an electric mixer at high speed until tripled in volume and at the heavy-ribbon stage. Lower the speed of the mixer to a little less than moderate and slowly drizzle in the warm milk. When you have finished, put the mixture into a heavy pan and place it over low heat, stirring with a whisk the whole time. The moment the mixture looks thicker than it started out to be, take it off the heat and pour it into a clean glass or stainless steel bowl to cool, uncovered, before putting it in the refrigerator.

When it is cold, cover the mixture and refrigerate it for about 6 hours or overnight. Follow the directions of your particular ice-cream machine.

Gelato di Vaniglia #2

MAKES 2 QUARTS

As good as the other ice creams in this section are, you probably will like this one best. The cream and egg yolks not only make a lusher version of ice cream but they seem to enhance the flavor of the vanilla. This ice cream would be a good choice for using in spumoni.

2	*cups whipping cream*	1½	*cups granulated sugar*
1	*quart whole milk*	2	*teaspoons salt*
6	*egg yolks from large eggs*	2	*tablespoons vanilla*

Scald the cream and milk in a large saucepan. If you are using a thermometer, the temperature should be about 180° F. Meanwhile, beat the yolks, sugar, and salt in an electric mixer until they become pale and thick. Add the hot cream and milk mixture and slowly mix again for about 1 minute. Put the mixture back into the saucepan over medium heat and stir constantly until the mixture just begins to simmer. Remove from the heat and stir in the vanilla. If there are any lumps, strain them out. Pour the mixture into a container and let cool in the refrigerator, uncovered, for at least 6 hours. *You can make the recipe up to this point 2 days ahead.*

Put the cold mixture into the freezing can of an ice-cream maker and churn it until it is thick and very heavy. Remove the dasher and put the ice cream into an ice-cold bowl with a cover and let it "cure" in the freezer for 1 day before using. *You can keep it frozen for up to 2 weeks.*

4 *cups whole milk*

⅓ *cup whole hazelnuts, well toasted and skinned*

10 *large egg yolks*

1¼ *cups sugar*

Gelato di Nocciole

Hazelnut Ice Cream

MAKES ABOUT 5 CUPS

Warm the milk in a pan over medium heat, but do not boil. When the milk is quite hot, approximately 180° F, put it into a blender, add the toasted hazelnuts, and blend on the highest speed your blender can produce. If your blender does not comfortably hold all of the amount shown, simply blend it in two separate batches. The nuts must be as finely ground as possible. It is possible to pulverize small amounts of the nuts in a food processor and add them to the hot milk. In either case, let the nuts steep in the hot milk for at least 15 minutes before proceeding with the recipe.

Beat the egg yolks with the sugar to the ribbon stage with an electric mixer on high. When the egg yolks have turned pale yellow and have tripled their volume, lower the speed of the mixer to quite low and drizzle in the hot milk and hazelnut mixture. When the mixture is well amalgamated, put it into a stainless steel or glass bowl and cool it in the refrigerator until it is quite cold. Cover and leave overnight.

When you are ready to make the ice cream, follow the instructions of your particular ice-cream machine.

NOTE: You may want to read the sections on Ice Creams (page 292), Ices (page 290), and Spumoni (page 296) before making this or any other ice-cream dessert.

Spumoni

THE DERIVATION OF THIS WORD IS "foam." If you are at all imaginative, you can see that ice cream of any type could be considered a foam. Foam is generally something that is bigger than the original parts or state. That definition is not from the dictionary. A *spumone* as known in this country is always like stratified tutti-frutti ice cream, served wedge-shaped and usually in a paper cup, such as you would find wrapped around a muffin.

Spumoni and *cassate* are in the same family. The biggest difference I can see is that a *spumone* always has as its first layer ice cream made with egg yolks beaten dense and stiff. The center is a semifreddo (page 286) or a lighter creamlike filling that probably would not have the strength to be a first layer. The *zuccotto* from Tuscany has a similar structure, except that cake is the armor or first layer, and flavored whipped cream is the filling. In *cassate gelati,* or ice-cream *cassate*, you find that there are usually more layers, and one layer, if not more, is *pan di Spagna* (page 269), or what we might call *genoise*, usually flavored with some kind of alcohol, rum being typical. The filling is made in the same way that a semifreddo would be made.

The following section gives a few different spumoni that can be made easily. Make up your own concoctions thereafter. As long as you have diversity of ice creams available, homemade or bought, you are always able to produce a stunning, delicious dessert, fit for even the most formal occasion you can think of.

In general the procedure is the same for all spumoni. For a 6-quart mold with 3 layers, you should have 1 quart of ice cream for the outer layer, 1½ pints of ice cream for the second layer, and about 1 cup of flavored whipped cream of any semifreddo mixture (page 286) you like.

The mold should be either tinned metal or glass that can be frozen. The shape easiest to deal with and that looks prettiest on the table is a charlotte mold. This mold is usually made of tinned metal and has two little heart-shaped handles on it. It can be purchased with a lid, but for making spumoni a metal lid is not necessary. You can use plastic wrap.

Freeze the mold for at least 1 hour before adding any ice cream. Scoop the first flavor of ice cream from its container and start lining the bottom of the charlotte mold with it. If the ice cream is very hard, let it soften out of the freezer for about 15 minutes or so. It is easier to mold when it is a little soft. The layer should be about ¾ inch thick. Be sure it is an even layer. Then start layering the sides, making them the same thickness. Again, be sure to get the layer as even as possible. I find that a thin rubber spatula or a slender metal spatula works well for gliding over the surface of the ice cream and smoothing it out. Put the mold, lined with the ice cream, into the freezer to harden for about 2 hours. Then take it out and add another flavor of ice cream as the second layer. Put the mold back into the freezer for another 2 hours.

Meanwhile, if you have not already prepared the semifreddo, do so while the second layer is freezing. Put the semifreddo into the remaining space in the mold and smooth out the bottom so that is even. Freeze it overnight. You can make it 1 or 2 weeks ahead and just leave it in the mold, well covered in plastic wrap, until you are ready to use it.

When you are ready to remove the *spumone*, dip the mold into cold, not warm, water, up to the top edges. Quickly dry the mold and put an ice-cold serving plate over the ice cream. Invert the plate and mold and gently shake the mold back and forth to dislodge the *spumone*. Remember, it is the vacuum that is holding it back. If it seems impossible to disgorge the *spumone* from its mold, try inserting a long, slender knife down the side and pulling the *spumone* back to let some air into the mold. Usually this does the trick, and you should hear a slurping sound, which means the *spumone* is on its way out. You may have to bang the mold on the serving plate several times. After you have turned out the mold, put the serving plate with the *spumone* on it into the freezer and freeze it again for about 1 hour to be sure it has not begun to melt and puddle up on the plate.

The usual way to serve *spumone* is to cut the molded ice cream in wedges, as you would a cake or a pie, with a very slender knife dipped in cold water and wiped with a clean cloth after every cut. I use a very thin carving knife.

Some of the combinations I like the best follow. If there are three flavors, it means that the first two are ice creams and the last is a semifreddo. If there are only two flavors listed, that means the outer layer of ice cream is twice as thick and the semifreddo is the filling. Proceed as described above.

Spumoni Diverse
Different Spumoni

Vanilla (page 294)
Raspberry
Coffee Semifreddo (page 287)

Strawberry
Strawberry Semifreddo (page 288)

Chocolate
Pistachio
Pastry Cream (page 260) and Hazelnut Semifreddo (page 289)

Coffee
Lemon Ice (page 291)
Strawberry Semifreddo (page 288)

Vanilla (page 294)
Hazelnut (page 295)
Coffee Semifreddo (page 287)

GLOSSARIO VINI
DEL SUD ITALIA

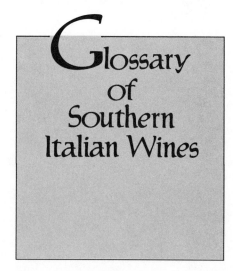

Glossary
of
Southern
Italian Wines

WINE IS LIFE. OR, RATHER, life is bigger than the sum of its parts if it includes wine. Wine may not always be of blue-ribbon quality, but almost without exception it is drinkable, and if you include it as a food, as you really must do, it is also a staple in the diet.

Italian wines should be seen not only for their enormous value-for-dollar ratio but as high-quality, diverse, complicated wines that, categorically, have world-class stature. With careful shopping and with some knowledge of the kinds of wine you like and why you like them, you can begin to enjoy them here in America the same way the Italians do, which is to drink modest, available, and affordable wines on an ongoing basis.

The wines of Southern Italy are good, solid, well-made products, and on their own these wines can be delightful, delicious, and abundantly available.

Soil that is rich in volcanic ash adds a dimension of flavor and intensity not found in Northern grapes. In Southern Italy, grapes have a very high sugar content because they are bombarded by the rays of the sun for a long period of time not only in the course of a day but in the course of a season. This is not to imply that all Italian wines are sweet. It is just that the more sugar the grapes have, the stronger the production of alcohol, which gives strength of character to the wine and also allows a long barrel and bottle life.

I give you here a mere hint of the range and scope of the various wines that are available in the United States. This listing is by no means complete.

There is a brief description of the character of the wine and a suggestion of foods that complement it and any other little insights that occur. No value judgment is intended by the listing and it will be by region (where applicable, there will also be province, city, or area or some other identification), status (government designation, i.e., D.O.C.), grape, and color. The Italian D.O.C. (*Denominazione dell'Origine Controllata*) is roughly equivalent to the French appellation *contrôlée* and means that certain of the Italian wines qualify to use this designation on their labels, assuring the buyer of certain rigid requirements. This designation applies to only about 12 percent of the Italian wines. Although these rigid standards are proudly met by the people entitled to use them, you should be aware that this does not by any means guarantee that you are going to like the results of their care and skill. The wine may meet or exceed all the requirements and yet not be the ultimate expression of that kind of wine. They say it is all "in the hands." I know that is true in cooking and I am ready to believe it is no less true in winemaking.

ABRUZZO

Montepulciano d'Abruzzo

Provinces of Chieti, L'Aquila, Pescara, and Teramo

D.O.C.

GRAPES: Montepulciano with the permissible addition of up to 15 percent Sangiovese

COLORS: Red and Cerasuolo (cherry red)

Robust with plenty of flavor and a softness that makes it a perfect choice for pastas, pizza, grilled pork, game, roast meat such as lamb or chicken and delicious with fresh ripe figs and peaches. Cerasuolo, while lighter in color, is equally good and perfect with dishes like stews and sautéed vegetables and *frittati*.

Trebbiano d'Abruzzo

Provinces of Chieti, L'Aquila, Pescara, and Teramo

D.O.C.

GRAPES: Trebbiano d'Abruzzo and/or Trebbiano Toscano with the permissible addition of up to 15 percent Malvasia Toscana

COLOR: White

Pale, dry, delicate, and fresh wine that can age a little. It is good with grilled fish and is particularly good with artichoke dishes.

APULIA

Aleatico di Puglia

Provinces of Foggia, Lecce, Brindisi, and Taranto (there are many zones in these provinces too numerous to mention)

D.O.C.

GRAPE: Aleatico, sometimes with the addition of Negroamaro, Malvasia Nera, and Primitivo

COLOR: Red (garnet)

Sweet, called *dolce naturale* with 15 percent alcohol, is best suited for eating with cookies, dessert breads, and simple unfrosted cakes. Another, *liquoroso dolce naturale*, if aged three years or more, may be called *riserva*. It has a more delicate, smoother taste and aroma, and has 18 percent alcohol.

Brindisi

Province of Brindisi in the Brindisi and Mesagne zones

D.O.C.

GRAPES: Negroamaro and Malvasia Nera, Sussumariello, Montepulciano and Sangiovese

COLORS: Red and *rosato*

Intense and winy, it is dry but well balanced with a slight bitter aftertaste; it is one of my favorite wines. The *rosso* is good with pasta and pizza dishes and with most kinds of pork. The *rosato* is slightly fruity but dry and is very good with seafood and some cheeses. This might be a good place to say that the name is constantly mispronounced. It is not Brin-di´-si; it is Brin´-di-si, with the accent on the first four letters.

Cacc'e Mmitte di Lucera

Province of Foggia in the Lucera, Troia, and Biccari zones
D.O.C.
GRAPES: Uva di Troia, Montepulciano, Sangiovese, and Malvasia Nera di Brindisi, alone or combined, and Trebbiano Toscano, Bombino Bianco, and Malvasia di Chianti alone or combined
COLOR: Ruby red
In Pugliese dialect, the name means either to "keep drinking" or "keep drowning"; freely translated, both could mean the same thing. This wine is at its best with salty cheeses and salami.

Castel del Monte

Province of Bari in the Minervino Murge and parts of many other zones
D.O.C.
GRAPES: For the white, Pampanato, but can also have Trebbiano Toscano or Giallo, Bombino, and Palumbo, and for the red, Bombino Nero or Uva di Troia and/or Montepulciano
COLORS: White, rosato, or red
The white is delicate, fresh, and dry and is very good with antipasti of cured pork, seafood, and some of the typical Southern sweet-sour dishes such as Sicilian Eggplant Relish. The rosato has a winy aroma and is rather intense. It goes well with shellfish or grilled light foods such as fish and vegetables. The red is nicely tannic and has a winy aroma. If aged three years it may be called riserva. Roasts and grills of meat and poultry are perfect with it.

Favonio

Estate name (meaning vento dell'ovest, or "wind of the west") of the following wines:

Favonio Bianco

Province of Foggia
GRAPE: Pinot Bianco
COLOR: White
The terms dry and fruity seem to contradict each other, but this wine has them both. It is as good as any northern Italian Pinot Bianco, which is high praise, indeed. Very good with pasta with Marinara Sauce, Tuna, Calabrian Style, Grilled Swordfish, Snails with Oregano or Tomato, or Fried Codfish, Roman Style.

Favonio Cabernet Franc

Province of Foggia
GRAPE: Cabernet Franc
COLOR: Red
This highly flavorful wine, reminiscent of bell peppers, and medium bodied, seems bigger than it is. Best drunk within three to five years, it is excellent with dishes such as Chicken, Potenza Style or with Rosemary; Braised Beef, Roman Style, and Skewered Pork Rolls; or Braised Rabbit, Sardinian Style.

Favonio Pinot Nero

Province of Foggia
GRAPE: Pinot Nero
COLOR: Dark red but not intense
Softer than the Cabernet Franc with a more pronounced vinous smell, this wine is almost imperceptibly bitter with

a hint of nuts and berries and should be drunk before it is four years old. It is good with foods that are not too acid and is very good with feathered game and some braised meats.

Five Roses

Province of Lecce, Salice Salentino zone
GRAPE: Negroamaro
COLOR: Rosé

Unlike most rosé wines, Five Roses is high in alcohol and is aged several years in the bottle before it is sold. First made around 1930, it may well be the first bottled rosé sold in Italy. Five Roses is good with light antipasto dishes such as *prosciutto* and melon or figs, Bread and Cheese Skewers, Roasted Roman Style, fish dishes such as shrimp cooked in brandy, or grilled fish with herbs.

Locorotondo

Province of Brindisi in the Locorotondo, Cisternino, and Fasano zones
D.O.C.
GRAPE: Verdeca, Bianco d'Alessano, Fiano, Bombino, and sometimes Malvasia
COLOR: Pale yellow

Dry and slightly fruity and nutty make this one of the best all-around whites you can buy. A bargain at almost any price, its price is never very high. It can be used with almost any kind of food such as pasta, vegetables, fish, fowl and meats, pan-fried, grilled, or roasted.

Moscato di Trani

Province of Bari in the Trani, Bisceglie, Andria, Canosa, Minervino, and parts of Cerignola, Trinitapoli, and Barletta, Terlizzi and Bitonto

D.O.C.
GRAPE: Moscato di Trani or Moscato Reale, and other grapes may be used
COLOR: White, actually a kind of gold

Dessert or after-dinner wine. It is unctuous but not overwhelming and goes well with hard cookies.

Primitivo di Manduria

Provinces of Taranto and Brindisi in the Manduria, Carovino, Monteparano, Leporano, Pulsano, and other zones
D.O.C.
GRAPE: Primitivo
COLOR: Red

This wine's hues change from violet to orange, and the alcohol level is high. It has a vinous aroma and taste, and, as it gets older it becomes smoother. It is best with furred game and dishes that have distinctive flavor and can withstand the 14 percent or higher alcohol content. There are also sweet versions with higher sugar and alcohol that are called *dolce naturale*, *liquoroso dolce naturale*, and *liquoroso secco*, all good after dinner or with midafternoon snacks of cookies.

Rosato del Salento

Salento area, all over:
GRAPE: Negroamaro, Malvasia Nera, and sometimes Ottavianello grapes
COLOR: Rosé

A very fine example of a rosé wine with an herbaceous and slightly bitter aftertaste, and much appreciated. It is quite good with dishes such as Chicken, Potenza Style, or Clay-Cooked Prawns, or Snails with Oregano, or pastas with tomato sauce.

Rosso del Salento

Salento and Brindisi zones

GRAPES: Negroamaro and Malvasia Nera

COLOR: Dark red sometimes with amber overtones

This wine, one of my favorites, is underrated. It is dark, vinous to the nose and mouth, tastes of pepper and a hint of juniper, and is very much like Amarone. Like Brindisi, this wine is noble and is perfect with roast game, feathered or furred, grilled or braised meat, and Chicken Roasted with Rosemary.

Salice Salentino

Province of Brindisi in the Salice Salentino, Veglie, Guagnano, S. Pancrazio Salentino, and Sandonaci zones

D.O.C.

GRAPE: Negroamaro with the addition of Malvasia Nera di Brindisi and Lecce alone or in combinations

COLORS: Red and rosato

The red is good with salty foods such as antipasto made with cured meats, grilled or baked sausages, and is very good with a variety of pasta dishes. The rosato is excellent with hot antipasti and fried foods and stuffed savory breads such as Sicilian Bread Roll in the Old Style and Fried Calzone.

San Severo

Province of Foggia in the San Severo, Torremaggiore, S. Paolo Civitate, and part of some five other zones

D.O.C.

GRAPES: For the white, Bombino Bianco, Trebbiano Toscano, Malvasia Bianca Lunga, and Verdeca; for the red or rosato, Montepulciano or Sangiovese

COLORS: White, red, and rosato

The white has a typical winy taste with no particular hints of other things. It is fresh and dry and goes well with pasta and pizza and with grilled fish and maybe minestrone. The red has a rather thin but grapey aroma and is of medium body. It is good with many kinds of food including antipasti, pasta, and all kinds of roasted meats with herbs. The rosato is best with grilled fish or Rabbit, Ischian Style.

Torre Quarto Bianco

Province of Foggia, Cerignola zone

GRAPES: Bombino Bianco, Trebbiano, and Greco

COLOR: Very white

The dryness of this wine is balanced by a deep, almost herblike aroma. It is served quite cold to assure smoothness and is good as an aperitivo wine as well as an accompaniment to fish and shellfish and chicken dishes with or without tomatoes.

Torre Quarto Rosso

Province of Foggia, Cerignola zone

GRAPES: Malbec and Uva di Troia

COLOR: Red/garnet with a tinge of orange

High alcohol with fruit and tannin make this dense and intensely flavored wine suitable for long aging. It is excellent with chicken dishes, roast and braised meats, feathered or furred game, and strong firm cheeses and bread.

BASILICATA (Lucania)

Aglianico del Vulture

Province of Potenza in the Rionero Vulture, Basile, Rapolla, Ripacandida,

Ginestra, Maschito, Forenza, Acerenza, Melfi, Venosa, Lavello, Palazzo S. Gervasio, and Banzo zones
D.O.C.

GRAPE: Aglianico

COLOR: Ruby red to garnet with orangy highlights

In all of Italy this wine deserves and gets respect, and it is held in high esteem for good reason. It is full, complex, austere, with a marvelous bouquet and ages extremely well. If aged two years in the barrel and one in the bottle, it is called *vecchio* ("old"), and if bottle aged two more years it is then called *riserva*. You can drink it relatively young or old or very old, and it has different characteristics at those different times, all good. When young it is good with light meats or with cured meats, and as it gets older it is marvelous with furred or feathered game and stuffed meat and poultry dishes. As in the case of Taurasi, there seems to be one producer who stands head and shoulders above the others: Fratelli D'Angelo.

CALABRIA

Cirò

Province of Catanzaro in the Cirò, Cirò Marina, Melissa, and Crucoli zones
D.O.C.

GRAPES: For the white, Greco Bianco, with some Trebbiano Toscano optional; for the red, Gaglioppo, Trebbiano Toscano, and Greco Bianco optional

COLORS: White, red, and *rosato*

The white is smooth, fruity, and full and makes a good match for shellfish, antipasto, and snails. The red when aged for three years and with an alcohol level of at least 13.5 percent (these wines often have more) is called *riserva*. It has a wonderful bouquet and some tannin and becomes elegant with age. This is a wine to have with game and lamb or grilled pork. The younger red and the *rosato* are everyday drinking wines that are perfect with fish stews, poultry, and light roasted meats and vegetables such as grilled eggplant.

CAMPANIA

Fiano di Avellino

Province of Avellino in the Avellino, Atripalda, Cesinali, Aiello del Sabato, and S. Stefano del Sole zones
D.O.C.

GRAPES: Fiano for the major part but Greco, Coda di Volpe Bianca, and Trebbiano Toscano can each be added or all of them or in any combination

COLOR: White

Dry and pleasant, this wine should be served cold. It is good with dishes that have herbs such as rosemary or fennel in them or mild fish dishes such Codfish Salad, or creamy dishes. It has been called elegant and aristocratic, both good descriptors. Fiano has the flavor of flowers and spice (and I want to say "everything nice," which is true), with the slightest hint of toasted almonds in the aftertaste.

Greco di Tufo

Province of Avellino in the Tufo, Patruso, S. Paolina, Montefusco, Chianche, Torrioni, and Altavilla zones
D.O.C.

GRAPES: Greco; but, optionally, may include up to 20 percent Coda di Volpe

COLOR: White

Greco grapes are ancient and have been described in many historical connections. Even fans of northern Italian wines have good things to say about this one. It is often served as an *aperitivo* and then continued with the first course, which, ideally, is fish that is not too assertive. It is light but with a certain strength, has a hint of bitter almond taste, and is very good with hot or cold *antipasti*, pasta, pizzas, and fish dishes. It should be served rather cool.

Per'e Palummo

Island of Ischia

GRAPES: Piederosso (Per'e Palummo) and sometimes Guarnaccia

COLOR: Ruby red with amber overtones

Tannin and fruitiness give this wine a long life. Its flavor is floral and intense and is excellent with feathered and furred game and with strong cheeses and bread. It would be ideal with macaroni and Rabbit, Ischian Style, and Braised Oxtails, Roman Style.

Ravello Bianco

Province of Salerno, Ravello, and di Scala zones

GRAPES: San Nicola, Coda di Volpe, Fiano Greco, Bianca Tenera, and others

COLOR: White with amber overtones

An excellent, fresh taste with almost imperceptible bitterness makes this a good sipping wine as well as a perfect companion to fish dishes such as Mussel or Oyster Soup, Taranto Style, or Mussels and Sausage, or Pepper Sprinkled Mussels.

Ravello Rosso

Province of Salerno, Ravello, and di Scala zones

GRAPES: Aglianico, Per'e Palummo, and Mangiaguerra

COLOR: Deep red with orange overtones

High alcohol, tannin, and full fruit assure a long and flavorful life to this wine. Perfect for feathered game such as Pomegranate Quail or with Chicken, Potenza Style, or Rolled Steak, Stuffed Sicilian Style. Strong hard cheese such as Parmesan or *pecorino* and bread with this wine could be dessert.

Solopaca

Province of Benevento in the Solopaca, Castelvenere, Gurardia Sanframondi, and Telese zones

D.O.C.

GRAPES: For the white, Trebbiano Toscano or Greco, Malvasia di Candia, Malvasia Toscana, and Coda di Volpe; for the red, Sangiovese (but locals refer to them as Montepulciano), Aglianico, Piedirosso, Sciascinoso, and perhaps others

COLORS: White and red (sometimes *rosato*)

The white is rather dry with a hint of bitter almonds, best drunk young and cool. It goes well with boiled or grilled shellfish and is very good with Sicilian Rice Dumplings. The red is sometimes ruby or as light as rosé. It is somewhat fruity, dry, with some tannin and has a nice perfume, excellent with roast chicken, pasta with tomato, roasted light meats such as veal and pork, and is awfully good with grilled mushrooms and some game.

Taurasi

Province of Avellino in the Taurasi, S. Angelo all'Esca, Luogosano, and Mirabella zones

D.O.C.

GRAPES: Aglianico primarily but may have up to 30 percent Piedirosso, Sangiovese, and Barbera

COLOR: Red

This noble wine qualifies in every way to stand with its brethren of the north, Barolo and, by extension, even farther north: Burgundy. Fresh-shot game, furred and feathered alike, would enjoy the company of this wine, equally good with fresh shelled walnuts and big shards of freshly broken Parmigiano-Reggiano cheese, or Sicilian *percorino pepato*, semihard sheep's cheese with whole peppercorns in it. The single best producer of this special wine is Mastroberardino.

Vesuvio

Province of Naples in the Boscotrecase, San Sebastiano al Vesuvio, and Ottaviano

D.O.C.

GRAPES: For the white, Coda di Volpe or Caprettone, Verdeca, Greco, and Falanghina; for the red, Piedirosso and Sciascinoso, and sometimes Aglianico are used

COLORS: White, red, and *rosato*

The white is pale gold and is very dry with up to 11 percent alcohol (if it has 12 percent or more it can be called Lacryma Christi). Excellent with grilled fish and pasta made with tomato sauces. The *rosato* and red are much like those described in the section on Lacryma Christi del Vesuvio wines.

LATIUM

Cesanese del Piglio

Province of Frosinone in the Piglio zone
D.O.C.

GRAPES: 90 percent Cesanese, the other 10 percent can be one of six or seven others including Montepulciano or Sangiovese

COLOR: Red in various hues

There are sweet and semisweet versions as well as a semidry and dry one. The latter two are good with most food, especially variety plates such as an antipasto or maybe Chicken Roasted with Rosemary, roasted meats, game, and mushrooms.

Colli Albani

Province of Rome in the Colli Albani zone

D.O.C.

GRAPES: Malvasia Rossa or Bianca di Candia about 60 percent with the remaining 40 percent made up of Trebbiano Toscano, Trebbiano Verde, Malvasia del Lazio, and finally Bonvino and Cacchione. The mixtures are arbitrary up to a point.

COLOR: White

Many wines come from the geographically large area of Colli Albani that are good everday wines. These wines can be drunk with almost any food, especially pastas and fish.

Est! Est!! Est!!!

Province of Viterbo in the Lago di Bolsena zone

D.O.C.

GRAPES: Trebbiano Toscano 65 percent Malvasia, about 20 percent, and the rest can be Rossetto

COLOR: White

There are dry and semisweet versions of this wine. In the Renaissance period it may well have been the best wine available in Latium. Although fruity, the dry has enough acid to make it good with shellfish and cured meats in *antipasti*, and with some soft cheeses.

Fiorano Bianco

Province of Rome

GRAPE: Malvasia di Candia

COLOR: Straw

Strength, elegance, and earthiness describe this high-ranking wine, which can age for several years. It is exceptional with such dishes as stuffed calamari, Mussels with Saffron, and trout with mushrooms.

Fiorano Rosso

Province of Rome

GRAPES: Merlot and Cabernet Sauvignon

COLOR: Ruby red with violet and gold overtones

The intense aroma confirms the taste of herbs and an insinuation of bitterness that characterize this prized wine. It can be aged for up to a decade if well cellared. A meal of Penne with *Porcini* in a Hot Tomato Sauce, Snails with Oregano followed by Lamb Chops, Calabrian Style gives you an idea of how to use this wine.

Frascati

Province of Rome in the area of Frascati

D.O.C.

GRAPES: Malvasia Bianca di Candia, Malvasia del Lazio, Greco, Trebbiano Toscano, 90 percent, and about 10 percent Bellone and Bonvino or Bombino Bianco

COLOR: White

This is probably the single most famous of the Lazio wines. It is light, crisp, and dry with a bit of fruit and a nice strawlike aroma. The *superiore* has 12 percent alcohol and is fruity and intense. The *amabile* (slightly sweet) can be good with cured meat such as prosciutto and fresh fruit and bread.

Lacryma Christi del Vesuvio

Province of Naples, Torre del Greco, and Boscoreal zones

GRAPES: Greco di Torre and some Fiano

COLOR: Gold with some amber tones

The most famous of the Greco wines, the best is known as Lacryma Christi. The name has been overused and indiscriminately used to pawn off some wines that are not all that worthy. The real thing is good indeed and has some of the character of Greco di Tufo but is not as intense and complex. It is very good with salads with eggs and shellfish and seafood stews. There are also a Lacryma Christi red and *rosato*, which are fairly stout wines; the red benefits from aging. These latter wines are very good with pasta with tomato or fish with tomato or light roasted meat, or they are good with herbed roasted chicken or pizza.

Marino

Province of Rome in the Marino and Falcognana zones

D.O.C.

GRAPES: Malvasia, Trebbiano, and Malvasia Puntinata

COLOR: White

Marino is esteemed by many Romans who actually put it above the beloved Frascati. There is a dry Marino, best drunk young, which can be used with most food and a semidry that can be used interchangeably. There is also a *superiore* that is like the preceding but with higher alcohol and a *spumante*, which is certainly in the dessert category.

Merlot di Aprilia

Province of Latina in Aprilia, Cisterna, and Nettuno zones

D.O.C.

GRAPES: Merlot

COLOR: Red

Relatively new wine developed in the 1930s when the Pontine Marshes were drained. It can be aged some and can be served with most any food, but especially dishes such as Chicken, Potenza Style, or Rabbit, Ischian Style.

Sangiovese di Aprilia

Province of Latina in the Aprilia, Cisterna, Latina, and Nettuno zones

D.O.C.

GRAPE: Sangiovese

COLOR: Medium red with orange overtones, some might even call it rosé

Winy odor with no particular other scents present. It is definitely dry and is good with pork and rice dishes. If well chilled it can be used as an *aperitivo*.

Torre Ercolana

Province of Frosinone, Anagni zone

GRAPE: Cabernet, Merlot, and Cesanese

COLOR: Ruby or Garnet

Very rare, expensive, high alcohol wine with vinous smell and taste, dry and robust. It should be well aged before drinking, and, generally, can be kept for several years if well cellared. Ideal wine with roasted meats and game.

Trebbiano di Aprilia

Province of Latina in the Aprilia, Cisterna, Latina, and Nettuno zones

D.O.C.

GRAPE: Trebbiano Giallo

COLOR: Deep gold

This wine has a Trebbiano flavor different from its northern counterpart of the same name. It has deeper color and is softer and smoother with a slight nutty flavor. It is a good choice for shellfish and fish dishes in general, and some chicken dishes made with herbs.

SARDINIA

Anghelu Ruju

Province of Sassari, Alghero zone

GRAPE: Cannonau

COLOR: Red with violet or garnet overtones

Some people think of Port wine when they drink Anghelu Ruju. It is at its best when drunk with dry fruit desserts like Golden Christmas Bread. It has 18 percent alcohol and a deep, robust, slightly sweet taste, a perfect accompaniment to an excellent cigar.

Cannonau di Sardegna

Provinces all over the island produce this wine; it is literally universal in Sardinia

D.O.C.

GRAPES: primarily Cannonau with up to 10 percent of other local grapes such as Pascale di Cagliari, Monica, or Vernaccia di San Gimignano

COLORS: Red and *rosato*

The red has up to 18 percent alcohol! When young it is good with almost all foods. It can be aged, which helps develop its character and depth. The range of flavor goes from very dry to *abboccato*. The *rosato* has 12 percent to 14 percent alcohol and is a multiuse wine that is smooth and tasty. There are other types of this wine such as *amabile*, which is on the sweet side, and *liquoroso*, which is semisweet with alcohol around 18 percent.

Girò di Cagliari

Provinces of Cagliari and Oristano in many different locations

D.O.C.

GRAPE: Girò

COLOR: Ruby red

When red and dry it is good with most hearty main dishes. The *liquoroso* or Girò di Cagliari Dolce, *liquoroso secco*, and the *riserva*, all sweet, must be aged at least two years and are wonderful for after-dinner sipping or with desserts and cookies.

Monica di Cagliari

Provinces of Cagliari, Oristano

D.O.C.

GRAPES: Monica

COLOR: Ruby, sometimes with orange overtones

Smooth and velvety, yet intense with 14 percent alcohol, it goes well with big meat dishes and sharp cheeses. There is also a *liquoroso dolce naturale,* and *liquoroso secco* and dry that are much like the previously described types. This is the type most people will respond to when you mention the name. In the menu suggestions, the sweet version is the usual one chosen.

Monica di Sardegna

Provinces all over the island produce this wine

D.O.C.

GRAPE: Monica with up to 15 percent Pascale di Cagliari, Carignano, Bovale Grande, and Bovale Sardo alone or in combinations

COLOR: Ruby red and variations

Sausage, game, and hearty meat dishes as well as cheeses and very spicy vegetable dishes are natural companions for this wine. Pasta with rich meat sauce is another good companion.

Nasco di Alghero

Province of Sassari, Alghero zone

GRAPE: Nasco

COLOR: White

Dry, semisweet, and sweet wines are made from Nasco grapes, thought to come from Spain around 300 years ago. The sweet has a slight bitter taste like *amaretti* cookies, high alcohol, about 14 percent, and is light sherry colored. The dry is excellent as an *aperitivo*, and all of them are good with hard cookies as a snack or after dinner.

Torbato di Alghero

Province of Sassari, Alghero zone
GRAPE: Torbato
COLOR: Straw with a shimmer of green
Intense aroma of vines and a touch of herbs make this dry wine good with fish dishes, some pork dishes, and can be a good *aperitivo* if served chilled.

Vernaccia di Oristano

Province of Oristano in many zones and also in Cagliari
D.O.C.
GRAPE: Vernaccia di Oristano
COLOR: Deep gold
This could easily be called Sardinian sherry, but I like it better than sherry. It has a hint of bitter almonds and is soft and delicious. While it is a great before and/or after dinner wine, you can also cook with it (see Trout Vernaccia, page 177).

SICILY

Bianco Alcamo (or just Alcamo)

Province of Trapani in the Alcamo zone
D.O.C.
GRAPES: Catarratto Bianco and/or Catarratto Bianco Lucido; some other grapes may be added
COLOR: White with green highlights
Fresh, slightly fruity, but dry and quite flavorful. It is good as an *aperitivo* and can then go right on to be served with the antipasto or with fish dishes.

Rapitalà

Rapitalà is a brand name of a wine noteworthy enough that I have included it separately. It is slightly fruity and herbaceous. It is regarded by most connoisseurs of Italian wines to be the best of the Alcamo wines, though it is named after a stream in the province of Palermo.

Corvo Bianco

Province of Palermo, Casteldaccia zone
GRAPES: Carratto and Inzolia
COLOR: White with tinges of green
Serve very cold with fish and antipasto dishes including cured meats. Although dry, this wine is not flinty, and it has a well-balanced, slightly fruity taste. It will age well several years in the bottle.

Corvo Rosso

Province of Palermo, Casteldaccia zone
GRAPES: Calabrese, Perricone, and Nerello Mascalese
COLOR: Ruby red with garnet and orange overtones
Stout wine with smooth vinous taste. Tannin and a slight fruitiness allow this wine to be cellared for several years, but there is no need to do so. It is consistently good and available. Very good with furred or feathered game, roasts, and strong, firm cheeses with bread.

Etna

Province of Catania in the Paterno, Giarre, Acireale, Trecastagni, Aci, Linguaglossa, and Milo zones
D.O.C.
GRAPES: For the white, Carricante Minimo, Catarratto, and others; for the *superiore*, Carricante Minimo, Catarratto Bianco, and others; for the red and *rosato*, Nerello Mascalese, Nerello Mantella, and others

COLORS: White, red, and *rosato*

The white is a good *aperitivo* wine that goes well with antipasto, fish, and eggs. The *superiore*, more alcoholic, is dry and fresh with a hint of fruit and is good with fish stews and pasta with fish. Etna wines are refreshing and meant to be drunk young and enjoyed. The red and the *rosato* have many of the same qualities as the *superiore* except in degree. They smell very winy and balanced and are warm and friendly wines with a certain robustness. These are good wines for roasted meats and big pasta casseroles; the *rosato* is very good with an antipasto.

Faro

Province of Messina in the Messina zone
D.O.C.
GRAPES: Nerello Mascalese, Nocera, Nerello Cappuccio, and some Calabrese, Gaglioppo, and Sangiovese added alone or in combinations
COLORS: Red and *rosato*

It is medium bodied, dry, full, very winy in aroma, intense, and brick red. It ages well. Good with most dishes but is probably the best with very rich dishes such as roasts with lots of herbs and oil flavors. The *rosato* is good with pasta dishes made with simple fresh sauces and most chicken dishes.

Malvasia delle Lipari

Province of Messina on the Lipari or Aeolian Islands and Salina
D.O.C.
GRAPES: Malvasia delle Lipari
COLOR: White

In the dessert-wine category, this is a classic. It is aromatic and beautifully amber and is good just to sip. It is a good finale to a meal simply as a wine, but a small glassful on ice cream, maybe melon flavor, but vanilla or chocolate will do, makes an unusually good dessert. Let the ice cream get very soft and creamy. If you don't want ice cream, drink Malvasia along with breads like *pangiallo* or with *cartellate*.

Marsala

Provinces of Trapani, Palermo, and Agrigento in scattered production sites all over
D.O.C.
GRAPES: Catarratto and/or Grillo and optionally not more than 15 percent Inzolia
COLOR: Amber to dark brown

Marsala started out being another alternative to sherry and Port. Exporting it as a business was started, in Marsala, by the Englishman Woodhouse around 1773. There are several types: Marsala Vergine, the choicest, very dry with intense aroma and flavor, good as an *aperitivo*, or with sharp cheese and nuts; Marsala Superiore, dry or sweet, excellent for sipping or used as above, the sweet with desserts or for making desserts; Marsala Fine, a less exotic quality that can be from sweet to dry for sipping and for use in general cooking.

Moscato di Pantelleria

Province of Trapani on the island of Pantelleria
D.O.C.
GRAPE: Zibibbo
COLOR: White

Classic Moscato that comes in variable alcoholic strengths and sweetness. This is a sipping wine at the end of a meal that has typical Moscato flavor, delicate but fragrant aroma, and is very smooth and mellow. This is not a wine for aging. It is quite good when it is one year old and has up to 18 percent alcohol.

Regaleali Bianco

Province of Palermo, Sclafani and Bagni zones

GRAPES: Catarrato, Inzolia, and some Sauvignon

COLOR: Pale straw

Dry but somewhat fruity wine with relatively high alcohol. It is very good with *antipasti* and most fish dishes and should be served cold but not icy.

Regaleali Rosso

Province of Palermo, Sclafani and Bagni zones

GRAPES: Calabrese or Nero d'Avola, Nerello Mascarese and Perricone

A fair amount of tannin and 13 percent alcohol give this wine a long life, although it is always drinkable when first bought. It is smooth and has a big, vinous flavor. Excellent with braised or roast meat or Breaded Lamb Chops (page 186) or Homemade Sicilian Sausage (page 188).

Boldface references indicate pages on which recipes appear.

Raisins, expelling natural sugars
     from, 245
Ramerino, 32
Rapitalà, 308
Rasaul, 140
Ravello Bianco, 303
Ravello Rosso, 303
Raviolatrice di legno, 38–39, 144
Ravioli, 127
     dessert, Teramo style, **283**
     Neapolitan, **144–145**
     pasta dough for, **124**
     Sardinian, **130–131**
Ravioli, 127
     culingiones, **130–131**
     alla napolitana, **144–145**
     pasta di, **124**
Ravioli cutters, 38–39
Recipe guidelines, 41–42
Red kidney beans, 21
Red pepper flakes, 31
     deviled broccoli, **217**
     pasta with toasted bread crumbs
          and, **142**
Regaleali Bianco, 310
Regaleali Rosso, 310
Relishes:
     roast onions, **233**
     Sicilian eggplant, **218–219**
Renaissance, 11–12, 73
Rendering lard, 24
Restaurants:
     Italian-American, 11
     in Italy, 15–16, 18, 19
Rice, 14, 31
     casserole Barese, **170**
     croquettes, "phone-wire," **96–
          97**
     dumplings, Sicilian, **152–153,**
          color plate 5
     as *minestra,* 16–17
     as *primo piatto,* 17
     risotto, 17
Ricotta, 14, 31
     artichokes stuffed with salami
          and, **227**
     crepes filled with prosciutto and,
          160

macaroni with sausage and,
     shepherd style, **137**
and salami calzone, 62
and spinach calzone, 62
Ricotta, 14, 31
     carciofi ripieni di, **227**
     crespelle di prosciutto e, **160**
     crostata di, **271**
Rigatoni, 128
Riso, 31
     arancini, **152–153,** color plate 5
     supplì al telefono, **96–97**
     teglia barese, **170**
Risotti, 17
Risotto, 17
Roast(ed):
     chicken with rosemary, **178**
     macaroni and, in natural juices,
          212
     mushrooms with pine nuts, **239**
     onions, **233**
     peppers with Italian-style tuna
          and clams, **104**
     stuffed squid, **175**
     tomatoes, **99,** color plate 2
Roasting pans, 38
Rolled steak, stuffed Sicilian style,
     166–167
Rolling pins:
     matterello, 36, 125–126
     raviolatrice di legno, 38–39, 144
Roma, romana:
     baccalà fritto, **190–191**
     bruschetta, **91**
     calamari con piselli alla, **193**
     coda alla vaccinara, **187**
     crostata di ricotta, **271**
     fettuccine alla, **132**
     manzo garofolato, **184–185**
     pollo alla, **180**
     spiedini alla, **93**
     spinaci alla, **245**
     stracciatella alla, **111**
     uova in trippa, **85**
Romanesca, pizza alla, **56**
Rome, Roman:
     braised beef, **184–185**
     braised oxtails, **187**

cheesecake, **271**
chicken, **180**
fettuccine, **132**
fried codfish, **190–191**
garlic bread, **91**
omelette in strips, **85**
roasted bread and cheese
     skewers, **93**
shredded egg soup, **111**
spinach, **245**
squid and peas, **193**
Root, Waverley, 12
Rosato del Salento, 300
Rosemary, 32
     chicken roasted with, **178**
Rose wheels, **264–265,** color
     plate 15
Rosmarino, 32
     pollo arrosto con, **178**
Rosso del Salento, 301
Russo, Luigi, 55

Saffron, mussels with, **103,** color
     plate 2
Sage, 32
Saint Agatha's nipples, **273**
Saint Joseph's Day, 255
Saint Joseph's Day fritters, **289**
Saint Vitus focaccia, **57**
Salads, 18
     cauliflower, **97,** color plate 10
     chick-peas in olive oil with
          tomatoes and herbs, 95
     codfish, **102**
     orange and lemon, **242,** color
          plate 8
     roast onion and tomato, 233
     savory bread, **94**
Salamanders, 39
Salami, 32
     artichokes stuffed with Ricotta
          and, **227**
     and Ricotta calzone, 62
Salami, 32
     carciofi ripieni di ricotta e, **227**
Sale, 32–33
Salice Salentino, 301
Salse, 69–78

About
the Author

Carlo Middione is a second-generation Sicilian-American and formerly *the* Italian specialist on the faculty of the California Culinary Academy for Chefs in San Francisco. His friendliness, culinary skills, and contagious enthusiasm for good Italian food have won him a wide following, and he has appeared regularly on local television. His Italian restaurant/delicatessen, located in San Francisco, has been praised by *Gourmet* magazine, which says, "Eating at Vivande is very much like being a guest in a large and friendly kitchen."